A PHOTO-LOCATION AND VISITOR GUIDEBOOK

PHOTOGRAPHING
THE PEAK DISTRICT

CHRIS GILBERT & MICK RYAN

fotoVUE
outdoor photography

PHOTOGRAPHING **THE PEAK DISTRICT**
BY CHRIS GILBERT AND MICK RYAN

First published in the United Kingdom in 2017 by fotoVUE.
www.fotovue.com

Additional photography: Andrew Marshall (p.44/342),
Craig Hannah (p.57), Stuart Holmes (p.482).

Edited by Stuart Holmes and Mick Ryan – fotoVUE Ltd.
Photo editing and layout by Stuart Holmes.
Design by Nathan Ryder – www.ryderdesign.studio

All maps within this publication were produced by Don Williams of Bute Cartographics.
Maps contain Ordnance Survey data. © Crown copyright and database right 2016.
Map location overlay and graphics by Mick Ryan.

Additional graphics by Xavier Ryan and Felicity Ryan.

A CIP catalogue record for this book is available from the British Library.

ISBN 978-0-9929051-5-6
10 9 8 7 6 5 4 3 2 1

Front cover: *Higger Tor from Carl Wark (page 270). Canon 6D, 17-40 at 25mm, ISO 200, 1/10s at f/14. Dec. © CG*

Rear cover left: *The Vale of Edale, the Great Ridge and Win Hill from Grindslow Knoll on Kinder (page 162). Sony A6000, 18-200 at 23mm, ISO 100, 1/5s at f/11. Nov. © MR*

Rear cover right: *Chatsworth House from the Three Arch Bridge (page 376). Canon 6D, 70-300 at 100mm, ISO 50, 1/4s at f/20. Oct. © CG*

Opposite: *Framing the Landscape at Holme Moss Summit (page 74). Canon 6D, 17-40 at 27mm, ISO 400, 1/160s at f/20. Aug. © CG*

Printed and bound in Europe by Latitude Press Ltd.

Framing the Landscape at Holme Moss Summit

CONTENTS

NORTHERN PEAK

WESTERN PEAK

CONTENTS

THE PEAK DISTRICT – AREA MAP

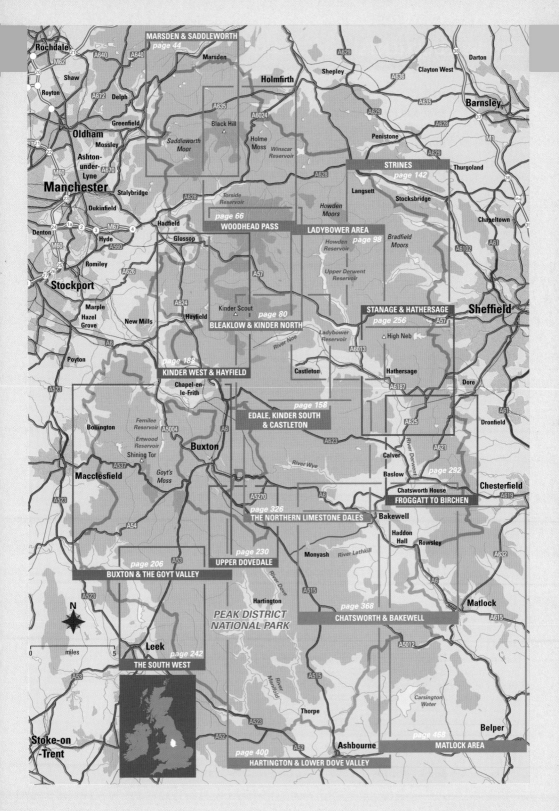

MARSDEN & SADDLEWORTH
page 44

WOODHEAD PASS
page 66

STRINES
page 142

LADYBOWER AREA
page 98

BLEAKLOW & KINDER NORTH
page 80

KINDER WEST & HAYFIELD
page 188

STANAGE & HATHERSAGE
page 256

EDALE, KINDER SOUTH & CASTLETON
page 158

FROGGATT TO BIRCHEN
page 292

THE NORTHERN LIMESTONE DALES
page 326

UPPER DOVEDALE
page 230

BUXTON & THE GOYT VALLEY
page 206

CHATSWORTH & BAKEWELL
page 368

THE SOUTH WEST
page 242

MATLOCK AREA
page 468

HARTINGTON & LOWER DOVE VALLEY
page 400

PEAK DISTRICT
NATIONAL PARK

N

0 miles 5

Rochdale
Shaw
Royton
Delph
Greenfield
Oldham
Mossley
Ashton-under-Lyne
Manchester
Stalybridge
Dukinfield
Denton
Hyde
Stockport
Marple
Hazel Grove
Poynton
Bollington
Macclesfield
Leek
Stoke-on-Trent

Marsden
Holmfirth
Shepley
Black Hill
Saddleworth Moor
Holme Moss
Winscar Reservoir
Torside Reservoir
Hadfield
Glossop
Howden Moors
Howden Reservoir
Upper Derwent Reservoir
Kinder Scout
Hayfield
New Mills
Chapel-en-le-Frith
Castleton
Ladybower Reservoir
Femilee Reservoir
Errwood Reservoir
Shining Tor
Buxton
Goyt's Moss
River Wye
Hartington
Monyash
River Lathkill
River Dove
Thorpe
Ashbourne
River Manifold

Holmfirth
Shepley
Clayton West
Darton
Barnsley
Penistone
Thurgoland
Stocksbridge
Langsett
Bradfield Moors
Chapeltown
Sheffield
High Neb
Hathersage
Dore
Dronfield
Calver
Baslow
Chatsworth House
Chesterfield
Bakewell
Haddon Hall
Rowsley
Matlock
Carsington Water
Belper

A640 A640 A672 A635 A6024 A629 A636 A635 A628 A629 A628 A629 A628 A670 A560 A626 A624 A57 A537 A5004 A623 A6 A623 A5270 A523 A54 A53 A5012 A515 A615 A632 A621 A625 A6013 A6187 A619 A6102 A61 A61
M62 M60 M67 M60 M1

PEAK DISTRICT – AREA MAP **9**

ACKNOWLEDGEMENTS

First and foremost my thanks go to Mick, for two reasons: firstly for knocking on my door a couple of years ago and asking me to join the fotoVUE project. Secondly for being with me on our consequent journey through the Peak District, a landscape that we both already knew and loved but which the project has allowed us to revisit with a new intent. It has often felt like we've been writing the biography of a close and dear friend and it has been a great excuse to revisit favourite haunts and finally check out places that we've known about for years but never had the chance to visit. Thanks also to Stuart for backing Mick's hunch about my work and my knowledge of the Peak District and agreeing to my joining the project.

fotoVUE have also provided me with an opportunity for validation. I first started walking in the Peak District in 1988 and have always carried a camera with me. Inevitably I have gained a considerable amount of knowledge and have taken hundreds of images in the intervening years. While in itself this is fairly satisfying it is nonetheless of little material worth unless it is put to good use. In this guidebook that knowledge has finally found a fitting purpose. I hope sincerely that the journeys that this book takes the reader on give the same delight as every single one of mine has through this beautiful landscape.

My thanks go to my lovely wife Jane, who has been my constant companion on my Peak District explorations since we first met at Edale Youth Hostel in 1990 and who herself has been exploring the Peak District since 1976. In the early part of our relationship she was very much my guide, first taking me on a day long walk through Dove Dale in the snow. Her patience over the last couple of years while I have revisited many of the places that we have explored together in our time in the Peak District has been immense.

Chris Gilbert
Cressbrook, July 2017

This guidebook and fotoVUE have joyfully taken up much of my life the last few years and I have several important people to thank for the collaboration, support, inspiration and friendship that they have kindly given.

First, thank you to my co-author Chris Gilbert who loves the Peak District and knows it better than most, Chris has been an absolute pleasure to work alongside. I am indebted to Stuart Holmes, my fellow co-director at fotoVUE who photo-edited and laid out this book beautifully. Thank you to Don Williams our cartographer, Nathan Ryder for our new book design, Jon Barton at Vertebrate who oversees our printing, Ola Stepien and Paul Phillips for our lovely website, and thank you to Alan James who I worked with at Rockfax guidebooks and UKClimbing.com where I learnt so much about modern media, working with creative teams, writing and publishing.

For five years – 2010 to 2016 – I lived in the Peak District with Caitlin Rimmer, Donna Claridge and my old school friend, Greg Rimmer, in their beautiful house above Bradwell. They had to put up with me leaving the house early to catch the sunrise and coming back late after sundown – and other bad habits. Their generosity and patience, the space they gave me, the many great meals and good cheer were appreciated every day and still are. Thank you to neighbours Steve Byers and Sally Pereira who were full of local advice and warmth as were my table-tennis partner Neil McAdie and family, Sue, Jake and Ellie. For the last year I have lived in Calderdale with another dear friend Craig Smith, thank you to Craig and his daughters Maddie and Sylvie for a great time. Thank you to my smart, wise and lovely partner Kate. I hope, that in between lots of gardening and daily walks in the woods and on the South Pennine moors, that it will be OK if I work on my next book Photographing Calderdale and the other imminent fotoVUE titles?

Thank you to my mother Rita and my late father Peter who, not only brought me up right, but bought me my first camera, an Olympus OM1n on my 18th birthday in 1979, I've been taking photographs ever since.

Finally and very importantly thank you to my children Xavier and Felicity who are my motivation and friends, you make your wonderful mother Gabriella Frittelli and myself very proud – and thanks for doing those graphics.

Mick Ryan
Hebden Bridge, July 2017

Ramshaw Rocks (page 248) . Canon 5D Mk 1, 17-40 at 17mm, ISO 50, 1/4s at f/20. Aug. © CG

Foreword by Ray Manley

It was my good fortune and privilege to be the official photographer at the Peak District National Park for 28 years.

When I first took up my post, I had a very limited knowledge of the Peak District and would have appreciated this excellent book to guide me to locations in, what was then, an unfamiliar landscape.

Fortunately, I had some help and inspiration from my predecessor at the National Park, Mike Williams. His black and white photographs in the National Park guide book *First and Last* perfectly captured the dramatic character of a landscape that I longed to explore and photograph.

My first few months involved taking photographs around the Edale valley and Kinder Scout area for a new display in the Edale Information Centre. What a dream job!

In my spare time and days off I loved nothing better than to walk and take photographs in those very same places. However, it was a long time before I succeeded in taking a photograph I was proud of, which was due to some very frustrating and unpredictable weather. I have aborted many a photographic mission because of the weather but there was nothing more rewarding when the conditions were favourable and I was in the right place, a treasured combination for a landscape photographer.

One such occasion was on Stanage Edge where I took one of my favourite photographs for a National Park poster. I waited for over two hours as dark clouds and dramatic shafts of light replaced a clear blue sky, providing the perfect image of wilderness and solitude I was hoping to achieve. A colleague of mine admired the photo but commented, 'What a pity you didn't have a better day with a blue sky.'

We all view the landscape in our own individual way and from the same locations we will rarely produce identical photographs. I have returned to my favourite places on many occasions but have always ended up with a totally different result each time.

For me, a passion for the Peak District was just as important as a passion for photography and it is obvious from the excellent and inspiring photos in this book, that Mick and Chris have both in abundance. The information and advice they have given will be of tremendous help to all aspiring photographers.

Ray Manley
Peak District National Park photographer (1979–2007)
July 2017

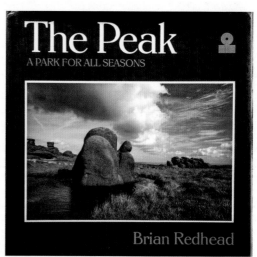

A Park For All Seasons is Ray's most well known and loved photographic book documenting the Peak District through the seasons. The broadcaster Brian Redhead wrote the introduction and Roly Smith the lyrical captions that accompany Ray's photographs –there are 83 of them – and it is still one of the most definitive photographic works about the Peak District.

Curbar from New Bridge at Calver Weir (page 314). Canon 6D, 70-300 at 120mm, ISO 50, 1/25 at f/14. Oct. © CG

The Peak District is one of the most beautiful regions in the UK, and one of the most accessible. The northern crown of the Peak, and its eastern and western flanks, are areas of tor-capped, windswept gritstone and heather moorland, known as the Dark Peak. The White Peak to the south is lush and green, crossed by limestone walls and cut by deep dales and crystal clear streams that flow beneath tall cliffs.

Beauty is all around on a grand scale, with viewpoints from gritstone edges, high plateaus and down into steep dales offering classic landscape compositions for the photographer.

For those who like to zoom in, the ecology of the area provides an astonishing variety of plant life, with many rare species, including several species of orchid, occurring here in abundance. Lonely isolated trees cap ridges, mysterious forests hide fungi whilst a walk through many Peak woodlands in the spring will be amongst carpets of ramsons and bluebells. On the moors there is a thriving population of mountain hares, replete with white coats in winter. Red deer rut in October on Big Moor, whilst down country lanes you may spot brown hares, foxes, buzzards, kestrels and owls.

The region's human history offers a tapestry of subjects for the camera. Stone circles and chambered cairns sit side-by-side with industrial architecture – in the South Peak the Industrial Revolution began in Richard Arkwright's mills. Old farms and barns neighbour ancient villages which in summer are adorned with the colours of celebration, with the quaintly parochial Well Dressing taking centre stage. A visit to the estates and stately homes of Chatsworth House and Haddon Hall will transport you back to medieval times.

Early appreciation of the Peak District came from Thomas Hobbes who in 1636 published a poem called *De Mirabilibus Pecci, Being the Wonders of the Peak in Darby-shire*. Later, in 1681 Charles Cotton published *Wonders of the Peak*, the Peak District's first-ever travel guide, although it wasn't until the advent of the railways in the nineteenth century that the Peak District became popular with visitors.

Photography has been practiced in the Peak since before the Kodak Brownie box camera. Gerald Hine from Macclesfield explored the western and southern Peak in the 1930s with a bulky glass plate camera. The upland landscapes that the trespass and rambler movements opened up were fertile places for early adventurous mountain photographers like W. A. Poucher to explore. The images Poucher created for his book *Peak Panorama: Kinder Scout to Dovedale* (1946), with Mam Tor on the cover, were key in forging the visual foundation upon which the photographic exploration of the Peak would be built. A significant pioneer was Ray Manley, who for 28 years was the Peak District National Park Authority's official photographer and if you leaf through his book, *The Peak: A Park for All Seasons*, many will recognise what have now become classic Peak District photographs. The creative torch they lit has been carried by photographers such as Jerry Rawson and more recently by Karen Frenkel, Fran Halsall and their contemporaries, and is now carried by every person who ventures into the Peak with a camera.

Whilst we have both explored and lived in the Peak District for many years, it has been a real treat, and lots of hard work putting this guidebook together. We hope you enjoy exploring, visiting and photographing the Peak District as much we have.

Chris Gilbert and Mick Ryan
July 2017

Upper Tor on Kinder looking down onto the Vale of Edale (page 166). Canon 6D, 17-40 at 21mm, ISO 200, 1/50s at f/13. Jul. © CG

Farmer Roger Brown drives his sheep in the White Peak. Drive cautiously and defensively on these narrow lanes. Sony A6000, 18-200 at 105mm, ISO 400, 1/1000s at f/8. Jul. © MR

A transect of the Peak District from Manchester across Kinder, Edale and the Eastern Edges to Sheffield in the east.

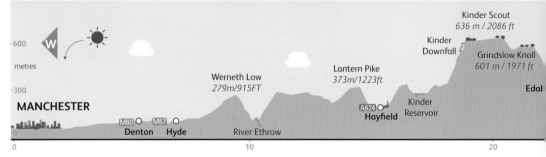

The 555 square miles (1,438 sq. km) of the Peak District National Park reaches into five counties: Derbyshire, Cheshire, Staffordshire, Yorkshire and Greater Manchester. It is the most accessible of the UK's 15 national parks positioned in the centre of England and being close to the cities of Manchester, Sheffield, Derby and Nottingham.

Getting to the Peak

The Peak is bordered by the M1 to the east, the M6 in the west, the M62 to the north and the A50 in the south. These are the main routes to reach the Peak District.

From the North

If coming down the M6 the best entry to the north and central Peak avoiding Manchester is from the M60 by the A628 Woodhead Pass road or Snake Road, the A57. The A6 from Stockport and the M60 is a good choice and leads to Chapel-en-le-Frith from where many points can be accessed. If coming down the M1 exit at junction 35a for the A628 Woodhead Pass road. For accessing the central and southern Peak from the M1 either go through Sheffield or travel south of Sheffield to exit at the M1 at Chesterfield, junction 29, and follow the A619 to Baslow.

From the South

Coming from the south east and London go north on the M1. For the south Peak exit the M1 at junction 28, Alfreton and go west following the A615 to Matlock. More popular is leaving the M1 at Chesterfield, junction 29, to follow the A619 to Baslow where you can access the central and north Peak District, through Sheffield is an option too. For the far north Peak it is better to continue past Sheffield to junction 35a and go west on the A616 Woodhead Pass road.

From the south west go north on the M6. For the south Peak exit at Stafford and follow the A518 and A515 to Ashbourne, or; exit the M6 at Newcastle-under-Lyme and through Stoke-on-Trent and follow the A53 to Leek and the south west corner of the Peak near the Roaches. For the northern reaches of the Peak it is best to avoid Manchester and exit the M6 at Sandbach to Congleton and the A54 to Buxton – one of several gateway to the Peak towns.

Main Roads within the Peak

The Dark Peak is traversed by the A628 Woodhead Pass road, linking the M67 on the outskirts of Manchester to South Yorkshire in the west. This often windy road tops out on the moors at 460m (it can close briefly in winter) and skirts the top of the Strines (Mortimer road) which is often quieter than other ways into the Peak. It pops you out at the Ladybower reservoir and close to Bamford. From the Woodhead Pass road you can also access locations in the far north Peak, including Holme Moss, West Nab and the Marsden locations.

Just to the south of the Woodhead Pass road is the infamous Snake Road, the A57, which is narrow, winding and summits at 512m. Take care on this road, it has a high accident rate. Be wary when parking as cars approach fast. It does provide access to some of the best photographic locations in the Peak passing over Bleaklow and by Kinder popping out at the Derwent reservoirs at Ladybower.

The A623 branches off from the A6 at Chapel-en-le-Frith and heads south east into the northern reaches of the White Peak passing by Tideswell and on to Baslow. The A6 just to the south is also important, it is a relatively uncongested road, linking Buxton to Bakewell and Matlock.

The A6187 which links Sheffield to Hathersage and carrying on to Castleton, and by a side road to the

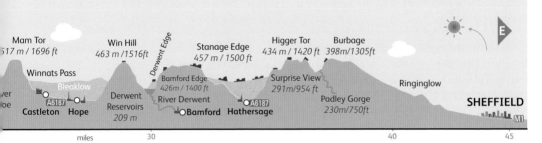

Vale of Edale, is an important road for getting to locations, especially Stanage and the Eastern Edges, Surprise View, Kinder South and Edale.

Finally two important north-south roads are the A53 Buxton to Leek road, passing by the Roaches and the A515 from Buxton to Ashbourne which takes you on a wonderful trip amongst some of the best high limestone plateau scenery and beautiful villages where you can access Hartington and Dove Dale.

In winter it can take several hours for these roads to be cleared of snow (sometimes days on the high roads) and careful driving is required, snow tyres are a big advantage especially if you are traveling to high ground.

Minor Roads

The Peak District is criss-crossed with country lanes and B roads, many used by farmers and walkers, and sometimes stray livestock. Drive cautiously and defensively on these narrow lanes. If you are not in a hurry, pull in and allow those who wish to go faster to pass. After heavy snow these roads can be blocked for several days or even weeks.

Parking

There is a mix of National Trust and Peak District National Park car parks near many locations with most being pay and display. Official car parks are marked on the maps by a blue parking symbol **P**. There are many informal parking spots – marked by a small letter ℗ on the maps – you park at these places at your own risk. Avoid driving up on grass verges and do not block any gates. Most of these 'pull outs' are fine and legal, some are lay-bys, but look out for no parking signs in villages.

Peak Times and Places

Places to avoid on bank holidays and sunny weekends include the Ladybower and Derwent reservoirs, the Hathersage area, around Bakewell and Chatsworth House, and southern Dove Dale near the village of Thorpe. These areas will be congested at peak holiday times, but are usually quiet first thing and late, avoid them between 9am-5pm. However, most can be by-passed by consulting a map and using minor roads. At home time, main exits from the Peak will be busy, often with traffic jams, it is best to wait until after 7pm to leave.

Public Transport

The Peak District has an extensive public transport network with many options. Go to **www.peakdistrict.gov.uk/ visiting/publictransport/peakconnections** for more information and for public transport information leaflets.

Train and Bus

If travelling to the Peak by rail the best stations to travel to are Manchester Piccadilly or Sheffield train station where you can take trains to Buxton, Edale, and Hathersage. From Burton-upon-Trent, Derby and Nottingham you can connect to trains which will take you to Matlock in the southern Peak. In the far north, Greenfield in the Saddleworth area, and Marsden, can be reached by trains from Manchester and Huddersfield. National Express Coaches serve all the cities and towns in and around the Peak District.

www.nationalrail.co.uk
www.nationalexpress.com

By Air

The nearest international airports to the Peak District are Manchester Airport and Doncaster Sheffield Airport.

Where to stay in the Peak

If you are staying in the Peak District for a weekend or a week you are spoilt for choice regarding accommodation. Where you stay of course depends on your objectives.

The heart of the Peak District is the Upper Derwent Valley from Ladybower – including Edale – to Chatsworth, and the Wye Valley from Millers Dale to Bakewell. These are the best areas to stay when visiting the Peak District giving easy access to some of the best photographic locations – important if you want an early start to catch the dawn, or are staying out late for sunset. You will also never have to drive far if you stay in or near one of the major centres such as Bakewell, Hathersage or Buxton with their convenient amenities.

Whilst giving individual recommendations where to stay is beyond the scope of this book, here are the best resources to help you find a bed and breakfast, hotel, pub, or holiday cottage.
www.tripadvisor.co.uk
www.visitpeakdistrict.com
www.peakdistrictonline.co.uk
As regards camping, there are over 40 campsites and caravanning parks. Search the Peak District listing at
www.pitchup.com

Breakfast, Lunch and Dinner

Cafes for Breakfast
- Top of the list is the Grindleford Station Cafe next to Padley Gorge, (S32 2JA).
- Colemans Deli (S32 1BB) and the Pool Cafe (S32 1DU) in Hathersage.
- High Nelly's Cafe, Peak District Parlour and the Vanilla Kitchen, Tideswell (SK17 8PF).
- The Yondermann Cafe at Wardlow Mires (SK17 8RW).
- The Edensor Tea Cottage at Edensor, (DE45 1PH).
- The Carriage House Restaurant at Chatsworth House, (DE45 1PN).

Pubs
The Peak has many great rural pubs, most with open fires that retain an old charm, and providing real ale and home-cooked food – from gastro to basic, often serving locally sourced produce.

On all the Section maps the nearest pubs to locations are marked by a pub symbol. Here are some favourites as chosen by the Facebook group, Peak District Photography and Chris and Mick – Google the pub name for location, opening times and menu.

- The Red Lion, Litton, SK17 8QU
- Farmyard Inn, Youlgrave, DE45 1UW
- The Lamb Inn, Hayfield, SK23 6AL
- The Barrel Inn , Bretton, S32 5QD
- The Bull's Head, Foolow, S32 5QR
- The Miner's Arms , Eyam, S32 5RG
- The Devonshire Arms, Pilsley, DE45 1UL
- Ye Olde Nags Head, Castleton, S33 8WH
- The George, Castleton, S33 8WG
- Strines Inn, Bradfield, S6 6JE
- The Packhorse, Little Longstone, DE45 1NN
- Thorn Tree, Matlock Bank, DE4 3JQ
- The Cheshire Cheese Inn, Hope, S33 6ZF
- The Cock and Pullet. Sheldon, DE45 1QS
- The Eyre Arms, Hassop, DE45 1NS
- The George, Alstonfield, DE6 2FX
- The Beehive, Combs, SK23 9UT
- The Paper Mill Inn, Chinley,SK23 6EJ
- Three Stags Heads, Wardlow, SK17 8RW
- The Royal Oak. Hurdlow, SK17 9QJ
- The Devonshire Arms, Beeley, DE4 2NR
- The Packhorse Inn, Crowdecote, SK17 0DB
- The Lamb Inn, Chinley Head, SK23 6AL
- Old Hall Inn, Chinley, SK23 6EJ
- Pack Horse at New Mills, SK22 4QQ
- The Peacock, Bakewell, DE45 1DS
- The Devonshire Arms, Peak Forest, SK17 8EJ

Indian Restaurants
- Curry Cabin, Hope, S33 6RD
- Sangams, Hathersage, S32 1BB
- Curry Cottage, Lover's Leap, Stoney Middleton, S32 4TF
- Rajas Indian Restaurant, Bakewell, DE45 1DS

Fish and Chips
- Bradwell Fisheries, Bradwell, S33 9JL
- Elliott's Fish & Chips, Tideswell, SK17 8NU
- Bakewell Chip Shop, DE45 1EW
- Longnor Fish & Chip Shop. SK17 0NT

Formally a farmstead and 17th century coaching inn, the Eyre Arms at Hassop is great to visit and photograph especially in the autumn. Landlord Nick Smith welcomes you. Canon 6D, 70-300 at 116mm, ISO 100, 1.6s at f/14. Oct. © CG

Which season to visit the Peak District?

WINTER – December, January, February

Winter arrives in the Peak District with a bit of a crash. Waves of wet stormy November weather blast away the remnants of autumn colours, although temperatures can hold up quite well in the run up to Christmas.

The first snows sprinkle the higher tops usually in early December but these rarely last more than a couple of days. As the year closes out look for high pressure days, which can result in a temperature inversion in the Derwent Valley resulting in low lying mist on the valley floor. If the temperatures are close to zero then there is an excellent chance that the misty inversions will coincide with air frosts that coat the trees and walls with ice.

In the new year the temperatures in the High Peak drop and may allow snow to persist long enough to entertain the photographer. Wrap up warm and pack a hand warmer next to your spare battery to stop the cold draining power.

Late January and early February in particular are good times for snowfall. How accessible the landscape is at these times depends on just how much snow falls. Heavier falls will quickly close many of the other high level major A roads such as the A515 and the A623. You need to be aware of this if you are planning to be out and about when the snow is actually falling.

In the White Peak strong winds can scour snow off the fields and dump it in between the dry stone walls that line the lanes, making them impassable for days. Once the snow has fallen and the major routes are open the snow ploughs turn their attention to other thoroughfares and the photographer can venture to more remote areas, even if it means a bit more walking than normal.

When the temperature remains below zero for prolonged periods and we have access to the magical snow-covered landscape, the low winter light at this time can create some stunning visual experiences.

The high moorlands offer genuine winter mountaineering experiences for the more adventurous. The trek to a frozen Kinder Downfall, typically after three consecutive days of sub-zero temperatures, is a favourite.

- After a hard frost or snow head to the accessible gritstone edges where a combination of brown bracken, yellow grasses and colourful sunsets and sunrises can give spectacular conditions.
- After snow head to the White Peak for photographs of snowy fields, barns, farmhouses and walls especially at sunset.
- If you are adventurous, fell fit and experienced head to the Kinder Plateau and Bleaklow which can be arctic-like. Look out for mountain hare in their white winter coats.
- Snowdrops appear in February

SPRING – March, April, May

How quickly spring gets going depends on what sort of winter the Peak District has had, although the predominant altitude means that it arrives significantly later here than at lower altitudes. The snowdrops get everything going in February with celandine coming in quickly after this.

The Peak often gets a curious mild period in March that can create colourful, hazy high pressure mornings but these usually disappear to be replaced once more by cold air. The air mass over the hills warms slowly. Spring creeps into the lower reaches of the Derwent Valley long before it manifests itself in the High Peak, with the daffodils in Derby having long gone over before they even in bud in Castleton and Buxton.

It is usually well into May before it feels warm in the High Peak. Photographically the early part of spring is mostly about the rocky summits and tors of the high moorlands but there is plenty to be made of the lines of bare trees that punctuate the skylines of the White Peak. Once the flowers kick in, however, it is the bluebells, ramsons and orchids that inevitably draw the eye. Trees come into leaf quite slowly, with the purple haze of silver birch buds colouring the flanks below the Eastern Edges around Easter time. For landscape photography this green budding contrasts well with the moorland where the heather and bracken are still in their winter coat of dark earthy tones. Ash, which dominates the White Peak woodlands often doesn't come into leaf until May.

The maples and oaks have an acid yellow with curious red quality, a colour that often lasts a week before creeping over into the more familiar green with blue quality of cholorophyll. On the moors the bilberry acquires a vivid lime colour that the evening light picks out brilliantly. A highlight is the slow tide of candyfloss hawthorn blossom that washes its way up the valleys and hillsides, topping out often in early June although a cold winter will see the highest trees flowering only weakly. Frosty mornings can still coincide with the occasional inversion as it does in winter so it is worth keeping an eye on high pressure and predictions for humidity and temperature at this time of year.

- Cold mornings produce temperature inversions.
- As the trees and meadows start to burst into life, their mosaic of green hues contrasts with the earthy-tones of the still dormant bracken and heather on the moorlands.
- April is bluebell time and the first orchids flower in May.

SUMMER – June, July, August

When spring ends and summer begins in the Peak District is open to debate – let's say the beginning of June in the White Peak and the end of June in the Dark Peak.

The spring orchids can still be flowering strong in some of the damp, cool corners of the limestone dales while the first summer orchids are making an appearance in the warmer and drier places, such is the overlap.

Summer is characterised by pale blue harebells and purple-pink scabious in the fields, tractors turning grass to make silage and hay. Hazy late afternoons layer up the landscapes beautifully. The bracken on the slopes below the gritstone edges shoot up to form a sea of green.

The rocks and tors of the higher moors can be visited late when the sun is low and still leave plenty of ambient light to make the walk out safe. If you are not inspired by the relative softness of the summer landscape then why not have a look at the many festivals and country shows that happen at this time.

Well dressings are plentiful and many villages have specific and very interesting fertility and religious festivals. Look out for open gardens events and the large country shows where character abounds in not only the animals that are shown at these events but also in the people who attend them. The long days mean that animals that would often only be out foraging at night show themselves in the early dawn and late evenings. Owls, hares and deer are all more likely to be see in the summer months than at other times of the year – just get up early.

In late summer the high moorlands turn spectacularly purple with the heather and there are some places that would at other times of year be quite uninteresting but when the heather arrives suddenly become utterly magical.

The bell heather (Erica cinerea) appears first at the end of July with its pinkness followed by the ubiquitous common heather or ling (Calluna vulgaris) with its rich purples appearing half-way through August and can stretch all the way through September.

- Hazy sunsets over Win Hill and Kinder from Stanage take on a Japanese layering quality.
- If you are traveling from afar for a visit, visit at end of August when the heather is in full flower. You will never regret it.
- Take a walk by a river or visit a waterfall.
- Walk down a green lane to get compositions of flower-filled limestone meadows and field barns.

AUTUMN – September, October, November

As the days shorten and cool the Peak District colours morph subtly toward yellow and rust. From mid-September through November get out with your camera when you can, this can be the best of times.

The heather fades from purple into an appealing russet colour that still photographs well when there is plenty of blue in the sky. Silver birch, oak and maple turn to gold and the beeches in Padley Gorge go swiftly from orange to red as the frosts approach, creating a riot of colour.

Other excellent beech woodlands include Ox Low Rake near Peak Forest, Musden Wood near Ilam, the southern flanks of Eldon Hill and the hillsides around the Goyt Valley, particularly Long Hill above Chapel-en-le-frith. The mainly ash of the White Peak does not colour up well but instead yellows and then promptly drops with the first frost. This means that the White Peak, where the ash predominates, is better for colour in the middle of autumn when there are still plenty of leaves on the trees. The Roaches in particular are a superb place to work in autumn, with the russet of the late heather combining with the mixed woodland well. The Back Forest to the west of the the Roaches is lovely at this time of year. In the Dark Peak the millstones at High Neb re-emerge as the bracken fades to gold.

In autumn the waters of the Derwent catchment create cool hollows into which the early morning mists pour, making the vantage points 'round here very attractive. Photographers rush to Winnat's Pass, Mam Tor, Bamford Edge and Curbar Edge where these events are presented very well. In the south west Tittesworth Reservoir does something similar for the Roaches and Ramshaw Rocks. The Wye Valley also catches autumn mists in a similar way to the Derwent Valley but on a smaller and more intimate scale. Monsal Head is a good place to witness and record Wye Valley mists and some of the views available from Longstone Edge on such mornings are outstanding.

- Autumn starts slowly but the changes are significant as the rest of the landscape is still in its summer coat. Peak autumn when the colour is at its height is hard to predict but is usually in October. As autumn progresses into early November don't give up hope, what little remains on the trees is usually very colourful but very distinct.
- Waterfalls and cascades are at their best in autumn as the water flow increases.
- This is the main season for temperature inversions; both misty and foggy mornings are common at this time of year. Check the forecast for clear still nights after a warm day with dropping temperatures. The Hope Valley and Upper Derwent, from Ladybower to Chatsworth, will not let you down. For the energetic get high on Kinder.

PEAK DISTRICT CLIMATE AND WEATHER

The Peak District lies at the geographic heart of England so its climate is a transition from the drier and warmer south, and the colder and wetter north. However as well as its latitude it is also an upland area, with much of the land above 300 metres – its highest points being Kinder Scout at 636 metres and Bleaklow Head (610 metres) – and because of this high elevation it can get some quite extreme weather conditions: intense rain, heavy snow, low temperatures, very strong winds and thick persistent hill fog.

Best times for photography

In general from September through to May are the best times for photography in the Peak District. At these times there is more contrast in the land, the sun is lower giving 'warmer' light, sunrise and sunset times are respectable, and you've a higher chance of valley mist. Saying that do not dismiss summer, witnessing an orange summer sunset from Kinder's North Edge whilst all around you is cotton grass, or watching the rising sun whilst on the limestone summit of Wolfscote Hill, are experiences not to be missed and you will return with great photographs.

If you were to pick a season to visit, it would be autumn, from roughly early October through to late November. This period is when the colours of the trees and moors will be at their most intense, and with the onset of the colder weather and long nights there will be a high chance of valley mists. If the forecast is for snow and frost, usually from November through to March, book yourself a bed and breakfast, and get yourself here – it can be magical.

The changeable weather of spring, from late March, April and May sees storms rush in from the west and south west and it is a time of rainbows and flashes of light, and you've still a good chance of valley mist.

The Month in the Captions

Look at the captions of the photographs in this guidebook – all have the month the photograph was taken and this will give you a good idea of the conditions experienced in a particular month.

Valley Mist

The Peak District is well know for its temperature inversions that produce valley mist and fogs (also sometimes called cloud inversions). Fog and mist, tiny droplets of water suspended in the air, occur often in the Peak all-year round, but frequently between October and May. Fog is denser when visibility is down to 200m, mist lighter when you can see further than 200m. Both fog and mist are great for photography, whether you are within it, but especially looking down on it from on high.

Temperature inversions

Normally the air is warmest near the ground as the sun heats the land that heats up the air, then if you gain elevation the temperature drops. If this temperature gradient is reversed, with cold air nearest the ground, the colder temperature causes moisture in the air to condense to form bigger water droplets and fog or mist.

The best conditions for this to occur are when you have a cloudy or moist day, or perhaps a moist wind coming in from the west, followed by a clear, cool, windless and long night. Check the forecast for these conditions.

Other Mist and Fog Types

Hill Fog

Upslope fog or hill fog forms when winds blow air up a slope (called orographic uplift). The air cools as it rises, allowing moisture in it to condense. You often see this Great Ridge or on the slopes of Kinder.

Evaporation Fog

Low lying mist forms when cold air passes over moist land and bodies of water, often seen at the Derwent Reservoirs.

Freezing Fog

Freezing fog is supercooled water droplets that remain as water even if the temperature is below freezing. This creates low-lying mist that surrounds the frozen land and vegetation.

A sea of cloud below you

If a low lying fog forms and high pressure comes in trapping the warmer lower air this can create a thick sea of fog that can last all day or several days. Get up high to witness this.

Best Locations for misty mornings

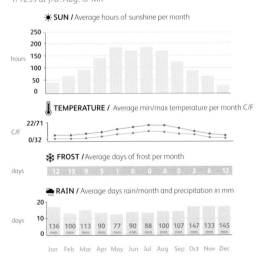

Moat Low (page 416). Sony A6000, 18–200 at 18mm, ISO 200, 1/125s at f/8. Aug. © MR

PEAK DISTRICT WEATHER STATION AVERAGES

The average maximum temperature is 11.5°C with the hottest months being July and August. The average minimum temperature is 5.3°C, the low average temperatures recorded in January and February. The average annual number of sunshine hours is 1334 hours. The highest average number of sunshine hours are in May (180 hours) and July (178 hours). The average annual rainfall in the Peak District is 1329mm. The months with the highest rainfall are December (145mm) and January (136mm). Wind direction for the area is predominantly from the south and south west. Winds of 100mph can be experienced at the summit of Mam Tor.

The Peak is wetter, colder and less sunny than the rest of the UK– although from July to September there are more sunshine hours on average than the rest of the UK, but also more rain in every month.

There are notable differences within the Park between the cooler wetter upland areas in the north and west and warmer drier south and east areas.

Opposite*: Peak Tor from Pilhough at the edge of Stanton Moor (p.392). Canon 5D, 17-40 at 20mm, ISO 100, 1/4s at f/20. Apr. © CG*

☀ **SUN /** Average hours of sunshine per month

🌡 **TEMPERATURE /** Average min/max temperature per month C/F

❄ **FROST /** Average days of frost per month

| 12 | 13 | 9 | 5 | 1 | 0 | 0 | 0 | 0 | 3 | 6 | 12 |

☁ **RAIN /** Average days rain/month and precipitation in mm

| 136 mm | 100 mm | 113 mm | 90 mm | 77 mm | 90 mm | 88 mm | 100 mm | 107 mm | 147 mm | 133 mm | 145 mm |

Jan Feb Mar Apr May Jun Jul Aug Sep Oct Nov Dec

USING THIS GUIDEBOOK TO GET THE BEST IMAGES

Great photographs require being in the right place at the right time regardless of whether you are using a digital, film or mobile phone camera. This is what fotoVUE photo-location guidebooks are about – giving you the information and the inspiration to get to great locations in the best photographic conditions.

In the right place

Each location chapter in this guide describes a place where you can take great photographs. Comprehensive directions are given including co-ordinates to the nearest car park or lay-by, nearest postal codes for sat navs and smart phones, and an OS map co-ordinate.

Before you set off walking study a map so that you know where you are going and give yourself plenty of time to get your destination. Also read the accessibility notes to check the distances and terrain to a location's viewpoints.

Maps

Whilst there are detailed maps in this guidebook which along with the directions will get you to a location and its viewpoints, for finer navigation we recommend a printed map to go in your rucksack or camera bag.

For the best detail, recommended maps for the Peak District are:

OS Explorer Map (scale 1:25 000): OL1 Dark Peak
OS Explorer Map (scale 1:25 000): OL24 White Peak
These maps cover almost all of the Peak District National Park but for the northern and southern reaches of the Peak District there is:

OS Explorer Map (scale 1:25 000): OL21 South Pennines
OS Explorer Map (scale 1:25 000): OL259 Derby

There are two 1:40,000 scale **British Mountaineering Council hillwalking maps**; one to the Dark Peak and one to the White Peak. These are printed on plastic which is durable, tear-resistant and waterproof.

More affordable and covering larger areas, but less detailed, are the **OS Landranger maps** (scale 1:50 000) and the AA's **Central Peak District Walkers Map** (scale 1:25 000).

Our Map Symbols

Our maps are detailed but with few symbols. The symbols that are important are:

A location chapter

A location chapter is marked by a numbered circle or pin and its name.

A viewpoint

A viewpoint is marked by a small circle sometimes with the name of the viewpoint by it.

Footpaths

Not all footpaths are marked on our maps, only footpaths that are useful to get to a location and its viewpoints.

Walking Man Symbol

If a footpath has a walking man symbol it means that the approach is strenuous and often involves steep uphill walking.

Open Access Land

Open Access Land is marked by the Open Access Land symbol. However the borders of Open Access Land are not marked. Open Access Land is shown as a yellow wash on the Ordnance Survey Explorer maps.

Pub Symbol

Pubs are marked with a pint symbol and the pub name. They are included as they are good way marks and provide excellent refreshment before or in between photographic excursions. Each pub has been individually checked by either Chris or Mick, more than once.

Opposite top: Carrhead Rock (page 266). Sony A6000, 18–200 at 18mm, ISO 400, 1/60s at f/9. Sep. © MR
Opposite bottom: From Shining Tor summit (page 214). Canon 5D Mk 1, 17-40 at 17mm, ISO 400, 1/30s at f/20. ND. Dec. © CG

The Great Ridge (page 168). Canon 6D, 17-40 at 17mm, ISO 100, 1/200s at f/14. Jan. © CG

At the right time

Great photographs usually depend on light, texture and colour. In each location chapter are detailed notes on the best time of year and day to visit a location to get the best photographic results. Good light can occur any time however and often the best times to visit any location is when conditions are rapidly changing like after a storm.

The topography, sun position and the weather determine how the light falls on the land. Use the sun position compass on the front flap of this guidebook for sunrise and sunset times, to find out where the sun rises and sets on the compass (it changes throughout the year) and sun elevation (how high the sun rises in the sky).

Useful websites for this include suncalc.org and the Photographer's Ephemeris.

Self Exploration

The photographic interpretation of viewpoints is entirely down to prevailing conditions as well as your personal style and skill as a photographer.

This guidebook will help you get to some of the best photographic locations in the Park District. The list is by no means exhaustive, use it as a springboard to discover your own photo locations. There are many other great places in the area both known or still waiting to be discovered and photographed. Study a map and look for locations or just follow your nose to discover your own.

The Wheel stones on Derwent Edge (page 126).
Canon 5D Mk 1, 17-40 at 17mm, ISO 100, 1/30s at f/14, Sep. © CG

Chris Gilbert

My images in this book were taken over a number of years with either a Canon 5D or Canon 6D with some of the oldest ones taken on a Canon 30D. Where filtering is required I use Lee Graduated Filters or a Hoya Circular Polarising Filter. I have a minimum number of lenses, preferring to not replicate focal lengths. My workhorse wide angle is a Canon EF 17-40mm f/4L and my zoom lens is a Canon EF 70-300mm f/4-5.6L. If I really need to bridge the gap in focal lengths between the two lenses then I also have a Kenko 1.4x teleconverter in my bag that I can tag onto the back of the 17-40. I also use a Sigma 105mm f/2.8 Macro lens for close-ups. My tripod is a robust but inexpensive Slik 400 Pro. I prefer a 3-way head to a ball head.

I spend a lot of time studying weather maps and satellite images to determine the best subjects to shoot given the available weather and, by that same token, what are the best conditions to shoot a particular location under. I enjoy observing and recording unusual phenomena and out of the way places. I also enjoy working with the drama offered by extremes of light, which often puts my compositions outside the dynamic range available in a single exposure. I much prefer exposure blending over HDR in these circumstances and often shoot brackets to capture the entire dynamic range quickly.

I use Adobe Photoshop for processing. I aim for as natural a presentation as possible and avoid over-saturation. The methods I use in image capture maximise image data quality. This minimises the need for over-processing.

Camera Bodies
Canon EOS 30D
Canon EOS 5D Mk 1
Canon EOS 6D

Lenses
Canon EF 17-40mm f/4L USM
Canon EF 70-300mm f/4-5.6L IS USM
Sigma MACRO 105mm f/2.8 EX DG OS HSM
Kenko DGX MC4 1.4x Canon AF Converter
Filters
Lee Graduated Filters
Hoya Circular Polarising Filter

Tripod
Slik Pro 400 DX Tripod with 3-Way Head.

The gate on the Great Ridge (page 168). Canon 5D Mk 1, 17-40 at 24mm, ISO 50, 1s at f/20. Sep. © CG

Mick Ryan

I like to travel light and be ready for any opportunity, so I have two APSC sensor, mirrorless Sony A6000s with a Sony E 10-18mm f/4 on one body and a Sony E 18–200mm f/3.5–6.3 on the other. I always carry a tripod, but only use it when I have to when the light is low preferring to shoot handheld when I can. I carry everything in a small rucksack or sometimes a shoulder bag.

I can be quite obsessive when after a shot, watching the weather and visiting a location several times when conditions look good. I often camp out if doing a summer sunrise shoot. I also like to wander when the light looks good, going on walks in an area with no specific goals and taking my chances. I always have my cameras with me. I am upgrading soon to full frame, more than likely a Sony, and also I am enjoying the iPhone 7 camera.

I don't use filters at the moment, preferring to bracket exposures and blend them. For processing I use Adobe CC Lightroom and Photoshop.

Camera Bodies
2 x Sony A6000's

Lenses
Sony E 10-18mm f/4 OSS
Sony E 18–200mm f/3.5–6.3 OSS LE
Sony E PZ 16-50mm f/3.5-5.6 OSS

Tripod
Manfrotto 290 Light

A White Peak summer meadow. Sony A6000, 10-18 at 10mm, ISO 200, 1/80s at f/8. Jul. © MR

Captions

The photo captions in fotoVUE guidebooks are in two parts:

1 Descriptive Caption
First is a descriptive caption that describes where the photograph was taken, mentioning any references to viewpoints (e.g., VP1) in the accompanying text and any other useful descriptive text.

2 Photographic information
The second part of the caption lists the Camera, Lens, Exposure, Filter, when taken and Copyright. This information is from the Exchangeable Image File Format (Exif data) that is recorded on each image file when you take a photograph.

Who
Photo credit in the captions has either: © CG for Chris Gilbert or © MR for Mick Ryan.

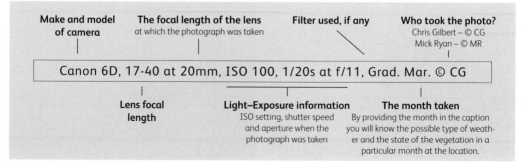

Make and model of camera | The focal length of the lens at which the photograph was taken | Filter used, if any | Who took the photo? Chris Gilbert – © CG Mick Ryan – © MR

Canon 6D, 17-40 at 20mm, ISO 100, 1/20s at f/11, Grad. Mar. © CG

Lens focal length | Light–Exposure information ISO setting, shutter speed and aperture when the photograph was taken | The month taken By providing the month in the caption you will know the possible type of weather and the state of the vegetation in a particular month at the location.

There are some photographs of the Peak that you will see a lot, often these are the classic viewpoints of the Peak District. Because of a combination of how the compositional elements are arranged; how the land lies and its vegetation cover, as well as the subject matter of the location, they just make great images. It is often familiarity or an emotional reason why some viewpoints at a location demand to be photographed, the reasons are often complex. Here is our bucket list of Peak District classic locations to visit.

Mount Famine & South Head from Swine's Back on Kinder (p.201). A6000, 18–200 at 18mm, ISO 100, 1/15s at f/11. Aug. © MR

The Anvil on Baslow Edge (p.316). Sony A6000, 18–200mm at 18mm, ISO 100, 1/13s at f/10. Sep. © MR

Haddon Hall from Haddon Fields (page 384) Canon 5D Mk 1, 17-300 at 115mm, ISO 100, 1s at f/20. Aug. © CG

ROADSIDE LANDSCAPE PHOTOGRAPHY LOCATIONS

While the Peak District rewards a wander away from the car there are many impressive landscape photography locations that are roadside, which are very useful if you have limited mobility, are rushed for time or just want an easier day. The same principles of light and weather that we have described throughout this book apply to these locations and they are usually best at dawn and close to dusk, or during the day when there is changeable weather. We have not included villages or valley bottoms in this list as these are usually good to explore with limited walking.

In book order, these are some of the most accessible viewpoints in the Peak, either roadside (marked with the wheelchair symbol &), or a short walk of less than 250m from the road (no symbol).

See each location's page for specific access details and location descriptions.

Boot's Folly taken from the road (page 156). Sony A6000, 18-200mm at 106mm, ISO 160, 1/60s at f/11. Early Sep. © MR

The Serpentine curve of the road to Edale. Taken from a short walk up the Mam Tor path. Sony A6000, 18-200 at 18mm, ISO 200, 1/400s at f/9. Jan. © MR

Derwent Reservoirs, Cave Dale, Calver Weir and Northwood Carr are all very accessible locations.

Almost all the Matlock area locations are close to the road with many suitable for wheelchair users.

The Peak District has over 1,600 miles of public rights of way – footpaths, bridleways and tracks – including 64 miles accessible to disabled people, and around 520 sq km (202 sq miles) is open access land – open to walkers without having to stick to paths.

Open Access Land

Open access was introduced by the Countryside and Rights of Way Act 2000 (CROW Act) in the Peak District on 19th September 2004. This gives everyone the freedom to roam off statutory paths over moors, heaths, commons, unimproved hills and dalesides and land above 600m – it doesn't usually apply to farmland where you have to stay on established paths and bridleways. The Peak District has a rich heritage of activism directed at liberating privately owned land for recreation that was once closed – see pages 188 and 198 for more information about some of the individuals and organisations involved.

Land mapped as open access is shown as a yellow wash on the Ordnance Survey Explorer maps and on Natural England's website and on the ground Access Land is marked at the point of entry with the Open Access Land symbol.

In the Peak such locations as Winnat's Pass, Chrome and Parkhouse Hills, the edges of Dove Dale, and much of the moorland and gritstone edges of the Dark Peak benefited from the CROW Act and many once-closed-off viewpoints are now available for photography.

Public rights of way on maps

Public rights of way are linear routes which fall into four categories. They are the legal responsibility of and maintained by Highway Authorities. Details of the routes are held on the Highway Authorities' Definitive Maps. The following symbols are used on OS 1:25,000 Explorer maps:

Footpaths ----------
For use on foot only.
Bridleways — — — — —
For use on foot, on a horse or on a pedal cycle.
Restricted byways -+-+-+-+-
For use on foot, on a horse or pedal cycle, or by horse drawn vehicle.
Byways -+-+-+-+
Open to all traffic, on foot, on a horse, on a pedal cycle or motorcycle, or in a motor or horse-drawn vehicle. However, they are mainly for use as footpaths or bridleways and are usually unsealed.

Then there are **Green Lanes** – unsurfaced rural roads – which have or may have the potential to carry motorised vehicle rights. Green Lanes are ancient routes that have existed for millennia, such as hollow ways, drover's roads, ridgeways and ancient trackways. There are many Green Lanes in the Peak and they are very beautiful to photograph and to photograph from, examples that you will encounter in this guidebook include the lanes to Three Shire Heads, Shatton Lane above Shatton and Monksdale Lane near Tideswell, there are many others.

Permissive paths are where a landowner gives agreement for public access. There is no statutory legal right to use these routes and permission may be withdrawn. They are shown on OS 1:25,000 Explorer maps as footpaths or bridleways and the agreement may be posted at the start of the path.

Maps in this book

Please note all paths and tracks are not marked on the maps in this guidebook, only the ones that are essential to get to a location or viewpoint. Including all rights of way would have made the maps indecipherable at their scale. It is essential that you use an OS map or similar with the guidebook maps for navigation.

The gate at Grindslow Knoll (p.160) on Kinder looking down to Edale. Kinder is Access Land. © MR

Impaired Access

If your movement is impaired, you can't walk far or up steep slopes, we have provided a list of accessible photography locations on page 38. If you use a wheelchair or have an injury and need to know whether a location is suitable for you, each location chapter has a brief Access notes section describing the terrain and distance from the road to a viewpoint. If a location has a wheelchair symbol part or all of it will be accessible by wheelchairs. ♿

Be a respectful photographer

The obvious is always worth stating: do not climb over walls or fences, shut all gates, drop no litter, pick up litter others have dropped, keep dogs at home or on lead, drive slowly in rural and urban areas, give way to cyclists, agricultural vehicles and horse riders, park considerably, don't scare livestock and keep quiet (don't play music or fly drones near others) but always say hello to fellow outdoor enthusiasts. In short follow the **Countryside Code**.

However, as photography becomes more popular some accessible locations and viewpoints can become busy at times of good light. In some circumstances this can cause conflict between photographers as they look for the best spot to compose their shot.

Some tips to avoid conflict

If high on your list is a photograph of the Mam Tor gate at sunrise with the Hope Valley veiled in mist – and why would it not be? – and conditions look good for the morning, you

Photographers at Curbar Edge. @ MR

can bet your last pound that you won't be the only one setting up their tripod at the gate just before sunrise. With that in mind, you can either go for it and risk being part of a crowd, or choose an alternative location – there are plenty of other options (see page 29).

Let's say you go for it and you are first to arrive at the gate. Does this give you any rights? Maybe morally, but not legally. Whist you may be considerate of others, some may not be so considerate of you and a conflict situation is something you may have to deal with. That good light may be fleeting and only last a few seconds, the pressure is on to get the shot.

The only answer is to talk. If you are first and in the prime spot greet whoever arrives after you with a friendly hello, let there be some chit chat, then explain to them the shot you are trying to take and that you will be as quick as possible. If they are reasonable, they shouldn't set up their tripod in front of you spoiling your composition.

Similarly, if you arrive at the gate, and someone is set up already, give them space and don't get in their way. Again talking and negotiating helps. They may be OK with you setting up next to them, or with you using their spot after they have done. Again, there are usually alternative viewpoints, but just make sure you aren't in their line of fire.

If there is a crowd at a particular spot, it is often best just to find another viewpoint.

An autumn mist in Edale taken from below Grindslow Knoll on Kinder (page 160).
Sony A6000, 18-200 at 18mm, ISO 100, 1/320s at f/11, Oct. © MR

NORTHERN PEAK

The Marsden area is the most northern outpost of the Peak District. We have been liberal with our definition of the Peak and include the cotton grass displays of Foxstone Moss near the M62 and the popular scenic viewpoint of Buckstones that overlooks the bronze swathes of Marsden Moor. Like their southern counterparts, the gritstone edges of Pule Hill, Standedge and West Nab supply wonderful textured rock as a foreground to dramatic compositions looking over endless moors. The small town of Marsden is a must visit for those who enjoy photographing old mills, terraced houses and canals, its visual heritage stretching back through the Industrial Revolution to when pack horses used to carry goods over the bleak landscape.

Saddleworth is the closest part of the Peak District to Greater Manchester and surprisingly its most mountainous, with steep rocky slopes and narrow valleys running down to Dove Stone Reservoir. On the rocky edge of Saddleworth Moor and its boggy mosses the views are dramatic and look down on over three million people. Up here however, you will often be alone. This is the most northern habitat of the mountain hare in the Peak and, along with them, you will share the endless moors with grouse, peregrine falcons and curlews. After photographing distinctive rock formations such as the famous Trinnacle – a Peak District classic, there are many impressive cascades to visit.

Maps

- OS Explorer Map OL21 (1:25 000) South Pennines
- OS Explorer Map OL1 (1:25 000) The Peak District: Dark Peak Area

You will find the mountain hare on the Saddleworth moor, Bleaklow and Kinder. Nikon D800E, 300 + 2x converter at 600mm, ISO 1000, 1/1600s at f/5.6. © Andrew Marshall

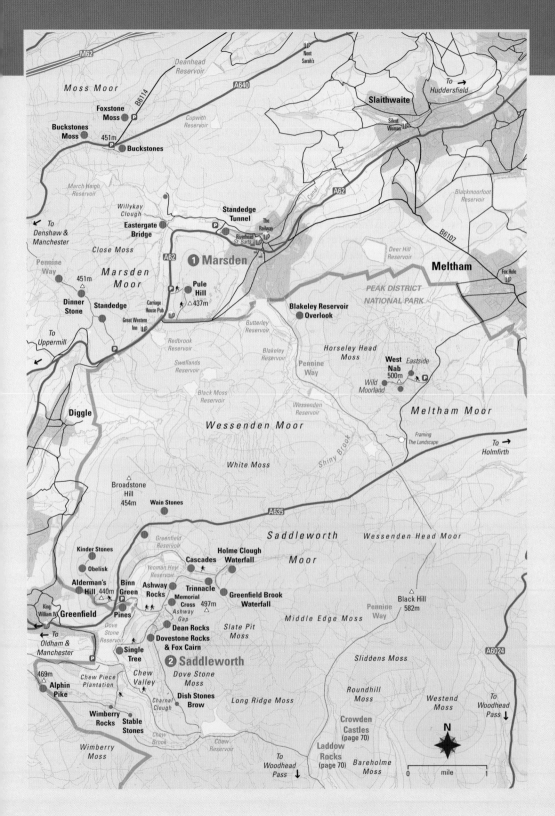

Moss Moor

M62

Deanhead
Reservoir

A640

To →
Huddersfield

B6114

Slaithwaite

Foxstone
Moss

Cupwith
Reservoir

Silent
Woman

Buckstones
Moss

451m

Buckstones

A62

March Haigh
Reservoir

Blackmoorfoot
Reservoir

Willykay
Clough

Standedge
Tunnel

To
Denshaw &
Manchester

Eastergate
Bridge

The
Railway

Riverhead
St. Bart's

B6107

Close Moss

A62

❶ Marsden

Meltham

Pennine
Way

451m

Marsden
Moor

Pule
Hill

Deer Hill
Reservoir

Fox Hole

Dinner
Stone

Standedge

Carriage
House Pub

437m

Blakeley Reservoir
Overlook

PEAK DISTRICT
NATIONAL PARK

To
Uppermill

Great Western
Inn

Butterley
Reservoir

Horseley Head
Moss

West
Nab
500m

Eastside

Redbrook
Reservoir

Swellands
Reservoir

Blakeley
Reservoir

Pennine
Way

Wild
Moorland

Diggle

Black Moss
Reservoir

Wessenden
Reservoir

Meltham Moor

Wessenden Moor

Shiny Brook

Framing
The Landscape

To →
Holmfirth

White Moss

Broadstone
Hill
454m

Wain Stones

A635

Saddleworth

Wessenden Head Moor

Greenfield
Reservoir

Moor

Kinder Stones

Cascades

Holme Clough
Waterfall

Obelisk

Yeoman Hey
Reservoir

Trinnacle

Black Hill
582m

Alderman's
Hill 440m

Binn
Green

Ashway
Rocks

Memorial
Cross

Greenfield Brook
Waterfall

Pennine
Way

King
William IV

Greenfield

Pines

497m

Middle Edge Moss

Dove
Stone
Reservoir

Ashway
Gap

Dean Rocks

Slate Pit
Moss

A6024

To →
Oldham &
Manchester

Single
Tree

Dovestone Rocks
& Fox Cairn

❷ Saddleworth

Sliddens Moss

469m

Alphin
Pike

Chew Piece
Plantation

Chew
Valley

Dove Stone
Moss

Dish Stones
Brow

Long Ridge Moss

Roundhill
Moss

Westend
Moss

To
Woodhead
Pass

Wimberry
Rocks

Stable
Stones

Charnal
Clough

Crowden
Castles
(page 70)

N

Wimberry
Moss

Chew
Brook

Chew
Reservoir

Laddow
Rocks
(page 70)

To
Woodhead
Pass

Bareholme
Moss

0   mile   1

Marsden is nestled in the Pennine Hills at the head of the Colne Valley surrounded by high moorland and gritstone edges. The Peak District National Park boundary stops just short of the village, but we have included several great locations to the north on Marsden Moor.

Marsden was a centre for the production of woollen cloth until the early 21st century. Bank Bottom Mill – once employing 1,900 workers – closed in 2003, and the area has a rich cultural and industrial history stretching back beyond Roman times. Marsden is on the Yorkshire side of the Pennines and several generations of tracks and roads pass this way crossing the high moors linking Manchester and Huddersfield, as well as the Standedge Tunnels that carry the Huddersfield Narrow Canal, and the Huddersfield and Manchester Railway.

Marsden village is worth a few hours with a camera as it retains much of its original architecture such as St Bartholomew's Church and its packhorse bridge,

terraced houses and the more industrial like Bank Bottom Mill. The village and surrounding area is popular as a location for television and film productions, and classics such as Last of the Summer Wine and The League of Gentlemen have been filmed here. Marsden was also the home of the poet Simon Armitage and he still lives locally. Just outside the village there is the packhorse bridge of Eastergate Bridge and Standedge Tunnel.

The surrounding moorlands, bleak and desolate on some winter days, are well served by a network of footpaths and free-to-roam Access Land. Buckstones, Pule Hill, Standedge and West Nab provide wonderful high viewpoints over the moors, often with a foreground of gritstone rocks. The moors are best experienced on frosty winter days with a low sun, or in high summer when the cotton grass and heather flowers, when you should look out for moorland birds such as golden plover, red grouse, curlew and twite.

On Buckstones moss looking west to March Hill. Sony A6000, 10-18 at 10mm, ISO 160, 1/160s at f/11. Nov. © MR

The view from Buckstones south, toward Pule Hill. Canon 6D, 17-40 at 20mm, ISO 200, 1/100s at f/14. Grad. Nov. © CG

BUCKSTONES

Buckstones is a small but significant gritstone edge by the A640 New Hey Road two miles north west of Marsden and a mile south of the M62. Its elevated position gives a tremendous view over Marsden Moor and down to the rocky escarpment of Pule Hill which rises above the moor, with West Nab in the distance.

What to shoot and viewpoints

The free-standing gritstone boulders and short cliff faces of Buckstones, a.k.a. Nont Sarah's after the nearby pub, provide perfect foreground for big landscape compositions that sweep down to March Haigh Reservoir and on beyond Marsden.

The best compositions point to the south east as the land slopes down towards the escarpment of Pule Hill. Significant are a large square block and the protruding flying fins of gritstone that point out over the moor. Explore the length of the edge, but the best viewpoints are where the car park path joins the clifftop where you can include March Haigh Reservoir in a composition.

Also explore along and above the road in the west especially on Buckstones Moss where there is another gritstone edge.

How to get here

From the west approach from Denshaw for 4 miles north east along the A640 to a car park at the junction of the A640 and B6114. From the north cross the M62 on the B6114 from Barkisland, and from Huddersfield follow the A640. There are connecting minor roads from Slaithwaite east of Marsden that lead to A640 New Hey Road. There is a small car park at the junction of the A640 and B6114 and once parked, the rocks of Buckstones are just in front of you to the south.

Parking Lat/Long: 53.619585, -1.975494
Parking Grid Ref: SE 017 136
Parking Postcode: HD7 6NG (2.5 km)

Accessibility ♿

This is a location for everyone. It gets busy at times being a popular local viewpoint – and popular with climbers and paragliders – but at sunrise you should be by yourself. The gritstone edge is 100m down a good path although there are great viewpoints all along the road. Boots are a good idea as the moor sucks up moisture.

Approach: 2 minutes, distance 100m, 0m ascent

Best time of year/day

Due to its high elevation and south west aspect the cliff's front face catches light from the setting sun all-year round and the rising sun from September to March. From October onwards both sunrise and sunset are the best times, the low winter light illuminating the rust hues of the moorland as the bracken, heather and grasses sleep for the winter. This location is especially good if there is a frost or light snow cover which increases the texture of the land.

FOXSTONE MOSS

This is the most northern location in this guidebook and it is stretching it to call it the Peak District. Just a few hundred metres north of Buckstones on the B1664 Ripponden Road and south of the M62, this flat moorland right by the road is home to one of the best displays of cotton grass in the Pennines. The moorland is flat, the display is extensive and flowers around late June and early July. If you go with a dog or another person you will have a focal point amongst the sea of white. Early and later in the day are best. This is a recovering blanket bog managed by the National Trust and is an SSSI.

What to shoot and viewpoints

This moorland is flat and featureless unless you go to the south edge of Buckstone Moss that overlooks Marsden Moor, or north to Way Stone Edge where the moor slopes down to the M62 and Ripponden. At the edge of the moor you can compose with cotton grass in the foreground with an interesting mid and background.

However, compositions of a sea of cotton grass as far as the eye can see can be powerful especially if combined with a colourful sky. A person, dog or fence posts can be used as focal points or leading lines to help compositions.

Also try getting low down, kneeling or lying, to shoot through the cotton grass trying different apertures. This is also the perfect place for macro images of cotton grass.

How to get here

From the Buckstone car park at the junction of the A640 and B6114, drive north up the B6114 toward the M62. After a third of a mile look left for some small lay-bys and park carefully off the road. Walk onto the moor.

Parking Lat/Long: 53.622842, -1.970790
Parking Grid Ref: SE 020 140
Parking Postcode: HD3 3FT

Accessibility ♿

The moorland is flat but tussocky, and walking poles can help on this type of terrain. Wellingtons, because of the wet nature of the moss, are a good idea at anytime of year here. You don't have to walk far for the cotton grass, a few metres, but the display does stretch for over a mile.

Best time of year/day

For the cotton grass in early June and July, the best times to visit are at either end of the day at sunrise or sunset or when the sun is low in the sky.

An endless sea of cotton grass at Foxstone Moss. Sony A6000, 10-18mm at 10mm, ISO 125, 1/350s at f/11. Jul. © MR

The Marsden end of the Standedge Tunnel. Canon 6D, Canon 17-40 at 17mm, ISO 200, 1/200s at f/8, Grad. Aug. © CG

STANDEDGE TUNNEL

The Huddersfield Narrow Canal linking Ashton-under-Lyne in the west and Huddersfield in the east travels under the Pennines by Standege Tunnel, the longest, highest and deepest canal tunnel in the UK. Completed in 1811 at great cost and labour it is three miles long and only wide enough for one way traffic. Narrowboats loaded with cargo had to be 'legged' through the tunnel. Leggers laid on the deck and pushed with their feet against the walls to propel the barge forward, they were paid one shilling and sixpence per journey. The tunnel was closed in 1944 and reopened with a visitors centre in 2001. For those interested in industrial heritage it is a great place to photograph. There is a canal basin here with moored narrowboats, an historical exhibition, walks along the canal and the tunnel itself. You can also go on a two hour trip through the tunnel.

What to Shoot and Viewpoints

It is worth walking to the tunnel down the canal from Marsden to photograph traveling and moored barges. Once at Standege Tunnel there is a canal museum to explore with your camera and the tunnel entrance.

How to get here

You can either walk half-a-mile down the canal from Marsden railway station to the tunnel or drive. Head into Marsden off the A62 down the main street (Peel Street) to Station Road and cross the bridge at the railway station and turn left down Reddisher Road for half a mile then left down to the car park.

Parking Lat/Long: 53.604616, -1.940823
Parking Grid Ref: SE 040 120
Parking Postcode: HD7 6NQ

Accessibility ♿

This is a location for everyone. The tunnel is 100m from the car park and is wheel-chair accessible.

Approach: 2 minutes, distance 100m, 0m ascent

Best time of year/day

This is an all-year-round location but is best in the summer and autumn when the area is at its most colourful.

EASTERGATE BRIDGE

Eastergate Bridge (marked as Close Gate Bridge on OS maps) is an attractive packhorse bridge built around 1800 that crosses Haigh Clough. Several streams drain off Marsden Moor here and form the source of the River Calder. The bridge is on the route of the old Huddersfield to Rochdale packhorse trail and is similar to Three Shires Head Bridge on Axe Edge Moor. As well as the bridge there is moorland, a ford and a unique parallel gritstone wall running up the hillside known as the Dark Lane.

What to Shoot and Viewpoints

Viewpoint 1 – Eastergate Bridge

Eastergate Bridge is a subject to work at trying several viewpoints. The two streams make an effective focal point and leading lines. The stream under the bridge runs west to east. Close Moss, the rise of land behind the bridge, can shade the bridge late in the day or in winter and the adjacent trees do shade the bridge most of the time. Overcast days may be best or anytime there is uniform light.

The ford on Redbrook Clough (VP2). Canon 6D, Canon 17-40 at 20mm, ISO 50, 1s at f14, ND, Grad. Aug. © CG

Autumn and winter are the best times to visit, especially after heavy rain with the stream in spate.

Viewpoint 2 – The Ford and Dark Lane

Just up south of the bridge the ochre-coloured waters of Redbrook Clough stain a ford and a small cascade. Across from the ford is the Dark Lane which is very worthy of exploration by walking up it right to the top of the hill or viewed from on the opposite slope. It makes a very strong image if composed well. Dark Lane is a public right of way being part of the Standedge Trail, although not marked as such on the OS map.

Viewpoint 3 – Up High – Drystone Wall Patterns

This valley has some striking wall patterns that are best photographed from a high viewpoint. As well as up the Dark Lane try walking up Willykay Clough, the drainage west of the bridge and also up Blake Lee Lane. For Blake Lee Lane go steeply up the road from the parking to where the road bends. From here there are elevated views down into the valley with great field wall patterns.

How to get here

Head into Marsden off the A62 down the main street (Peel Street) to Station Road and cross the bridge at the railway station and turn left down Reddisher Road which turns into Waters Road. Park a mile from the railway station in front of a big house and next to a farm track or at Tunnel End car park and walk. Head west down the footpath by the stream (Haigh Clough) for 300m to Eastergate Bridge where Redbrook Clough joins Haigh Clough.

Parking Lat/Long: 53.606907, -1.955238
Parking Grid Ref: SE 028 121
Parking Postcode: HD7 6NG (0.5km

Accessibility

The path to the bridge is narrow and sometimes slippery but should be accessible to most. Photographing the bridge from some angles requires walking over slippery rocks. The path up Dark Lane is steep.

Best time of year/day

This area can be very photogenic in winter, especially with snow around, or in autumn and spring. At these times of year there is more contrast in the landscape giving stronger, more atmospheric images. The bridge gets light late morning/early afternoon in the autumn.

Bank Bottom Mill in Marsden from the road. Sony A6000, 18-200 at 43mm, ISO 400, 1/125s at f/6.3. Aug. © MR

Above: *The view down Dark Lane and up Haigh Clough (VP2). Canon 6D, 17-40 at 20mm, ISO 100, 1/30s at f/14, Grad. Aug. © CG*

Below: *The elegant Eastergate Bridge (VP1)). Canon 6D, 17-40 at 20mm, ISO 100, 1/60s at f/14, HDR. Aug. © CG*

BLAKELEY RESERVOIR VIEW

Wessenden Brook drains the high moorland south of Marsden and has been dammed to form four reservoirs. This viewpoint looks up the valley above and toward the reservoirs. From the A62 at Marsden take Fall Lane south to Binn Lane and follow this road passing terraced houses and a mill up the hill by Owles End Farm, now a single lane minor road, to a turnaround at the end of the road. The viewpoints are right in front of you looking up the valley.

Parking Lat/Long: 53.606907, -1.955238
Parking Grid Ref: SE 028 121
Parking Postcode: HD7 6NG (0.5km

Great views from the end of Binn Lane, toward Blakeley Reservoir. Canon 6D, 17-40 at 20mm, ISO 100, 1/30s at f/14, Grad. Aug. © CG

PULE HILL

Pule Hill's steep west side topped by a gritstone edge and quarry with a commanding position overlooking Marsden and the surrounding moorland. There are views in all directions with the best overlooking Marsden Moor toward Saddleworth in the west.

The name Pule Hill is from the Celtic and Old English, pol, peol, and pul which means quite aptly, the hill in the marsh. In 1896 George Marsden discovered urns containing human ashes, arrowheads, tools and flints from this Bronze Age burial site.

What to Shoot and Viewpoints

Viewpoint 1 – Stanza Stones

The Stanza Stones Trail links Marsden to Ilkley (a 47 mile walk) with poems by Marsden's Simon Armitage carved onto stones by Pip Hall at six locations along the walk. Each poem has a theme and the Stanza Stone theme at Pule Hill is Snow.

Park in the lay-by north of the Carriage House pub below the quarry and near the derelict quarry building. From the lay-by walk south, through the gate and follow the path between the derelect building and the air shaft to follow the old quarry incline up the hill to the quarry of Pule Hill. The Stanza Stone is found in some quarry blocks behind the stone seat at the front of the quarry – they are tricky to see (and find).

Viewpoint 2 – Cliff Top

The cliff top can be accessed near the quarry or by walking up the hill near Carriage House pub on Mount Road. The gritstone edge stretches for 500m along the hill top and there are various platforms and features including a rock arch with a window, called Flying Buttress, to include in compositions. Being west facing these stones and the land in front of them are illuminated by low sun for most of the day in the winter.

How to get here

Pule Hill is by the A62 – the Huddersfield-Manchester Road between Marsden and Diggle. From Marsden head west for 2 miles on the A62 and park in a lay-by on the road where a quarry track meets the road – recognisable by some buildings and spoil heaps – or take a left at the Carriage House pub and park by a path on Mount Road. Both parking spots are by the start of paths that lead to the cliffs and a path that traverse the summit area above them.

Parking Lat/Long: 53.592493, -1.958010
Parking Grid Ref: SE 028 106
Parking Postcode: HD7 6NL

Accessibility

It's a stiff up hill walk of 20 minutes on rough paths to the top of Pule Hill by either route.

Approach: 20 minutes, distance 300m, 70m ascent

Best time of year/day

A place for all times of day as its summit has views in all directions. Autumn and winter are the best seasons when the moorland has more colour and the sun is low in the sky.

The natural arch on Pule Hill's west face (VP2). Canon 6D, Canon 17-40 at 20mm, ISO 400, 1/200s at f/14. Dec. © CG

Simon Armitage's Stanza Stone in Pule Hill Quarry(VP2). Canon 6D, 70-300 at 200mm, ISO 800, f5.6, 1/800s. Dec. © CG

STANDEDGE

South west facing Standedge at the edge of Marsden Moor includes Millstone Edge and the Dinner Stone overlooking the Castleshaw Reservoirs and the Saddleworth villages of Diggle, Delph and Dobcross. This is a big vista anchored by superb featured gritstone formations which is best suited for winter photography. There is lots of potential at this accessible location and if it was in the central Peak it would be a major location.

The view from The Dinner Stone on Standedge down toward Castleshaws Reservoirs below. Canon 6D, 17-40 at 20mm, ISO 200, 1/200s at f/14, Grad. Dec. © CG

How to get here

The gritstone edges at Standedge are a short walk over the moors from the A62, three miles drive from Marsden. Park at a car park on A62 Huddersfield – Manchester Road opposite Brun Clough Reservoir where the Pennine Way/Bridleway leads up to Millstone Edge. You can also park on a minor road near Bentley Farm for even quicker access.

It is a 1.5km walk to the highest point at 451m with 60m of elevation gain, give yourself 20 minutes from the car to the viewpoints..

Parking Lat/Long: 53.582252, -1.975408
Parking Grid Ref: SE 017 095
Parking Postcode: OL3 5LT

WEST NAB

West Nab is an accessible elevated moorland hill with magical vistas in most directions from its rock-strewn plateau. Humans have been visiting here since Stone Age times when the area was used as flint 'workshops'. If you are lucky you may find a microlith, small worked pieces of flint that were used to form the points of arrows and spears. Some also believe that because of its position West Nab was a 'Temple of the Sun' for Bronze and Iron Age people.

For the photographer West Nab has wide compositions in most directions, especially around its east and south-facing summit crags and boulders. To the east you look down on the village of Meltham, over to the Victorian tower on Castle Hill and Huddersfield. In all other directions the view is of high moorland with the Wessenden Reservoirs and the Pennine Way to the west and the road snaking off in the south. There is great photographic potential all around on this rocky moorland summit and its slopes particularly at sunrise, sunset and when the weather is changeable.

What to Shoot and Viewpoints

A path on the west side of the road leads up the hill to the eastern rocks of West Nab.

Viewpoint 1 – Eastside Rocks

The boulders and small cliff faces of the east side of West Nab overlook Meltham and in the distance Huddersfield. These interesting features get light from sunrise all year around, but are better from September onwards when the sun rises in the east to south east and they are side lit if you are shooting to the north east.

Viewpoint 2 – Summit

From the east side of West Nab path leads unto the summit passing a small stone shelter. At the summit cairn there are shapely rocks scattered around, some catching water, with views in all directions. To the west the moorland slopes down to Wessenden Reservoir and the Pennine Way then rises up to form Black Moss.

Shapely outcrops at the western end of West Nab, overlooking Wessenden (VP3). Canon 6D, 17-40 at 20mm, ISO 100, 1/20s at f/14, Grad. Aug. © CG

Looking down on Meltham (VP1). Sony A6000, 10-18 f/4 at 10mm, ISO 100, 1/100s at f/11. Mar. © MR

Seat anyone? Curious weathering of one of the West Nab boulders (VP1). Canon 6D, 17-40, ISO 100, 1/30s at f/14, Grad. Jul. © CG

Viewpoint 3 – Wild Moorland

Follow the path from the summit to the west to more gritstone outcrops and eventually a fence line. The view back to the summit is particularly photogenic and is best in late afternoon to sunset. The road can be included as a beautiful serpentine leading line. There are many outcrops here sculpted by the elements.

Viewpoint 4 – Framing The Landscape

Just north of the junction of the A635 and the West Nab/Meltham road is a lay-by with a footpath leading down to Wessendon Reservoir. In late afternoon light and at sunset this can be a great composition looking down the drainage to the reservoirs. There is a Framing The Landscape installation at the start of the path.

Opposite left: Looking south from West Nab's summit (VP2).Sony A6000, 18-200 at 30mm, ISO 100, 1/60s at f/11. Mar. © MR

Opposite right: Looking west at sunset (VP3).Sony A6000, 10-18 at 15mm, ISO 200, 1/100s at f/10. Mar. © MR

How to get here

West Nab is located just west of the Wessenden Head Road which links the A635 Saddleworth Moor road to Meltham. There is a small lay-by down the road on the Meltham side of the road – next to a sometimes graffitied rock known as the Cock Crowing Stone.

A path leads from here over a stile and up the slope to the east facing rocks of West Nab's summit; a 20 minute gentle up hill walk.

Parking Lat/Long: 53.575895, -1.879625
Parking Grid Ref: SE 080 088
Parking Postcode: HD9 4HW (1km)

Accessibility

It is a short uphill approach up a good but sometimes rocky path. There are good paths on the flat summit, but once off the paths the going gets tougher. In winter wear Muck Boots or similar as this moor is boggy.

To West Nab summit: 15 minutes, distance 550m, 58m ascent.

Best time of year/day

Late autumn and winter sunrises and sunsets are the best times with stormy weather giving atmosphere and mood anytime of year. If there is snow this is a wondrous place to be.

Saddleworth Moor sucks up over a metre of rain each year and this eventually tumbles steeply down ravines over rocky steps to collect in the reservoirs of the Chew Valley. This valley is a cirque or a cwm, surrounded by hills except for a gap in the west where it opens toward Oldham and Manchester. At an elevation of 1500ft/460m the edges of the moorland plateau are lined with gritstone cliffs, boulders and pinnacles; perfect pedestals and foreground subjects. These are accessible locations with a mountain feel to them. In the valley bottom there are woodland and lake locations, and a little higher some very special cascades and waterfalls.

What to shoot and viewpoints

Viewpoint 1 – Alderman's Hill
Location Grid Ref: SE 014 046
Approach: 30 minutes, distance 1km, 135m ascent

From Binn Green car park cross the road and take the path opposite that weaves its way up to the rocky summit of Alderman's Hill. It's a short and steep approach but with

dramatic views in all directions particularly to the north east where a composition could include Yeoman Hay Reservoir and the snaking line of the Holmfirth Road. Winter sunrises are good here. Off the summit the rocks tumble down the south east slope providing interesting foreground. At sunset the moor and cliffs opposite light up.

A 15 minute walk north from the summit of Alderman's, overlooking the seven villages of Saddleworth, is the obelisk, a stone memorial to the fallen of the First World War next to Pots and Pans Rocks and near the Kinder Stones. These moorland locations look down on the terraces, semis and mills of Uppermill and beyond.

Viewpoint 2 – Binn Green Pines and Dove Stone Reservoir
Location Grid Ref: SE 018 043
Approach: 15 minutes, distance 0.5km, 40m descent

Below Binn Green car park follow the path down to a dense pine woodland which extends down to the waters edge and along Yeoman Hey Reservoir. This is an autumn place when the low winter's sun filters through the woods. Calm windless days at this time of year offer potential for reflections of the golden moorland in the still waters.

Along the road to Dove Stones car park. Sony A6000, 16-50 at 50mm, ISO 200, 1/200s at f/11. Jan. © MR

Above: The spectacular view over Dove Stones Reservoir from Alderman's Hill (VP1). Canon 5D Mk 1, Canon 17-40 f/4 at 20mm, ISO 200, 1/40s at

Below: The lone tree by Dove Stones reservoir (VP2) Try to spot it in the above image. Canon 7D Mark II, 100-400, ISO 100, 1/4000s at f/5.6. © Craig Hannah

Wassenden Moor

Ravens Stones Brow & the Trinnacle (hidden)

Ashway Rocks

Memorial Cross

Ashway Stone

Dove Stone N

Dean Rocks

to Holme Clough and Greenfield Brook Waterfalls

Greenfield Reservoir

Ashway Gap

Yeoman Hey Reservoir

Bill 'o Jacks Plantation

Access Land

A635 to Holmfirth via Isle of Skye Road

Bin Green Car Park

m
Cairn on Fox Stone
Charnel Stones
Dish Stones Brow
Great Dove Stone Rocks
Little Dove Stone Rocks
To Chew Reservoir (and Laddow Rocks)
Chew Brook and Track
Stable Stones Brow
Wimberry Rocks
Wimberry Moss
Alphin
469m
Chew Piece Plantation
the lone tree
Sailing Club
Dove Stone Car Park
P
path around reservoir
Dove Stone Reservoir
to Oldham and Manchester
Alderman's Brow

How to get here

The parking for most locations is at the pay and display Binn Green car park on the A635 (the 'Isle of Skye' Holmfirth road) next to Dove Stone and Yeoman Hey reservoirs. If coming from the west, Manchester, from the M60 take exit 22 and the A62 to Oldham. Once through Oldham take the A669 Lees Road/Oldham Road to the Chew Valley Road, which leads to Greenfield. Take the A635 Holmfirth Road for 1.1 miles to Binn Green car park below Alderman Hill and Rocks between Dove Stone and Yeoman Hey reservoirs. If coming from the east from Holmfirth take the A635 west for nearly 9 miles to Binn Green parking. For viewpoints 6 and 7 park at Dove Stones car park.

Parking Lat/Long: 53.537024, -1.974958
Parking Grid Ref: SE 017 044
Parking Postcode: OL3 7NN (0.2 km)

Accessibility ♿

The Pine woods and reservoirs have short approaches and can be accessed by wheel chairs by the access road below Binn Green car park. Also for those with limited mobility driving up the Holmfirth Road has some great roadside locations when the light is good. For other locations here a good pair of legs are needed for the 30-50 minute uphill hikes on good paths. Navigation may be needed when up on the moor as some paths are indistinct.

Opposite: *Looking down at Greenfield Brook from Raven Stones Brow (VP4). Sony A6000, 18-200 at 18mm, ISO 100, 1/16s at f/11. Aug. © MR*

Best time of year/day

The high elevation moorland locations, Ashway Rocks, the Trinnacle and Dove Stones are good at or before summer sunsets, Any time during the winter when the sun is low especially at either end of the day works well too. In autumn the summer greens turn to bronze and russet brown creating delightful contrast.

The waterfalls are good on summer afternoons especially when the fox gloves and heather bloom in August, and during the shorter days of autumn and winter when they will be in full spate – light will be limited at this time. Autumn is the best time for the pine woods and the reservoir, on still cold mornings with perhaps some mist floating around. If the clag descends you can get great atmospheric misty compositions.

The cairn on the Fox Stone above Great Dove Stone Rocks (VP6). Canon 6D, 17-40 at 21mm, ISO 200, 1/60s at f/14. Feb. © CG

Viewpoint 3 – Ashway Rocks and Memorial Cross
Location Grid Ref: SE 028 048
Approach: 50 minutes, distance 2km, 191m ascent

Approach by Ashway Gap. From Bin Green Car Park follow the path through the woods and left down the road to the dam between Yeoman Hey Reservoir and Dove Stone Reservoir. Follow the road over the dam which goes right and at a bridge turn left up the path with the man-made waterway on your right. This path arches left gradually climbing the slope straight to Ashway Rocks. This is a stiff 40-minute walk from the car park: just over a mile/1.7km with 203m/650ft of ascent.

The compositions from these rocks can include foreground rocks lit by a setting sun at most times of year looking down to south west down to Dove Stone Reservoir or north west to Yeoman Hay.

From Ashway Rocks walk uphill and east to a path, turn right down the path to the James Platt Memorial Cross. The cross commemorates James Platt, an MP for Oldham who in 1857 accidentally shot and killed himself here whilst grouse shooting. It makes an interesting subject with an atmospheric sky or at night.

Ashway Rocks looking down on Dovestones reservoir (VP3). Canon 5D, 17-40 at 20mm, ISO 200, 1/40s at f/20, Grad. Mar. © CG

Viewpoint 4: Raven Stones and the Trinnacle
Location Grid Ref: SE 037 048
Approach: 1hr 10 minutes, distance 3km, 234m ascent

The Trinnacle is composed of three joined gritstone pinnacles that sit just below Raven Stones Brow looking breathtakingly down to Greenfield Brook and Reservoir. The formation is hidden at the west end of Raven Stones Brow which themselves offer many impressive views over the valley and moorland.

The easiest way to get there is to make your way to Ashway Rocks as described in the previous viewpoint and follow a path that heads initially north along the edge, then turns right (west). Continue along this path all the way to where the plateau descends to Greenfield Brook – a walk of 1km. The Trinnacle is situated at the edge of the cliffs here. You can also approach from Greenfield Brook, a steeper and trickier approach, not for the feint of heart.

The best times to be here are between May and August (heather flowers) at sunrise, early afternoon and sunset when the Trinnacle and the valley below will be illuminated. Winter can be good as well when there is more contrast in the landscape. Thoughtful composition is needed so as not to block out the reservoir and the track. If you get the light, both straight on and from the side both work well.

***Opposite middle**: The Dish Stones on the north side of the Chew Valley (VP7). Canon 6D, 17-40 at 20mm, ISO 100, 1/5s at f/13. Jan. © CG*

Above: The Trinnacle on Raven Stone Brow. A stunning location with a remote feel (VP4). Canon 5D, Canon 17-40 at 20mm, ISO 200, 1/40s at f/20, Grad. Mar. © CG

Below: Ashway Cross, a memorial to James Platt MP. Canon 5D, 17-40 at 20mm, ISO 400, 1/200s at f/8. Grad. Mar. © CG

Above: The approach to Greenfield waterfall (VP5). Sony A6000, 18-200 at 18mm, ISO 100, 1/125s at f/11. Aug. © MR

Viewpoint 5: Greenfield and Holme Clough Waterfalls

Greenfield Waterfall Approach: 1hr 10 minutes , distance 3km, 147m ascent

At the head of the valley Holme and Birchen Clough tumble steeply down through gritstone boulders and join to form Greenfield Brook above Greenfield Reservoir. Here there are several impressive waterfalls and cascades that are very worthwhile to photograph.

Approach from Binn Green car park down through the woods and left down the access road to follow the road north along side Yeoman Hay Reservoir and passing Greenfield Reservoir (1.2 miles/2km to here).

The first cascades (SE 032 051) are either side of a small packhorse bridge, the lower cascade – on the left – being the tallest. Explore either side of the bridge for many pleasing compositions, both close up and including the steep sided slopes of the valley – you can include the Trinnacle in a composition. Most of these initial cascades are easy to get do being right by the track, others require scrambling down slopes.

Holme Clough Waterfall

Location Grid Ref: SE 039 051
Approach: 1hr 10 minutes, distance 3km, 234m ascent

Continue up the valley to a weir (1.8 miles/3km from the car park). The valley splits here and the going gets a little tougher. The left fork is Holme Clough. Go right at the weir until just above it and head back left across the brook and navigate up Holme Clough to the beautiful 10ft high segmented waterfall surrounded by boulders. This valley faces south-west and can be very sunny.

Birchen Clough – Greenfield Waterfall

Location Grid Ref: SE 038 047
Approach: 1hr 10 minutes, distance 3km, 234m ascent

This is the shadier right fork for that leads up steeply to the south east. As you navigate up through rocks and a narrow steep path the impressive multi-stepped cascade of Greenfield Brook reveals itself with the biggest drop at its head. Take care when hopping around in the water. Beware after heavy rain, this valley floods.

Opposite: Holme Clough waterfall (VP5). Sony A6000, 18-200 at 18mm, ISO 100, 1/6s at f/11. Aug. © MR

Greenfield waterfall (VP5). Sony A6000, 18-200 at 18mm, ISO 100, 1/4s at f/5. Aug. © MR

Viewpoint 6: The Chew Valley – North Side
Dish Stones – Charnal Clough – Fox Stone – Dovestone Rocks
round trip: 3hr, distance 7.2km, 286m ascent

The northern side of the Chew Valley is dominated by the edge of Dove Stones Moss. This dramatic skyline is not only easy to access but it also offers the photographer considerable interest.

From Dove Stones reservoir car park follow the Chew Road up toward Chew Reservoir as far as the disused quarry before the reservoir (a 1.7km walk). A clear path that is not marked on the map ascends the far lip of the quarry and double-backs around the top, leading directly to the edge of the hill at Dish Stones, which dominate the view above as you reach the top of the Chew Road. The main 'Dish Stone' is a shapely pinnacle which composes up well in winter light against Stable Stones Brow beyond.

The path continues beyond Dish Stones and is often quite boggy but after 500 metres meets the top of Charnal Clough. From this position Stable Stones and Wimberry Stones have now separated and they compose together well with some great wind-carved foreground rocks that are here at the top of Charnal Clough. Spring mornings and summer evenings work well.

A further 250 metres along the path and at an un-named point on the edge you reach an obvious and dramatic pinnacle. Just before this and slightly down from the path at SE 026 029 there is a fantastic collection of wind-sculpted rocks, threaded through with some old, broken down walls. Again Stable Stones and Wimberry Rocks offer excellent background with Dove Stones Reservoir now becoming a more important compositional component.

A further 300 metres along the path brings you to the Cairn on Fox Stone and beyond that Great Dovestone Rocks themselves. At this position Alderman's Hill on the far side of the valley starts to play a more important role than Wimberry Edge but given the twin aspect here – both north west and south east – the position has excellent potential at all times of year.

From Fox Stone there is an obvious path that leads directly and steeply down to rejoin the Chew Road where it meets Chew Brook at SE 019 031.

Viewpoint 7: The Chew Valley – South Side
Alphin Pike – Wimberry Rocks – Stable Stones Brow round trip:
3hr, distance 7km, 327m ascent

The high brow south of Dove Stone reservoir is a great place to look down over the reservoirs north toward Saddleworth Moor, and in the opposite direction down toward Manchester. This rocky edge of Wimberry Moss is good for photography all year round, especially in the afternoon and at sunset. It is however quite a slog to get up high. Two routes are recommended, first by a long ridge, Alphin Brow, starting just south of Greenfield, that takes you to the summit of Alphin Pike. From its summit are great composition south to Manchester, north west down to the village of Greenfield and north east over the reservoirs. This path along the edge of the brow takes you to Wimberry Rocks (aka Indian's Head) and Stable Stones Brow, both providing great foreground boulder subjects.

You can also approach from Dove Stone reservoir by taking the path up the Chew Valley to the small bridge where a path heads right and south up through the plantation and roughly up the slope by big boulders to a gully on the left of Wimberry Rocks and Wimberry Moss. All approaches are rich with photographic interest and you could think that you were in the Lake District or North Wales.

Manchester from the summit of Alphin Pike (VP7). Sony A6000, 15-50 at 34mm, ISO 100, 1/200s at f/11. Jan. © MR

Wilderness Gully from below Wimbery Rocks. Climbers Graham West and Michael Roberts died in an avalanche here in 1963. Sony A6000, 16-50 at 40mm, ISO 100, 1/250s at f/13. Jan. © MR

From Wimberry Rocks (VP6) looking down on Dovestones reservoir and beyond to Oldham, Manchester and 3 million people. Sony A6000, 10-18 at 10mm, ISO 100, 1/250s at f/11. Jan. © MR

The Woodhead Pass and its locations are wild and have a big atmosphere, yet they are not far from the vast sprawl of Greater Manchester to the west. The A628 Woodhead Pass road is frequently closed in the winter due to snow or strong winds, and the high moorland either side of the road is a place where you will easily find solitude, or find that you are lost. The River Etherow cuts the Longdendale Valley where there are now six reservoirs known as the Longdendale Chain: Woodhead, Torside, Rhodeswood, Valehouse, Bottoms and Arnfield; as well as several small scattered settlements.

The Pennine Way descends off Bleaklow down the side of Torside Clough to the pass and then ascends by Crowden Great Brook to Laddow Rocks with its long history of rock climbing and hiking. Both these locations are breathtaking for photography but do require a big effort and good pre-planning.

Black Clough is a Peak favourite for its waterfalls and cascades especially in the autumn and when there is a freeze. Care is needed in this narrow valley as the terrain gets rough higher up. Then there is the accessible Holme Moss Summit and its wonderful view down to Holmfirth.

Whilst we have pin-pointed some of the best locations here, this area is great for exploring when the light is good. On the map we have marked the crags of Shining Clough, south of the pass which, for the adventurous photographer, are well worth a look.

Maps

- OS Explorer Map OL1 (1:25 000)
  The Peak District: Dark Peak Area

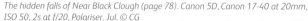

The hidden falls of Near Black Clough (page 78). Canon 5D, Canon 17-40 at 20mm, ISO 50, 2s at f/20, Polariser. Jul. © CG

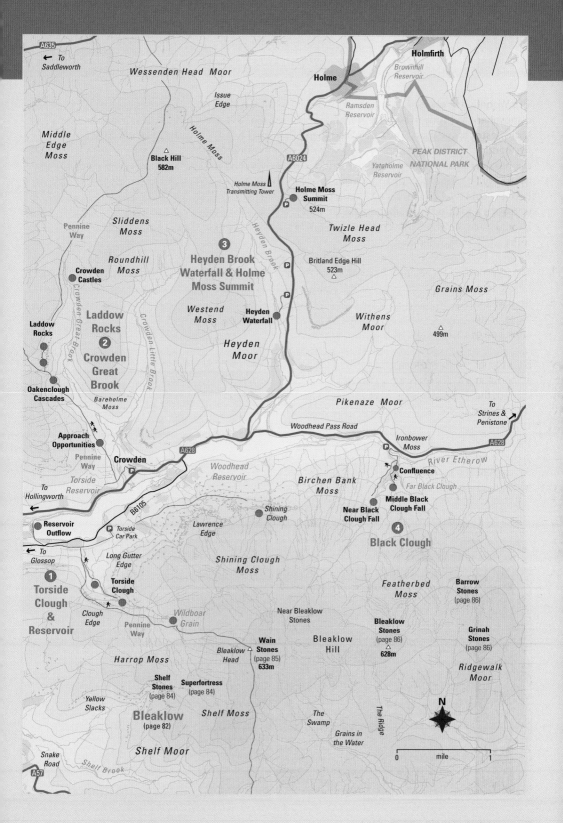

Torside Clough and Reservoir are two contrasting locations by the A628 just west of Crowden. The reservoir is a testament to Victorian industry and ingenuity, the clough and its cascades, a wild place full of risk and adventure, and yet very close to civilisation.

What to shoot and viewpoints

Viewpoint 1 – Torside Reservoir

Walk along the Longdendale Trail from Torside Car Park, then follow the Pennine Way across the dam to the culvert.

The architects of Victorian large scale engineering invariably attempted to incorporate some elegance and style into their work and on the Woodhead Road side of the dam between Rhodeswood and Torside Reservoirs is a very good example. Here is a graceful, curving brick-built culvert that protrudes out into the reservoir. This is best photographed when the reservoir is full and running, the regularity and conformity of the obviously man-made structure offers an excellent counterpoint to the apparently untamed nature of the surrounding hills. A calm day will give you some excellent reflections.

Viewpoint 2 – Torside Clough

Almost directly opposite Crowden is Torside Clough, which descends the northern flank of Bleaklow. The fall in height for Torside Clough is slightly greater than that for Crowden

Great Brook in about half the distance. This makes Torside a much more dramatic proposition than Crowden and an excursion into it must be undertaken with care.

The central section of the gorge, about a mile's walk from the road (at SK 073 970), is particularly dangerous. A great cascade of rock staircases which are bounded by vertical walls make access problematic, it can however be photographed from below. The brook below the staircase offers occasional interesting detail but the stream above is more interesting. There is a particularly fine waterfall at SK 074 969. Above, on the Wildboar Grain arm of the brook, there are some lovely cascades with often dramatically inclined rock planes. The Pennine Way crosses the top of Clough Edge, which has a number of good rock buttresses.

Torside Clough, Upper Cascades (VP2). Canon 5D, Canon 17-40mm at 20mm, ISO 50, 4s at f/20, Polariser. Apr. © CG

How to get here

For both locations park at Torside Car Park opposite Glossop Sailing Club on the B6105 Crowden to Glossop road which can accessed up the road from Crowden between Torside and Crowden Reservoirs, or from the south from Glossop or Hadfield.

Parking Lat/Long: 53.482211, -1.898976
Torside Clough Grid Ref: SK 063 979
Parking Postcode: SK13 1JF

Accessibility

The walk to Torside Reservoir is a pleasant walk along a good footpath. The walk to the Wildboar Grain in Torside Clough takes about an hour and requires some moderate scrambling over rocks with steep drop offs.

Torside Reservoir Approach: 40 min, distance 2km, ascent 0m.
Torside Clough Approach: 1 hour, distance 2km, ascent 200m.

Best time of year/day

Both morning and evening light is particularly good for Torside Reservoir. Illumination for Torside Clough is more problematic as it runs to the north west and is dog-legged. Cloudy days for the cascades can be perfect and various aspects of this valley receive illumination for most of the day when the sun is high. In spring the vegetation in the Clough is lucent green then purple in August when the heather flowers.

Above: Victorian architectural flamboyance in the outflow to Torside Reservoir (VP1). Canon 6D, 17-40 at 20mm, ISO 100, 1/2s at f/20, Grad. Mar. © CG

Opposite left: Torside Clough, Middle Cascades (VP2). Canon 5D, 17-40 at 20mm, ISO 50, 1/2s at f/20, Polariser. Apr. © CG

Opposite right Torside Clough, Cascades detail (VP2). Canon 5D, Canon 17-40 at 20mm, ISO 50, 2s at f/20, Polariser. Apr. © CG

Worth the walk. The view into Crowden from Laddow Rocks (VP3).
Canon 6D, 17-40 at 20mm, ISO 100, 1/40s at f/14, Grad. Apr. © CG

Crowden Great Brook descends the southern flank of Black Hill and has cut a wide valley out of the moors. On the valley's western edge the Pennine Way traverses above Laddow Rocks. Here there are much sought after compositions including gritstone promontories and pinnacles which provide foreground detail as a counterpoint to the grand vista down Crowden Great Brook and beyond to Bleaklow. Even further up the valley are Crowden Castles, gritstone tors that are well worth visiting.

Crowden Great Brook has few interesting features but its tributary Oakenclough Brook is significantly more interesting with some very good falls and cascades on its steepest sections although these are quite awkward to get to. Be prepared for a full but great day out.

What to shoot and viewpoints

From the car park at Crowden go through the trees to the far end of the campsite and turn left along a wide track, follow this back on yourself and cross Crowden Great Brook by a bridge and up the hill. 300m from the bridge turn right and follow the Pennine Way path.

Viewpoint 1 – The Approach to Laddow

The track that carries the Pennine Way into the valley is punctuated with detail. There is a very picturesque stand of larches at SK 066 997, while the flanks of Hey Edge to the east have many deciduous trees, particularly silver birch.

Viewpoint 2 – Oakenclough Brook

Soon after you pass Black Tor, the cliff band on the left, the path starts to ascend until it crosses Oakenclough Brook where there are several east-facing cascades. These are awkward to descend to but are well worth the effort.

Viewpoint 3 – Laddow Rocks
Laddow Rocks Grid Ref: SE 056 015
Approach: 1 hour, distance 3.2km, ascent 294m

After Oakenclough Brook you will soon arrive at the path which traverses the edge of the valley to the prominent pinnacles and tors of Laddow Rocks (a path splits off west to Chew Reservoir here). Laddow is a famous cliff for rock climbers, although it is now out of fashion, and in the early 20th century members of the Kyndwr Club and the Manchester YMCA made this remote place their own on Sunday excursions from the mills of Manchester. This really is one of the grandest views in the Peak District. Walk a little further on for some impressive towers of rock with head-spinning drops down to Crowden Great Brook. Be careful, the footpath passes close to the edge in places. It is worth getting an early start or camping to catch the sunrise.

Viewpoint 4 – Crowden Castles
Crowden Castle Grid Ref: SE 062 022
Approach: 1.5hrs, distance 4.2km, ascent 297m

If you continue by the top of Laddow Rocks for a kilometre the valley narrows and on the east side of Crowden Great Brook are Crowden Castles, two Dartmoor-esque tors formed of weathered gritstone. They are attractive from below and particularly close up looking from above down the valley.

Opposite middle: The larches on the walk into Crowden (VP1). Canon 5D, 17-40 at 20mm, ISO 100, 1/40 at f/20. Grad. Apr. © CG

How to get here
The access for Laddow Rocks is best from the hamlet of Crowden next to Torside Reservoir on the Woodhead Pass/A628 which, if coming from Manchester, is 5 miles along the A628 from the junction with the A57 at Hollingworth. Park at the National Park car park at Crowden just north of the A628. You can also approach on foot from Holme Moss summit and Black Hill, and from Dove Stone Reservoir in the Chew Valley.

Parking Lat/Long: 53.490765, -1.893011
Parking Grid Ref: SK 071 993
Parking Postcode: SK13 1HZ

Accessibility
This is a stiff up hill walk on the Pennine Way and is often boggy. Prepare well by pre-planning your route, taking a map and compass, a charged-up phone, food and drink, and protective clothing and footwear.

Best time of year/day
The valley of Crowden Great Brook aligns north-south and needs early morning or late afternoon light to reveal its grand topography. Whilst good at most times of year, heather time in August and winter are the best times to visit.

Above*: Crowden Castles dominate the head of the valley (VP4). Canon 6D, Canon 17-40 at 20mm, ISO 400, 1/200 at f/14. Nov. © CG*

Below*: Waterfall detail on Okenclough Brook (VP2). Canon 5D, Canon 17-40 at 20mm, ISO 50, 2s at f/20. Polariser. Apr. © CG*

Above*: The weir on Crowden Brook above the field centre (VP1). Canon 6D, 17-40 at 20mm, ISO 50, 3s at f/14. Nov. © CG*

Heyden Brook drains south from Holme Moss and follows the A6024 down to Woodhead Reservoir. About half way down it drops down a shale step forming a beautiful 18ft/5.5m south-facing waterfall that plummets into a large pool. This is one of the Peak District's prettiest waterfalls to photograph, especially in August and later in the year. The bilberries here in August are some of the biggest and sweetest in the region.

At the top of the A6024 is Holme Moss Summit (1,719ft/524m) home to Holme Moss Transmitting Station built in 1951 to transmit BBC radio and TV. The views down to Holmfirth and beyond are well known and impressive.

What to shoot and viewpoints

Viewpoint 1 – Heyden Brook Waterfall
From the lay-by go through the gate and head west down the slope towards the brook. It is better to traverse diagonally down south – across two drainages and by small walls – to where you can see a gap in the clough. After reaching some small outcrops and two short parallel drystone walls, follow the walls steeply down to the waterfall.

Access to the base of the waterfall is down a steep stepped path. There are many compositions to be explored at the base of the waterfall and pool, on both sides of the brook and in the brook itself. Also explore higher up the slopes, downstream and from above. The falls have ferns growing by them and there is heather higher up.

Viewpoint 2 – Holme Moss Summit
It almost feels like cheating: such a magnificent view for so little effort if you came by car. For good photography you need good light here, or perhaps try at night. It is also a challenging composition but with much opportunity. Try a wide angle approach and also zoom in. The 'Framing The Landscape' installation here can be used very effectively. Any time of day can yield good conditions. Of note are various spots on the roads up to Holme Moss Summit, especially the south side down to the Woodhead Pass.

The Framing The Landscape installation at Holme Moss Summit viewpoint. Very well positioned (VP2). Canon 6D, 17-40 at 30mm, ISO 400, 1/300s at f/8. Aug. © CG

How to get here

For Heyden Waterfall park at the lower lay-by on Woodhead Road/A6024 which is 1.7 miles from the Woodhead Pass Road/A628. There is a gate at the lay-by which leads to Access Land.

Holme Moss Summit is at the top of the Woodhead Road/A6024, 4.5 miles south of Holmfirth and 2.8 miles from the Woodhead Pass Road/A628. Park in the car park across the road from the radio mast.

Heyden Waterfall Parking Lat/Long: 53.516402, -1.852279
Parking Grid Ref: SE 096 017
Parking Postcode: HD9 2QH (2km)

Holme Moss Parking Lat/Long: 53.531725, -1.854773
Parking Grid Ref: SE 096 017
Parking Postcode: HD9 2QH (2km)

Accessibility ♿

The approach to Heyden Brook is across and down rough moorland for 0.5 km and the path around the waterfall is narrow and above a drop, but it is relatively easy to get to its base. Holme Moss summit is a roadside location suitable for all

Heyden Brook Approach: 20 min, distance 500m, 70m descent
Holme Moss Summit Approach: Roadside..

Best time of year/day

Heyden Waterfall is south facing but is enclosed in a steep-sided clough. It gets sun from mid-morning to mid-afternoon in the summer. Cloudy but light conditions can be ideal for photographing waterfalls. The views from Holme Moss Summit north to Holmfirth are illuminated all day with the land falling into shadow earlier in the winter due to a lower sun. Head here if it is a mix of sun and showers, you may get lucky.

Top left: Holme Moss Summit on a winter evening (VP2). Sony A6000, 18-200 at 21mm, ISO 800, 20s at f/5. Nov. © MR

Top right: A rainbow on Holme Moss. Sony A6000, 18-200 at 18mm, ISO 160, 1/800s at f/3.5. Aug. © MR

Bottom left: Heyden Brook Waterfall (VP1). Sony A6000, 18-200 at 18mm, ISO 160, 1/100s at f/5. Jul. © MR

Bottom right: The approach to Holme Moss from Woodhead Pass. A6000, 18-200 at 21mm, ISO 100, 1/160s at f/8. Jan. © MR

Cascade detail in Near Black Clough. Canon 5D Mk 1, 17-40 at 25mm, ISO 100, 4s, at f/20, Polariser. Aug. © CG

Black Clough is recognised when driving on the A628 above the Woodhead Reservoir by looking to the south where you will see a densely wooded birch and oak clough coming down off the heather-clad moorland of Bleaklow. This is home to the eight metre drop of the Middle Black Clough waterfall, a popular photographic subject at most times of year, and one of several cascades in this richly featured gorge eroded from Bleaklow Grit. A good pair of wellington boots are useful here.

What to shoot and viewpoints

Black Clough consists of three streams in a narrow valley – Far, Middle and Near Black Clough – that join just before they emerge from the hills. The main attraction is the eight metre waterfall on Middle Black Clough and although further interesting material lies higher up.

Once on the track into the clough follow it to an open grassy area where Far Black Clough joins the main stream.

Viewpoint 1 – The Confluence of Far Black Clough

The dark stream cascades gently through a beautiful grove of birch trees. There are plenty of shots here for those who lack the confidence for a more adventurous trip. Far Black Clough is the narrow clough opposite.

Viewpoint 2: Middle Black Clough Waterfall

Walk about 100m up the main stream from Far Black Clough and cross the stream into Middle Black Clough on the left. Navigate up a sometimes distinct path on the left side of the stream with some awkward steps. Around 250m up this clough is the eight metre high Middle Black Clough waterfall. Access is tricky and the rocks around the fall are slippery.

A wide angle lens is useful as you are close to the falls and a tripod mandatory as light levels will be low. A neutral density filter will help if you want to blur the water. Be careful with exposure if it is a bright day, the sky above the falls may blow out your highlights, consider exposure blending by taking multiple exposures or using a graduated neutral density filter.

Viewpoint 3 – Near Black Clough Cascades

Near Black Clough is a very deceptive location. Its outflow merges with Middle Black Clough and appears to be no more than a trickle at the best of times. This is deceptive because much of the water that descends Near Black Clough never reaches the confluence but disappears under ground through a series of geological faults, not before it has cascaded its way spectacularly off the moor over a series of beautiful rock shelves. Access is tricky up this clough and it can be better taking the path through the trees onto the moor and following this path until you spot something of interest down in the clough below.

How to get here

Black Clough is accessed from a service road a mile beyond the western end of the Woodhead reservoir. The service road descends south off the main A628 Woodhead Pass at SK 117 996. There is sufficient parking for several cars or park on the main road at a lay-by. Follow the service road down the hill, cross the River Etherow and turn left. At about 450m before crossing Black Clough turn right into the clough up a good track.

Parking Lat/Long: 53.492960, -1.823625
Parking Grid Ref: SK 117 996
Parking Postcode: SK13 1JE (0.5 km)

Accessibility

A photographic excursion into Black Clough is not for the faint hearted and a bit of mountain experience can be a useful asset. It is tricky and in parts dangerous, requiring both route finding and risk assessment. As with all gorges, extreme caution needs to be exercised particularly during times of heavy rainfall when spate waters can catch the unwary.

Approach: 40 minutes, distance 1.5km, 135m ascent.

Best time of year/day

Black Clough is north-facing and you have to be wary of sunny days when you could blow highlights. Bright overcast days with less dynamic-range are better. Bring a tripod and if you are after swirly patterns in pools and milky ethereal effects, an ND filter. Autumn, when the colours of the birch and oak leaves lend a bit of welcome additional colour is a good time to visit. After a heavy freeze is also a good time to visit but come prepared with mountain boots, walking poles and a friend.

Above: The top fall on Near Black Clough (VP3). Hard won but worthy. Canon 5D MK1, 17-40 at 20mm, ISO 50, 6s at f/20. Polariser, ND. Mar. © CG

Opposite left: The 8m fall on Middle Black Clough. Canon 5D Mk 1, 17-40 at 30mm, ISO 50, 3s at f/20. Polariser, ND. Nov. © CG

Opposite right: Black Clough from Woodhead Pass. The obvious cleft in the moor. Canon 6D, 17-40 at 40mm, ISO 200,1/60s at f/8. Grad. Aug. © CG

Bleaklow and Kinder are part of the High Peak and home to the area's highest peaks including Kinder Scout (636m), Bleaklow (633m) and Higher Shelf Stones (621m). All three are considered mountains – by Whittow's Dictionary of Physical Geography – as they are above 2,000ft/610m. They are however unlike the shapely steep-sided mountains of the Lake District with their distinct summits, these are vast expanses of raised bog and moorland with gritstone outcroppings.

The terrain and conditions can be very much mountainous however and extremes of weather are common, which is a good thing for photographers. Kinder especially does have some distinct mountain features of ridges, steep-sided cloughs and precipitous slopes guarding its featureless, but beautiful plateau.

The Snake Pass road splits Kinder and Bleaklow and provides easy access to the moorland from several points on good, well-maintained paths – the Pennine Way traverses both Kinder and Bleaklow – and these moors have long been popular with hikers and climbers, especially from nearby Manchester and Sheffield.

Bleaklow is very accessible, the Snake Road and your car doing most of the elevation gain for you. But to get to some of its distinctive features: gritstone edges, boulders, and endless vistas, does require good navigation skills to traverse its deep groughs, peat hags and bogs.

You have to work harder for the delights of Kinder's Northern Edge as you will be starting in the Ashop Valley east of the Snake's summit and will have to gain 300m in height up steep paths to reach its gritstone-lined plateau, but once there you will experience a dramatic landscape equal to those of the Lake District, North Wales and Scotland.

Maps

- OS Explorer Map OL1 (1:25 000) The Peak District: Dark Peak Area

Looking at Manchester from near the Boxing Gloves on Kinder North (page 92). Sony A6000, 18-200 at 57mm, ISO 200, 1/320s at f/11. Jul. © MR

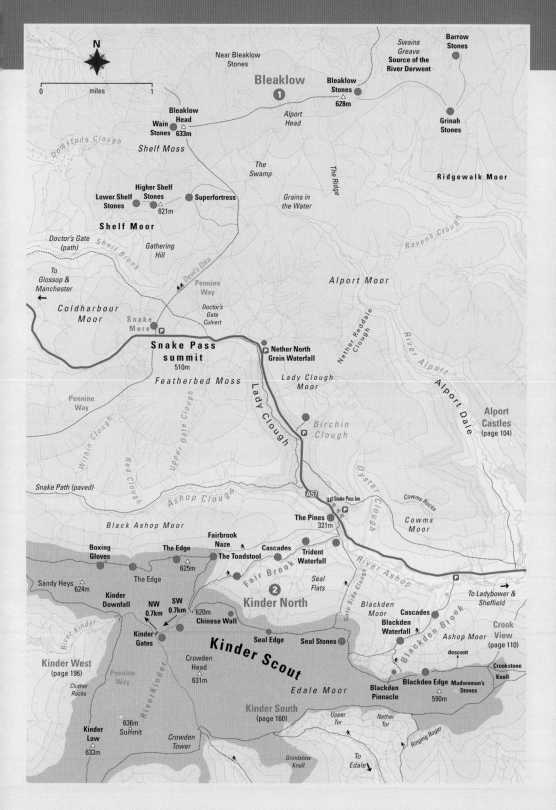

N

0 miles 1

Near Bleaklow Stones

Swains Greave
Source of the River Derwent

Barrow Stones

Bleaklow ①

Bleaklow Stones 628m

Alport Head

Grinah Stones

Bleaklow Head 633m
Wain Stones

Shelf Moss

The Swamp

Grains in the Water

The Ridge

Ridgewalk Moor

Higher Shelf Stones
Lower Shelf Stones
Superfortress 621m

Dowstone Clough

Shelf Moor

Doctor's Gate (path)

Gathering Hill

Shelf Brook

Devil's Dike

Ravens Clough

Alport Moor

To Glossop & Manchester

Pennine Way

Doctor's Gate Culvert

Nether Reddale Clough

River Alport

Coldharbour Moor

Snake Mere

Snake Pass summit 510m

Nether North Grain Waterfall

Featherbed Moss

Lady Clough Moor

Alport Dale

Alport Castles (page 104)

Pennine Way

Within Clough

Red Clough

Upper Gate Clough

Lady Clough

Birchin Clough

Oyster Clough

Cowms Rocks

Snake Path (paved)

Ashop Clough

A57

Snake Pass Inn

Cowms Moor

The Pines 321m

Black Ashop Moor

Boxing Gloves

The Edge

Fairbrook Naze
The Toadstool

Cascades

Trident Waterfall

River Ashop

The Edge 625m

Fair Brook

Seal Flats

Gate Side Clough

To Ladybower & Sheffield

Sandy Heys 624m

Kinder Downfall

NW 0.7km

SW 0.7km

620m

Kinder North ②

Chinese Wall

Blackden Moor

Cascades

Crook View (page 110)

River Kinder

Kinder Gates

Seal Edge

Seal Stones

Blackden Waterfall

Ashop Moor

descent

Crookstone Knoll

Kinder West (page 196)

Crowden Head 631m

Kinder Scout

Blackden Pinnacle

Blackden Edge 590m

Madwoman's Stones

Cluther Rocks

Pennine Way

Edale Moor

Kinder South (page 160)

Upper Tor

Nether Tor

636m Summit

Kinder Low 633m

Crowden Tower

Grindslow Knoll

To Edale

Ringing Roger

The wreckage of the B29 Superfortress 'Overexposed' on Shelf Moor (VP1). Canon 6D, 17-40 at 20mm, ISO 100, 1/200 at f/4.5. Grad. Apr. © CG

The River Derwent has shaped the Peak District in many ways. Important in the Upper Derwent Valley for agriculture and tourism, further south from Matlock toward Derby the river powered Richard Arkwright's cotton mills and was the centre of the industrial revolution which dramatically changed the world. The Derwent and its tributaries begin their journey on Bleaklow; a wild rolling high-elevation plateau of peat bogs, moorland grasses, heather and gritstone outcrops. It is skirted by roads but is wild and desolate. For the adventurous hiker-photographer this moorland provides dramatic landscape compositions at all times of the year and is home to the beautiful mountain hare.

What to shoot and viewpoints

The starting point is at the summit of Snake Pass (1673ft /510m) on the Snake Road/A57 by a small mere where the Pennine Way crosses.

Viewpoint 1 – Higher Shelf Stones and the Superfortress
Higher Shelf Stones: SK 089 947   **Superfortress:** SK 09062 94890
Approach: 1 hour, distance 3.2km, ascent 102m

Higher Shelf Stones (SK 089 947) is the low looking hill topped with a gritstone edge north of the Snake Road. This is the third highest hill in the Peak District at 2,038ft/621m. The views from its summit rocks down to Glossop are impressive and the wreckage of the Superfortress is sombre.

Park at the Snake Pass summit by the small tarn where

The Horror of Bleaklow

If you are in the middle of this moor when the mist comes down you are surrounded by 50 square miles of almost featureless moorland and it will be a minimum of three miles to the nearest road, which are themselves remote. You will have to walk over undulating terrain and when it isn't boggy your progress will be slowed by thick heather and maze-like head-height groughs (water-worn channels); you will get tired and cold quickly. It is difficult to navigate in thick clag and some of the bogs will swallow you whole. The moor is the grave of many unfortunate airmen; UFOs and ghost planes have been sighted here and the area is inhabited by a ferocious species of werehare. You may not return alive. It's not surprising that this moor has mountain rescue call outs almost every week of the year. On a fine summer day however it can feel like a desert, bring plenty of water.

the Pennine Way crosses the road. Follow the flagged path north for 2.4km to just before Hern Clough. Turn left here with the stream on your right. Head west and contour round to the toward the summit of Higher Shelf Stones. The wreckage is on the south east slope of the hill 200m from the summit cairn at SK 09062 94890.

The wreckage site of the USA's Boeing Superfortress, a B-29, known as 'Over Exposed' is a thoughtful place for making poignant images. Thirteen airmen lost their lives here when the plane crashed in thick fog on a flight from Lincoln to Cheshire on 3rd November 1948. The wreckage is extensive, well-preserved and is strewn across the slope often dotted with memorial crosses.

The four engines of the B29 Superfortress are the most prominent features of the crash site (VP1). Canon 6D, Canon 17-40 at 20mm, ISO 100, 1/20 at f/14. Grad. Apr. © CG

A cascade just off the road at Upper North Grain, east of the Snake summit. Canon 6D, 17-40 at 20mm, ISO 100, 4s at f/20. Apr. © CG

Shelf Stones (VP1). Canon 6D, Canon 17-40 at 20mm, ISO 200, 1/150s at f/14. Grad. Apri.l © CG

Higher Shelf Stones summit is a well-visited place and rocks here are carved with names and dates. The gritstone is lit up in the late afternoon and at sunset and the hill slopes down steeply to the Shelf Valley and Glossop. You can reach Lower Shelf Stones by contouring west from the summit cairn with the perspective here very dramatic.

Viewpoint 2 – Wain Stones
Wain Stones Grid Ref: SK 091 959
Approach: 1 hour, distance 3.7km, ascent 113m

I've been over Snowdon, I've slept up on Crowdon;
I've camped by the Wain Stones as well.
I've sun bathed on Kinder, been burned to a cinder,
And many more tales I can tell.
Manchester Rambler – Ewan McColl

The kissing Wain Stones at Bleaklow Head (633m) sit on a ledge 3.7km along the Pennine Way from the summit of the Snake Pass Road. Stay on the main path following Hern Clough until you reach three stones on a low gritstone shelf that from some angles appear to be kissing.

How to get here

Bleaklow is situated east of Glossop between the Snake and Woodhead Passes. Described here is access from the Snake Road/A57 at the Snake Pass Summit where the Pennine Way crosses over from Kinder. Park at the side off the road in several lay-bys near the Snake Mere.

Snake Pass Parking Lat/Long: 53.432959, -1.869390
Parking Grid Ref: SK 087 929
Parking Postcode: SK13 7PQ (3.5km)

Accessibility

Before you venture on to Bleaklow pre-plan and plot a route using a 1:25000 OS Explorer map and Google Earth. Bringing a map and a compass with you is essential (and/or GPS). Described are routes giving an approximate mileages and grid references. Navigation is difficult because of the lack of features especially if you wander off the main footpaths.

Best time of year/day

This is an all-year round area that is best appreciated when there is 'weather' that creates moody big skies. Vegetation changes are important to consider with autumn, winter and early spring providing the best contrast when the heather, bilberries, bracken and grasses transition. The best times of day are described in each viewpoint, but for the energetic early and late will produce the best conditions; just remember to bring a headtorch or consider camping/bivouacking. If accessible this is a very worthwhile area after snow and frost, and with a low winter sun can be rather special. Mountain hares are common and change from brown to white between October and April.

Viewpoint 3 – Bleaklow Stones
Bleaklow Stones Grid Ref: SK 112 963
Approach: 1 hour 20 minutes, distance 6km, ascent 117m

From the Wain Stones at Bleaklow Head head east (turn right) on the path across the plateau for 1.6km to Bleaklow Hill (2067ft/630m) and the source of the River Alport at Alport Head. On the east side there is a cluster of wind-sculpted boulders on the edge of the moor which slopes down to the drainages that collect to form the River Westend. The Bleaklow Stones are quite extensive and there is a variety of amazing formations including an anvil-shaped rock and three boulders that point over the sloping moor toward the Grinah Stones. These formations make good photographic studies by themselves or as foregrounds to the compositional narratives around you. Look out for ghostly Roman legionnaires (the nearby Doctor's Gate path is an old Roman Road), UFOs and rocks moving.

For the description of an alternative walk to Bleaklow Stones from the Howden reservoir illustrated with photographs visit **www.fotovue/viewpoints**.

The Wain Stones, or Kissing Stones at Bleaklow Head (VP2). Canon 6D, 17-40 at 40mm, ISO 100, 1/20 at f/8. Grad. Apr. © CG

Viewpoint 4 – Grinah Stones
Grinah Stones Grid Ref: SK 130 962
Approach: 1 hour 40 minutes, distance 7.6km, ascent 129m

The Grinah Stones are a significant gritstone edge and boulder field to the east of Bleaklow Stones, you can see them in the distance. From the Bleaklow Stones so as not to lose too much height contour to the north east then east on an indistinct path that follows shallow groughs. It is a 1.6km of hard but level walking. You will lose about 50m in elevation.

Although the Grinah Stones arc around the nose of a hill, they generally face south-west. Like many of the boulders on the moor their elevated position means that some of the rock faces will always get the available sun light. This is a place to take landscapes of the moorland with interesting sculpted and heavily textured rocks in the foreground with the most prominent and interesting rocks on the south-west.

Viewpoint 5 – Barrow Stones
Barrow Stones Grid Ref: SK 134 969
Approach: 1 hour 40 minutes, distance 8.5km, ascent 146m

The Barrow Stones are a short flat walk behind or north from the Grinah Stones. This boulder-field is not that extensive but its position is impressive. There are low sculpted boulders scattered around and one impressive south-facing, tall collection of boulders by a gate and fence with the path you approached on snaking away into the distance. Return the way you came.

Barrow Stones (VP5). Canon 5D Mk 1, 17-40 at 20mm, ISO 100, 1/20s at f/4. Grad. Jan. © CG

Above: The wonderfully weathered rocks of Bleaklow Stones (VP3). Canon 6D, 17-40 at 17mm, ISO 100, 1/40s at f/14. Apr. © CG

Below: The Bleaklow Stones (VP3) looking at the Grinah Stones (VP4). A6000, 18-200 at 19mm, ISO 160, 1/160s at f/7.1. Jan. © MR

Beautiful summer evening light on the stones of Blackden Edge (VP4, page 94).
Canon 5D Mk 1 / Canon 17-40 at 20mm, ISO 100, 1/40s at f/20, Grad. Aug. © CG

Kinder Scout's Northern Edge is a lofty perch on the edge of the Kinder Plateau lined by gritstone edges and tors with sweeping ridge lines that draw the eye down to the Ashop Valley and the Snake Road. The land then rises up again forming the Howden and Bleaklow Moors. For landscape photography this combination of foreground, mid-ground and background with narratives of ridges, cloughs and valley presents many aesthetic opportunities for the energetic photographer.

Within its two main drainages are tumbling rocky streams that provide some of the Peak Districts' best photography locations for wild cascades and waterfalls. If all this wasn't enough described here is a roadside pine woodland for more ethereal and intimate compositions.

Despite Kinder Downfall being fully described in the Kinder West chapter (p. 200), a recommended approach starts here from the north, see next page.

Larches in autumn off the Snake Road. Sony A6000, 18-200 at 80mm, ISO 100, 1/160s at f/7.1. Nov. © MR

What to shoot and viewpoints

Viewpoint 1 – Snake Pass Inn Pine Woods
Across the road from the Snake Pass Inn is a pine woodland which can be atmospheric especially on sunny or cold misty mornings and is worth a visit to photograph if passing. In autumn you will find a variety of fungi, toadstools and mushrooms here. Also look out for a variety of moss beds, especially amongst decaying fallen trees.

Viewpoint 2 – Fair Brook Trident Waterfall
Approach by Fair Brook
Waterfall Grid Ref: SK 109 899, distance 1.5km

Climb over one of the two stiles on the Snake Road and follow the path down through the woods and right over a wooden board, head straight down from here (not left) to the footbridge (hidden at first and hard to see if dark) over the River Ashop. Go left after footbridge and follow to where Fair Brook joins the River Ashop at a ford.

The stone sheep pen (pinfold) opposite can make a good photograph with a background of heather and fern slopes, a grove of trees and a track that contours up the hill (the Gate Side Clough approach). This area is very green in summer, this is a subject for when the foxgloves (June/July) and heather (August) blooms, and later when the ferns and trees turn golden (October).

Continue right following Fair Brook up the valley on the path which stays on the stream's right side. You will pass some small pools and cascades, then a side valley on your left. After less than fifteen minutes walk up the valley with a mature silver birch on your left, and just before the path steepens, look down to a pool and the 1.5m high 'trident' waterfall, a classic Peak District photograph.

Getting into position for a good composition can be tricky, both in the stream and on the bank work. The main problem is that you may be shooting into the sun. Using a graduated filter or exposure blending will work in such conditions. Heather time in August and September on a cloudy bright day after rain is the best time to visit.

There are many more cascades and falls further up the valley which are just as good as the Trident, especially where this valley splits in two.

***Opposite left:** The Trident waterfall on Fair Brook VP2). Canon 5D Mk 1, 17-40 at 40mm, ISO 50, 1s at f/20. Polariser. Grad. Sep. © CG*

How to get here

Described are three ways up to the Kinder Plateau from the north: Fair Brook (Viewpoints 1 to 3), Gate Side Clough (Viewpoint 4) and Blackden Brook (Viewpoint 5) all starting from the Snake Road (A57) in the Ashop Valley.

Snake Pass Inn Lay-bys: For Fair Brook, the Seal Stones and Blackden Edge (Viewpoints 1-4) park in one of three lay-bys below the Snake Pass Inn, the lower one is the best as it is nearer the path that goes through the pine woods to Fair Brook. Alternatively park Wat Birchen Clough car park half-a-mile up the road from the pub.

Parking Lat/Long: 53.411720, -1.832397
Parking Grid Ref: SK 112 905
Parking Postcode: S33 0AB (2.3km)

PARKING DANGER WARNING: Traffic travels fast on the Snake Road and just below the Snake Pass Inn the road curves making traffic difficult to see when you are leaving the lay-bys. Do not park facing up hill in the lay-bys, if coming from the direction of Sheffield turn around in the pub car park. If you arrived from the Glossop direction when leaving the lay-bys do not turn and go the way you came but travel 1.2 miles/2km toward Sheffield and turn-around at the parking lay-by for Blackden Brook.

Blackden Brook Lay-By: For Blackden Brook Waterfall park at the Blackden Brook Lay-by, half-way between the Ladybower lights and the Snake Pass Inn on the Kinder side of the road.

Parking Lat/Long: 53.402384, -1.805739
Parking Grid Ref: SK 130 895
Parking Postcode: S33 0AB (1.2km)

Above middle: Fair brook detail. Canon 5D Mk1, Canon 17-40 at 20mm, ISO 50, 2s at f/20. Polariser. Mar. © CG

Above right: There are numerous cascades up Fair Brook. Canon 5D Mk1, 17-40 at 40mm, ISO 50, 1s at f/20. Polariser. Apr. © CG

Accessibility

Kinder Scout's Northern Edge rises up from 300m on the the Snake Road to just over 600m. Expect stiff up hill hikes gaining nearly a 1,000ft over rough ground but on well travelled paths with a minimum round trip of 4 miles/6.5km. The pine woodland is roadside and a quick hit. For the waterfalls Fair Brook is the easier option over the more rugged Blackden Brook. Whilst the Kinder Plateau may be benign on hot summer days be prepared anytime of year for cold conditions, especially early and late. If the ground is wet, and it often is, you will be grateful for a good pair of waterproof boots (wellies are good) and a walking stick or poles for descents and checking bog depths.

Best time of year/day

This edge of Kinder here faces north with Fairbrook Naze and parts of the Seal Stones facing east. The sun falls on the gritstone tors and edges of Kinder's northern edge and the valley below it when the sun sets in the north west (April to August) and rises in the east to north east (March to September). The plateau and the back of the edges and tors get sun for most of the day throughout the year. While sunset later on in the year won't light up the valleys below the last rays do illuminate the plateau and its rocks.

If the weather is dynamic, sun and showers for example, this can add drama and contrast to the plateau. Both Blackden Clough and Fair Brook run from the south west down to the north east and are very dark in mid-winter. The best times to photograph their cascades are on bright but overcast days from spring to autumn, particularly in August when the heather flowers. Cotton grass flowers in June and July.

Winter. If it snows and the forecast is for cold clear weather, take a day off work, wrap up warm, pack a hearty lunch and head up to Kinder. Almost anywhere you point your camera will yield great results, especially if you stay until sunset; anywhere between 4pm and 6pm depending on the month. Don't forget a head torch.

Getting to Kinder Downfall and Exploring The Plateau: Kinder River and Kinder Gates

This is the quickest way to the Kinder Downfall with the least elevation gain (2.7 miles/4.25km, 1,000ft), although if you are coming from the west (Manchester) starting from Hayfield is probably best (see page 194). It is also great way to explore the plateau especially in summer when the cotton grass flowers.

Starting from the Snake Pass Inn go up Fair Brook to its head then south west for 0.7km across the plateau (sometimes there will be a several feint paths, but you are on your own) navigating through and over groughs until you reach Kinder River (fantastic to photograph) and hopefully the Kinder Gates (SK 088 886), two 20ft high rock buttresses either side of the river. Follow this beautiful river north west for 0.7km//0.4m to the Downfall.

Note: Do not stay in a grough and follow it thinking you are going in the correct direction, they twist and turn and may lead you in the wrong direction. It is easy to get lost.

Viewpoint 3 – To Fairbrook Naze and The Edge
Approach by Fair Brook
Grid Ref: SK 096 897, distance 3.7 km

Carry on up Fair Brook beyond the Trident Waterfall which is easy-angled at first. The path turns right where the valley splits. Stay on the path which eventually steepens with an easy scramble over rocks in a last push to the top. There are fine views looking up the brook with the valley sides and the jutting nose of Fairbrook Naze. At the final rocky exit to the plateau there are several cascades.

Emerging on the plateau follow a path around right towards the Naze (nose) of Fair Brook. Outcrops of rock both on the plateau and at its edge abound here and there are many great sweeping compositions back down Fair Brook to the Ashop Valley from this east facing edge – good at sunrise and later when the whole scene will be lit. At the Naze the east facing edge turns to north facing and there is a small top-heavy tor, the Naze Toadstool (SK 096 897) slightly down from the path. This photographs well at both sunrise and sunset in the summer.

The Edge and the Boxing Gloves

West of Fairbrook Naze is The Edge (SK 086 897), a line of north facing gritstone buttresses that look down onto Featherbed Moss and the summit of Snake Pass and, in the west, Manchester. Good at sunset in the summer, however during the day the back and sides of these gritstone cliffs are illuminated along with the moorland beyond them.

There are many interesting rock formations and cliffs if you follow the path west from Fairbrook Naze. There are two small tors (free-standing pinnacles) of interest, the first just after Nether Edge Brook at 1km from the Naze, and the second, the Boxing Gloves (SK 079 897) a further 500m along the path at Upper Red Brook.

Left top: Sunrise at the toadstool (VP3). Sony A6000, 18-200 at 18mm, ISO 400, 1/640s at f/10. Sept. © MR

Left bottom: Cotton grass on the Kinder Plateau in early summer. Sony A6000, 18-200 at 18mm, ISO 125, 1/320s at f/7.1. Jul. © MR

Opposite top: The Boxing Gloves on Kinder's North Edge. Canon 6D, 17-40 at 20mm, ISO 100, 1/40s at f/14. Grad. Jul. © CG
Opposite middle left: Fly Agaric toadstools in Snake woodlands (VP1). Canon 5D Mk 1, 105mm, ISO 100, 1/5s at f/11, Nov. © CG
Opposite middle right: Manchester from near the Boxing Gloves. Sony A6000, 18-200 at 186mm, ISO 320, 1/400s at f/11. Jul. © MR
Opposite Bottom right: Looking down on the Snake from Fair Brook (VP3). Sony A6000, 18-200 at 18mm, ISO 160, 1/100s at f/10. Sept. © MR

Bottom left: *Snow-filled groughs on Kinder Scout. Canon 5D Mk 1, Canon 17-40 at 40mm, ISO 400, 1/200s at f/8. Feb. © CG*

Viewpoint 4 – Seal Stones, Seal Edge & Blackden Edge

Approach by Gate Side Clough
Seal Stones Grid Ref: SK 114 889, distance 2km

The quickest and easiest of all the ways up to the Kinder Plateau is by a grouse shooting track by Gate Side Clough which takes you direct to the Seal Stones (40 minutes). Walk to the junction of the River Ashop and Fair Brook from the Snake Road and ford Fair Brook. Go through the gates in the stone sheep pen to follow the track that leads diagonally across the slope. Follow it round the corner where it traverses above Gate Side Clough. Higher up where the steep clough shallows it crosses the stream by a small plank bridge, continue onward and upward as the path becomes indistinct to emerge at the gritstone rocks on the skyline, continue above these rocks to the plateau and a double path that traverses the edge of the plateau.

Seal Stones & Seal Edge

Seal Stones are the rocks all around you as you emerge at the plateau, some facing north and if you walk east some that look down onto Blackden Brook. In good light possibilities are endless using interesting rocks as foreground subjects for grand vistas. The path provides a wonderful leading line and moorland grasses (not heather at this spot) and cotton grass cover the ground. Looking west is

particular impressive with the strong lines of Fairbrook Naze ridge and several drainages leading down to the Snake Road – the sun rolls down these ridges as it sets in the north west in the summer.

It's a half a mile flat walk west along the edge to Seal Edge a significant – 40ft high – gritstone cliff between the Seal Stones and Fair Brook. It provides a good subject for landscapes and close up is highly carved and weathered.

Blackden Edge & Pinnacle

You can approach Blackden Edge by going up Blackden Brook but that approach is only recommended if your objective is the Blackden Brook Waterfall. For the highly sculpted Blackden Pinnacle and the scattered boulders approach up Gate Side Clough (described above) to the Seal Stones and follow the path to the top of Blackden Brook and continue west where you will see the small towers of Blackden Pinnacle down from the path. This formation and others here get great light at summer sunrises, and at sunset for most of the year.

The Seven Minute Crossing

Of note is that from Blackden Edge if you head due south for 0.4km, if you navigate well, you will arrive at the south edge of Kinder overlooking Edale emerging near Nether Tor.

The Seal Stones VP4. Sony A6000, 10-18 at 10mm, ISO 100, 1/45s at f/11. May. © MR

Above: Looking west near Blackden Clough at sunset. Sony A6000, 18-200 at 51mm, ISO 100, 2s at f/10. Oct. © MR

Below: Blackden Pinnacle overlooking Blackden Clough (VP4). Canon 5D Mk 1, 17-40 at 20mm, ISO 100, 1/20s at f/20, Grad. Apr. © CG

Viewpoint 5: Blackden Brook Waterfall
Approach by Blackden Brook
Blackden Brook Waterfall Grid Ref: SK 121 883, distance 1.6km

Blackden Brook is one of the less frequented Kinder drainages, probably due to its dark nature; it is narrow and runs east to north east. It is also hard to walk up, with several stream crossings, often steep drop-offs next to the path, it is frequently boggy and at its higher reaches it is rocky and requires some moderate scrambling.

For those who do venture up it you will find one of the most beautiful true waterfalls in the Peak District.

Starting from lay-by above Blackden Barn near Wood Cottage and up Blackden Brook emerging near the Seal Stones is 1.2 miles/2km (an hours walk). Park on the south side of the road in the small car park, go through the gate down through the field to cross a bridge and up through a gate where the walls join. Follow the path above the brook and almost immediately below you are some stone walls with a beautiful waterfall below at SK 127 889.

The path eventually goes down to the brook crossing it several times (it's boggy) and you see several small cascades of interest. At just over a kilometre from the road as you turn a corner you will see the 30ft high Blackden Brook Waterfall. If Thomas Hobbes had visited this wonder it would have surely made it into his 1678 poem, De Mirabilibus Pecci, (Being The Wonders of the Peak In Darby-shire). Approach the waterfall from below as it is surrounded by broken cliffs and steep banks close up. The light can be tricky here, choose a bright day as the waterfall gets little sun, there are three great times to be here: August when the heather is purple, October when the surrounding trees will be wearing their autumn coat, and when it freezes.

Above the Waterfall and onto the Plateau

There are more cascades above Blackden Brook Waterfall, the path is narrow, slippery and has steep drop offs and toward the top you will have to scramble a little. It is better to go up the grassy slope to the plateau avoiding the rocky top section.

If you have had an afternoon at the waterfall this is a good way to go to photograph Blackden Edge and Pinnacle at sunset. If you do go up to the plateau, descent down Blackden Brook is arduous, especially at night, better to go down and follow your nose across the heather slopes east of the brook (see the arrow on the map marked descent). On these slopes you will get a great view of the Fairbrook Naze ridge as the sun sets. Your descent should lead you to the lower reaches of Blackden Brook and back to the road.

Sprouting ferns at Blackden waterfall. Sony A6000, 18-200 at 30mm, ISO 100, 1/60s at f/5.6. May. © Kate

***Opposite**: The beautiful 8m waterfall on Blackden Brook (VP5). Canon 6D, 17-40 at 20mm, ISO 50, 2s at f/14, Polariser. Apr. © CG*

The Upper Derwent Valley around Ladybower reservoir is one of the most diverse areas for photography in the Peak District. Locations include the Upper Derwent reservoirs, high moorland and rocky summits, distinctive gritstone pinnacles, barns, a village, weirs and waterfalls, agricultural shows, well-dressings, and even a stone circle.

If conditions are good: a morning mist, a stormy day or a colourful sunset you will be spoilt for choice. There are several classic Peak District compositions here including Ladybower from Bamford Edge, the arches of Ashopton Bridge, Alport Castles, the Salt Cellar, Bamford Weir and several more, lesser known locations that deserve classic status.

It is a place for all photographers too. If you aren't up for hiking to the Crow Stones or along Derwent Edge there are many great roadside, or near-to-road locations here, that are good year-round except on the dreariest of days.

Maps

- OS Explorer Map OL1 (1:25 000) The Peak District: Dark Peak Area

Ladybower from Bamford Edge. A classic Peak District view and wonderful all year (page 136). Canon 6D, Canon 17-40 at 20mm, ISO 200, 1/120s at f/11, Grad. Aug. © CG

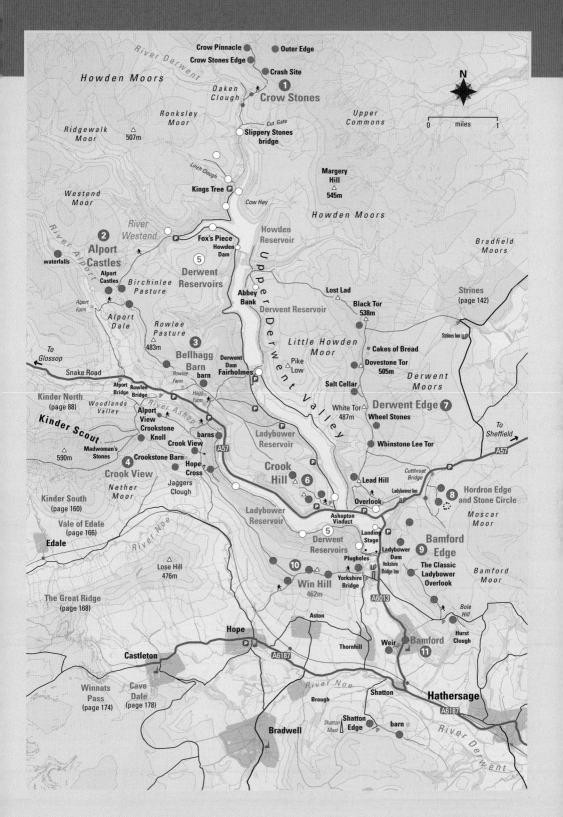

Crow Pinnacle · Outer Edge
Crow Stones Edge
Crash Site

River Derwent

Howden Moors

Oaken
Clough

1

Crow Stones

Ronksley
Moor

Cut Gate

Upper
Commons

Slippery Stones
bridge

Ridgewalk
Moor
△ 507m

Linch Clough

Margery
Hill
△ 545m

Kings Tree

Cow Hey

River
Westend

Howden Moors

2

**Alport
Castles**

River Westend

Fox's Piece

Howden
Reservoir

Howden
Dam

Bradfield
Moors

waterfalls

Alport
Castles

Birchinlee
Pasture

5

**Derwent
Reservoirs**

Abbey
Bank

Lost Lad

Strines
(page 142)

Alport
Farm

Alport
Dale

Rowlee
Pasture
△ 483m

3

**Bellhagg
Barn**

Derwent Reservoir

Black Tor
538m

Little Howden
Moor

Cakes of Bread

Dovestone Tor
505m

Derwent
Moors

Strines Inn

To
Glossop

Snake Road

Rowlee
Farm

Derwent
Dam
Fairholmes

Pike
Low

Salt Cellar

Alport
Bridge

Rowlee
Bridge

barn

Hagg
Farm

White Tor
487m

Wheel Stones

Derwent Edge **7**

Kinder North
(page 88)

Woodlands
Valley

Alport
View

barns

Ladybower
Reservoir

To
Sheffield

Kinder Scout

Crookstone
Knoll

Crook View

Whinstone Lee Tor

△ 590m

Madwoman's
Stones

4

**Crook
View**

Crookstone Barn

Hope
Cross

**Crook
Hill**

△ **6**

Lead Hill

Cutthroat
Bridge

Hordron Edge
and Stone Circle

8

Nether
Moor

Jaggers
Clough

Overlook

Ladybower Inn

Moscar
Moor

Kinder South
(page 160)

Ladybower
Reservoir

Ashopton
Viaduct

5

**Derwent
Reservoirs**

Landing
Stage

Ladybower
Dam

**Bamford
Edge**

9

Bamford
Moor

Vale of Edale
(page 166)

Edale

River Noe

Lose Hill
476m

10

Plugholes

Yorkshire
Bridge Inn

The Classic
Ladybower
Overlook

The Great Ridge
(page 168)

Win Hill
462m

Yorkshire
Bridge

Bole
Hill

Hope

Aston

A6013

Castleton

A6187

Thornhill

Weir

Bamford

11

Hurst
Clough

Winnats
Pass
(page 174)

Cave
Dale
(page 178)

Brough

River Noe

Shatton

Hathersage

A6187

Shatton
Mast

Shatton
Edge

barn

Bradwell

River Derwent

The Crow Stones. Remote and spectacular (next page). Canon 5D Mk 1.
Canon 17-40 at 20mm, ISO 100, 1/30s at f/20, Grad. Aug. © CG.

If you want to visit somewhere special where paths are rarely trod and the views seldom seen, head to the Crow Stones. It's a 3.6km/2.5 mile hike to these high gritty oddly-eroded stones, the latter half a calf-burning stomp up hill – the same distance as the walk to the Salt Cellar. These rocks are sat high on the moors facing west with superb views to the south over the reservoirs of the Upper Derwent Valley toward Win Hill. Good at most times of year but especially when the heather flowers or in the midst of winter when the sun is low. Whilst the Crow Stones may be the objective, the walk to these rocks is rich with photographic opportunities.

What to shoot and viewpoints

From the King's Tree parking follow the track through the pines northwards to the Slippery Stones bridge. Cross the bridge and continue north/straight ahead – don't go up the right hand track, the Cut Gate path. A few hundred metres up this track turn right up a track that goes up and round into Broadhead Clough just before Oaken Bank – great photos in autumn looking up this valley. Follow this broad rutted path up the clough until on moorland where it peters out. Turn left here and head north following an indistinct trod to the crash site and beyond then follow a narrow trod north west to the Crow Stones Edge (low gritstone boulders) then the bigger Crow Stones and the distinctive Crow Pinnacle.

Viewpoint 1 – Icelandic Airlines Airspeed Consul

You may stumble on the remains of Icelandic Airlines TF-RPM Airspeed Consul (Grid Ref: SK 174 966) and they may leave a lasting impression. Especially in the dark when your mind may wander to that fateful night when the crew of three became disorientated in cloud and flew into the hill. Their souls are now memorialised by wooden crosses.

Viewpoint 2 – Crow Stones Edge

The first rocks you encounter are a series of low buttresses with a small pinnacle at their southern end. These rocks get illuminated at sunset and provide good foreground subjects for a composition to the south over the reservoirs. But don't forget to turn around and look north.

Viewpoint 3 – Crow Stones and the Crow Pinnacle

500m north of Crow Stones Edge are the most interesting rocks here: the buttress of the Crow Stones (SK 169 970) and the fantastically shaped Crow Pinnacle. If the light is good there are a number of good compositions here. Try behind, to the north were the land slopes down and in front of these formations. If you get here late, the silhouettes of the formations are attractive against a colourful sky.

The higher elevation **Outer Edge Rocks** (SK 177 968) are worth a look to the east and the **Rocking Stones** (SK 167 974) below and to the north west of the Crow Stones. If you go north then contour west around Stainery Clough you will find an interesting formation of rocks called the **Horse Stones** (SK 159 976).

How to get here

Park at the Kings Tree by Howden Reservoir at the end of the road, 5 miles beyond Fairholmes Visitor Centre. This road is not open to cars at weekends and bank holidays when you have to take a bus (or walk or bike) from Fairholmes to the Kings Tree; the bus runs every half hour, last bus at 6pm. Mid-week in August drive to the Kings Tree for 4.30pm and after a 40 minute to two hour hike depending on your fitness and route finding skills you should be in position at the Crow Stones for the golden hour (7.00pm onwards). You can also approach from the Dog and Partridge Pub on the A628 in the north, a stiff hike of around 4 miles..

Kings Tree Parking Lat/Long: 53.442935, -1.748991
Parking Grid Ref: SK 167 940
Parking Postcode: S33 0BB (2.4 km)

Accessibility

Whilst the first half of this 3.6km/2.5 mile walk is mellow, the latter half is tough going up and over moorland where paths can be tricky to find. If you have gone up for a sunset shoot, make sure you have a head torch with fully charged batteries and a beer waiting for you at the car. **Approach**: 1 hour+, distance 3.6km, ascent 239m..

Best time of year/day

The Crow Stones face west and because of their high elevation, 521m/1700ft, get sun for most of the day making them suitable for sunrise and early morning photography, but especially late afternoon and at sunset when they are lit directly. August is great with flowering heather and winter sees the heather, bracken, bilberries and grasses turn golden to dark brown that is especially attractive with a low winter sun. Critical for compositions down the Upper Derwent Valley is that the sun has to be high enough to partially illuminate this impressive background.

Opposite bottom: Crow Stones Edge looking down to the reservoirs (VP2). Sony A6000, 18-200 at 19mm, ISO 100, 1/3s at f/13. Aug. © MR

In Broadhead Clough looking up to Horse Stone Naze and the Howden Moors. Sony A6000, 18-200 at 18mm, ISO 320, 1/60s at f/9. Oct. © MR

Dramatic late afternoon light on Crow Pinnacle. Canon 6D, Canon 17-40 at 20mm, ISO 100, 1/20s at f/14.,Grad. Aug. © CG

Late winter afternoon sunshine at Alport Mere, near Alport Castles (next page)
Canon 5D Mk 1, Canon 17-40 at 20mm, ISO 100, 1/20s at f/20, Grad. Apr. © CG

The narrow valley of Alport Dale – cut by the River Alport draining off Bleaklow – has a remote and big feel. Views from up high on the moor above the dale take in the best hilly wildness the Peak has to offer. Situated in this valley above an old farm is a west-facing cliff called Alport Castles, a geological landslip feature where softer shales have eroded away leaving harder gritstone rock. Debris from this landslip has formed the Tower, a free-standing pinnacle of gritstone which resembles a motte and bailey castle. Below the Tower is Alport Mere, a small tarn. This area has been compared to the Storr on Skye and is unlike anything in the Peak District.

What to shoot and viewpoints

Viewpoint 1 – Alport Dale

If parked at Alport Bridge on the A57 cross the road carefully and go through a gate by the bridge on the left side of the river. Follow the path gently upwards through a field to join an unpaved road and a mile/1.6km to Alport farm. You will pass conifer plantations and sheep pasture before dropping down to Alport farm. The farm was once home to Hannah Mitchell (b.1871) who despite only two weeks schooling became a suffragist and a founder of the Manchester labour movement. Depending on conditions there are good compositions here on the way to the farm.

When just at the farm and cottages go through a gate on the right and follow the footpath down to the river and back right following the river downstream and cross the footbridge. Follow the path uphill and left to follow a fence line up the slope. As you ascend impressive views up and down the valley provide great landscape photography.

Viewpoint 2 – Alport Mere

At over half way to the cliff top you will come to a steeper section of path with a small cascade running down next to some trees. Look left and on the skyline is a distinct tree at the edge of a small curved dip of a small hill. Leave the main path and head for the tree and through the dip to discover the hidden Alport Mere, a beautiful frying pan shaped tarn that sits at the base of Alport Castles.

The mere catches the reflection of the castle above on calm days which along with the a drystone wall on the slope make great photographic subjects. Head further north west to find compositions of the mere and the castle combined with the rest of the landscape.

If you are heading to the cliff top, a worn path leads you from the mere gently up the slope to the west to join the main path (no need to retrace your steps).

Viewpoint 3 – The Tower: Little Moor

The main path skirts the bottom of Little Moor, a crevassed gritstone plateau, and leads you through a gate, the path then curving round left to the cliff top – again great views down the valley. Before you summit at a dip is a stile on your left. Go over the stile and navigate your way carefully through landslips passing boulders and small cliffs to a great viewpoint looking over Alport Castles, the mere and up Alport Valley. This viewpoint is best late afternoon or just before sunset in early spring, autumn and winter.

Viewpoint 4 – The Tower and the Cliff Top

If you continue on the main path it leads to the cliff top and the moorland of Birchinlee Pasture. Turn left for various viewpoints looking down onto Alport Castles (Grid Ref: SK 140 914) and the shale-grit banded cliff. Depending on the time of year and your position at sunset you may be shooting into the sun. If you do have problems with flare, consider changing position. This is the point you arrive at if coming from Howden Reservoir.

Follow the River Alport for 2km beyond Alport farm to this cascade. Canon 5D Mk 1, 17-40 at 19mm, ISO 100, 1/4s at f/20, Grad. Mar. © CG

How to get here

Alport Dale is 13 miles from Sheffield, 19 miles from the M61/M67 junction at Denton, and 6 miles from Hathersage. There are two main approaches, a 3km /2.5 mile walk from the Snake Road/A57 up Alport Dale to Alport Farm then steeply up to Alport Castles. You can also go direct to the Alport Castles overlook at the cliff top by a 1.8km/1.2 mile gentle uphill walk from Howden Reservoir.

Alport Bridge parking, Snake Road: Alport Dale Approach

1 hour+, distance 3km, ascent 262m

Park at Alport Bridge on the A57, Snake Road. If coming from the east Alport Bridge is 4.7 miles from Ashopton Bridge at Ladybower Reservoir or from the west 2 miles down from the Snake Inn.

Parking Alert: There is parking for four cars south of the bridge – don't block the gate. Be alert when both entering and leaving the parking spot as there is a bend near the lay-by and traffic approaches quickly.

Parking Lat/Long: 53.402600, -1.789278
Parking Grid Ref: SK 141 895
Parking Postcode: S33 0BJ (0.1km)

From Howden Reservoir: Ditch Clough approach

40 minutes , distance 1.8km, ascent 185m

On Monday to Friday you can drive beyond Fairholmes Visitor Centre to Howden Reservoirs (weekends you can catch a bus or bike this road). Park at the end of the left fork of Howden Reservoir after Howden Dam known as Fox's Piece. Take the path into the woods that starts with an old footpath sign that says Peak District and North Counties Footpaths Preservation Society no.118 1953. Public Footpath via Alport Castles, Alport, and Hayridge Farm to Hope Cross and Edale. Head left and up at the fork then through the trees to moorland. This path, by Ditch Clough, leads straight to the cliff top overlooking Alport Castles: a 1.8km/1.2 mile walk.

Parking Lat/Long: 53.431438, -1.768550
Parking Grid Ref: SK 154 927
Parking Postcode: S33 0BB (1.5km)

Accessibility

If approaching from the Snake Road this is a 8km/5 mile plus round trip on an unpaved road then rough steep ground, often with steep drop offs. This approach is only for the hill fit and you need to be prepared for cold weather at anytime of year. When snow is on the ground the approach is arduous but do-able – you'll need big boots and full mountain kit.

The shorter 1.8km/ 1.2 mile approach from Howden Reservoir, the Ditch Clough approach, is more country walking (unless there is a gale blowing) and is useful if time is short. But you can only park at the start of this path Monday to Friday.

Best time of year/day

The half-mile long cliff, the main Tower and the scree slope of boulders face south west and so are illuminated by the afternoon and setting sun for most of the year. Sunset is the best time to visit. This valley runs north west to south west and gets low winter sun in the early morning in December. Autumn and winter are the best times to visit for photography when the vegetation changes or when snow has fallen, although it worth visiting Alport Mere in the summer on windless days for reflections.

Alport Castles in winter raiment (VP3). Canon 5D Mk 1, 17-40 at 20mm, ISO 100, 1/10s at f/20, Grad. Jan. © CG

Bellhagg Barn sits hidden away above the Snake Road below Bellhag Tor and Rowlee Pasture. The barn itself is a very attractive photographic subject but also this is a good way up to Rowlee Pasture which commands a great position overlooking views and grand vistas to the south (Win Hill), the north (Upper Derwent) and the west up the Snake toward Kinder.

What to shoot and viewpoints

The track and walls by the barn provides a leading line for close up compositions. The slope above the track is Access Land and positions to the north west have useful perches for sunset shots and to north east for sunrise when the whole of the Ashop Valley and Kinder will be lit up. Back toward Hagg Farm along the track is a steep path by a fence line which gives access to the boulders and cliff bands of Bellhag and Pasture Tor, and the Rowlee Pasture path; from all of these higher positions compositions will show the barn in its wider landscape.

Late afternoon in the larches above Hagg Farm Outdoor Centre.
Canon 6D, 70-300 at 150mm, ISO 800, 1/120s at f/8, Nov. © CG

How to get here

There are three main approaches. First, park at the small car park 600m before Fairholmes Visitor Centre. Walk up the track through the pines to emerge at a footpath which is followed north west (cross the path junction) to the barn.

Better is to park at lay-bys on the Snake Road – be aware of fast traffic – either below Hagg Farm Outdoor Centre or Rowlee Farm and follow tracks upward by these buildings to the track to the barn. By Hagg Farm is the quickest approach. From the lay-by on the Snake Road walk up Hagg Farm drive to a gate, follow the path beyond through the pine trees until you reach a track, head left here to Bellhagg Barn.

Parking Warning: Care is always needed on the Snake Road as traffic approaches quickly and there are many blind bends..

Hagg Farm Lay-Bys Lat/Long: 53.395351, -1.7593682
Bellhag Barn Grid Ref: SK 159 892
Parking Postcode: S33 0BJ (2km)

Accessibility

This is a short walk on good paths and a track but initially it is steep. Beyond the barn you are on open moorland.
Approach: 30 minutes, distance 0.8km, ascent 99m

Best time of year/day

The barn has a southerly aspect and is lit at sunset from June to August when the sun sets in the north west to west. Get here a few hours before sunset so that the valley is lit. Sunrise is best here in February and October, but just after sunrise in April and August. Because of the surrounding trees autumn can be spectacular.

From the slope above the barn looking up the Snake. Sony A6000, 18-200 at 34mm, ISO 100, 1/25s at f/11. Sep. © MR

Below: *Bell Hagg Barn is located in a secluded position above the Woodlands Valley. Canon 5D Mk1, 17-40 at 20mm, ISO 100, 1/40s f/20, Grad. Apr. © CG*

Crookstone Barn is a 400-year old barn now used as an activity centre. It is situated on the eastern slope of the Kinder Plateau, known collectively as Crookstone Moor, and above the terminus of the west fork of Ladybower Reservoir. The barn is a good landmark from which to explore the multitude of great viewpoints and compositions nearby including: Crook and Ladycrook Hills, the pines of the Woodland Valley, Jaggers Clough and views into Edale and Alport Dale. The approaches to the moor also offer many great subjects and views.

What to shoot and viewpoints

From Hagg Farm Lay-Bys. From the lay-by below Hagg Farm go down the path and cross the river by Haggwater Bridge. Once over the bridge go right up a path then back left and up a good path through the pines. Go right and up at a junction to emerge from the pines in a field below Crookstone Barn. Follow the path to a junction of paths near Hope Cross, a 7ft-high stone marker or stoop on an old Roman road/packhorse route. The date 1737 is carved on the shaft, the date when this medieval stoop was restored and on its square capstone are the names of Edale, Glossop, Hope and Sheffield. From here you can access several viewpoints.

Viewpoint 1 – Crookstone Barn
Walk up to Crookstone Barn and just below and above it are good compositions of Crook and Ladycrook Hill in the north east above the pine trees. Good at sunrise in late summer and autumn.

Viewpoint 2 – Jaggers Clough
Jaggers Clough is the steep and deep wooded ravine just south of Crookstone Barn. There are good compositions down into it, and across Edale to Lose Hill and the Great Ridge.

Viewpoint 3 – Crookstone Knoll
It is a short up hill walk to Crookstone Knoll and the Kinder Plateau from Crookstone Barn, which depending on conditions are worth exploring. Especially on the plateau before the rise up to the Knoll where there are some distinctive trees amongst the relatively flat grassland. From Crookstone Knoll, the narrow east end of Kinder, you have a choice to follow paths that skirt the north and south edges of Kinder.

How to get here

Two approaches are described from the lay-bys on the A57 below Hagg Farm Outdoor Education Centre and from Rowlee Bridge just off the A57 below Rowlee Farm. You can also reach Crookstone Barn by going from Win Hill, or from Edale.

Hagg Farm lay-bys Lat/Long: 53.395351, -1.7593682
Parking Grid Ref: SK 160 887
Parking Postcode: S33 0BJ (2km)

Rowley Bridge parking Lat/Long: 53.398697, -1.775649
Parking Grid Ref: SK 150 891
Parking Postcode: S33 0AQ

Above: *The sycamores below Crookstone Knoll (VP3). Sony A6000, 18-200 at 18mm, ISO 100, 1/90s at f/8. Jul. © MR*

Opposite: *From below Crookstone Barn looking at Ladycrook and Crook Hills (VP1). Sony A6000, 18-200 at 68mm, ISO 100, 1/4s at f/11. Nov. © MR*

Accessibility

The approach from the Hagg Farm lay-bys is up hill on good paths, with some tricky navigation in the pine forest. Check your approach on a good map before you set off. Bring a head torch, especially for sunrise shoots. It can be very boggy on the moorland and it is often tough going. The approach from Rowlee Farm is straightforward on a good track in open country.

Approach to Crookstone Barn from:
Hagg Farm lay-bys: 45 mins, distance 1.2km, ascent 124m/406ft.
Rowlee Farm: 1 hour, distance 2km, ascent 157m/516ft

Best time of year/day

Whilst August will see the heather flowering, the best times are from September until June at sunrise and after, especially if there is mist in the valley.

Viewpoint 4 – Ladybower Pines

From Hope Cross below Crookstone Barn if you follow the path toward Win Hill you can go through a gate into the mixed-pine plantation above Ladybower. In the summer and early autumn the rising sun illuminates these trees and there is a network of forestry paths to explore which not only give great views to the north east, but also give you access into the woods for tree photography. These woodlands have a very Canadian forest feel to them.

Viewpoint 5 – The west fork of Ladybower Reservoir and Old Barns

If you are in the Ladybower Pines head on paths down hill to pick up the path on the south side of the reservoir which can be followed back to Hagg Farm and in autumn is a kaleidoscope of colours.

Heading back to the Hagg Farm lay-bys just downstream from Haggwater Bridge below the lay-bys is an open meadow in the trees which is home to two old barns which make beautiful studies, especially in the morning.

From Rowlee Bridge. You can reach all the viewpoints above by parking at Rowlee Bridge but this approach also gives magnificent views up the Alport Valley to Alport Castles. Rowlee Bridge is situated down from the A57 by the River Ashop, 3.5 miles up the Snake Road from Ashopton Bridge, below Rowlee Farm. Park near the barn.

Viewpoint 6: Alport Valley View

Approach To Crookstone Barn. Walk over the bridge down from the barn, up the paved track and turn left at the track junction. This track leads east up the slope all the way to Hope Cross with magnificent views north and north west up the Alport Valley to Alport Castles. You can leave the track before Hope Cross and go cross-country following grouse shooting tracks to above Crookstone Barn. Here the land flattens out and there are a few singular trees (Viewpoint 3) with the summit of Loose Hill popping its head out.

Blackley Hey Approach to Crookstone Knoll. For a fit person, going straight up Blackley Hey, the steep slope above Rowlee Bridge, is a fast but strenuous way up to the Kinder Plateau. There is a runners' 'trod' (informal single track path) up this slope used by the Dark Peak Fell Runners for hill reps, but it can be tricky to find. After 0.8km and 260m/853ft of elevation gain you should emerge at Crookstone Knoll.

Opposite far right top. Back down at the head of Ladybower reservoir (VP 5). Sony A6000, 18-200 at 32mm, ISO 100, 1/60s at f/9. Nov. © MR

Sunrise and the pines on the ridge near Hope Cross (VP4). Sony A6000, 18-200 at 200mm, ISO 100, 1/25s at f/11. Nov. © MR

Alport Valley from the walk up from Rowlee Bridge (VP6). Sony A6000, 18-200 at 18mm, ISO 100, 1/60s at f/11. Jul. © MR

The west fork of Ladybower (VP5). Sony A6000, 18-200 at 32mm, ISO 100, 1/60s at f/9. Nov. © MR

From Jaggers Clough looking at Lose Hill and Back Tor (VP2). Sony A6000, 18-200 at 26mm, ISO 100, 1/10s at f/11. Nov. © MR

Derwent Dam overflowing. Canon 6D, Canon 17-40 at 20mm, ISO 50, 1s at f/14, Dec. © CG

The Landing stage (VP1). Sony A6000, 10-18 at 18mm, ISO 100, 1/60s at f/11. Jul. © MR

The Upper Derwent Reservoirs of Ladybower, Derwent and Howden were built between 1901 and 1945 to supply water to the Midlands. Their construction flooded the villages of Derwent and Ashopton.

Since completion of the dams the woodlands planted on the surrounding slopes have softened the industrial nature of the area while the dams themselves – built from local materials – have weathered and seem as much a part of the local geology as the overlooking gritstone tors of Derwent Edge.

The whole area, from Ladybower Dam northwards, is a recreational focus for this part of the Peak District. There is much here for the photographer, including photographers with limited mobility. Almost the entire perimeter of the three reservoirs is accessible and when the wind drops, the three large bodies of water become giant mirrors. The planting in the overlooking woodlands is very mixed, featuring colourful deciduous trees, massed ranks of dark conifers and lots of wonderful larch which makes it a very special place in the autumn.

What to shoot and viewpoints

This location has been subdivided into three areas each with several significant viewpoints described. You can access the perimeter of the reservoirs by foot on their east side or by a road on their west side.

LOWER LADYBOWER RESERVOIR

The Lower Ladybower Reservoir is all of that reservoir south of Ashopton viaduct/bridge by the A57. Park at Heatherdene car park (charge) or for free roadside parking opposite Heatherdene car park and just above the Yorkshire Bridge Inn, both on the Ashopton road (A6103) at the east end of the reservoir. There is also free parking by Ashopton Viaduct/Bridge on the A57.

Viewpoint 1 – The Landing Stage
At the eastern end of Ladybower reservoir just north of Heatherdene car park is an angler's landing stage and often boats moored on the water (please note access over the wall is not allowed without permission). This is a perfect place for sunsets – especially if people are fly fishing – or early in the morning with mist on the water.

Viewpoint 2 – The Plugholes and the Dam
The walkable dam of Ladybower and its two plug holes (bellmouth overflows) are situated at the south end of the reservoir above the Yorkshire Bridge Inn, one plughole at each end of the dam. The plug holes overspilling with water are a Peak District photography right of passage usually taken with a slow shutter speed using a ND filter,

From the Ladybower Inn overlook (VP4). Sony A6000, 10-18 at 18mm, ISO 100, 1/80s at f/10. Nov. © MR

Ashopton viaduct in autumn with Bamford Edge beyond (VP5). Canon 6D, 70-300 at 150mm, ISO 200, 1/100s at f/14, Oct. © CG

with a moody sky above or at sunrise with an orange sky. If the water level is low, water won't be flowing down the plugholes. The dam itself offers architectural detail and on a calm summer or autumn morning the reflections of the woodlands on the flank of Win Hill offer great potential.

Viewpoint 3 – Wiseman Hey Clough Plantation Walk

You can walk the western arm of Ladybower reservoir on its south side using an unpaved road. This walk offers great views of across the reservoir to Ashopton Viaduct, Crook Hill and its farm, and the deciduous woodlands on the >>

How to get here

The Derwent reservoirs are situated alongside and near the A57 Snake Road at the junction of Ashopton Road (A6013), 2 miles north of Bamford, 9 miles west of Sheffield and 25 miles from Manchester. For parking, a mix of paid and free, see each area section.

Ashopton Bridge A57 Parking Lat/Long: 53.374684, -1.707819
Parking Grid Ref: SK 195 864
Parking Postcode: S33 0AX (0.1km)

Fairholmes Visitor Centre and Derwent Dam Lat/Long: 53.402531, -1.741765
Parking Grid Ref: SK 172 892
Parking Postcode: S33 0AQ (1km)

Accessibility ♿

The majority of locations described are accessible to all and are wheelchair friendly. This is a low elevation area and you are never far from your car.

Best time of year/day

Spring, autumn and winter are all good, summer can be very green and busy. The reservoirs run north to south east and are enclosed by hills. They are better for sunrises in the late autumn, winter and early spring when the sun rises in the south-east and rarely get direct light at sunset but sunset can cast colour on the water. Facing south they do get direct sunlight for most of the main part of the day at most times of the year, when the sun is low being the best times. Autumn is a must.

The eastern bellmouth overflow of Ladybower dam (VP2). Canon 6D, 17-40 at 20mm, ISO 50, 2s at f/14, Grad. Feb. © CG

north side of the reservoir. Cross the Ladybower Dam turn right and follow the road, the views start to open up after half-a-mile and if you continue for another half-a-mile there are excellent views up the Woodlands Valley/Snake Pass. This walk is best done on calm autumn or spring morning with the sun on your back. The colours are spectacular in the autumn. Retrace your steps rather than doing a circular walk as the Snake Road is usually very busy.

Top: Derwent Reservoir dam railway construction foundations. *Canon 6D, 17-40 at 40mm, ISO 50, 4s at f/13. CPL, ND. Jul. © CG*

Above: A pike fisherman on Ladybower. Sony A6000, 10-18 at 18mm, ISO 100, 1/500s at f/8. Nov. © MR

Viewpoint 4 – Ladybower Inn Overlook
If there is mist on the water, a woodland path starting by Ladybower Inn allows you to gain height quickly to an excellent clear viewpoint of the reservoir which can be followed all the way to Ashopton viaduct with various viewpoints down to the reservoir and interesting subjects on the way.

Viewpoint 5 – Ashopton Viaduct
Another classic Peak photograph is of the seven arches of the Ashopton viaduct over the A57. Park at the free parking on the road by Ashopton Viaduct. Walk over the viaduct and turn right up the road to Fairholmes (the road that follows the northern spur of Ladybower). Follow a path down to the waters edge to several viewpoints of the arches; calm mornings or evenings work best. On the eastern side a good spot is by the water's edge, this is good at sunset.

UPPER LADYBOWER AND UPPER DERWENT RESERVOIR
You can access the Upper Ladybower and Upper Derwent Reservoir, north of the A57, by foot on their east side or by a road on their west side. Described here are specific viewpoints starting from the visitor centre at Fairholmes (run by Peak District National Park Authority and Severn Trent Water) including the Derwent Dam and the view of the Howden Dam from the elevated position of Abbey Bank – a classic Peak District photograph.

Approach. The visitor centre at Fairholmes is situated 2.2 miles up the road on the west bank of Ladybower reservoir, accessed up a minor road from Ashopton Bridge on the A57. The parking is pay and display with a cafe, gift shop and interactive exhibitions about the area. There is free parking just before Fairholmes and five minutes walk away at Hagg Side car park.

Evening light on Ashopton Viaduct (VP5). Canon 6D, 17-40 at 30mm, ISO 100, 1/8s f/13. Grad. Nov. © CG

From Abbey Bank toward Howden Reservoir (VP2. page 120). Canon 6D, 17-40 at 20mm, ISO 100, 1/30s at f/14. Grad. Sept © CG

The visitor centre at Fairholmes will be very busy at weekends and holidays but there are a number of delightful woodland walks that start here including a complete circumnavigation of Derwent and Howden reservoir, all with many photographic subjects. Maps are available at the visitor centre. Described here are two interesting locations.

The Road to Fairholmes

Look out for spots by the reservoir and in the woods on your left as you drive to Fairholmes as there is much potential. There are three parking areas to stop.

Viewpoint 1: The Derwent Dam at Fairholmes

From Fairholmes walk north following the footpath sign that says 'To The Dams', from here walk through a wooded area before it opens up to reveal Derwent Dam (10 minutes walk). This high dam is a magnificent feat of engineering and construction, which is even more impressive when the water overflows down the outside dam wall – this occurs when the dam capacity is over reached usually after heavy rain. The overspill can freeze in winter and also has potential for night shots. Both detail and wide shots are effective here.

Across the Derwent Reservoir from the roadside to the east shore. Canon 6D, 70-300 at 250mm, ISO 50, 2s at f/18. Oct. © CG

Across the water to Nether Hey (VP2). Canon 5D, Canon 17-40 at 20mm, ISO 100, 1/30s at f/20. Grad. Jun. © CG

HOWDEN RESERVOIR

Viewpoint 1: Howden Dam

Howden Dam is 4.4 miles from the A57, 2.2 miles beyond Fairholmes Visitor Centre. The road beyond the visitor centre is closed to cars at weekends and public holidays until 6pm. A regular bus service runs to the Kings Tree parking/turnaround where the paved road ends when the road is closed. This end of the Derwent Reservoirs is a very special place, especially when not busy, and is more reminiscent of remote wild areas in the Lake District or Scotland.

Viewpoint 2: Abbey Bank and Howden Reservoir

A classic Peak District photograph is of the Howden Dam from the edge of the Howden Moor at Abbey Bank. Midday in autumn is a good time. To get here walk to below the Derwent Dam and continue at its far end up steps to reach the east side road (foot traffic only). Turn left and walk for 2.4km/1.5 miles until just before a bridge and after that the Howden Dam. The footpath to Abbey Bank starts before you go around the corner to the bridge. A small 4x4 track heads off the track you are on marked by a sign. Walk 40ft up this track and turn right up a feint path which bears slightly right up the hill through trees. Go through the gate onto the moor and take the right diagonal steep path up the hill. As you get high, the Howden Dam and the island in front of it reveal themselves. It is worth exploring the high moorland above for more viewpoints and wildlife.

Viewpoint 2: Fox's Piece and the River Westend

Just after the Howden Dam is the left fork of the reservoir where there are several viewpoints, especially looking across the water toward Nether Hey on the Howden Moors. Significantly this fork points west and because of a dip in the hills it can receive direct light from sunset in spring and autumn, and late afternoon sun in summer. The fall and rise of the reservoir here creates interesting curved features of the mud banks. The inflow here is the river Westend and its gentle cascades, shaded by trees, are worth exploring in the autumn. It will be a lot quieter than Padley Gorge.

Although deliberately planted, the Ladybower Woodlands are mature and very attractive. © CG

Opposite: Howden Dam from Kings Tree (VP3, page 122).
Canon 6D, 70-300 at 280mm, ISO 200, 1/2s at f/14, Oct. © CG

Viewpoint 3: Kings Tree to Slippery Stones

The road stops at 7 miles from the A57, 5 miles from Fairholmes, at a place called Kings Tree where there is a turnaround and parking for several cars.

Just down from the parking area a fence line becomes submerged in the water (water level dependent) and looking down to the dam when calm with the surrounding slopes reflected; you could almost be photographing at Derwentwater in the Lake District. There are several spots by the reservoir where you get good reflections with converging diagonal lines, which are even better if there is a colourful sunset or mist on the water.

Walk along the unpaved road to Slippery Stones and its bridge for another good photograph. From near the King's Tree you can also access Linch Clough (small waterfall) and Ronksley Moor for an elevated viewpoint of the reservoirs.

The attractive bridge at Slippery Stones (VP3). Canon 6D, Canon 17-40 at 20mm, ISO 50, 2s at f/14, Polariser. Jul. © CG

Autumn colours on the Westend River (VP2, page 120). Canon 6D, 17-40 at 20mm, ISO 50, 2s at f/14. Polariser. Oct. © CG

Supports for the old railway submerged in the reservoir. Canon 6D, Canon 70-300 at 200mm, ISO 50, 3s at f/20, Nov. © CG

Lancaster Bombers from Whinstone Lee Tor on Derwent Edge. Sony A6000, 18-200 at 30mm, ISO 200, 1/250s at f/11. Sept. © MR

The Dambusters at Derwent Reservoir

In 1943 the RAF and other commonwealth air forces came together for operation Chastise, where a number of important dams in the German industrial heartland were targeted by Lancaster Bombers. The squadron carried the bouncing bomb designed by Barnes Wallace. The whole project was immortalized in the 1955 film The Dambusters.

The aircrews underwent training prior to the operation at the reservoirs of the Upper Derwent and in particular the Derwent Reservoir dam because of its resemblance to the target dams in Germany's Ruhr valleys. The events of 1943 are regularly commemorated in the Peak District with fly-pasts of the Derwent Dam by the Battle of Britain Memorial Flight and other guest aircraft from the current 617 Squadron.

The planes fly down the length of the three Derwent reservoirs and over the dams from the north and it is a great opportunity to photograph these splendid aircraft in incredible scenery.

When?

The flights usually take place every five years. Check the Battle Of Britain Memorial Flights website: **www.raf.mod.uk/bbmf**, as well as social media and local press for dates. There were fly-bys in 2012, in 2013 on the 70th anniversary of operation Chastise and in 2014 and 2017. Hopefully it will happen more frequently, it is an important memorial of remembrance and thanksgiving to those who lost their lives for our freedom.

Get here early

These events are popular and parking is always a problem. Bring a packed lunch and get here early. Wait until well after the flypast to leave.

Where from?

If you want photographs of the bombers near the Derwent Dam, which is by the Fairholmes Visitor Centre, the best places are either side of the dam on the roads which will allow you to take close ups of the bombers and the dam. If you prefer an elevated position walk up Pike Low hill on the east side of the dam which also ensure that you get good views of the bombers approaching down the valley as well as above the dam. You can also try below the dam, but this will restrict you to one viewpoint. Also popular is from Whinstone Lee Tor, various spots on the Derwent Edges and on Crook Hill, which is good to get the bombers against the sky

Light and lens

The fly past usually takes place at midday or early afternoon when the sun is in the south, so if you are shooting towards the north or from the east or west the scene is usually well-illuminated.

A mid-telephoto lens is preferable to get both wide and close up shots. The fly past is over quickly and you have to make sure you are ready. They do often make several fly passes so you may have several chances.

Crook Hill (374m) and Ladycrook Hill (382m) are a little overshadowed by the surrounding Derwent Edge and Win Hill. But these twin peaks stand proud above Ladybower reservoir and have views and a character that is unique, as well as being very accessible. On the south west sides of their summits are small gritstone outcroppings that run down the slope to the Snake Road as scree. On the short uphill approach through fields you pass by Toadhole Cote Barn to the beautiful Crookhill Farm – a working sheep farm owned by the National Trust. The views on this approach down to Ashopton Bridge over to Bamford are classic, and the summits vistas are very special.

When there is an inversion with mist in the valley this is one of the best locations in the Peak; it's fast to get above the mist and there is plenty to photograph.

What to shoot and viewpoints

On the left 100m up the Fairholmes Reservoir road from the junction of A57 Snake Pass road is a stile and a National Trust sign before a cattle grid. This is the start of the path to the summit of Crook Hill.

Viewpoint 1 – Ashopton Bridge
The arches of Ashopton Bridge are often photographed from the banks of the reservoir, another alternative is from above. Follow the path through the first small field and near the top of the second larger field – Toadhole Cote Barn is on your left looking down – there are good viewpoints down to the reservoir and beyond to the profile of Bamford Edge.

Continue through the next field – please shut all gates – to Crookhill Farm, a delightful old sheep farm. The path skirts the farm or you can go through the farm to reach a farm track and go either left or right then direct up the slope. Almost immediately follow a footpath that rises gently to a point between the two hills where the summits are accessible.

Halfway to Crook Hill (VP1). Sony A6000, 18-200 at 18mm, ISO 100, 1/160s at f/11. Sep. © MR

Opposite: *Dawn light on Crook Hill, Ladycrook Hill beyond. Canon 5D Mk 1, 17-40 at 20mm, ISO 100, 1/15s at f/20. Grad. Mar. © CG*

How to get here

Crook Hill is situated by Ladybower reservoir, just above the junction of the A57 Snake Road and the Fairholmes Road at Ashopton Bridge. Park either at Heatherdene car park on the Bamford Road, at Ashopton Bridge or by the cattle guard at the start of the Fairholmes Road where the path begins. A path leads through fields leads to Crookhill Farm and onwards to the summit of Crook Hill.

Parking Lat/Long: 53.374599, -1.7082882
Parking Grid Ref: SK 195 864
Parking Postcode: S33 0AX (0.1km)

Accessibility

From the road it is uphill for just short of a mile on a good path then tougher going near the summit. This ridge catches the weather, especially the wind. Wrap up well.
Approach: 40 minutes, distance 1.2km, ascent 140m

Best time of year/day

Both sunset and sunrise are favourite times here, especially mornings when there is mist in the valley. In July the sun sets in the north west providing golden hour illumination if you are photographing Ladycrook Hill from Crook Hill straight into the sun, or Crook Hill will be illuminated if you are on Ladycrook Hill. The rocky outcrops of both summits are lit by late afternoon sun most of the year. This is a good location for photographing Ladybower and Bamford edge at sunrise or when the weather is stormy.

Looking to the east and Crookhill farm (VP2). Sony A6000, 10-18 at 10mm, ISO 100, 1/100s at f/10. Oct. © MR

Viewpoint 2 – From Crook Hill

The summit rocks of Crook Hill (SK 184 868), especially the square block, make interesting subjects. Once on top the potential opens up in most directions. The most obvious angle is toward Ladycrook Hill with Crook Hill summit and its rocks and moorland grasses as foreground subjects. It's worth exploring further down the slope toward the Snake Road. Evening and morning light is good at most times of year. Also consider down the slope to a rock shelf toward both Bamford and just above Crookhill Farm.

Viewpoint 3 – Ladycrook Hill

From the top of Ladycrook Hill there are good views looking back to Crook Hill and also across to the Derwent Edge.

Derwent Edge is a high moorland escarpment lined by gritstone tors, boulders and pinnacles sitting high above the Ladybower and Derwent reservoirs. Once you are on the well-maintained path that traverses this moorland the views and compositions are continually dramatic in all directions. The Edge is home to several weather-sculpted gritstone blocks, one of the most well-known is the Salt Cellar, so-named due to its resemblance to an old-fashioned salt cellar.

As well as rock formations there is much to photograph on and from this moorland. It is a great place for panoramas especially when the weather is changeable. This area is also home to grouse, mountain hares and the rare bird of prey, the goshawk. This is a location to visit again and again; it will lift your spirits.

What to shoot and viewpoints

The LadyBower Inn Approach. For this approach park at Ashopton Bridge or at Heatherdene car park on Bamford Road, then make your way to the Ladybower Inn (pints only allowed on the way back). On the right of the Inn is a rocky track, follow this then cut left to a path behind the Inn through woods and a gate to continue along the path by a wall to the first viewpoint.

Viewpoint 1 – Ladybower Overlook (SK 201 865)

All along the wall are great views looking south across Ladybower towards Bamford and Bamford Edge. This is a great stop off before the steep ascent to Lead Hill, or a place to nip up to if there is morning mist over the reservoir. If you aren't going up to Lead Hill you can continue along this path at a low level checking viewpoints down to the reservoir to emerge near Ashopton Bridge.

Viewpoint 2 – Lead Hill (SK 196 871)

Just after where the wall starts is a steep and eroded path on your right, follow this up through the ferns to the top of the Lead Hill where the path thankfully levels off and contours round to the west and the views open up.

This is where you will get some of the best views of Ladybower from the Edge. Look out for a coffin-shaped boulder carved with the letters FW; this rock points toward the north fork of Ladybower. This is a great early afternoon and sunset location.

From Lead Hill carry on north to the junction of six paths just below Whinstone Lee Tor (viewpoint 3) and beyond.

How to get here

Derwent Edge and moor is above and north of the A57, the Snake Road. Parking is at Ladybower Reservoir or Cutthroat Bridge which is 11 miles from Sheffield, 22 miles from the M61/M67 junction at Denton, and 4 miles from Hathersage. An alternative approach starts from the Strines Inn on the Mortimer (Strines) road.

Cutthroat Bridge Parking Lat/Long: 53.382894, -1.680455
Parking Grid Ref: SK 213 873
Parking Postcode: S33 0AX (2km)

Strines Inn Parking Lat/Long: 53.411976, -1.666647
Parking Grid Ref: SK 222 906
Parking Postcode: S6 6JE

Which Approach?
Where you park depends on which approach you are going to take and whether or not you want to take in Viewpoint 1 – The Ladybower Overlook and Viewpoint 2 – Lead Hill, and how fit you are. Three approaches are suggested. The first two take you to below Whinstone Lee Tor on Derwent Edge, the third to Back Tor.

The Ladybower Inn approach (1.6km/ 1mile) to Whinstone Lee Tor is the steepest approach (elevation gain roughly 200m/ 600ft) but on the way gives you a great overview and photographic viewpoints of Ladybower Reservoir, Bamford Edges, Win Hill and all views west plus it takes in the fantastic viewpoints of the Ladybower Overlook and Lead Hill

The Cutthroat Bridge approach (1.6km /1 mile) is less steep (elevation gain 100m/300ft) and takes you gently across Derwent Moor to Viewpoint 3: Whinstone Lee Tor; watch out for the grouse on the way up. The views are limited until on the edge itself.

The Strines Moor approach takes you (2.5km/1.6 miles) to Back Tor (elevation gain 217m/711ft) along a bridleway. Then a further 2km/1.3 miles to the Salt Cellar. Easy access to the Strines Pub afterwards. This is the most direct route to Back Tor.

Accessibility

Plan your visit with a map. Wrap up well, take a rain jacket, a hot drink and food, a pair of sturdy boots and legs. It's just short of an hour up to the edge, and an hour along a good path to the Salt Cellar and other attractions. The walking is on good paths and once on the edge near the Salt Cellar the path is paved with recycled mill flagstones (providing attractive 'leading lines' to photograph as well as pleasant walking).

Best time of year/day

Derwent Edge faces west so gets back-lighting in the morning, side-lighting in the afternoon and direct light in the evening, depending on the time of year. The most popular time to photograph the Salt Cellar is an hour or so before sunset in late July and August when the heather flowers and the sun sets in the north-west.

In early summer the grouse are docile and easily photographed, they are more flighty in August and September. The mountain hares are common but most distinctive when they get their white coat or pelage in winter from December until April. They stand out most prominently when there is no snow on the ground. The goshawks are usually seen in spring when they do an aerial display high over woodland. This rolling, austere but inspiring place is great to visit when the weather is stormy or changeable and is often best photographed in winter.

Above: Ladybower from the coffin boulder near Lead Hill (VP2). Sony A6000, 10-18 at 10mm, ISO 200, 1/50s at f/13. Nov. © MR

Opposite: Ladybower from below White Tor on Derwent Edge (VP3, page 130). Canon 6D, 70-300 at 300mm, ISO 200, 1/200s at f/8. Sep. © CG

Cutthroat Bridge appraoch. This is the gentle approach that takes you direct to Whinstone Lee Tor. Cutthroat Bridge parking is on the A57 a quarter-of-a-mile north east of the Ladybower Inn toward Sheffield. Parking is at a large lay-by 200m up the road beyond the bridge. Walk back down to the bridge and go through the gate on the moorland side of the road (opposite are pine trees that are worth exploring and Hordron Edge page 132) and follow the broad rocky path by Highshaw Clough (a stream), ignore the path that branches off sharp left early on, go straight on. The path arches round left and takes you gently up moorland to the junction of the six paths just below Whinstone Lee Tor. You can reach Viewpoint 2 – Lead Hill from here by taking the main path on the left back to Lead Hill.

Viewpoint 3: Whinstone Lee Tor (SK 198 875)

Whinstone Lee Tor is a major landmark on Derwent Edge as it is just above where the six paths meet. It is worth noting if you have parked at Ashopton Bridge there is a good alternative route from here down the steep gully in the notch which passes through a pine forest, with good photo opportunities, back to the Ladybower parking. From the junction of the six paths walk north uphill to the jumble of rocks that is Whinstone Lee Tor. The rocky outcrops here point towards Ladybower and could be used to anchor a composition.

From Whinstone Lee Tor continue on the path that heads uphill to the north. The path eventually levels off and in the distance – just short of a mile – is the significant profile of the Wheel Stones. Follow the path past some smaller rocks, cross a footpath (signposted Moscar to Derwent) to a sandy area before the Wheel Stones, this is Viewpoint 4.

Viewpoint 4: Approaching the Wheel Stones

The eroded patch of moorland were peat is exposed and many small rocks litter the ground. This is good foreground interest for a shot of Wheel Stones. Recently this area has been spoiled somewhat by the construction of a new path which hopefully will meld in with the landscape.

Last glow of light over the Upper Derwent, from Whinstone Lee (VP3). Canon 6D, 17-40 at 20mm, ISO 100, 1/40s at f/14. Grad. Sept. © CG

The Salt Cellar (VP7). Sony A6000, 10-18 at 14mm,
ISO 100, 1/30s at f/11. Aug. © MR

Viewpoint 5: Wheel Stones (SK 201 885)

The Wheel Stones are a significant gritstone formation on Derwent Edge and can be seen from many miles away on the A57 coming from Sheffield or from Mortimer (Strines) Road. As their name suggests, they are shaped like wheels stacked on top of each other. They catch the evening sun and are a good stop off point to explore if heading to the Salt Cellar for sunset. Flowering heather makes a good foreground to these stones, the rocks themselves can also be good for abstract or close up detail compositions.

Viewpoint 6 – White Tor (SK 198 887)

White Tor is the cliff face on the edge of the moor beyond the Wheel Stones. Its profile works well against the sky, especially at sunset.

Continue up the path past White Tor then down past some small rocks on your left. Continue down until the path levels and in the distance you'll see a spiky rock and a turtle-like rock on the left skyline. The path goes up a little to a knoll and on your left, before the path goes down again, is a small path which leads to the Salt Cellar alongside a stone wall.

Late autumn colours around Grainfoot Clough below Whinstone Lee Tor. Canon 5D Mk 1, 17-40 at 40mm, ISO 100, 1/20s at f/14. Grad. Nov. © CG

Viewpoint 7 – Salt Cellar (SK 195 892)

Approach: 1 hour+, distance 4km/2.5 miles ascent 186m/609feet

One of the best times for photographing the Salt Cellar is just before sunset in August (8:20pm) when the heather is vibrant purple. It is good at other times of year at or just before sunset. Give yourself two hours to get here. Composition can be challenging but there are many options. Most popular is from the south shooting to the north-west with a foreground of heather and rocks. But also consider the opposite side beyond the Salt Cellar where there is a drystone wall that can be used as a leading line. Get here early and try compositions with different focal lengths and viewpoints.

Viewpoint 8 – Dovestones Tor (SK 196 898)

Continue on the main flagged path beyond the Salt Cellar to the next clump of rocks: Dovestones Tor. There are several viewpoints here. First looking back at the Salt Cellar using the flagged path as a leading line (it glistens when wet). A panorama here could include Wheel Stones, White Tor and the Salt Cellar; best taken early morning or late afternoon. There is also much foreground interest if shooting toward the west down the the valley and north toward Cakes of Bread, the two pinnacles on the right,

Looking west from Dovestone Tor (VP8). Canon 5D Mk1, 17-40 at 24mm, ISO 50, 1/6s at f/18. Grad. Nov. © CG

Below top: The Cakes Of Bread on Derwent Edge (VP9). Canon 5D Mk1, 17-40 at 20mm, ISO 100, 1/40s at f/20. Grad. Jan. © CG

and the varied rocky profile of the distant Back Tor. The Dove Stone itself is set below the Tor and isn't visible from the path. You have to go down the side and around to the front. It's a smaller version of the Salt Cellar.

Viewpoint 9 – Cakes of Bread and Back Tor (SK 197 909)

The flagged path carries on all the way to Back Tor, about a mile away in the distance. Before you reach Back Tor just east of the path is a ring of low boulders known as the Cakes of Bread, some of which are often surrounded by a moat-like pool of water which can be used for reflections.

Direct approach to Back Tor From The Strines Inn. The quickest approach to Back Tor is from near the Strines Inn on Mortimer Road (locally known as the Strines Road). From here it is a 2.5km/1.6 mile walk to Back Tor with an height gain of 217m/711ft. Park down the hill from the Strines Inn at a bend where there is a small lay-by next to the woods. Go through the gate opposite and follow the paved bridleway, Foulstone Road. There is much to photograph on this approach including grouse shooting butts and a stream. Follow this road through felled pines passing a house, Foulstone Delf, then out onto open moor following a path to a junction with the main path on Derwent Edge. Turn right for Back Tor – the jumble of rocks, or left to go to the Salt Cellar.

Back Tor includes many small cliff faces, fingers of rock and pinnacles, including a formation quite similar to the Salt Cellar and is the highest point on this part of the moorland at 538m/1,765ft.

Back Tor at the northern end of Derwent Edge (VP9). Canon 5D Mk 1, 17-40 at 20mm, ISO 200, 1/80s at f/20. Grad. Jan. © CG

Back Tor isn't as popular as the Salt Cellar but it's quicker to get here. Its rocky edge faces west and arches around to the north west with expansive views, so parts of it receive the setting sun for most of the summer.

Lost Lad, Abbey Bank and Howden Dam

For the energetic it is worth the short walk to Lost Lad, if only for the name. You can also descend from Lost Lad by Abbey Bank to Howden Dam, and return by the east side path back to Ashopton Bridge.

'The view from here is one of the best in the Peak: west is Win Hill and Mam Tor; to the right, the broad, bleak weight of Kinder Scout; at my back, the crisp blocks of Crow Chin set against the gathering darkness.'
Ed Douglas, Nature writer, in The Guardian.

Just above Cutthroat Bridge on the edge of Moscar Moor is a delightful location just ten minutes from the road and like Ed wrote, home to one of the best views in the Peak. Hordron Edge is a small gritstone cliff that looks down on Ladybower Reservoir and up to Win Hill through Ladybower gap giving a magnificent composition. Close by on the moorland is the mysterious Seven Stones of Hordron and below a conifer-deciduous woodland perfect for intimate autumn studies. If there is morning radiation fog over Ladybower this is a good choice of location perhaps after you have photographed the reservoir close up or after a session on Crook Hill.

What to shoot and viewpoints

Viewpoint 1 – Hordron Edge (SK 215 871)
From the Cutthroat Bridge lay-by take the bridleway south up through the pines. Once just through the pines you can either go direct through the ferns up the slope passing some boulders to the moor top and the small gritstone cliffs, or go left and diagonal up the slope to the edge. Once at the intermittent gritstone edge the view down to Ladybower is seen. There are several viewpoints to explore here, some with gritstone cliff/boulders as foreground. Further along the path the woods below are revealed with some attractive Scot's pines to include in a composition. Both a wide-angled approach as well as isolating parts of the view with a telephoto is recommended.

Viewpoint 2 – The Seven Stones of Hordron
This small stone circle is set back from the gritstone edge 300m south from the main rocks of Hordron Edge. There are actually eleven stones but seven is a more magical number, three more stones are buried. The largest stone on the south west is called the Fairy Stone and at Halloween (31st October) the setting sun appears to roll down this stone. It has a notch in its top which can be

aligned with the moon. Some say the circle also aligns with the summit of Win Hill in the distance. The moor beyond and Stanage Edge form a backdrop to the stones, which are better photographed in the autumn.

Viewpoint 3 – The Woodlands
From Cutthroat Bridge stay on the bridleway that takes you through the first pine plantation, this is in itself good for early morning photography as the light streams through the trees. Continue along the bridleway for 500m and below you are mixed woodlands which are great to explore with a camera at first and last light in summer, but especially in the autumn when the colours are quite vivid. If you follow the bridleway further it eventually takes you up Jarvis Clough onto Moscar Moor and you can reach the stone circle and Hordron Edge this way.

Top: Looking at Win Hill from Hordron Edge. (VP1). Sony A6000, 10-18 at 18mm, ISO 100, 1/100 at f/10. Oct. © MR

Middle: The Seven Stones at a winter sunset (VP2). Sony A6000, 10-18 at 10mm, ISO 100, 1/30 at f/9. Jan. © MR

TBottom: In the woods below the edge (VP3). Sony A6000, 18-200 at 35mm, ISO 160, 1/200s at f/5.6. Oct. © MR

How to get here
Park at Cutthroat Bridge on the A57 in the small lay-by 0.8 miles up the hill from the Ladybower Inn, or further up the road at the big lay-by (a footpath joins these two lay-bys so no need to walk down or cross the road).

Parking Lat/Long: 53.382765, -1.6804147
Parking Grid Ref: SW 698 505
Parking Postcode: S33 0AX

Accessibility
It's a short steep ascent to Hordron Edge and the stone circle. If you stay on the bridleway to visit the woodlands it is a flat walk. The bracken is particular high here and after rain you will get drenched if you walk through them. This is Access Land and you are free to wander but do not climb over fences and close any gates.
Approach: 15 minutes, distance 700m, ascent 60m

Best time of year/day
This is a great autumn location after sunrise, it takes a while for the sun to rise above Stanage. From May to July when the sun rises in the north east this area gets light at sunrise, but it will be early (5am). Sunset at anytime of year is special here as the stone circle and the edge catch the evening light. This is a prime location for night photography at a full moon or when the Milky Way is visible.

Toward Ladybower from Bamford Edge with the August heather in full bloom (VP3, next page). Canon 6D, 17-40 at 20mm, ISO 100, 1/20s at f/13. Grad. Aug. © CG

Bamford Edge sits above the village of Bamford in the Hope Valley and sweeps round in an arc overlooking Win Hill all the way round to fine views of Ladybower Reservoir – a classic Peak District photo location. The cliff's steep rocky profile, known as Great Tor, can be viewed from Ladybower, this gritstone cliff is a favourite of rock climbers. The cliff face has a very appealing texture and up close sometimes resembles stacks of pancakes.

What to shoot and viewpoints

From the parking lay-by go over the stile and up a well-worn grassy path straight up the hillside, steep at first with good views across to Win Hill and the profile of the Edge. As you reach the crest onto Bamford moor turn left to follow a path – then left at a fork – that eventually reaches the edge of the gritstone cliff. Look to the right for great views of Stanage Edge as you traverse the moor. There is a lower approach that branches off left just after the initial stile and traverses more gently up the hillside and emerges at the start of Bamford Edge.

Viewpoint 1 – Win Hill and Mam Tor
There is a great view over to Win Hill and Mam Tor from the start of the edge with good rock platforms on which to rest your tripod.

Viewpoint 2 – The Edge (SK 207 848)
The Edge itself is convex meaning that is actually quite hard to photograph Bamford Edge from Bamford Edge, unlike Stanage, which wiggles in and out like a snake.

There are however some textured buttresses that are worthy of attention.

Look out for abandoned millstones below the edge, which are predominantly runner stones (the top stones) rather than bed or base stones.

Below the edge there is a stand of ancient weathered and stunted oaks which are challenging to photograph but are worth exploring, especially in autumn.

Viewpoint 3 – The Classic Ladybower Overlook
The best viewpoints from Bamford Edge are where the cliff starts to peter out and descend, looking down onto Ladybower Reservoir. The viewpoints are easily recognisable – set your tripod up on one of the rock platforms at the cliff edge – you just have to choose one. Gritstone rocks and heather add foreground interest. This composition is good most times of the year, but the best time is in August when the heather flowers and the sun sets in the north west.

How to get here
On Ashopton Road between Ladybower Reservoir and Bamford village is the Yorkshire Bridge Pub. Down the road 200m from the pub toward Bamford is the narrow New Road that goes up a hill. Take this road for one mile, through an avenue of trees to open moorland and stunning views across the Hope Valley to a lay-by on the left just after a small plantation of pine trees. The footpath up to Bamford Moor and its Edge starts here.

Parking Lat/Long: 53.352051, -1.677837
Parking Grid Ref: SK 215 839
Parking Postcode: S33 0AN (0.6km)

Accessibility
The grassy path up to Bamford Edge is initially steep and takes your breath away. The terrain is level but rocky once on the moor near the Edge and walking boots are recommended. Beware after summer rain as the tall ferns will drench your legs. There are steep drop-offs, take care if you set your tripod up close to the cliff edge. The round trip walk is just over two miles. Bamford catches the weather, be prepared if it is stormy. This is a very accessible location, it takes about 30 minutes to get in position. This is a great elevated viewpoint for relatively little elevation gain. **Approach**: 40 minutes, distance 1.5km, ascent 100m.

Best time of year/day
Two to three hours before sunset is the best time to catch the glorious warm light that can bathe the edge and the surrounding countryside. The sun casts direct light on parts of the edge throughout the day. The heather flowers in August. Because of its aspect Bamford Edge can be challenging at sunrise but good results can be achieved.

Millstones at the south end of Bamford Edge (VP2). Canon 5D Mk 1, 17-40 at 20mm, ISO 50, 1/13s at f/18. Grad. Mar. © CG

Morning inversion in the Derwent Valley from VP3. Canon 5D Mk 1, 17-40 at 20mm, ISO 100, 1/20s at f/18, Grad. Mar. © CG

Flare from the sun can be a problem. As well as the wider landscape composition this is a good position to zoom in on the twin peaks of Crook Hill.

Viewpoint 4 – Further toward Ladybower

Also consider continuing down the path to the north west. As you lose height more of Ladybower reservoir will be in view as it snakes up the Woodlands valley. In the autumn the larches and pines above Heatherdene parking next to Ladybower add rich colours.

Viewpoint 5 – Hurst Clough (SK 220 839)

To the south of Bamford Edge, Hurst Clough is a great bowl-shaped valley full of trees whose mixed planting provides a riot of colour in autumn. Drive up the road and around the corner from the Bamford Edge lay-by for 0.2 miles to below Bole Hill. Photograph from the road or from the footpath that cuts across the top of the Clough below the road. Best in late afternoon in autumn when the sun cuts through the trees dramatically and accentuates the superb colour here.

Autumn colours in Hurst Clough (VP5). Canon 5D Mk 1, 17-40 at 20mm, ISO 100, 1/13s at f/20, Grad. Oct. © CG

From many miles away Win Hill (463m/1519ft) is one of the most recognisable hills in the Peak District with its distinctive summit pimple. Its northern slopes are covered in pine trees ending at the dark waters of Ladybower Reservoir. The south side is softer, the fields of the Hope Valley touching its moorland topping and gritstone summit. There are great photographs to be had from the summit pimple, but its summit ridge and slopes are fantastic to explore with a camera in most conditions.

Reputedly in 626 an Anglo Saxon battle took place here. The Saxon King Cyengils of Wessex with superior forces on Lose Hill tried to storm the Northumbrian held Win Hill. The Geordies beat the Southerners by rolling large boulders down the hill; hence the names Win Hill and Lose Hill, although there is no written record of the battle.

What to shoot and viewpoints

Viewpoint 1 – Win Hill from Hope village
From Hope village walk up the Edale Road for 300 metres and turn right down Bowden Lane. Follow this road across a river and under the railway bridge. Go right here and follow the lane steeply up to Twitchell Farm half-way up Win Hill. Go through the farm and holiday cottages yard and steeply uphill through the field and over bridleway which crosses the hillside.

There is a good viewpoint here to the west of the Great Ridge: Lose Hill to Mam Tor that favours early morning light. Continue up through another field with a plantation of

Approaching Win Hill from the west. Sony A6000, 18-200mm at 18mm, ISO 160, 1/13s at f/11. Apr. © MR

trees on your left. Traverse up and right across moorland to join a ridge path and the rocky summit of Win Hill. Again there are many compositions to explore before the summit with useful fences, walls, some lone trees and paths to use as leading lines and subjects.

Viewpoint 2 – The Summit (SK 186 851)
The moorland plateau and summit of Win Hill has a 360 degree panoramic view. In the west is Lose Hill, Back Tor, Mam Tor, Rushup Edge and Kinder; to the north is Ladybower Reservoir, the Snake Pass and the Derwent Edges, and in the

How to get here
Win Hill is situated above Ladybower Reservoir in the north, and above the village of Hope and the Hope Valley in the south, 4 miles west off Hathersage.

Two hikes up Win Hill are described: from the village of Hope in the Hope Valley and from the Yorkshire Bridge and Ladybower Reservoir (the steep approach via Parkin Clough).

Hope Village Parking Lat/Long: 53.348208, -1.742672
Parking Grid Ref: SK 172 835
Parking Postcode: S33 6AA

Parkin Clough/Yorkshire Bridge Parking Lat/Long: 53.361246, -1.704220
Parking Grid Ref: SK 197 849
Parking Postcode: S33 0BP (0.2km)

Accessibility
The walk up Win Hill from Hope is gentle on good paths with one final steep section. It's 2.5km /1.5 miles to the summit with an elevation gain 275m/902ft. it will take an hour to the summit. The ascent up Parkin Clough is steep and rocky; it is extremely treacherous when wet and in the dark. It is just over half a mile/1.2km, with 258m/846ft of ascent from the Yorkshire bridge. In good weather the hill is quite benign, but if the weather turns you will be exposed to the elements. Walking shoes and waterproofs are a good idea.
Hope Village Approach: 1 hour+, distance 2.5km, ascent 275m
Parkin Clough Approach: 40 mins, distance 1.2km, ascent 258m

Best time of year/day
Win Hill catches both sunrise and sunset. In evening light the hills northern flanks, the Great Ridge of Mam Tor and the vastness of the Kinder plateau are lit up by direct and side light. In autumn and winter the moist valleys and Ladybower Reservoir ensure there is a mist surrounding the hill in early mornings and the rising sun can give spectacular light. Don't discount later in the day, especially when stormy as the sun in the south will light up the Derwent Edges to the north. August sees the flowering of the purple heather and is a special time. If you are up to it this is a great place when there is frost or snow on the ground.

Top left: On the approach from Hope looking at Lose Hill (VP1). Sony A6000, 18-200 at 40mm, ISO 160, 1/320s at f/10. Mar. © MR

Top right: Heather and stormy light on the summit (VP2). Canon 5D Mk 1, 17-40 at 20mm, ISO 200, 1/320s at f/18. Grad. Aug. © CG

east is Bamford Edge and Stanage. In contrast to this upland moorland to the south is the farmland of Hope Valley and Derwent Valleys – Hathersage to Castleton, with a backdrop of the plateaus, dales and low hills of the White Peak.

Both sunrise and sunset are great times on the summit. Sunset lights up the valley and moorland in the east and shooting direct into the setting sun can be spectacular. Rocks and the summit pimple can be used as foreground interest and paths as leading lines. Also explore down the path west toward the Great Ridge on Hope Brink where there are fences, gates, walls, heather and sheep. You can walk from Win Hill along a ridge to Crookstone Barn and Hope Cross (page 110).

Viewpoint 3 – Win Hill up Parkin Clough

This approach is fast, but is only for the agile and the surefooted. Its advantages apart from speed is that it starts near the waterfall of Yorkshire Bridge (page 140) and does pass another waterfall in the clough itself.

Above left: Winter on Win Hill (VP2). Sony A6000, 18-200 at 18mm, ISO 100, 1/80s at f/16.3. Feb. © MR

Park near the Yorkshire Bridge Inn and walk along the road south toward Bamford passing some houses, then turn right down Lydgate Lane to the the Yorkshire Bridge over the River Derwent (possible parking here, although limited) turn right just after the bridge. Go through a gate and on your left is a footpath sign, Win Hill. (Opposite the start of this path is the Yorkshire Bridge waterfall on the River Derwent, (page 140).

Follow the steps up by the stream to a carriage road, cross this and continue steeply up a rocky path by the stream for about 100m to a small waterfall on your left. This hidden waterfall only forms after heavy rain and the best time is October after rain and when the leaves have turned – or in the first flush of spring. Continue through the trees to open moorland and follow a path direct to the summit of Win Hill. If you return this way in the dark make sure you have a head torch. There is also a switch back which gets you back to the Yorkshire Bridge half-way down the clough which is a safer descent option.

Above right: South edge of Win Hill across to Abney Moor (VP2). Canon 5D Mk 1, 17-40 at 20mm, ISO 200, 1/60s at f/18. Grad. Jan. © CG

Bamford was mentioned in the Domesday Book of 1086 as a small centre for agriculture. A weir and corn mill were built on the River Derwent which passes by the village. Around 1780 the corn mill was converted to a water-powered cotton mill. Today Bamford is a thriving village with a strong community. Bamford's weir, the Yorkshire Bridge and Parkin Clough waterfalls are local highlights. Also described are two village events and a nearby hill with fine views and a funny name.

What to shoot and viewpoints

Viewpoint 1 – Bamford Mill and Weir

Park carefully in the centre of the village. Down from the Country Store and across from the village green walk down the Hollow, an unpaved road passing terraced houses to a right turn at Bamford Mill (now private apartments) then left down a path to the weir. A narrow bridge crosses the River Derwent in front of the weir. The weir is 150ft/50m across and there are good viewpoints on either side and on the bridge. Early morning in the summer or near sunset are the best times to visit, there are often ducks there.

Viewpoint 2 – Bamford Sheep Dog Trials

Bamford sheepdog trials are held on Bank Holiday Monday at the end of May at the Bamford with Thornhill Recreation Ground off Water Lane just south of the village centre (7.30am – 6pm). There is a small admission fee. As well as the sheepdog trials, there is a competition for the best sheep and a demonstration of sheep shearing. At 1pm there is the fell race up and down Win Hill (1,000ft, 4.5 miles). A long lens is useful for the sheep dog trials. This is a great celebration of rural life and very photogenic.

Viewpoint 3 – Bamford Well Dressing

Each year Bamford hosts a carnival week and one feature is the annual well dressing. The wells are presented the second Saturday in July and are usually up for a week. (also see page 478 for more on well dressing locations).

Well dressing at Bamford, Tour de France year (VP3). Sony A6000, 18-200 at 18mm, ISO 250, 1/125s at f/5.6. Jul. © MR

Viewpoint 4 – Yorkshire Bridge Waterfall

North of Bamford village and below the Ladybower reservoir embankment dam is the hamlet of Yorkshire Bridge with a pub of the same name and a collection of houses that were built to rehouse people who lived in the villages of Ashopton and Derwent that were flooded by the reservoir in 1943. The Yorkshire Bridge is a former packhorse bridge and near it is a delightful waterfall to photograph.

To get there walk south of the pub by the houses and walk down Lydgate Lane, follow this to the bridge and a junction with Carr Lane. Carr Lane leads to the village of Thornhill, go right here along a track and through the gate to the waterfall on the River Derwent on your right. Choose an overcast but bright day in autumn or spring to visit.

Parkin Clough Waterfalls. Follow steps uphill opposite the Yorkshire Bridge waterfall and across the carriage road up the steep path that follows Parkin Clough to the summit of Win Hill. Up this path are several waterfalls, the most significant being 100m up the path. This location is only worthwhile after heavy rain, and is best in autumn and spring.

Viewpoint 5 – Shatton Edge (SK 201 815)

Go less than half a mile from the Sickleholme Garage toward Hope on the A6187 and turn left over a bridge (viewpoint) into the village of Shatton – the name means 'farmstead in the nook of land between streams.' Continue

Morning mist above Offerton from Shatton Edge (VP5). Canon 5D Mk 1, 17-40 at 20mm, ISO 50, 1/2s at f/20, Grad. Oct. © CG

through the village and take the second left turn up Shatton Lane for half a mile. Please note, Shatton Lane turns into a bridleway at the second bend and cars are not allowed up to the Shatton Mast.

The view from various places up on Shatton Moor and Edge are spectacular in good conditions. You can see the whole of the Hope Valley, Mam Tor, Win Hill and beyond. It is however not so easy to photograph because of the lack of foreground and expansiveness of the vista; use walls, the lane and gates to anchor your composition. It has much potential and, importantly, if you think it's going to be good – when there is valley mist for example – it is easy to access quickly. This is also a good place to access viewpoints overlooking Hathersage. From the bend follow the footpath east toward Hathersage until the hill starts to descend.

How to get here

Bamford is on the Ashopton Road between Ladybower Reservoir and the Hathersage Road, nestled between Win Hill and Bamford Edge. It is 11 miles west of Sheffield and 25 miles east of Manchester.

Bamford Village Parking Lat/Long: 53.348516, -1.689532
Parking Grid Ref: SK 207 835
Parking Postcode: S33 0AA

Shatton Edge Parking Lat/Long: 53.330041, -1.699596
Parking Grid Ref: SK 201 815
Parking Postcode: S33 0BG (1km)

Accessibility ♿

Except for Parkin Clough all the locations described are on good paths with very short approaches. There is wheelchair access to Bamford Weir, but not across its narrow bridge. For the less mobile Shatton Ridge is a great high place some good drive-able viewpoints.

Yorkshire Bridge waterfall is fed by a reservoir. (VP4). Canon 6D, 17-40 at 20mm, ISO 50, 10s at f/14, Polariser, ND. Dec. © CG

Bamford Weir (VP1). Sony A6000, 18-200 at 18mm, ISO 160, 1/80s at f/10. Oct. © MR

The Derwent and Howden moors rise up steeply from the upper Derwent Valley to form a ridge with a high point at Margery Hill (546m/1,791ft); a vast area of moorland then farmland slopes gently down to Sheffield. Crossed by Mortimer Road, a 17th century toll road, this area is known collectively as Strines, a name that dates back to the 13th century where streams that collected down into Bradfield Dale were recorded as Water of the Strynds.

West of Mortimer Road is high moorland cut by several streams forming deep cloughs, and despite being within view of Sheffield, and to the north close to the steel town of Stocksbridge, this area has a remote and wild feel. Below Mortimer Road to the east is a network of country lanes, small villages and farmhouses, 19th century reservoirs and pine plantations.

Apart from the lovely village of Bradfield, this area rarely gets busy or crowded, although the new tarmac on Mortimer Road laid for the Tour de France has increased the number of cyclists – give them space. If you are new to this area, take a trip along Mortimer Road and in some places you would be forgiven for thinking that you were somewhere in the Highlands of Scotland.

Maps

• OS Explorer Map OL1 (1:25 000)
  The Peak District: Dark Peak Area

A friendly red grouse near Sugworth Hall (page 156). Sony A6000, 18–200 at 37mm, ISO 160, 1/250s at f/10. Sep. © MR

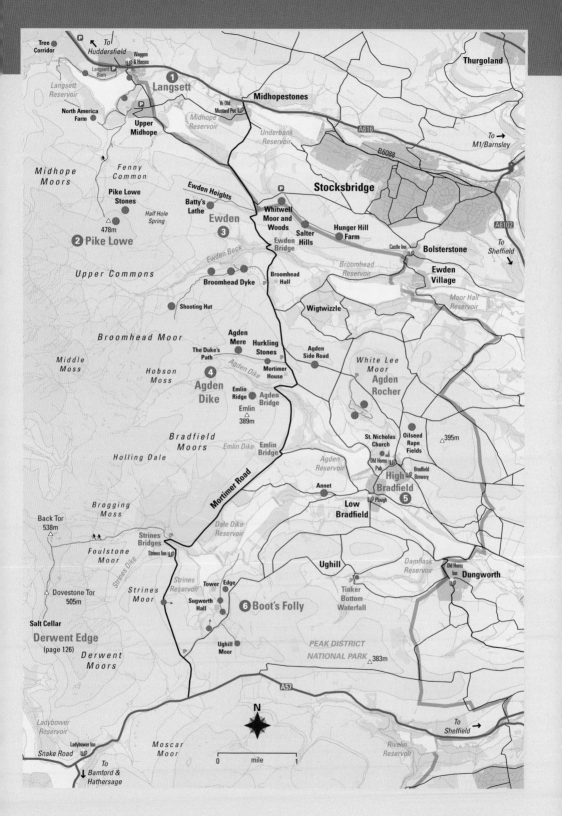

Tree
Corridor

To
Huddersfield

P

Waggon
& Horses

Langsett
Reservoir

Langsett Barn

1

Langsett

Midhopestones

Ye Old
Mustard Pot

A616

To →
M1/Barnsley

North America
Farm

P

**Upper
Midhope**

Midhope
Reservoir

Underbank
Reservoir

B6088

Stocksbridge

*Midhope
Moors*

*Fenny
Common*

Pike Lowe
Stones

Ewden Heights

P

Ewden

A6102

Batty's
Lathe

Whitwell
Moor and
Woods

Hunger Hill
Farm

To
Sheffield
↓

478m

2 Pike Lowe

Half Hole
Spring

3

Salter
Hills

Ewden
Bridge

Castle Inn

Bolsterstone

**Ewden
Village**

Upper Commons

Ewden Beck

Broomhead
Hall

*Broomhead
Reservoir*

*Moor Hall
Reservoir*

Broomhead Dyke

Shooting Hut

Wigtwizzle

Broomhead Moor

Agden
Mere

Hurkling
Stones

Agden
Side Road

*White Lee
Moor*

*Middle
Moss*

The Duke's
Path

*Hobson
Moss*

4

*Agden
Dike*

Mortimer
House

**Agden
Rocher**

Agden Dike

**Agden
Dike**

Emlin
Ridge

Agden
Bridge

△395m

Emlin
△
389m

*Bradfield
Moors*

Emlin Dike

Emlin
Bridge

St. Nicholas
Church

Oilseed
Rape
Fields

Holling Dale

*Agden
Reservoir*

Old Horns
Pub

Bradfield
Brewery

**High
Bradfield**

*Brogging
Moss*

Back Tor
538m
△

Annet

Plough

5

**Low
Bradfield**

*Foulstone
Moor*

Strines
Bridges

Strines Inn

*Strines
Dike*

*Dale Dike
Reservoir*

Ughill

*Damflask
Reservoir*

Old Horns
Inn

Dungworth

△ Dovestone Tor
505m

*Strines
Moor*

*Strines
Reservoir*

Tower

Edge

Sugworth
Hall

6 Boot's Folly

Tinker
Bottom
Waterfall

Salt Cellar

Derwent Edge
(page 126)

*Derwent
Moors*

Ughill
Moor

*PEAK DISTRICT
NATIONAL PARK*

△383m

A57

N

To
Sheffield →

*Ladybower
Reservoir*

Ladybower Inn

*Moscar
Moor*

*Rivelin
Reservoir*

Snake Road

To
↓ Bamford &
Hathersage

0   mile   1

The Little Don River (aka Porter) drains from the Langsett Moors to the south east of the Woodhead Pass and is temporarily trapped en route by Langsett Reservoir before its confluence with the River Don below Stocksbridge. The reservoir is surrounded by Langsett Woods, once a pine plantation, it is now being replaced by oak and birch trees. This is a great place for woodland and water photography, with some adjacent wild moorland.

What to shoot and viewpoints

Despite depletion by recent forestry activities, and replanting of deciduous trees, there is still plenty of colour and texture to be had. Paths follow the entire circumference of the reservoir so it is possible to consider every aspect of its shore and woodland. Newer plantations offer order and patterns while older woodland offers random interruptions of textures and colours. A long lens is required to make compositions from the patterns available on the opposite shores but the reservoir is not particularly big. There are also two specific places worth highlighting.

Viewpoint 1 – Corridors of Trees

The more southerly of two paths in the woods north of the reservoir, and across from Whams Road car park, is very attractive as it threads its way through the pine trees forming narrow corridors of trees. The horizontal shadows from a low south westerly sun combine very well with the verticals of the trees here to create some very pleasing patterns.

Viewpoint 2 – East End of the Reservoir

The dam and road at the east end of the reservoir and by Langsett village provide many good viewpoints over the reservoir and to the east down to the hamlet of Midhopestones. Here the outflow of the reservoir consists of a series of steps down which the waters tumble in a very attractive fashion but make sure you visit after a prolonged wet spell if you want to photograph this as the reservoir needs to be full.

There is also limited parking across the dam toward Upper Midhope where a footpath gives access to the woods lining the edge of the reservoir.

From the reservoir path (VP2). Canon 6D, 70-300 at 221mm, ISO 100, 1/30 at f/13. Jan. © CG

How to get here

Langsett Reservoir is located on the southern side of the A616 approximately 3 miles west of Stocksbridge and at the northern end of Mortimer Road (Strines). There are two good car parks, each located on the A616.

Langsett Barn Parking Lat/Long: 53.500348,-1.684150
Parking Grid Ref: SE 210 004
Parking Postcode: S36 4GY

Langsett Barn Parking Lat/Long: 53.506190,-1.697947
Parking Grid Ref: SE 201 010
Parking Postcode: S36 4GY (750m)

Accessibility ♿

Yorkshire Water own the site and have made considerable investment in making Langsett accessible. There are very good paths through the woods on the northern shore. A forest track traverses the low hill on the south-eastern shore while there are less formal footpaths that follow the south-western shore through the woods and which are not advisable for people with limited mobility.

Best time of year/day

This is a subtle landscape whose true merits are only revealed on calm days when the water offers back the reflections of the surrounding woodlands. Autumn colours are best.

Corridors of trees (VP1). Canon 6D, 17-40 at 20mm, ISO 100, 1/30s at f/14. May. © CG

[2] PIKE LOWE

There are two Pike Lowes, one above Fairholmes at Ladybower Reservoir (spelt Pike Low) and this moorland summit, Pike Lowe (478m) above Langsett Reservoir. There are no major gritstone edges here, just a large loose-stone summit cairn and a large scree of gritstone boulders on a forever moorland with good views down to Langsett and Midhope Reservoirs, with the 1,000ft Emley Moor transmitting station in the far distance. This is a place to take photographs that reflect the vastness of the moors. Be prepared for an adventure and self-exploration.

Warning: Be very careful out here, the area was used extensively during the Second World War for training and people still find high explosive shells that are live and have to be detonated by the Royal Engineers. If you find any munition, do not pick it up. Note its location, take a photograph and give the police a call. For more information go to **www.langsettandmidhopeatwar.co.uk** to find out about the wartime history of this area.

What to shoot and viewpoints

Thickwoods Lane is a permissive lane. Walk along it and turn left up another track where the pine plantation starts. Follow this track onto the moor to where the track splits, take the right hand fork then pass a gamekeepers hut down to a bridge across the stream and follow the path up Sugden Clough. The path peters out, the going gets tougher, go up the hill slightly left rising toward the triangular summit cairn of Pike Lowe with the scattered boulders of Pike Lowe Stones on the shoulder of the rise north west of Pike Lowe Summit. Best plan this approach on Google Maps aerial view and an OS map. A 1.5 mile walk.

Viewpoint 1 – Pike Lowe Summit (SK 209 973)
Pike Lowe Summit is marked by a man-made stone cairn summit made by walkers from a Bronze Age burial cairn that was here. There are other features close by including a stone sheepfold and particularly bare areas of peat covered in bleached stones which are very striking. Go west from here for views down to Ewden, the reservoirs and the north of Sheffield.

Viewpoint 2 – Pike Lowe Stones
This extensive scree of gritstone blocks and boulders sits on the slope 300m north east of the summit cairn. Apart from in the depths of winter these stones are lit by the setting sun with great views to the north.

Viewpoint 3 – North America Farm, Langsett (SK 202 997)
The ruins of North America farm overlooking Langsett Reservoir are worth visiting. Use the same approach as described above but continue along Thickwoods Lane through the pine forest then following its edge through a gate and the ruins. A walk of one mile from the parking.

The summit of Pike Lowe (V1). Sony A6000, 18–200 at 18mm, ISO 100, 1/100s at f/9. Aug. © MR

How to get here

This walk starts between Langsett and Midhope Reservoirs south of the A616. Park at the bend where Stocks Lane changes to Low Moor Lane – 200m west of the hamlet of Upper Midhope at the end of Thickwoods Lane before a gate across this lane.

Thickwoods Lane Parking Lat/Long: 53.492093, -1.6790843
Parking Grid Ref: SK 213 995
Parking Postcode: S36 4GX (0.4 km)

Accessibility

This is a round trip of over 5km/3 miles initially on a good track and path, then over rough moorland. It can be very boggy here after rain. Remember to take a head torch.
Approach: 1 hour, distance 2.7km, ascent 194m

Best time of year/day

A dry sunny day in July/August from late afternoon to sunset will offer colour, or for dramatic big skys venture out when stormy anytime of year.

Pike Lowe stones (V2). Sony A6000, 18–200 at 18mm, ISO 100, 1/10s at f/11. Aug. © MR

Top: An old army track near North America Farm (V3). Sony A6000, 18–200 at 18mm, ISO 100, 1/125s at f/9. Aug. © MR

Ewden Beck forms the second major drainage valley on Strines, this time feeding the Broomhead and More Hall reservoirs. It bares a strong resemblance to Agden Dike and it is easy to be confused between the two with their similar bridges and hairpin dips in the road.

Ewden Beck runs to the north east, has steeper sides and is bigger than Agden. It also has more variety in locations with old barns and farmhouses, a grouse-shooting access road that takes you across the moors, pink-flowering rhododendrons, a Bronze Age stone circle and embankment, a spooky woodland and tremendous views. If you get a chance, try to find the woodland of Wigtwizzle, especially in autumn.

What to shoot and viewpoints

Viewpoint 1 – Broomhead Dyke (SK 235 964)

Approach: 20 minutes, distance 1.4km, ascent 50m
From the lay-by take the footpath/track toward the north west and onto moorland. The track turns left and on your right – in the grass and bracken – is a stone circle with several large and smaller stones arranged in a circle. To the left of the track is Broomhead Dyke, a kilometre long Bronze Age earthen and stone embankment. The embankment is marked by a long drystone wall. Follow the track with many opportunities for compositions of the track as it curves up the moorland of bilberries, bracken and very extensive heather.

The drystone wall on your left seems to go on for miles up the moor – it ends near the grouse hut. Eventually on your right you can access the the rhododendrons with great views across the beck to fields and an old barn. You can go down the slope to get better vantage points amongst the rhododendrons. If you continue along the track it eventually leads to a shooting hut, but before you get there you leave the rhododendrons and the valley opens up with some tremendous views and compositions up and down the beck. The track itself makes a good compositional figure and there are a few boulders and mountain ash on the slopes to use as foreground subjects. Spectacular in autumn because of all the trees, the rhododendrons flower in June and the heather in August.

Ewden Clough, from the Salter Hills (VP3). Canon 5D Mk 1, 17-40 at 40mm, ISO 100, 1/10s at f/20. Grad. Nov. © CG

The remains of the farm at Batty's Lathe (VP2). Canon 6D, 17-40 at 20mm, ISO 100, 1/20s at f/14. Grad. Aug. © CG

Below: Derbyshire Gritstone sheep on the approach track (VP1). Sony A6000, 18–200 at 200mm, ISO 200, 1/125s at f/10. Aug. © MR

How to get here

Ewden Beck valley on Mortimer Road is 2 miles north of Agden Dike and 2 miles south of the A616 at Midhopestones.

Broomhead Dyke Parking
Park on Mortimer Road on the south side of Ewden Beck, 0.5 miles from Ewden Bridge in a small lay-by opposite Broomhead Hall.

Parking Lat/Long: 53.477780, -1.633055
Parking Grid Ref: SK 244 979
Parking Postcode: S36 4GG (0.9 km)

Ewden Heights and Batty's Lathe Parking
Park on Mortimer Road on the north side of Ewden Beck, 0.6 miles north of Eweden Bridge, up the hill, in a small lay-by by a gate and opposite a pine plantation. This is at the brow of the hill before the road descends.

Parking Lat/Long: 53.474281, -1.641080
Parking Grid Ref: SK 239 975
Parking Postcode: S36 3ZA (0.5 km)

Whitwell Moor and Woods Parking
Whitwell Moor is north east of Ewden Beck. Park at a small car park by woods 0.4 miles down Long Lane from Mortimer Road. Long Lane is the minor road which leaves Mortimer Road to the east at the brow of the hill north of Ewden Beck.

Parking Lat/Long: 53.461993, -1.637604
Parking Grid Ref: SK 241 962
Parking Postcode: S36 3ZA (0.9 km)

Accessibility ♿

All these locations are on good footpaths or tracks never further than 1km from the car – unless you explore further. Both Broomhead Dyke and Whitewell Moor are suitable, for the most part, for the adventurous wheelchair user.

Best time of year/day

These are year-round locations with moors being best in August when the heather blooms, through autumn, winter to spring. Whitewell woods are good when they have a full canopy in the summer (low-light photography), in the autumn and when they are stripped of leaves in the winter. The rhododendrons at Broomhead Dyke flower purple in June. Sun information is given in each location section.

The Grouse Shooting Hut (SK 222 956)

Approach: 50 minutes, distance 2.4km, ascent 300m

It's 2.4km/1.5 miles along the track from the road to the Grouse shooting hut. This is a good sunset location at most times of year and this stone building makes an excellent photographic subject surrounded by a sea of moorland and the wooded slopes of Ewden Beck.

Viewpoint 2 – Ewden Heights and Batty's Lathe

Batty's Lathe: SK 229 977.

Approach: 20 minutes, distance 1.2km, ascent 20m

Cross the road from the lay-by (see parking on p.149) and over the stile to follow the track alongside a pine plantation. When you leave the pines you will go by a drystone wall and reach the highest point here, Ewden Height 375m (1,230 ft). If it is stormy the ridge is a great vantage point for compositions in most directions. On your left a track leads down to an abandoned farmhouse known as Batty's Lathe. It is three-quarters of a mile/1.2km from the road

This is a tremendous location and is particularly good on August evenings and anytime in stormy weather with good light. We couldn't find out much about the farmhouse unfortunately. The views here are expansive in most directions with lots of interest and the area is worth exploring. The savanna-like birch stand to the south west is known as Half Hole Spring. Beyond the birch trees is Pike Lowe Stones at an elevation of 478m (1,568ft) which is very much worth a visit (see page 146) and beyond that Margery Hill, 546m (1,791 ft). Above the track to Batty's Lathe are some long brick and concrete structures that were built for target practice and as decoys intended to divert enemy planes away from the Stocksbridge Steel Works during World War II.

Viewpoint 3 – Salter Hills, Whitwell Moor and Woods

Approach: 15 minutes, distance 0.6km, ascent 10m

From the spacious lay-by with an interpretive sign on Long Lane cross the road and take the path by the woodlands. In the first part of the wood are old gnarled oak trees with very little ground vegetation. This is one of the best places in the Peak for taking portraits of individual and densely packed oak trees. Exposures can be problematic because of the low light although the light does rush in when the sun is out, especially early and late.

Further on the woodland changes to mixed species with some pine, beech and birch surrounded by drystone walls. Here there is much potential for studies of woodland vegetation. The moor by the path is a riot of purple in August and a wonderful bronze in late autumn. Continue along the path to an open area with stunted Scot's pine trees. Below this is an elevated viewpoint from which to photograph Ewden Beck to the south west with Salt Springs farmhouse in the foreground. (SK 247 973).

From here it is short walk to the cairn of Salter Hills and if you continue down the track to Hunger Hill Farm, there is an attractive composition with a curving track leading down to the farm with Wharncliffe Woods in the distance.

Opposite middle left: Autumn colours in Whitwell Woods. Canon 5D Mk 1, Canon 17-40 at 40mm, ISO 200, 1/100s at f/8. Oct. © CG
Opposite middle right: The Salter Hills (VP3). Canon 6D, Canon 17-40 at 20mm, ISO 100, 1/50s at f/14. Grad. Aug. © CG

Opposite bottom left: August heather and bilberry on Whitwell Moor (VP3). Canon 6D, Canon 17-40 at 20mm, ISO 100, 1/40s at f/14. Grad. Aug. © CG
Opposite bottom right: Whitewell woods (VP3). Sony A6000, 18–200 at 18mm, ISO 100, 0.4s at f/8. Aug. © MR

The track to the grouse shooting hut. Sony A6000, 18–200 at 18mm, ISO 400, 1/50s at f/9. Jul. © MR

The grouse shooting hut. Sony A6000, 18–200 at 18mm, ISO 100, 0.4s at f/9. Aug. © MR

Stunted, windswept pines on the Salter Hills (VP3). Canon 6D, Canon 17-40 at 20mm, ISO 100, 1/50s at f/14. Grad. Aug. © CG

Agden Dike is one of two major drainages that flow off the moors and with Emlin Dike it is the main source of water for Agden Reservoir. Agden Dike is surrounded by beech and oak woodlands with its slopes rising up to heather moorland. The views from either side of the Dike down to Sheffield and up across the moors are beautiful. The locations described are very accessible but have a remote feel to them. Agden Rocher is a land-slip formed cliff composed of coal measures sandstone. Facing south west the crag overlooks Agden Reservoir and at its base is a mature oak and beech woodland that offers splendid colours in autumn. The views from the cliff top are superb and there is enough foreground interest to make excellent compositions here.

What to shoot and viewpoints

From the lay-bys make your way to the Dukes Path on the west side of Mortimer Road between Penistone Road and Rocher Flat Farm.

Morning light at Agden Rocher. (VP3). Canon 5D Mk1, Canon 17-40 at 20mm, ISO 200, 1/20s at f/20. Grad. Nov. © CG

Viewpoint 1 – Hurkling Stones, The Dukes Path and Agden Mere

The Dukes Road is named after the Duke of Norfolk who owned the grouse moors here. This area was also the site of a mass trespass by walkers in 1932 protesting against the lack of public access to the moors. Walk up the Dukes Road for 500m and on your left are a group of low gritstone boulders, the Hurkling Stones (SK239946), which are perfect for foreground interest in a composition either looking down to Sheffield or up Agden Dike, good at both sunrise and sunset. Continue for another 500m following a broken drystone wall; a great lead-in line along with the track. On your right are a group of small ponds, Agden Mere (SK 235 949), which are particularly good to use in a composition when the heather is flowering or on a bleak winters day.

Viewpoint 2 – Adgen Side Road and Emlin Ridge

Agden Side Road is accessed just up from Agden Bridge on the bend before the farm and has great views down to the reservoirs. Also worthy of exploration is the south side of Agden Dike known as Emlin Ridge which is accessed 100m (Strines Pub side) up the hill from Agden Bridge through a gate in to woods (Access Land) and onto high moorland.

Viewpoint 3 – Adgen Rocher

From the parking cross the road and follow the path across the field (Access Land) staying on the top contour of the hill and veering leftwards to the cliff-top path. Below you is the cliff and the woodland. This is the point you return to if you do a circuit of the cliff-top and the woodland at its base. The views overlooking the trees in all directions are apparent immediately, especially the four reservoirs of Agden, Dale Dike and Strines, with Damflask to the south west. Once through a kissing gate the cliff reveals itself more with a prow of rock sticking out to the west making a great vantage point to look over the moors and down to the trees. The oak and beech woodland at the base of the cliff is mature and full of characterful trees and can be accessed by paths descending from either end of the cliff.

The Hurkling Stones (VP1). Canon 6D, 17-40 at 23mm, ISO 50, 1/8s at f/14. Aug. © CG

How to get here

Agden Dike: The main parking is up from Agden Bridge on Mortimer Road near the junction with Penistone Road where you will find small lay-bys, two miles from High Bradfield.

Parking Lat/Long: 53.447198, -1.632240
Parking Grid Ref: SK 245 945
Parking Postcode: S6 6JN (0.3 km)

Agden Rocher: The parking for Agden Rocher is on the Penistone Road that links High Bradfield to Mortimer Road. Park near a 4-way crossroads at a gate on the north of the road next to a pine forest (access to White Lee Moor) and opposite a footpath sign. The parking lay-by is a half a mile north west of High Bradfield.

Parking Lat/Long: 53.444028, -1.611126
Parking Grid Ref: SK 259 942
Parking Postcode: S6 6JN (1.3km)

Agden Mere (VP1). Sony A6000, 18–200 at 18mm, ISO 400, 1/160s at f/11. Aug. © MR

The Dukes Path (VP1). Sony A6000, 18–200 at 62mm, ISO 400, 1/200s at f/11. Aug. © MR

Accessibility   ♿

Short walks on good paths with some off-path traipsing across heather moorland. The Dukes Road (a grouse shooting access road) above Agden Dike is suitable for robust wheelchair users. The approach to Agden Rocher is flat, but it is a steep descent if you decide to explore the cliff base.
Approach: 20minutes, distance 1km, ascent 35m.

Best time of year/day

These are all-year round locations but best from August to May for colourful vegetation including bilberry, heather and sapling silver birch. Agden Dike runs from the north west to the south east and is lit directly by sunrise in the winter and sunset in the summer, with side light at other times. The morning light tends to flatten the subtle topography here so evenings are better. Agden Rocher faces south west and gets sun for most of the day throughout the year from dawn until dusk, except in high summer when the sun sets in the north west.

Low Bradfield and High Bradfield are twin villages in the Agden Valley below Agden Reservoir. Both villages, linked by the steep Woodfall Lane, are worth wandering around with a camera to record their architecture, a village cricket pitch and an original village shop. High Bradfield is home to St. Nicholas Church, a Gothic Perpendicular style church dating from the 1480s. Its burial ground is crowded with large and densely-packed gravestones. It is a most curious and photogenic place situated high over the surrounding farmland. The cultivated fields above High Bradfield are one area in the Peak District where you are highly likely to find extensive fields of yellow-flowering oilseed rape in June.

What to shoot and viewpoints

Viewpoint 1 – St. Nicholas Church, High Bradfield

Park near the Old Horns Pub (well worth a visit) and Jane Lane in High Bradfield. The old houses here and in particular the Watch House, built in 1745 to guard against grave robbers, are particularly attractive. The best places to photograph the exterior of the church and its gravestones are behind the church up high. The graveyard is extensive and is worth a wander around. In the summer there is sometimes a flock of pet lambs in residence (best to leave dogs at home). Some of the victims of the Great Sheffield Flood of 1864 are buried here. Dale Dyke Dam in the valley below broke as it was being filled and the waters flooded all the way to Hillsborough in Sheffield demolishing houses and killing 230 people and 700 animals. If open, the interior of the church contains a Saxon cross and behind the church is Bailey Hill, the site of a Norman motte-and-bailey castle.

Viewpoint 2 – Oilseed Rape Fields

In June, between High Bradfield and Oughtibridge in the east the fields are often bright yellow with oilseed rape which make fantastic subjects both during the day and at sunrise and sunset. One particular good spot is by Delf Road and Onesacre Road a half-mile drive from High Bradfield. The fields, often used in rotation, are easy to spot and an exploratory drive will yield results. Some of the fields are split by drystone walls. Look out for a field full of horses and ponies, a pond and a wood. You'll find them.

Viewpoint 3 – Annet Bridge Corridor of Trees

Early morning as the sun rises light pierces through this corridor of trees situated on Dale Road that links Low Bradfield with Mortimer Road.

Low Bradfield Post Office. Sony A6000, 18–200 at 18mm, ISO 100, 1/125s at f/9. Jun. © MR

How to get here

Low Bradfield and High Bradfield are situated between Agden and Damflask Reservoirs 6 miles north west of Sheffield. They can be reached from Mortimer Road or along the B6077 from Sheffield. There is good parking in both villages, but are likely to be busy at weekends.

Parking Lat/Long: 53.428634, -1.598478
Parking Grid Ref: SK 267 925
Parking Postcode: S6 6LH

Accessibility ♿

All viewpoints are roadside and on good pavements.

Best time of year/day

These are all year round locations with spring and autumn being the best seasons and either end of the day for the best light. The yellow-flowering oilseed rape is at its peak in June and is harvested soon after.

Above: High Bradfield Church. A Gothic masterpiece. Canon 5D Mk 1, Canon 17-40 at 25mm, ISO 100, 1/100s at f/20. Grad. Nov. © CG

Below: The rape fields above High Bradfield (VP2). Sony A6000, 18–200 at 54mm, ISO 100, 1/125s at f/10. Jun. © MR

Sugworth Hall is situated on Sugworth Road at the south end of Strines. Next to it is Boot's Folly, a 45-foot-high square tower with a castellated top that overlooks Strines Reservoir. There has been a hall here since 1560.

Charles Boot, a Sheffield-born civil engineer and housebuilding contractor, lived at the hall from the early 1900s and extended much of the building. He built the tower in 1927 using stone from demolished farms. The interior, now bare, was originally wood-panelled with a large furnished room at the top from which to enjoy the view. The Hall is surrounded by rhododendrons. Above the folly is Sugworth Edge – a small heather-shrouded gritstone outcropping – and above the road Ughill Moor. Close by is the wonderfully named Tinker Bottom Waterfall.

What to shoot and viewpoints

At the gates of Sugworth Hall take the public footpath on the left side of the gates and follow the driveway until half-way down to the Hall where a footpath leads off right.

Viewpoint 1 – A Tunnel

This path leads through a tunnel of rhododendrons, you may have to duck, until you arrive at a wrought-iron gate and can see Boot's Folly. This tunnel especially near its end can make some interesting photographs.

Viewpoint 2 – Sugworth Edge

Go through the gate at the end of the tunnel and into the field towards Boot's Folly which begs to be explored. Up to your right is Sugworth Edge, small gritstone outcroppings which provide a useful vantage point. There are great views down to Strines Reservoir and west up to the moors

Viewpoint 3 – From The Strines Road

Many good compositions of the Hall and its Folly can be made from afar. The section of Mortimer Road toward the Strines Inn gives a great view of the Folly in its landscape, especially at a bench on your right as you travel toward the pub.

Ughill Moor

It is worth a wander up on Ughill Moor– especially in August – which can be accessed by a footpath going south before Sugworth Hall. This moor gives an elevated vantage point over Sugworth Hall.

How to get here

Park at the junction of the Strines Road and Sugworth Road a half mile north of the A57 Sheffield Road. From here walk to the gates of Sugworth Hall or find a small lay-by nearer.

Parking Lat/Long: 53.400681, -1.650951
Parking Grid Ref: SK 233 893
Parking Postcode: S6 6JA (0.2km)

Accessibility ♿

Good footpaths and roadside.

Best time of year/day

The purple rhododendrons start to flower around the Hall in June through to July. Light is the key here for landscape photographs of the Folly and down to Strines Reservoir or across to Bole Edge pine plantation, or up to the Derwent Moors. Spring is good, the heather flowers in August, autumn can be magnificent and the roads are usually open after snow.

Top: Boots Folly from just below Sugworth Road (VP2). Canon 5D Mk 1, Canon 17-40 at 20mm, ISO 100, 1/2s at f/20. Grad. Nov. © CG

Left: A friendly red grouse on Sugworth Road. Sony A6000, 18–200 at 37mm, ISO 160, 1/250s at f/10. Sep. © MR

Opposite: Boot's Folly from the Sugworth Road (VP2). Sony A6000, 18–200 at 18mm, ISO 160, 1/100s at f/11. Sep. © MR

EDALE, KINDER SOUTH & CASTLETON – INTRODUCTION

Kinder's South Edge, Edale and the Great Ridge are home to several classic Peak landscape photographs. Most notable are the Great Ridge at sunrise from Mam Tor's famous gate, the perilous perch on the rocky edge of Winnat's Pass looking down the Hope Valley, the medieval Peveril Castle in Cave Dale and of course, the Hope Cement Works chimney from above Pin Dale on Siggate Lane. All these should be high on anyone's list of 'must get' shots.

These easy to get to and popular gems contrast with Kinder's South Edge where more planning, luck with conditions and effort is required to get an amazing photograph. Several visits and long walks have to be invested to get to Upper Tor or the Wool Packs. But that's not a bad thing, the experience on Kinder is always life affirming, the exertion healthy and you may come away with a photograph that few have. Intimacy with the landscape is needed to get the best out of Kinder and that takes commitment.

In contrast to these high places, the Vale of Edale is a landscape of pastures and flower-filled meadows lined with dry stone walls, home to small hamlets or booths, a church spire and barns, all surrounded by steep slopes. Early on a spring or summer morning, or in autumn with a light morning mist, it is a delight to be there with a camera, before it gets busy later in the day.

To the south is Peak Forest, here we have compiled several diverse locations from a quiet limestone dale with a barn, one of the biggest quarries in the area, to a remote and lonely high plateau that looks down on the limestone dales of the southern Peak.

Maps

- OS Explorer Map OL1 (1:25 000)
  The Peak District: Dark Peak Area
- OS Explorer Map OL241 (1:25 000)
  The Peak District: White Peak Area

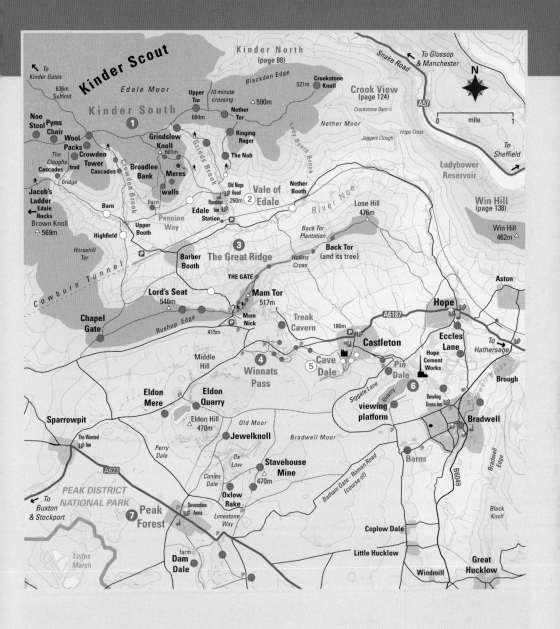

Kinder Scout

Kinder North
(page 88)

To Glossop
& Manchester

Snake Road

N

To
Kinder Gates

636m
Summit

Edale Moor

Kinder South

Upper
Tor
604m

10 minute
crossing

Blackden Edge

521m

Crookstone
Knoll

△590m

Crook View
(page 124)

A57

0   mile   1

Nether
Tor

Crookstone Barn

Noe
Stool

Pyms
Chair

Wool
Packs

Crowden
Tower

The
Cloughs
Cascades

trod

Broadlee
Bank

Grindslow
Knoll
601m

Meres

walls

Ringing
Roger

The Nab

Nether Moor

Jaggers Clough

Nether
Moor

Hope Cross

To
Sheffield

Ladybower
Reservoir

Win Hill
(page 138)

Cascades

bridge

barn

Old Nags
Head
260m

Vale of
Edale

Nether
Booth

River Noe

Win Hill
462m △

Jacob's
Ladder
Edale
Rocks

Brown Knoll
△569m

Barn

Highfield

Horsehill
Tor

Edale
Station

Upper
Booth

Pennine
Way

Rambler

Lose Hill
476m

Back Tor
Plantation

Aston

Cowburn Tunnel

Barber
Booth

The Great Ridge

THE GATE

Hollins
Cross

Back Tor
(and its tree)

Lord's Seat
546m

Mam Tor
517m

Treak
Cavern

180m

Hope

A6187

Eccles
Lane

To
Hathersage

Chapel
Gate

Rushup Edge
415m

Mam
Nick

Castleton

Middle
Hill

Winnats
Pass

Cave
Dale

Pin
Dale

Hope
Cement
Works

Brough

Eldon
Mere

Eldon
Quarry

Eldon Hill
△470m

Old Moor

Bradwell Moor

Siggate Lane

viewing
platform

quarry

Bowling
Green Inn

Bradwell

Sparrowpit

The Wanted
Inn

Perry
Dale

Jewelknoll

Ox
Low

Stavehouse
Mine
△470m

Barns

Bradwell
Edge

B6049

A623

Conies
Dale

Batham Gate - Roman Road
(course of)

Black
Knoll

PEAK DISTRICT
NATIONAL PARK

To
Buxton
& Stockport

Peak
Forest

Devonshire
Arms

Oxlow
Rake

Limestone
Way

Coplow Dale

Lodes
Marsh

Dam
Dale

farm

Little Hucklow

Windmill

Great
Hucklow

Opposite: *The gate on the Great Ridge. Canon 5D Mk 1, 17-40
at 24mm, ISO 50, 1s at f/20. ND. Sep. © CG*

The southern edge of Kinder Scout's moorland plateau extends from Crookstone Knoll in the east to Jacob's Ladder in the west rising over a thousand feet above the Vale of Edale. The edge is featured with gritstone cliffs, tors and boulders for almost all its length with expansive views south and east over Edale to the Great Ridge and beyond.

Pym Chair, the Wool Packs, Crowden Tower, Grindslow Knoll, Upper Tor and Ringing Roger lend themselves well to winter light when the low sun reveals these fabulous, craggy locations as well as the mid-ground and more distant hills. Grindslow Knoll is rapidly gaining classic status as a sunrise location on misty autumn mornings for its view down into the Vale of Edale toward the Great Ridge and beyond. The locations described can be visited individually or linked. Three approaches are described from the Vale of Edale, all taking just over an hour – depending on fitness – to reach the plateau. This is a wild place often with dramatic light and weather. Photography and just being there are great on most days and at most times of year.

NOTE: Because of the longer approaches and some navigational challenges give yourself plenty of time to get in position and carry a torch just in case.

What to shoot and viewpoints

GRINDSBROOK CLOUGH

Viewpoint 1 – Ringing Roger
Grid Ref: SK 126 873

The ascent up the Nab to the rocks of Ringing Roger is comparatively quick and is a good choice for a winter sunrise/sunset or summer sunset.

Park just before Edale village at the pay and display car park near the railway station. Exit the car park and walk past the Rambler Inn and the church into Edale village, continue past the Old Nags Head (the official start of the Pennine Way) for 200m and on your right just after two cottages follow a footpath down into the woods signposted Grindsbrook Clough. Cross the bridge and up the steps and turn left up the flagged path in the field.

Once in the field go right off the flagged path up through the field to a gate by the pine plantation, then up the steep switchbacks of the Nab then direct all the way to the small cliffs and boulders of Ringing Roger.

There are good views on the ascent (Edale church spire) but the rocks of Ringing Roger offer some great compositions with a foreground of rocks, both looking west to Grindslow Knoll and south east to Lose and Win Hill.

Above Edale, looking along the crest of Ringing Roger toward Dale Head (VP1). Canon 6D, Canon 17-40 at 25mm, ISO 400, 1/100 at f/11, Grad. Jul. © CG

How to get here

Kinder's southern edge is accessed from the Vale of Edale. For the Grinds Brook approach to Ringing Roger and Grindslow Knoll approach park just before Edale village at the pay and display car park next to the railway station. For the Crowden Brook and Jacob's Ladder approach to the Wool Packs and Pym Chair park at the car park between Barber Booth and Upper Booth at the west end of Edale.

Edale Rail Station Parking Lat/Long:
53.366833, -1.816621
Parking Grid Ref: SK 123 855
Parking Postcode: S33 7ZA

Barber/Upper Booth Parking Lat/Long:
53.359380, -1.839302
Parking Grid Ref: SK 107 847
Parking Postcode: S33 7ZL (0.5km)

Accessibility

This is steep hill walking with 1,000ft/300m of ascent over rough ground on good paths and round-trips of over 4 miles/6km. Give yourself an hour plus from the parking to reach the locations on the Kinder plateau and just less than an hour to descend. Even on sunny days in summer it can be cold. Bring a jacket, hat and gloves, and something to eat and drink. Plan your trip with google maps and an OS paper map. Bring a mobile phone and tell someone your plans and estimated time to back home. Carry a charged head torch.

Best time of year/day

The locations described align east to west and face south. They are illuminated at sunrise and sunset between September and March when the sun rises east trending to the south and sets in the west trending to south. Generally because of the topography sunrises are best from Grindslow Knoll and locations to the east, with sunsets being better to the west of Crowden Tower.

In the summer the formations are back lit by the rising (north east) and setting (north west) sun. In winter the sun stays low on the southern horizon and often conditions can be dramatic for most of the day, especially if stormy. If it snows it can be magical but sometimes hard work to get up high, frosty days can be very special adding even more texture to the land. June sees cotton grass flowering and in August the swathes of intense purple flowering heather on these moors can be incredible to witness. The texture and colour contrast increases in the autumn as the ferns and grasses change colour.

Above: *Looking across Edale to the Great Ridge and beyond (VP4, p.162). Sony A6000, 18–200 at 23mm, ISO 100, 1/30s at f/10. Oct. © MR*

Viewpoint 2 – Nether Tor and Upper Tor
Nether Tor: SK 121 876. 50 minutes, distance 2.8k, ascent 329m
Upper Tor: SK 114 876. 1 hour +, distance 3.7k, ascent 367m

From Ringing Roger continue up to the plateau. Nether Tor and Upper Tor are small gritstone cliffs and pinnacles to the west along the plateau path. Both offer higher viewpoints than Ringing Roger – but only Upper Tor (see map p.159) is more expansive – and both formations get the sun slightly earlier and later than the lower rocks. Upper Tor is the better choice with its several shapely pinnacles, and wider views. The best times are around sunset in summer (back light) and at sunset and sunrise later on in the year (side light).

Viewpoint 3 – Crookstone Knoll
Grid Ref: SK 144 883.
An hour plus, distance 4.5km, ascent 311m

Crookstone Knoll is just over a mile walk from Nether Tor at the eastern end of the Kinder Plateau. The Knoll presents some fabulous views and opportunities for longer focal lengths where the end of the vale of Edale, bracketed by Win Hill in the east and Lose Hill in the west is better seen. Crookstone Knoll also offers a great view to the north across the Woodlands valley and into the Alport Valley. However if this is your sole objective see page 110, the Crookstone Barn and Crook View chapter.

Viewpoint 4 – Grindslow Knoll
Grindslow Knoll Summit: SK 109 868
50 minutes, distance 2km, ascent 344m

This is a great autumn and winter sunrise location rivalling the Great Ridge for compositional excellence – but with a slightly longer approach. Grindslow Knoll (601m) is best approached from Edale village following the Pennine Way from the Nags Head west for 300m, the Pennine Way goes left through a gate here but continue north west through the field following a rutted track to a gate and the beginning of a steeper climb. Follow this path up.

The best viewpoints are on a grassy plateau and below that (various sheep trails to follow) half-way up to the summit of Grindslow Knoll at around 1km at SK 112 864. It's only 30

Edale church spire from Grindslow Knoll (VP4). Sony A6000, 18–200 at 81mm, ISO 100, 1/125s at f/9. Oct. © MR

Looking across to Back Tor from Grindslow Knoll (VP4). Sony A6000, 18–200 at 66mm, ISO 100, 1/50s at f/11. Nov. © MR

At the top of Broadlee Bank near Grindslow Mere. Sony A6000, 18–200 at 28mm, ISO 100, 1/60s at f/11. Jan. © MR

minutes to this spot from Edale village. These viewpoints are closer to the Vale of Edale (and the church spire of the The Holy and Undivided Trinity) but still high enough to see the Great Ridge and the hills and ridges behind it. Go left off the main trail across the hillside to various spots.

Grindslow Knoll summit and its south ridge are very worthwhile with some interesting gritstone outcrops and a tremendous view.

Grinds Brook

An alternative but longer approach is to follow Grinds Brook up the broad valley of Grindsbrook Clough which is home to several small waterfalls, a wooden bridge, an attractive stand of silver birches and good views down the clough down into Edale and the Great Ridge. It is best for photography later in the day. At the top of of the clough, the valley splits, direct is path that follows a steep boulder choke and to the north or up the right fork the going is slightly easier and there is a series of cascades between the rocky crags (SK 106 874).

Approach as for the Nab and Ringing Roger but for Grindsbrook Clough stay on the flagged path up the field, through the trees and up the steep path following the brook.

BROADLEE BANK AND THE GRINDSLOW MERES

The path up Broadlee Bank to Grindslow Knoll is also a great approach to viewpoints looking into Edale and to the south east. Importantly however the path up Broadlee Bank itself has significant viewpoints of barns, walls and great compositions looking both east and west along and down into Edale – good during the day if weather is changeable.

From the telephone box at Upper Booth go through the farmyard opposite and take the second right along the Pennine Way toward Edale village. The path goes gently uphill to a barn (a great subject) and just after turn sharp left and go up the slope then slightly right to the path that goes direct, no switchbacks, up the hill. It's a calf-burner, but relatively short lived. There are great views up this path – any excuse for a breather – and once at the top are some great drystone walls which can be used as foreground in multiple compositions. Just beyond are two significant bodies of water, the Grindslow Meres, and beyond those Grindslow Knoll. These meres are rare bodies of water on Kinder and are great for reflections on a calm day.

Opposite bottom: *From Ringing Roger into Edale (VP1). Sony A6000, 18–200mm at 112mm, ISO 160, 1/125s at f/10. Jan. © MR*

A cascade on the upper part of Crowden Brook (VP1, p.164). Canon 5D, Canon 17-40 at 20mm, ISO 50, 1s at f/20, Polariser. Sept © CG

Crowden Tower (VP2, p.164). Canon 5D, Canon 17-40 at 20mm, ISO 100, 1s at f/14, Grad. Jan. © CG

The Woolpacks (VP3, p.164). Canon 5D, 17-40 at 20mm, ISO 100, 1/2s at f/20, Grad. Nov. © CG

163

CROWDEN CLOUGH AND JACOB'S LADDER

Crowden Clough is a longer and harder approach to the plateau but gives access to some great formations including Crowden Tower, the Wool Packs, Noe Stool and Edale Rocks. This is a serious approach especially in the dark, it's hard to navigate and strenuous. An easier alternative, but longer is to approach by the popular Jacob's Ladder path which lands you at Edale Rocks, by the approach from Hayfield (see page 194) or by Broadlee Bank described above.

For Crowden Clough park at the small car park between Barber Booth and Upper Booth at the west end of Edale. From here walk up the road toward Upper Booth and Jacob's Ladder. At half a mile and just after Lee Farm/the telephone box, in the dip, there is a right turn up a path through a gate (not toward the campsite). Follow the path through trees on the left side of the stream then into fields to a path which follows Crowden Brook up the clough to Crowden Tower at its head on the left.

For the Jacob's Ladder approach (5km to Crowden Tower) stay on the main path passing Lee Farm.

These viewpoints are described from the Crowden Clough approach, they are in reverse order if you approached by Ringing Roger or Hayfield.

Viewpoint 1 – Crowden Brook

Crowden Brook is a very pretty, energetic stream with many falls, tumbles and pools. Visit after a good rain or when frozen. The falls are found once the moor opens up intermittently as you gain elevation, with more rocky falls once you reach the plateau.

Viewpoint 2 – Crowden Tower

Grid Ref: SK 094 871
50 minutes, distance 3.4km, ascent 345m

When nearing the top of Crowden Clough, don't follow the stream but take the distinct steep rocky path well to the left of the stream which lands you at the Crowden Tower rock formation. This jumble of boulders looks south west down the clough toward the Great Ridge and is illuminated for most of the day from September to March. The top of the rocks make a great tripod stand.

Viewpoint 3 – Wool Packs

Grid Ref: SK 091 869
1.5+ hours, distance 3.7km, ascent 355m

Follow the path west beyond Crowden Tower to the Wool Packs – named because of their resemblance to wool fleeces that are packed in bails. The Wool Packs is an incredible moor of hundreds of gritstone boulders and

The Moat Stone at the Wook Packs (VP3). Canon 5D, 17-40 at 20mm, ISO 100, 1/2s at f/20, Grad. Nov. © CG

groughs (water cut channels). Some are named; the Moat Stone has water around it. This boulder field is in a slight hollow surrounded but exposed on their south side, hence September to March is the best time to photograph them in the late afternoon/sunset. This is an area for exploration rather than specific viewpoints. Individual boulders are attractive to take portraits of as well as attempting to photograph the whole boulder field. Sunrise photography here is problematic because of the topography, Grindslow Knoll sticks out and obscures the view down Edale. A good spot is by and in front of Pym Chair looking to the south east across the Wool Packs. Winter sunsets are best as the boulders catch the setting sun.

Quick approach to the Wool Packs – The Cloughs

1+ hour, distance 3.5km, ascent 339m
You can also approach the Wool Packs direct by going to the bridge at the bottom of Jacob's Ladder. Cross the bridge, walk upstream to where the stream narrows and cross it, then follow a worn trod up the slope by an old fence direct to the Wool Packs. If your objective is the Wool Packs, especially if has snowed, this is the best way. In frosty or snowy conditions walking crampons will make life a lot easier.

Viewpoint 4 – Pym Chair

Grid Ref: SK 087 870
1.5+ hours, distance 4km, ascent 355m

Further west along the path from the Wool Packs is the Pym Chair – a significant gritstone formation that looks like a giant's chair. Pym Chair is exposed to the west and receives evening and sunset light for most of the year, even when the sun sets in the north-west. There are several great compositions here, a favourite being to the south west with the hilly profile of Swine's Back as background.

Beyond Pym Chair are two significant gritstone formations (both also accessible by ascending the Jacob's Ladder approach path). **Noe Stool** (SK 083 869), a top heavy gritstone tor, is situated west of Pym Chair. **Edale Rocks** (SK 079 867) is situated at the top of Jacob's Ladder on the Pennine Way path which is described in the Kinder West chapter (page 198). Both offer a different perspective looking east down the Vale of Edale toward the distinctive summits on the Great Ridge.

Opposite: Noe Stool from near Edale Rocks. Sony A6000, 18–200 at 20mm, ISO 160, 1/125s at f/10. Jan. © MR

The Vale of Edale has a remote feel despite being only an hour's drive from two major cities. This valley has been grazed by cattle and sheep since medieval times when herdsmen's shelters or booths were built, these have now grown into hamlets and the village of Edale. The area still retains a landscape of pastures, meadows, dry stone walls and barns.

Edale is connected to Sheffield and Manchester by the Hope Valley Line and this rail link has been very important, giving ramblers access to the hills since the late 19th century. Edale today is popular with adventurous hill walkers. The 256 mile long Pennine Way has its official start at the Old Nags Head pub in the village of Edale. Recently Ray Cooper's farm Highfield at Upper Booth featured in the BBC historical drama, The Village.

What to shoot and viewpoints

Viewpoint 1 – Back Tor view near Nether Booth

If you drive into Edale from Hope village the first 'booth' you come to is Nether Booth, a small collection of houses and a farm (3.5 miles from Hope). Park in Nether Booth and walk just beyond the hamlet to where the road parallels the railway, here, and on the other side of the railway bridge are good vantage points to photograph the steep profile of Back Tor with farmland and woodland in the foreground. Grid ref: SK 137 856, postcode S33 7ZH. You can get closer by taking a footpath south passing Back Tor farm accessed by a footpath beyond the railway bridge.

Viewpoint 2 – Mam Nick

The road at Mam Nick (SK 125 836) at 455m (1500ft) looks down on the Edale valley. This is a great viewpoint in certain conditions for wide or zoom shots of the valley; misty mornings or at the golden hour.

Viewpoint 3 – Edale Railway Station

Built in 1894 the Hope Valley Line links Manchester to Sheffield and is important for walkers from those two cities, who ramble around Kinder and Edale. The line emerges in Edale from Manchester at the two-mile-long Cowburn Tunnel. Steam trains regularly pass through Edale. The most convenient place to photograph the trains (they run every two hours) with a backdrop of the valley and hills is at the railway station, the bridges west of the station near Barber Booth or on the road up to Mam Nick.

Viewpoint 4 – Edale Village

As you walk into Edale village good subjects include the Holy Trinity parish church and the graveyard, the Old Nags Head pub – the official start of the Pennine way – Pennine ways signs, red telephone box, and various cottages especially beyond the Nags Head pub toward Grindsbrook Clough.

Beyond Upper Booth looking at the Ridge. Canon 5D Mk 1, Canon 17-40 at 17mm, ISO 500, 1/30s at f/20. Feb. © CG

Short walks

Grindslow Knoll down to the village

This high viewpoint is perfect if you are after a photograph of Edale village and the spire of the Church of the Holy and Undivided Trinity from above. This is good on misty mornings or later in the day as a low late sun illuminates the village, and it is quick to get in position – 30 minutes.

From Edale village follow the Pennine Way from the Nags Head west for 300m, the Pennine Way goes left through a gate here but continue north west through the field following a rutted track to a gate and the beginning of a steeper climb. Follow this path up. Half-way to the summit of Grindslow Knoll at around 1km from the village at SK 112 864 are various viewpoints down to the village. How high you go will depend on mist level and light.

The Start of the Pennine Way

Across from the Old Nags Head pub is the start of the Pennine way. Follow this between farm buildings to a stone path through hedges and trees. At the gate turn left and follow the flagged path through fields with much to photograph, especially the leading line of the flagged path itself. This path takes you to Upper Booth Farm. Retrace your steps or return to the village along the road.

Edale Valley – Barns, Meadows and 'The Village'

A short walk up any of the many footpaths that thread their way through the fields in the valley offers just enough of a height advantage to allow the photographer to pick out many interesting compositions. In June and July the meadows start to flower in Edale – one particular good place for this is the fields around Upper Booth and if you walk toward Jacob's Ladder there is a particularly attractive barn set back in a field. Highfield Farm which featured in the BBC's The Village is by a footpath that goes south from Upper Booth where you will have the opportunity to frame the farm with the Great Ridge in the background.

Top right: An Edale barn and meadow. Sony A6000, 18–200 at 18mm, ISO 400, 1/200s at f/8. Jul. © MR

The Tin Bath steams through Edale (VP3). Canon 6D, Canon 70-300 at 80mm, ISO 500, 1/640s at f/10. Nov. © CG

How to get here

Edale is 20 miles from Sheffield and 30 miles from Manchester. Access is from the village of Hope on the A6187 by a narrow road or over Mam Nick. It is just short of 5 miles from Hope to Edale village. Park at the pay and display car park across from the railway station.

Edale Rail Station Parking Lat/Long: 53.366833, -1.816621
Parking Grid Ref: SK 123 855
Parking Postcode: TS33 7ZA

Accessibility ♿

Exploring Edale, its villages and country walks with a camera is perfect for all, especially for those with limited mobility. Many viewpoints are on roads, country lanes and level paths and are often suitable for wheelchairs.

Best time of year/day

The Vale of Edale is L-shaped, with most of its area aligning east-west. It is effectively closed in on all sides by hills but nonetheless receives a lot of interesting illumination. The light along the valley is at its most sympathetic when the sun is low. This is when the topography is best revealed and the details in the landscape are picked out. On summer evenings the sun in the west rakes along the valley beautifully and in particular reveals the details on the northern flank of the Great Ridge, which at other times of the year remain in shadow.

On Lords Seat, high above the early morning mists. Canon 5D Mk 1, 17-40 at 20mm, ISO 50, 1/40s at f/20. ND. Oct. © CG

Across the Vale of Edale from Kinder runs the **Great Ridge, a wonderful roller-coaster of shale grit hills stretching from Lord's Seat in the west to Lose Hill in the east. It is a fabulous and very popular day walk and its accessibility and compositional strength means that it is also a very popular subject with photographers keen to capture its beauty, particularly in the dawn light.**

Shooting east toward Lose Hill from below the summit of Mam Tor gives an excellent leading line in the form of the paved path. The gate part-way down the descent from Mam Tor to Hollins Cross presents a wonderful foreground at dawn, shot with the sun rising over a mist-filled Hope Valley – a classic British Landscape composition.

What to shoot and viewpoints

All viewpoints are accessed from Mam Nick. If parked in the National Trust car park follow the steps at the back of the car park up to the road to Mam Nick where on your right is the path to Mam Tor summit (322m). Just over the Nick by the lay-bay on the right is the bridleway to the Gate (0.5km) and on your left before the Nick is the path up Rushup Edge to Lord's Seat (1.2km).

Viewpoint 1 – The Serpentine Curve (SK 126 836)

A classic composition is of the serpentine curve of the road snaking down into Edale from Mam Nick. This can be taken in several places. One is just off the main flagged path on the way to Mam Tor summit. It is such a strong composition that it works in varied light conditions and all seasons.

Viewpoint 2 – Mam Tor Summit (SK 127 836)

The Mam Tor summit cobbles, path and trig point make great subjects. There are several viewpoints toward where the slope steepens (beware the cliff and gully) looking down into the Hope Valley and at the Hope Cement Works and its chimney. To the south looking toward Winnats and Old Moor with its rolling hills and trees in the right conditions using a telephoto can work well. Below the summit is Mam Tor Gully with a path to the right of this steep broken cliff that offers a whole new perspective if you descend it.

Viewpoint 3 – The Gate (SK 131 843)

The Gate is down the flagged path from Mam Tor summit where the ridge levels out before Hollin's Cross. The quickest way to The Gate is by following the bridleway that starts from the lay-by down from Mam Nick on the Edale side. This path contours around Mam Tor, misses out the ≫

How to get here

The car park for Mam Tor and the Great Ridge is on the Sheffield Road below Mam Nick 2 miles from Castleton. From Castleton drive west up Winnats Pass. At the top of the pass turn right at the T-junction and follow the road round, passing the first turning on the right. The National Trust car park is on your right.

Alternatively continue past the car park and take the next right to Mam Nick where there is a small lay-by for several cars on the Edale side of the ridge – useful if you don't want to walk up the steep steps to Mam Tor summit or if you are in a rush at sunrise.

Parking Lat/Long: 53.345484, -1.815892
Parking Grid Ref: SK 123 831
Parking Postcode: S33 8WA

Accessibility

There are good viewpoints for the less mobile from the road at Mam Nick. Whilst there isn't much elevation gain from Mam Nick to most points on the ridge and distances are relatively short – it's 300m (with 36m of ascent) from Mam Nick to the summit of Mam Tor – do come prepared. 60-100mph winds are not uncommon on the ridge at anytime of year and it can be extremely cold. Wrap up well and bring gloves and a hat. The paths are usually paved but can be slippy. If the winds are extreme and you get caught out on the ridge, bob off the ridge to shelter down the slope.

From the NT car park
To Mam Tor Summit: 20 mins, distance 0.7km, ascent 74m
To Mam Tor Gate: 20 minutes, distance 1km, ascent 50m
To Lord's Seat: 30 minutes, distance 1.5km, ascent 123m

Best time of year/day

The ridge runs from west to east. Sunrise at most times of year is special here especially when there is valley mist or radiation fog in the Hope Valley. Mist is most frequent between September and April although valley mist can occur in summer after a hot humid day and a significant drop in temperature at night. The fog can vary in depth from just wisps in the valley to over 400m thick with Mam Tor's summit (517m) just popping its head out – walk up to Lord's Seat (546m) in such conditions. Frosty mornings and when covered in snow are also good times to visit.

Bear in mind that in the evenings in late spring and early summer the sun dips below the summit of Mam Tor, putting the part of the ridge immediately to the east in shadow and flattening the contrast along the along the ridge toward Lose Hill.

In midsummer however the sun sets behind the north west corner of Kinder Scout, meaning that the northern flank of the ridge is well illuminated, especially the dip at Hollins Cross.

Mam Tor Alternatives

Because Mam Tor is so good at sunrise when there is valley mist or low cloud, it can be very popular, especially at weekends in the autumn. If it is busy conside the nearby alternative locations listed on page 36.

Top: The road into Edale from Mam Nick (VP1). Canon 5D Mk 1, 17-40 at 17mm, ISO 100, 1/125s at f/20. Dec. © CG

Opposite: The Hope Valley from Mam Tor's summit (VP2). Sony A6000, 18–200 at 46mm, ISO 100, 1/400s at f/11. Oct. © MR

summit and emerges 200m before The Gate. Get here well before sunrise, at weekends you will have company. This is a classic viewpoint with its foreground, leading line, diagonal converging lines, the regression of the hills, strong compositional figures and narrative from ridge to summit to valley. Best photographed before and at sunrise from September through to spring when there is often a thin mist in the valley and a touch of cloud in the sky.

Viewpoint 4 – The Ridge toward Back Tor and Lose Hill

There are many great photographs to be had along this ridge and it rewards revisits. There is a lone Caledonian pine that sits on top of Back Tor and a pretty hawthorn and birch copse below its summit on the northern side.

From the ridge, Kinder Scout's southern edge to the north presents a level horizon, with all of the details hidden below the skyline but a longer focal length allows the photographer to pick out details on both sides of the ridge.

If the ridge has a weak point then it is perhaps Lose Hill itself, which is a bit lacking in foreground interest but should still be included in a traverse of the ridge.

Viewpoint 5 – Lord's Seat and Rushup Edge

Lord's Seat (SK 113 834) is 29m higher than Mam Tor and the ridge of Rushup Edge that leads up to it offers a superb perspective of diagonal slopes sweeping down to bulk of Mam Tor and the continuation of the ridge all the way to Lose Hill and beyond. It even has it's own gate. Take the western path just below Mam Nick that gains the ridge and follow it upwards to discover multiple viewpoints.

Opposite top: Dramatic weather at Back Tor (VP4). Canon 5D Mk 1, Canon 17-40 at 20mm, ISO 100, 1/20s at f/20, Grad. Dec .© CG

Opposite middle left: Along Rushup Edge, looking towards Mam Tor (VP5). Canon 5D Mk 1, Canon 17-40 at 20mm, ISO 100, 1/30s at f/20, Grad. Oct. © CG

Opposite middle right: Traversing the Ridge (VP4). Sony A6000, 18–200 at 18mm, ISO 160, 1/400s at f/9. Jan. © MR

A longer lens shot from Lords Seat, gathering Mam Tor, Back Tor and Lose Hill together in a single frame (VP5). Canon 5D Mk1, Sigma 105mm, ISO 100, 1/30s at f/20. Oct. © CG

The path before the gate (VP3). Sony A6000, 10-18 at 10mm, ISO 100, 1/30s at f/11. Oct. © MR

Early snows on the Great Ridge (VP2). Canon 5D Mk 1, Canon 17-40 at 20mm, ISO 100, 1/8s at f/20. Grad. Dec. © CG

The road down Winnats Pass to Castleton. Sony A6000, 18–200 at 45mm, ISO 200, 1/200s at f/11. Oct. © MR

Winnats Pass is a dramatic and craggy gorge on the edge of the limestone plateau above the village of Castleton. It looks down on the head of the Hope Valley and its drystone wall-enclosed farmland, reaching out to Lose and Win Hill in the background. It is thought to be a collapsed cavern or a ravine between coral reefs.

This cliff-lined pass with its limestone pinnacles and ribs used to carry an infrequently used farm track but was promoted to an important through route when the main road below Mam Tor collapsed irreparably in 1975. Until the CROW Act of 2000 photographing Winnats used to be a tricky option because of access restrictions but all of its splendid and precipitous vantage points are now available to explore and photograph.

What to shoot and viewpoints

From the lay-by at the top of the Pass go over the stile and diagonally leftwards through the field and a gate, then head left and over a stile. Turn right to reach the pinnacles.

Viewpoint 1 – The Pinnacles and Gullies
The limestone pinnacles jut out into the gorge separated by steep grassy concave gullies. The initial pinnacles are best as they catch the rising sun and you get the sweeping arc of the road in your composition. A wide-angle lens (10-24mm) will yield the best results. The concave gullies can be used to frame a composition. Look out for the rocky ribs opposite as they catch the sun first thing. Also compose up the pass as well as down it. To add a sense of scale wait for a car to drive up the road – good at twilight for long exposure light streaks. Zooming in to particular features, especially in June and July when the slopes are covered in flowers can be very effective.

Viewpoint 2 – Big Cliff
If you follow the drystone wall passing the pinnacles and the last gully you come to a flat area at the top of the biggest cliff. This is a great viewpoint for looking up the pass with the steep slopes of both sides of the pass in a composition. This can work at sunset May to July but is better at sunrise.

The North Side
It is worth exploring the north summit of the pass for something different.

VP 3 – Drystone Walls from Speedwell Cavern
If you park at Speedwell Cavern and walk up the road the lower pass and its pinnacles are revealed in all their splendour. Walk downhill from the cavern parking to find a footpath on your right, go down this to get a great vantage point of the parallel drystone walls and the trees around Peak Cavern and Castleton, especially effective in autumn.

Viewpoint 4 – Treak Cliff Cavern
There are a number of show caves near Castelton area and most will entertain photographers by prior arrangement. Owners are usually nervous about the combination of visitors and tripods in poorly lit areas with limited access. Treak Cliff Cavern will permit photographers without prior arrangement but they prefer it if you visit out of the peak tourist season, early in the morning, soon after opening, or later in the afternoon when there will be fewer people around. There is an entrance fee and there is a cafe at the cave head. The cave itself contains a mixture of mining archaeology and natural flowstone including stalagmites and stalactites. A tripod is useful for the low light conditions and/or use a high ISO; the cave is artificially lit.

Treak Cliff Cavern, Buxton Road, Castleton, Hope Valley, Derbyshire, S33 8WP, tel: 01433 620571. Open daily from 10.00am except 24th to 26th December , Adults £9.50. Other show caves around Castleton include Blue John, Peak Cavern and Speedwell. The latter do not permit tripods.

Looking toward Mam Tor from VP2-the Big Cliff. Sony A6000, 18–200 at 18mm, ISO 400, 1/80s at f/5.6. Jun. © MR

Natural flowstone features in Treak Cliff cavern. Canon 6D, 17-40 at 20mm, ISO 100, 13s at f/20. Mar. © CG

The Hope Valley at dawn from VP1. Canon 5D Mk1, 70-300 at 70mm, ISO 100, 1/200s at f/14. Sep. © CG

How to get here

Park in a lay-by at the top of Winnats Pass. From Castleton drive west up Winnats Pass. At the top of the pass turn left at the T-junction and park immediately on the left in a small lay-by by a stile before the bridleway. It is also possible to approach from the cattle grid near the top of the pass before the Winnats Head Farm.

Parking Lat/Long: 53.340898, -1.811278
Parking Grid Ref: SK 126 826
Parking Postcode: S33 8WA (1.5km)

Accessibility ♿

Access is short and flat. It is a third of a mile/500m through two fields to the rim of the south side of the pass. The going is tougher at the edge of the pass with many steep cliffs and slopes – an impressive place. For the less mobile the bottom of Winnats Pass has roadside locations.

Best time of year/day

Its topography and alignment make the Pass a tricky proposition to photograph. Winnats' highest pinnacles face north, meaning that for much of the year its depths are in shadow, only illuminating properly in the summer months. A good time to shoot is at dawn, eastwards out through the rocky gates when the valley beyond is filled with mist. The bottom of the pass looks north east and in May, June and July the rising sun shines directly up the pass from the north east. The sheer scale of its crags however mean that at any time of year there is detail to be found as the light scrapes across its high edges. The pass can look very alpine after snow and freezing temperatures. Mist can often tumble through the pass off the limestone plateau behind, the pinnacles casting great, fanning shadows into the depths below.

At the bottom of Winnats Pass (VP3). Canon 6D, 70-300 at 150mm, ISO 125, 1/1250 at f/5. Sep. © CG

Cave Dale is a beautiful craggy limestone dale that slopes down to the village of Castleton. The remains of the medieval Peveril Castle (1176) sit on the edge of a cliff high on the dale's west edge. The topography of the dale gives you a high viewpoint over the castle into the Hope Valley and beyond to the Great Ridge.

When conditions are favourable this is one of the classic Peak District landscape locations. But there is more to this place than the castle, it is full of potential for excellent compositions with its steep sides, characterful trees and winding path.

What to shoot and viewpoints

Cave Dale (signposted) is accessed from Castleton village through a narrow passageway between Dale Cottage and Cave Dale Cottage at the start of Pindale Road which leads off south/uphill from the villages 'market place cross.

Viewpoint 1 – Lower Cave Dale

Beyond the cottages a path leads through a limestone slit and then opens out into the broad dale lined by steep grass slopes and cliffs. Follow the path as it curves up the dale with Peveril Castle high on your right. Before the path turns left there is a good viewpoint of the steep sided dale and the castle with Lose Hill in the background. This is a low viewpoint and only gets the sun when it is relatively high, although it can be great early if there is a shallow mist creeping up the dale. An ultra wide-angle lens (10-20mm) is needed to get the whole view.

The village and castle view through the gap (VP4). Sony A6000, 18–200 at 18mm, ISO 100, 1/100s at f/9. Jun. © MR

After the left turn continue up the dale path and there are good compositions looking down the dale with the path as a leading line and the diagonals of the slopes. When you reach some trees on your left this is the point where you can access the two viewpoints on the rim of the dale.

Viewpoint 2 – West Side

Turn right at the trees and head diagonally up the slope following an indistinct path. As you ascend there are many good compositions that include Lose Hill, the village and the fields beyond. The castle can be somewhat obscured by trees. Nearer the top Win Hill starts to appear. On the rim of the dale by the wall you get a 'bowl' effect as both sides of the dale slope down. In late June and early July the rising sun shines up the dale, but sunrise will be very early. Return the way you came or:

From this side there is a grassy path which leads down to Castleton through a field and by trees and it is a good viewpoint for the barns and field patterns that run up to Winnats Pass. This path, that starts near Peak Cavern, is a good approach to the top of the west side of Cave Dale.

How to get here

Cave Dale is situated by Castleton village in the Hope Valley. Use the car park in Castleton at busy times, or road parking if you get here early.

Parking Lat/Long: 53.341457, -1.775448
Parking Grid Ref: SK 150 827
Parking Postcode: S33 8WQ

Accessibility

The approach from Castleton village into the dale is short – 5 minutes. The base of the dale has a good path, accessing the rim of the dale is by steep slopes.
Approach to top of the dale: 20 mins, distance 1km, ascent 138m

Best time of year/day

Cave Dale runs from a highpoint in the south west down to Castleton village in the north east. The dale and the castle get sun for most of the day. Peveril Castle is illuminated at sunrise for most of the year except in mid-winter. The castle is shaded by the higher east side of the dale when the sun is low. A favourite time is early autumn when the leaves change colour, valley mists become common in the morning and the sun rises in in the east to south-east. Much of the dale is in shadow at sunset. This location is also worthwhile on a mid-summer afternoon when you can photograph 'England's pleasant pastures seen' hopefully under an atmospheric sky.

Peveril Castle from Cave Dale (VP1). Canon 6D, 17-40 at 20mm, ISO 125, 1/10s at f/14, Grad. Sep. © CG

Viewpoint 3 – East Side

At the top of the dale turn left at the trees up a sometimes-wet stream bed a short way to a low drystone wall. Turn left and follow the wall gradually gaining elevation with the northerly aspect revealing itself. The view includes the full northern sweep from Mam Tor in the west to Win Hill in the east. Peveril Castle shows its south side and is not obscured by trees. This scene works well in summer after midday. Its strength however is in autumn (late October/early November) when the leaves have turned and the valley full of mist as the sun rises in the south-east. The relics of the castle are illuminated by golden side-light and hopefully a colourful morning sky. There are several rock pinnacles and curved side dales that can be used as foreground. Here you can combine both the castle and Mam Tor in your composition.

Note: there is a narrow path that traverses the east side of the dale that starts half-way up the main dale path. At a ventilation shaft, a grilled cave entrance on your right, turn sharp left and follow the single-track sheep path across the slope through the cliffs. It's safe but a bit airy.

Viewpoint 4 – East Side Village View

If you descend from the highest point of the east side more compositions appear. Further east and lower down is a good view 'through the gap' of most of the village. It is very steep to descend from here and is only for the agile. You can reach this point from the dale bottom by ascending the steep slope on your left when entering the dale; an easier – but calf-busting – option.

The castle and village from the south side of the dale, showing the Great Ridge from Mam Tor to Lose Hill. (VP3). Sony A6000, 10–18 at 10mm, ISO 100, 1/100s at f/11. Oct. © MR

The lower section of Cave Dale (VP1). Canon 6D, 17-40 at 20mm, ISO 125, 1/10s at f/14, Grad. Sep. © CG

A winter hike above Cave Dale. Sony A6000, 18–200 at 18mm, ISO 250, 1/320s at f/9. Jan. © MR

Hope Cement Works divides opinion. It has sat in the Hope Valley since the 1920s providing us all with road stone and construction materials, and employment for generations of Derbyshire folk. On the other hand this industrial complex sits in one of the most beautiful valleys in the Peak District and its chimney and the vast quarry behind it can be seen from miles around – featuring in many photographs from Stanage to the Great Ridge.

This juxtaposition makes it an intriguing photographic subject, especially close-up from Siggate Lane. Like several viewpoints around the Hope Valley, it is a classic Peak District landscape photograph but with an industrial flavour. If you have done a dawn shoot from Pin Dale, there are various spots around the village of Bradwell with much to offer.

What to shoot and viewpoints

Viewpoint 1 – Pindale Overlook

From the lay-by on Siggate Lane walk across the road through a gate to open land above the cement works and Pin Dale, the craggy dale below you. There are various viewpoints here and the best spot depends on the level of the valley fog and the position of the sun.

Viewpoint 2 – Above The Road

Near the parking spot a path leads up the hillside offering a higher elevation viewpoint.

The classic (VP1). Sony A6000, 10-18 at 18mm, ISO 200, 1/250s at f/11. Sep. © MR

Viewpoint 3 – The Steep Bit of Siggate Lane

Where Pindale Road goes left Siggate Lane rises up with the trees forming a tunnel. This is a great place most times of the year as the sun gets higher and filters through the trees.

Alternative Viewpoints of the Hope Cement works from Bradwell

There are several different close-up viewpoints of the cement works off the Smalldale Road near the village of Bradwell. When entering Bradwell from the north through Brough take the first right turn after the Samuel Fox Pub. This leads to Smalldale Road that climbs steeply passing the Bowling Green Inn.

From Mich Low

Park near the Bowling Green Inn and walk down the lane to a left down Michlow Lane (a footpath). This eventually leads to a small hill on your right with a position that overlooks the cement works to the west and is particularly good at night or when misty. The cement works is lit up with multi-coloured lights at night. The path continues by the cement works for even more intimate photographs. Please keep to rights of way.

Parking Lat/Long: 53.330450, -1.7453402
Parking Grid Ref: SK170815
Parking Postcode: S33 9JQ (Bowling Green Pub)

Hope Quarry Viewing Platform

From the Bowling Green in Bradwell continue to the top of Smalldale Road and park at the junction with Siggate Lane. Walk down the quarry road heading north, just around a bend on the left is a viewing platform overlooking the vast hole of the quarry. The sun hits it at sunrise in summer but it can be good anytime.

A long lens shot into the heart of cement works (VP1). Canon 6D, 70-300 at 270mm, ISO 400, 15s at f/13. Mar. © CG

Eccles Lane and the Ponds

Eccles Lane links Bradwell to Hope, starting at the Samuel Fox Pub. Down this road are ponds that provide a good view of the cement works (from the road, the ponds are private). In addition, nearer to Hope where it joins Pindale Road are footpaths where you can get a good photograph of Hope church spire and Win Hill.

How to get here

The Pin Dale overlook on Siggate Lane is situated near Castleton. In Castleton village turn off the A6187 at the bend and down Back Street passing the church to Market Place. Bare left on to Pindale Road and follow this going right at the fork steeply up Siggate Lane and around the hairpin bend to a parking spot on the right three-quarters of a mile from the village.

Parking Lat/Long: 53.338677, -1.763797
Parking Grid Ref: SK 158 824
Parking Postcode: S33 6RP (The cement works)

Accessibility

This is a roadside location suitable for all.

Best time of year/day

Early morning, before, during and after sunrise is best, especially from September until April when there is valley mist. Temperature inversions can also occur in summer. Anytime at night when the cement works is lit up.

Bradwell

Bradwell is a small village mostly built on a steep slope. Lead miners cottages line Town Gate by the White Hart Inn. It is however the spring-fed Bradwell Brook which is good for photography. This limestone brook flows along a walled channel and under several bridges within the village and in summer is full of white flowering water crowfoot. Downstream of the village the brook meanders through meadows and can be followed along a path, a barn providing an idea focal point. The brook is home to water voles.

Above: Hope Valley Cement Works from Siggate Lane (VP1). Canon 6D, 17-40 at 20mm, ISO 125, 1/80s at f/14. Grad. Sep. © CG

Hope church and Win Hill from Eccles Lane. Sony A6000, 18-200 at 55mm, ISO 200, 1/160s at f/8. Oct. © MR

Peak Forest is a pretty village which is worth a wander around with a camera, especially the graveyard of the Charles King and Martyr Church. Out of sight in the quiet hills high on moorland to the north of Peak Forest are some diverse locations to photograph: from a vast savannah-like limestone moorland at 1500ft to remnants of the lead mining industry, groves of beech trees that turn copper in the autumn, limestone heath, the massive Eldon Quarry, and the delightful Eldon Mere, there is no shortage of photographic subject material.

What to shoot and viewpoints

Viewpoints are accessed from or near Peak Forest.

Viewpoint 1 – Oxlow Rake, Stavehouse Mine and Old Moor
Grid Ref: SK 142 808
Approach: 40 minutes, distance 1.8km, ascent 77m

Park in Peak Forest and walk through the village northwards on a minor road to a road junction. Take the righthand fork and follow this lane for 500m and turn left up to farm bearing right before the farm up the lane into the delightful stand of beech trees – Oxlow Rake – which make good photographic subject close up. Continue up the lane gaining a height to look down and the beeches within the landscape. At a path junction head back right and up to the remains of Starvehouse Mine (not much there) but with great views down to Peak Forest or continue onto Old Moor and distant views of Win Hill to the north.

Eldon Mere (VP3). Sony A6000, 10-18 at 18mm, ISO 200, 1/250s at f/11. Sep. © MR

Viewpoint 2 – Jewelknoll Plantation
Grid Ref: SK 123 807
Approach: 40 minutes, distance 1.3km, ascent 106m

Park in Peak Forest and walk through the village northwards to the road junction. Continue straight on up a track passing Conies Farm and up the hill skirting Conies Dale to the beech plantation. As well as being a good photographic vantage point the beech trees and limestone walls provide great subjects, particularly when the sun is low late afternoon in the winter or early evening in the summer. It is possible to continue to Eldon Hill and Quarry from the plantation by continuing on the path then heading left (west).

Viewpoint 3 – Eldon Mere and Quarry
Grid Ref: SK 111 814
Approach: Roadside

From the main A623 in Peak Forest turn into the village then left for 1.4 miles down the dale to a junction.. Turn right and drive half a mile to park by a small road on your right. Walk back down where you have come from and through a gate to Eldon Mere, a small tarn. In summer this area is rich in flowers and insects. At sunset from May to early August the sun sets in the north west and lights up the waters.

For Eldon Quarry, walk up the small lane beyond the mere and the quarry is revealed. In May to early August from late afternoon to sunset the faces of the quarry are illuminated. it is worth walking around this vast old quarry and it will provide many striking compositions.

Viewpoint 4 – Dam Dale
Dale Dam Barn Grid Ref: SK 117 780
Approach: 30 minutes, distance 1.3km, ascent 0m

South of Peak Forest are limestone dales surrounded by fields with a dense network of drystone walls. This is a great area to explore. One worthwhile location nearby is Dam Dale which is within walking distance from Peak Forest. One way is to take the footpath – a road initially – between the church and the playing fields to Dam Dale Farm where Dam Dale begins. Better is to park at the sharp bend on the A623 above Peak Forest (SK 121 787) and take the footpath down the hill through fields to Dam Dale Farm as this gives access to good photographic viewpoints overlooking field patterns. At Dam Dale Farm take the footpath by the cow sheds into the north-south running dale. This is a narrow

*Top left: Jewelknoll Plantation (VP2). © CG **Top right:** Oxlow Rake (VP1). © CG **Bottom left:** Dam Dale (VP4). © MR
Bottom right: Eldon Quarry (VP1). © MR*

flat-bottomed open dale with a steep east side and gently sloping west side. It has a field barn,
a network of walls and flower-filled meadows; reminiscent of the Yorkshire Dales. Walk up the steep east slope above the footpath at various points for great viewpoints.

How to get here

Peak Forest is on the A623 Chapel-en-le-Frith to Chesterfield road 5 miles north of Buxton. Viewpoints are accessed from or near Peak Forest. See individual viewpoints for directions.

Parking Lat/Long: 53.310629, -1.830845
Parking Grid Ref: SK17 8EL
Parking Postcode: SK 113 793

Accessibility

Most of these viewpoints are photographic walks on good footpaths sometimes with hills to walk up and stiles or gates to pass through. Eldon Mere is a roadside location with a short walk, as is the overlook for Eldon Quarry.

Best time of year/day

These are all year-round locations but are particularly good in high summer, autumn and winter.

Eldon Mere Nature Reserve (VP3) is home to blue butterflies. Canon 6D, Canon 70-300 at 300mm, ISO 800, 1/4000s at f/5.6. Jul. © CG

On White Brow above Kinder Reservoir (p.199). Canon 6D. 17-40 at 20mm.
ISO 100, 1/50s at f/13. Grad. Mar. © CG

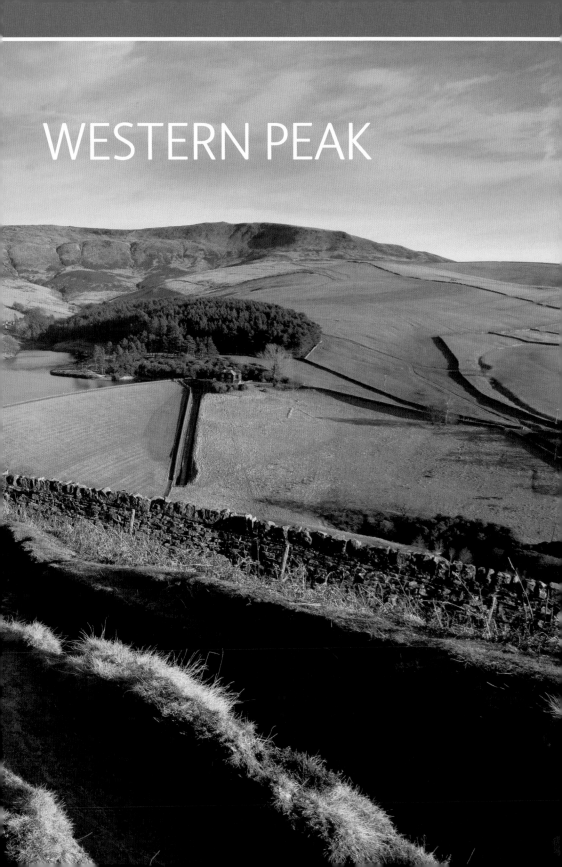

WESTERN PEAK

KINDER WEST & HAYFIELD – INTRODUCTION

To the west of Kinder West and Hayfield is Manchester, a place where lives of quiet desperation have long played out in its rows of terraced houses and dark satanic mills. The western Dark Peak – for many from Manchester, the North West and Sheffield – meant and still means freedom.

On Sundays in the late 19th and early 20th century – on their one day off from work – individuals and walking clubs made their escape from the smoke, long hours of labour and overcrowding. They hopped on the Dore and Chinley Railway, now known as the Hope Valley Line, and got off at Chinley or Edale, then marched, hob-nail clad, sandwiches and flasks in their canvas rucksacks, over the moors and hills.

The gentry owned this land, it was their firing range where they could shoot grouse, and these landowners had long resisted the determination of Manchester and Sheffield walkers to enjoy their rights along ancient ways, with calls of 'get off my land' and worse.

It was on 18th August in 1894 that the Peak District and Northern Counties Footpaths Preservation Society was formed, to fight for our freedom to wander the land. Two years later it had its first major success.

From the 'Manchester Guardian on 24th September 1896:
'The Peak District and Northern Counties Footpaths Preservation Society has happily succeeded in its first enterprise. The favourite route over Kinder Scout, from Hayfield to the Snake Inn, has been secured for ever to the public. All that remains to be done is to form a path, erect signposts, and build a small bridge over the Lady Brook near the Snake Inn. Everyone will then be able to take this delightful walk through some of the finest and wildest scenery in the Peak District without let or hindrance. This peaceful victory over the landowners who threatened for a time to close the path, although within the memory of man the public had always enjoyed the right of way, speaks volumes for the energy and tact displayed by the officials of the Society.'

This was the first of many footpaths opened that the now renamed Peak and Northern Footpaths Society secured. Later, the mass trespass of Kinder by the Manchester Ramblers in 1932 led by Benny Rothman put even more pressure on landowners and the government, and today we owe a lot to these pioneers.

We follow in the footsteps of the giants of the access movement to walk, enjoy and photograph these great places.

Maps

• OS Explorer Map OL1 (1:25 000)
The Peak District: Dark Peak Area

Plaque commemorating the mass trespass on Kinder Scout in 1932. © MR

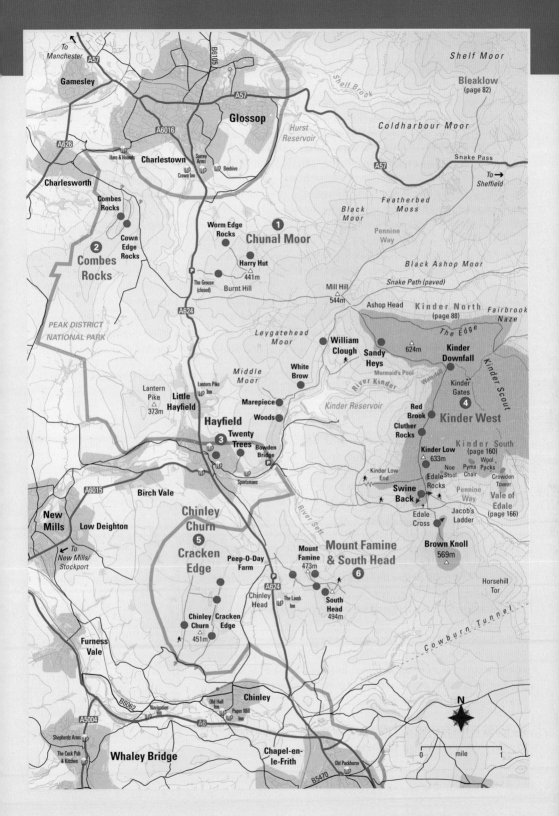

To Manchester

Gamesley

Glossop

Charlestown

Hare & Hounds
Surrey Arms
Beehive
Crown Inn

Charlesworth

A626

Combes Rocks

Cown Edge Rocks

②

Combes Rocks

PEAK DISTRICT NATIONAL PARK

Worm Edge Rocks

①

Chunal Moor

Harry Hut
△ 441m

The Grouse (closed)

Burnt Hill

A624

Leygatehead Moor

Middle Moor

White Brow

Lantern Pike
△ 373m

Lantern Pike Inn

Little Hayfield

Marepiece

Woods

Hayfield

③

Twenty Trees

Bowden Bridge

Sportsmans

A6015

Birch Vale

New Mills

Low Deighton

To New Mills/ Stockport

B105

A57

A6016

A57

Hurst Reservoir

Shelf Brook

Shelf Moor

Bleaklow
(page 82)

Coldharbour Moor

Snake Pass

A57

To Sheffield

Black Moor

Featherbed Moss

Pennine Way

Black Ashop Moor

Mill Hill
△ 544m

Snake Path (paved)

Ashop Head

Kinder North
(page 88)

Fairbrook Naze

The Edge

William Clough

Sandy Heys

Mermaid's Pool

River Kinder

Kinder Reservoir

△ 624m

Kinder Downfall

Kinder Gates

Kinder Scout

Waterfall

Red Brook

Cluther Rocks

④

Kinder West

Kinder Low
△ 633m

Kinder South
(page 160)

Noe Stool

Pyms Chair

Wool Packs

Crowden Tower

Kinder Low End

Edale Rocks

Swine Back

Pennine Way

Vale of Edale
(page 166)

Edale Cross

Jacob's Ladder

Brown Knoll
569m
△

Horsehill Tor

Chinley Churn

⑤

Cracken Edge

Peep-O-Day Farm

A624

Chinley Head

The Lamb Inn

Chinley Churn

Cracken Edge
△ 451m

River Sett

Mount Famine
473m
△

⑥

Mount Famine & South Head

South Head
494m
△

Cowburn Tunnel

N

Furness Vale

B6062

Navigation Inn

A5004

Shepherds Arms

The Cock Pub & Kitchen

Whaley Bridge

Old Hall Inn

Paper Mill Inn

Chinley

A6

Chapel-en-le-Frith

Old Packhorse

B5470

0   mile   1

Chunal Moor is a broad stretch of moorland that sits between the A624 and Kinder's Western Edge, just south of Glossop. Its highest point is Mill Hill (544m). Closer to the road is Harry Hut Hill (441m) and, 700m north of this small summit is the western edge of Whitethorn Clough that breaks into a gritstone tor called Worm Edge Rocks. This offers lovely views north down to Glossop and across to the Snake Road.

The moor is best visited in August when it is covered in purple-flowering heather. There are many informal tracks here, including an obvious one that goes from Harry Hut Hill to Mill Hill, from where there is an excellent view of Kinder's north western extremities, but the path can get very wet and boggy. There is an alternate route just south that goes from Burnt Hill to Mill Hill and this is paved, offering a sensible winter alternative.

What to shoot and viewpoints

Go over the stone wall at the lay-by and walk across the moor following a narrow cut path through the heather with splendid elevated views.

Across the snow-covered wastes of Mill Hill (VP1). Canon 5D Mk 1, 17-40 at 30mm, ISO 100, 1/30s at f/20, Grad. Feb. © CG

Viewpoint 1 – Approach to Harry Hut Hill

The heather and bilberry on the first stretch of moorland is perfect in the evening sun for close ups of the vegetation as it is lit by the evening sun, the path providing a leading line. There are isolated patches of bilberry, bell heather and of wet moss. This is big sky moorland terrain; nothing but moor and a big wonderful sky with distant hills.

Viewpoint 2 – Harry Hut Hill Summit
Grid Ref: SK 044 907
Approach: 25 minutes, distance1.8km, ascent 120m

The path descends to a wall. Go through the gate and up the rough narrow path beyond. As you gain height the hills in the distance to the south appear. Eventually a white summit cairn is reached which provides an attractive subject to place amongst the landscape. It is quite a beguiling place in certain conditions.

Viewpoint 3 – Worm Edge Rocks
Grid Ref: SK042914
Approach: 25 minutes, distance 1.7km, ascent 120m

From the summit cairn follow the path north west down towards Glossop. The path follows the edge of Whitethorn Clough to the small but distinctive buttresses of Worm Edge Rocks. Near and at sunset in summer these rocks are lit and the views in most directions are good. There is a small shooting hut beyond Whitethorn Clough in the west.

Worm Edge Rocks (VP3). Canon 6D, 17-40 at 20mm, ISO 100, 1/2s at f/14, Grad. Jul. © CG

West from Worm Edge Rocks toward Harry Hut Hill (VP3). Canon 6D, 17-40 at 20mm, ISO 100, 1/20s at f/14, Grad. Jul. © CG

How to get here

Chunal Moor is accessed from the large lay-by on the A624 two miles south of Glossop from which a path leads directly to Harry Hut Hill. (The lay-by is near the closed pub, The Grouse).

Parking Lat/Long: 53.415173, -1.951376
Parking Grid Ref: SK 033 909
Parking Postcode: SK13 6JY

Accessibility

It is 0.7miles/1 km to Harry Hut Hill along a narrow path through the heather, the latter half has a slight incline and is a little rougher. It is then a further 700m/0.4 miles down hill to Worm Edge Rocks.

Best time of year/day

Summer evenings in August when the moor is a blaze of purple and Glossop is lit by the setting sun.

Nestling in the very top left hand corner of the national park is Coombes Rocks and the Mares Back, a hilly ridge that dominates the southern skyline above Glossop. The craggy amphitheatre of Coombes Rocks face west receiving late afternoon light and the setting sun, with expansive views across to Greater Manchester. On the eastern aspect is Cown Edge Rocks, a quarried gritstone edge overlooking Rocks Farm. This gives moorland views east across to Kinder Scout and in the south down to Lantern Pike with valleys and hills snaking away into the distance. This is a spectacular and very accessible location.

What to shoot and viewpoints

The start of the footpath is downhill of the lay-by on the south of the road. Go through the gate and follow the path up the old sunken quarry road (or by the side of it) toward the pine plantation and the start of Coombes Rocks. You can also go up hill from the lay-by and around the corner and on your right a footpath goes uphill leading more directly to the northern end of Cown Edge Rocks.

Viewpoint 1 – Coombes Rocks
The path leads uphill to the pine plantation where the cliffs begin, a path traverses along the top of the edge taking you around the cirque. On this path are many good wide-angle viewpoints. The Banks, a grassy ridge to the north creates a curving leading line, buttresses of rock protrude out creating foreground subjects and sometimes the edge is scooped out providing a window to the view. There are three ponds in the quarry spoil heaps below, and half-way along the cliff top path there is a small gritstone tower. Heather flowers here in August and it would be a good place for night photography of the distant lights of Manchester and Glossop.

Viewpoint 2 – Cown Edge Rocks
You can add on a visit to Cown Edge Rocks by doing a circular walk; turn left at the end of Coombes Rocks. Alternatively head there directly by going uphill from the lay-by and around the corner, on your right a footpath goes up hill leading more directly to the northern end.

The northern end of Cown Edge has been quarried over the years and offers foreground interest but the middle ground is somewhat cramped by the high col between here and Churnal Moor to the east. The middle and southern end of Cown Edge is more interesting. The land here drops away toward Rowarth, beyond which rises the pretty, stepped flank of Lantern Pike with the crests of Chinley Churn and Coombs Moss above retreating into the distance. The foreground interest is provided by the rocks of Cown Edge itself, and at one point Rocks Farm below. The edge is best photographed in late afternoon when the sun is still high enough to illuminate the foreground rocks and light rakes pleasingly across the flank of Lantern Pike.

The west-facing cirque of rocks of Coombes (VP1). Canon 6D, 17-40 at 20mm, Tripod, ISO 100, 1/100s at f/13, Grad. Mar. © CG

The Mares Back from Coombes Rocks (VP1). Canon 6D, 17-40 at 20mm, ISO 100, 1/20s at f/13. Oct. © CG

How to get here

Coombes Rocks and Cown Edge Rocks are situated high above Glossop and are accessed by a minor road, Monk's Road, from the village of Charlesworth just south west of Glossop or from the same road by the A624, 2.2 miles north of Hayfield. The lay-by parking is on the Glossop side of the hill north of the road.

Parking Lat/Long: 53.430184, -1.979399
Parking Grid Ref: SK 018 923
Parking Postcode: SK13 5HH (0.3 miles)

Accessibility

It is half-a-kilometre to both Coombes Rocks and Cown Edge Rocks from the lay-by on good paths, but it is not suitable for wheelchairs. There is great roadside photography on many points on the minor road for those with limited mobility. If you do a circuit of both edges total distance is 3km.
Approach: 15 minutes, distance 0.5km, ascent 15m

Best time of year/day

These locations are all-year-round with the best times from August when the heather blooms through autumn – when the ferns start to turn golden brown – and in winter and spring. When there is snow and the weather fine it is worth the trip. Coombes Rocks facing west is best in late afternoon and at sunset, whereas the east facing Cown Edge Rocks is best at sunrise and late afternoon.

Top: Cown Edge Rocks south to Lantern Pike (VP2). Canon 5D Mk 1, 17-40 at 17mm, ISO 100, 1/25s at f/13. Mar. © CG

The pinnacle on Coombes Edge Rocks (VP1). Canon 6D, 17-40 at 40mm, Tripod, ISO 200, /160s at f/11, Grad. Mar. © CG

The Peak has many characterful trees to photograph and one interesting group is Twenty Trees a short walk from the village of Hayfield along the Snake Path. Locals are quick to point out that there are only 19, but we aren't sure if locals round these parts can count above 19.

Joking apart, there used to be 20 trees until 1944 when two young lads were sent by a local farmer to saw one of the trees down for gate posts. After they felled the tree they pulled the roots out with two horses, hence there is no evidence of the twentieth tree. Whilst here the old packhorse village of Hayfield retains much of its history and is a lovely village to walk around and photograph.

What to shoot and viewpoints

Follow the Snake Path up the hill through two restored kissing gates to the trees. The backdrop of the trees is the view toward Lantern Pike and Chinley Churn. There are many ways to compose the trees: on the approach including the path and kissing gate, from below, above and up close. A good sky will really help most compositions.

A. Hankins, Greengrocer and Fruiterer, Hayfield. Sony A6000, 10-18 at 18mm, ISO 100, 1/320s at f/7.1. Aug. © MR and detail © CG

How to get here

From the village of Hayfield drive up Kinder Road toward Bowden Bridge and Kinder Reservoir for 0.2 miles and park across from the Snake Path, the *Peak District and Northern Footpath Society path #30*. Or alternatively park in the village and walk.

Parking Lat/Long: 53.378286, -1.940904
Location Grid Ref: SK 039 868
Parking Postcode: SK22 2LD

Accessibility

It is 500m gentle up hill walk to Twenty Trees from the road.
Approach: 20 minutes, distance 0.5km, ascent 70m
Hayfield village is good for all.

Best time of year/day

Twenty Trees can be photographed at any time of year, although care should be taken with the sun position as the shooting direction is predominantly to the west. In July and August the meadow near the trees may be in flower. This is an accessible location in winter when there is snow on the ground and can be very atmospheric during stormy weather.

Above: The locals are right. The dramatic stand of 19 trees above Hayfield. Canon 6D, 17-40 at 40mm, ISO 100, 1/100s at f/13, Grad. Mar. © CG

The wind makes faces in the grit stacks:
totems and gargoyles squint and grimace.
The air here is half water: mouths suck
and gape in the rock. Bristle grass,
brown, bone-pale, shudders like hide,
grips each edge and cleft.
It is endless, a stranded reef
which seeps and surges indefinitely.
Paths slip under streams; pools hover;
stones become sheep become stones.

Look out. Follow the water's drop
into green distance. There is sun
glinting the reservoir, its drafted edges
bright as a chalk horse; there is a town
in the hills' shade that was once
a gathering place.
The wind is hard from the west,
a skein of voices in it, thin but clear
as curlews'. Their songs' rising
crests the brown moor and flies

Kinder Downfall, 24 April 1932 | Rob Hindle

Kinder Downfall (VP5, p.200). Sony A6000, 18–200 at 18mm,
ISO 1000, 1/100s at f/5.6. Jan. © MR

Plaque commemorating the mass trespass on Kinder Scout in 1932 at Bowden Bridge car park. © CG

The Western Edge of Kinder Scout above Hayfield is some of the most accessible wild land in the North of England. This accessibility and the freedom to enjoy and walk along footpaths and over the uncultivated land is the result of long battles, both legal and by direct action, by many individuals and organisations.

This activism and protest contributed to the passing of the National Parks and Countryside Act in 1949, when the UK's National Parks were created – the first being the Peak District 1951. While this freed up some land for recreation, it wasn't until 50 years later in 2000 that the Countryside and Rights of Way Act (CRoW) was passed granting access on foot to mountain, moor, heath and down ('open country') known as Access Land.

Approaches here aren't the roadside attractions of the eastern gritstone edges near Hathersage but they do offer something worth sweating for. Kinder provides a change from compositions of foreground rocks on high, flat moorlands over a valley toward a level horizon. Here in the north-west corner of the Peak District, the grit and shale layers break up into discrete hills to create large compositional figures in both the mid-ground and the distance that form multi-layered landscapes.

We have described Kinder West as a walk from Bowden Bridge just outside Hayfield, taking in Kinder Reservoir and climbing up William Clough to the gritstone cliffs and boulders of Sandy Heys on Kinder Scout. The route then leads to the 30m waterfall of Kinder Downfall and over to the boulder-strewn Kinder Low. It's an 7.5m/12km walk with over 1400ft/430m in elevation gain, topping out at just over 2,000ft/615m.

This is roughly the route taken by the Manchester Ramblers in 1932 on their protest walk across Kinder over the lack of access to Peak District moorland. Find out the full history at **kindertrespass.com**.

What to shoot and viewpoints

Park at Bowden Bridge National Park car park on Kinder Road, just over a mile east from Hayfield village. This is as far as cars are allowed along this road. At the back of this car park on a rock is a plaque commemorating the Kinder Trespass of 1932.

Viewpoint 1 – Bowden Bridge; Kinder Bank Woods

Beyond Bowden Bridge along the road to the Kinder Reservoir path is a bank of old oak and birch trees which are replaced by pine further along the road. Whilst there is no public access to most of these woods they do provide interesting subjects when the light shines through them Autumn can be perfect and in the midst of winter when they are stripped of their leaves and cast long shadows.

Opposite top: Beautiful early autumn colours in Marepiece Plantation, looking over to Kinder Reservoir (VP2). Canon 6D, 17-40 at 20mm, Tripod, ISO 100, 1/20s at f/14, Grad. Oct. © CG

High above Kinder Reservoir on the approach to Sandy Heys (VP4). Canon 6D, 17-40 at 20mm, Tripod, ISO 100, 1/100s at f/13, Grad. Apr. © CG

Viewpoint 2 – Kinder Reservoir by White Brow and Marepiece

Grid Ref: SK 054 882
Approach: 30 minutes, 1.7km, ascent 100m

From Bowden Bridge walk along Kinder Road (don't go over the bridge) to its end, go through gates into woodland with the Kinder River on your right, up to the reservoir gates and the cobbled path signed White Brow. Go up the cobbles to where it levels off and where there is a view of Kinder Reservoir at an interpretive sign. To the south over woodland is the Sett Valley and the twin peaks of Mount Famine and South Head. Switch back left here up a steep short path to the White Brow path. On reaching the path if you go left here and up it leads to two shooting cabins where there >>

How to get here

Park at Bowden Bridge National Park car park on Kinder Road, just over a mile east from Hayfield village. This is 8 miles from Glossop and 21 miles from Manchester. The parking is pay and display but there is often free parking across from the car park on the road side.

Parking Lat/Long: 53.379361, -1.931291
Parking Grid Ref: SK 046 869
Parking Postcode: SK22 2LH (0.3 km)

Accessibility ♿

This is a long hill walk and you need to be hill fit and well prepared. For those not prepared to go high and far the woodlands around Bowden Bridge and Kinder Reservoir are great locations.

Best time of year/day

Kinder West faces south west to north west and receives sun for most of the afternoon until sunset all year with variations due to season and topography. Of note are the two large, embracing arms that wrap themselves around Kinder Reservoir. The northern arm is

Sandy Heys to Middle Moor and the southern arm is Kinder Low to South Head. This topography must be accounted for when calculating when the sun hits where.

For example: Kinder Downfall, a very attractive subject to photograph, faces south west and is hidden from summer sunsets by the rise of Sandy Heys but is illuminated all year by afternoon sun, at sunset only between September and March.

Elevation is also an important consideration – there is a 400m/ 1200ft height increase from Hayfield to Kinder Scout. Use the sun compass in this book, the Photographer's Ephemeris and a detailed map to work out the best times – or just go for it and follow your nose.

Winter sees more contrast with the heather and ferns golden brown, and the grasses yellow when lit by low winter sun. Summer is a combination of pale green grasses and intense green bracken, but in August splashes of colour are added by purple flowering heather and bilberries. Cotton grass wave their white heads in July and August. If you are up to it when it snows and freezes, this area is an adventure and a must for spectacular winter photography.

The Kinder River and the top of Kinder Downfall (VP5). Sony A6000, 18–200 at 18mm, ISO 160, 1/80s at f/9. Sep. © MR

is an elevated all-encompassing view up to Kinder Downfall – worth the diversion. Late afternoon and sunset are best.

If you head to above Marepiece Woods there are gritstone outcrops that you can use as foreground for wide compositions, and many distinctive trees.

Turn right along the White Brow path that traverses above the reservoir to where the path starts to descend. You have two choices here either walking up William Clough or the steeper path direct to the crags and boulders of Sandy Heys.

Viewpoint 3 – William Clough
Grid Ref: SK 060 894
Approach: 1 hour+, 3.2km, ascent 184m

William Clough is the longer, less steep option and offers a small number of interesting falls along its path. At its head is a junction of paths and tremendous views including down Kinder's northern edge and the Ashop Clough down to the Snake Road. Turn right here up the last climb to the Kinder plateau.

Viewpoint 4 – Sandy Heys
Grid Ref: SK 072 892
Approach: 1.5 hours, 5.2km, ascent 388m

The area of the Kinder Plateau path from above Ashop Head to Kinder Downfall is known collectively as Sandy Heys and has much to offer. Boulders, pinnacles and prows nuzzle together and present themselves well on summer evenings when the sun is in the north west, or at sunset later in the year, with the the backdrop of the view down to Kinder Reservoir. Continue along the path south east to the Kinder Downfall.

Viewpoint 5 – Kinder Downfall
Grid Ref: SK 082 889
Approach: 2 hours, 6.4km, ascent 416m

Kinder Downfall is impressive and can be photographed from many points from afar, close up is a little more challenging. A distinctive characteristic of this waterfall is when a westerly wind blows the water falling down the drop blows back, this can be sometimes a gentle spray to full blown white horses. A good position to photograph this whole scene is to cross the Kinder River above the falls (south side) and go south a little and down amongst rocks with care to look back at the Downfall. You may be lucky and see a rainbow in the spray.

A more precarious perch is to scramble down amongst the rocks of the Kinder River and approach the edge of the falls. If the sun is reflecting back from the water make sure you expose for these highlights rather than the darker background to avoid blowing highlights. The Golden Goose is to take a photograph of the Downfall blow-back when the sun is setting in the west or south west from September to March. In this case you must also consider the flow of the Kinder Downfall which often runs dry, it is best after heavy rain. Bring plenty of lens wipes in case the spray is fierce.

Manchester is often visible in the distance from here and all along the western edge of Kinder – a zoom lens is useful.

Kinder is open access land and you are free to wander where you like. For something different, a recommended option is to follow Kinder River from Kinder Reservoir to Kinder Downfall.

Viewpoint 6 – Kinder Low
Grid Ref: SK 078 871
Approach: 2.5 hours, 8km, ascent 453

From the Downfall the path continues south and one drainage worth looking at is Red Brook, a bouldery and rocky drainage with great views down to the reservoir and across to Mermaid's Pool. Cluther Rocks is the next area with with lots of soft, grassy fall-offs punctuated by the occasional shapely boulder or small buttress. These 'set pieces' catch the afternoon sun and sunset all year.

The next major feature is the trig point of Kinder Low (elevation 633m). From here you have two options: either descend south to Edale Cross, a medieval cross that marked the boundaries of three wards of the ancient Peak Forest

From here traverse round Kinder Low End to Broad Clough and back to the reservoir. Or: descend steeply down Kinderlow End to Broad Clough. If you return to the car park from here you will have done a walk of 12km/7.5 miles.

Viewpoint 7 – Swine's Back, Lower Edale Rocks and Brown Knoll

This is a significant photographic viewpoint. Just north of Edale Cross and south of Kinder Low, below Edale Rocks, is Swine's Back, a small plateau lined by Lower Edale Rocks which offers great photographic opportunities looking down to the Vale of Edale in the east (best at/near sunrise), and of South Head and Mount Famine in the west (best at/near sunset).

If you want to get here direct you have two choices both similar in distance.

First from the Vale of Edale up Jacob's Ladder (4km/2.3 miles/ascent 318m) starting at Barber Booth or; from Bowden Bridge at Hayfield (4km/2.3 miles/ascent 363m) by going over the bridge and right just after the car park at Bowden Bridge and traversing below Kinder Low to Edale Cross and up. Plan your route on a map.

Depending on fitness give yourself an hour to two hours plus to get in position. There are various viewpoints: close to rocks just above Edale Cross is best for looking west, and higher by east-facing rocks for the Vale of Edale. Upper Edale Rocks and the Noe Stool are more problematic to photograph at the golden hour and lend themselves better in stormy afternoon light with the sun in the south.

Also consider walking over to Brown Knoll for another perspective into Edale, this can be spectacular at sunrise.

Looking into Edale from Swine's Back (VP7). Sony A6000, 18–200 at 27mm, ISO 100, 1/400s at f/11. Sep. © MR

Getting low at Kinder Low (VP6), cotton grass at sunset. Sony A6000, 18–200 at 54mm, ISO 400, 1/400s at f/9. Aug. © MR

The views from the high moorland of Chinley Churn (451m) and the quarries of Cracken Edge looking east down to Chinley Head and across to the Kinder Downfall are stunning and an unsung gem of Peak landscape photography. It is a short but steepish approach over moorland.

What to shoot and viewpoints

Follow the bridleway north that starts next to the drive of Throstle Bank cottages. Go through a gate and follow the track by the wall.

Viewpoint 1 – The Moorland

From the moorland, which is full of flowers in summer, there are great views to the south west to Whaley Bridge and Toddbrook Reservoir, and to Chapel-en-le-Frith in the south west. There are drystone walls for foreground subjects and leading lines.

Go through two gates then turn right up across the field and then down to a gate. The holes that you may pass are old trial holes used to explore for minerals and rock, some fill with water. Once through the gate you are at Cracken Edge.

Viewpoint 2 – Cracken Edge

This natural gritstone edge was once an active quarry that has been softened by nature but the scars of industry have left a pleasingly photogenic legacy. Tumble-down walls and buildings, spoil heaps, exposed crags, quarry tracks, precariously positioned solitary trees and the remains of old equipment dot the landscape and are there for the

Remains of quarry buildings on Cracken Edge (VP2). Canon 6D, 17-40 at 20mm, ISO 100, 1/60s at f/13, Grad. May. © CG

photographer to discover. Of course to add to this is the view down to Chinley Head, the valley below with its field barns and farms, and across to the majestic Kinder West with the Downfall at its head.

This whole edge is worth exploring. Follow a quarry track through the levels to a high point in the north with views down to Hayfield.

Viewpoint 3 – Chinley Churn Summit

You can return the way you came but better is to go south and visit Chinley Churn summit and the quarry by returning back to Over Hill Road by dropping down a path below the edge and more stunning views. If you parked at Throstle Bank cottages turn right up the hill.

How to get here

Chinley Churn is approached from a minor road that starts in the village of Chinley. Once in Chinley take the main road to a bridge over the railway – the station is 250m to the west. Drive over the bridge – there is a war memorial in front of you – and turn left passing houses up Stubbins Lane which bares right up the hill and turns into the narrow Over Hill Road. There is a lower footpath that goes up to Chinley Churn from here but recommended is to go to the top of this lane and park in a bigger lay-by on the right before Throstle Bank Cottages. There is a bridleway path just beyond the cottages' driveway that leads onto the moor and Access Land.

Parking Lat/Long: 53.345018, -1.955774
Parking Grid Ref: SK 030 831
Parking Postcode: K23 7NP

Accessibility

It's a round trip of 2 miles to Cracken Edge on Chinley Churn, gently up hill on paths and over rough moorland.
Approach: 30 minutes, distance 1.6k, ascent 100m.

Best time of year/day

Anytime of year will yield great results, especially in summer when the moorland grasses are yellow and the valley below a lush green dotted with trees and farms. More important is the time of day. The light is best when the sun is still slightly higher in the sky in the late afternoon in summer, or earlier in winter. Once the sun drops below the hill it casts a shadow to the east and detail and features are lost. If you time it right sun beams will shine through the gap or col between the Churn and Ridge Top illuminating Chinley Head below as well the expansive landscape of Kinder West. This is a fantastic place if there is snow on the ground, although you will probably have to park in Chinley.

Above: The great views north west from Cracken Edge (VP2). Canon 6D, 17-40 at 20mm, ISO 100, 1/60s at f/13, Grad. May. © CG

Below: Cracken Edge – Industry softened over time by nature (VP2). Canon 6D, 17-40 at 20mm, ISO 100, 1/60s at f/13, Grad. May. © CG

The River Sett rises from the moors below Kinder's south west corner where it has cut a deep valley that for the most part is hidden from view by its high, southern flank. Cresting this flank are the twin shapely hills of Mount Famine and South Head. Both hills are visible from nearly everywhere in this western area of the Peak District. They are very accessible and offer some great vantage points.

Mount Famine's eastern side lacks character and it could be easily overlooked but a walk along its crest reveals its true nature, with some lovely gritstone crags that hang out over the drop toward the River Sett. Kinder rises majestically above it and there are some great compositions that set the foreground against the background. Turning to the south, the crest path leads to South Head and again the foreground rocks offer the counter to the nearby hill. There is also a good path here with some tumbledown walls that create excellent leading lines. Described is a three mile walk taking in the best photographic viewpoint and both summits.

What to shoot and viewpoints

Viewpoint 1 – Between Mount Famine and South Head (SK 059 846)

As you walk between Mount Famine and South Head the views open up to your left toward Kinder down to the River Sett with the craggy top of Mount Famine and its sweeping slopes.

Don't go up the moorland path to South Heads summit, continue on the track for more compositions looking back from where you came – passing a distinctive wall that runs up South Head to a highpoint after a path shoots off left. A path from here heads direct and steeply – but short – to the summit of South Head.

Opposite: Looking toward Kinder from Mount Famine (VP3). Canon 6D, 17-40 at 17mm, ISO 50, 1/10s at f/20. Mar. © CG

The path from Mount Famine to South Head in (VP3). Canon 6D, 17-40 at 20mm, ISO 100, f14, 1/100s at f/14, Grad. Mar. © CG

Viewpoint 2 – South Head Summit (SK 060 846)

South Head Summit is a flat narrow ridge with a drystone wall running along it and some from it. There is a 360-degree panorama and just to be here in good conditions is enough to lift the spirits. The summit cairn and drystone wall provide good foreground subjects for many possible compositions featuring the surrounding land.

Head down the steep grassy path toward Mount Famine to the track you walked along, turn left on the track and up the steep grassy path on your right up to the rocky ridge of Mount Famine.

Viewpoint 3 – Mount Famine Summit (SK 059 850)

Mount Famine has a spectacular rocky summit ridge of small gritstone crags that overlook the Sett valley. The gritstone formations are creased horizontally and are perfect foreground for compositions to the north – a patchwork of fields and then the bulky moorland of Kinder and south looking back at South Head.

Turn left from the summit ridge over improved moorland back to the track which will take you back to the A624 and your car.

How to get here

Park in the Peep-o-Day lay-by on the east side of the A624 a mile and a half south of Hayfield. Sometimes there is a very good mobile catering van here. The bridleway to Mount Famine and South Head starts just over the brow of the hill from the lay-by just beyond Peep-o-Day farm heading east.

Parking Lat/Long: 53.359439, -1.9274274
Parking Grid Ref: SK 049 847
Parking Postcode: SK23 6AJ

Accessibility

An uphill walk on a very good track with two short but steep climbs over moorland. A three and a half mile round trip.
Approach: 1hr, distance 3km, ascent 150m.

Best time of year/day

Timing matters here, particularly with the westerly compositions; winter afternoon sun offers a very sympathetic angle. There are strong compositions everywhere, but they are intensified on stormy days anytime, but especially later in the year when there is more contrast in the landscape as the vegetation changes. Because of their short approaches and commanding viewpoints these locations are a good choice after snow and in freezing conditions.

There is a piece missing from the Peak District National Park, a corridor of land that runs from New Mills to Buxton was excluded from national park status because of quarrying and built up areas. This is still the Peak District however, and the historic spa town of Buxton, one of the 'gateways to the Peak District', is worth exploring. Being at 300m/980ft above sea level it is also has a 'healthy' climate and a local cricket match had to be abandoned in June 1975 because of a snow storm.

To the west of Buxton the national park begins again and rises up to Shining Tor, and the Cheshire region of the Peak District. This high ridge of Chatsworth Grit looks down to Macclesfield and the Cheshire Plain in the west, and to the east moorland dips moderately down to the Goyt valley, where the River Goyt begins its journey to the River Mersey and the Irish Sea.

Access is straightforward to the locations here by the spectacular Cat and Fiddle Road, which itself has several great photographic viewpoints, especially of Cheshire's Matterhorn, Shutlingsloe (506m).

To the south we venture to the mysterious wooded Lud's Church and Back Forest, and the two packhorse bridges of Three Shire Heads and its cascades.

Maps

• OS Explorer Map OL24 (1:25 000) The Peak District: White Peak Area

The path to Shining Tor with a snowstorm approaching (VP4, p.216). Canon 5D, 17-40 at 20mm, ISO 100, 1s at f/20, Grad. Dec. © CG

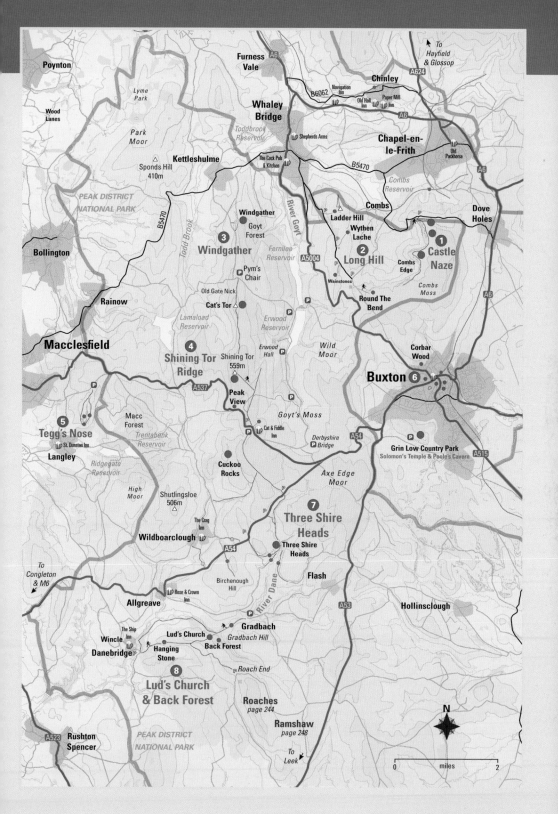

Castle Naze is the jewel in the crown of the Goyt Valley. Nowhere in the Peak can you get to such a splendid high, wild place for relatively little effort – although the short, steep approach is a bit of calf burner.

The gritstone ramparts of Castle Naze and Combs Edge sit at 443m/1400ft lining the north west tip of the moorland plateau of Combs Moss. They overlook the villages of Combs and Chapel-en-le Frith. A remote high moorland, a featured gritstone crag, an Iron Age fort, luminescent purple heather in August; with a view looking down steep slopes to a patchwork of fields, drystone walls and trees, winding roads, villages, farms and country houses, a reservoir and in the distance Manchester. If the light is right it doesn't get much better than this for landscape photography.

What to shoot and viewpoints

There are a variety of compositions to explore, some including Combs Reservoir and the farmland below, others concentrating on the sweep of moorland and slope to the south. Look out for the serpentine curve of the road going by Broadlee Farm in the south west, and in the north west the profile of Manchester (a telephoto lens needed). From the lay-by walk a few metres east and through a gate to follow the path up the hill to the rocks of Castle Naze. The lower path by the bench contours round to the gritstone scree and the base of lower slopes below the crag. The left hand path goes to the the cliff through a cleft where you can access a good path above that runs along the edge of Combs Moss, and just below, a climbers path traverses the foot of the cliff.

Viewpoint 1 – The scree at the base

A steep slope runs down from the cliff, littered with gritstone blocks to more gritstone blocks at the base of the slope. To access this area take the lower path by the viewing bench and around the corner. This viewpoint gives perspectives to the south around the cirque and also looking north where the steep edge of Castle Naze can seen in profile, all using an interesting foreground of scree and vegetation in a composition.

Viewpoint 2 – Climbers Path

The higher path takes you to the west end of the Castle Naze cliffs. Head along a path just below the cliff for compositions using the cliff as a side subject.

Viewpoint 3 – Castle Naze Top

The path up through the notch leads to a good path which traverses the top of Comb Moss often by a drystone wall. Where you initially emerge are many interesting features formed by the top of the cliff and various compositions can be made in many directions. On the moss above are the remains of an Iron Age hillfort.

Viewpoint 4 – Combs Edge and Combs Edge Pinnacle

From the top of Castle Naze head south (turn right) along the cliff top path. Several breaks in the rocks appear and there are many viewpoints where a succession of good foreground features lends narrative to a longer composition toward the Naze now in the north. About 300m from Castle Naze another significant grit edge begins known as Combs Edge. At the end of the continuous section of gritstone edge go down the slope to discover the Combs Edge pinnacle, a 30ft detached tower of rock which makes an interesting subject. Combs Edge continues beyond Pyegreave Brook and is worth exploring.

Viewpoint 5 – Short Edge

To the left, east, from where you emerge at the cliff top path is the northern edge of Combs Moss which falls down to Chapel-en-le-Frith and views of Eccles Pike, Chinley Churn, South Head, Mount Famine and beyond. The view is tremendous and an evening in summer finds the sun side-lighting the landscape beautifully. A long lens works well here, picking out the wealth of detail, or go wide with some some rocks in the foreground.

The Manchester skyline from Castle Naze. Sony A6000, 18–200 at 200mm, ISO 160, 1/100s at f/10. Aug. © MR

North from an old quarry to Castle Naze, Combs Reservoir beyond (V4).
Canon 6D, 17-40 at 20mm, ISO 200, 1/40s at f/13, Grad. Feb. © CG

How to get here

There is limited parking in a small lay-by (three cars) on a narrow, high-elevation minor road linking the villages of Combs and Dove Holes, north of Buxton and south of Chapel-en-le Frith. Further parking is possible down the road toward Combe at Whitehills. From the Beehive Pub (worth a visit) in Combs head due east up the hill. From Dove Holes north of Buxton take Station Road off the A6 and a left up the narrow Cowlow Lane. Park in the lay-by at the start of the worn swathe of a path going up the hill to the rocks.

Parking Lat/Long: 53.304788, -1.922665
Parking Grid Ref: SK 052 786
Parking Postcode: SK23 9UB (0.4 km)

Accessibility

Castle Naze is 200m up hill from a small lay-by with 30m of ascent. A short and steep 10 minute ascent to an elevation of 443m/1400ft. Once on the plateau there are good paths. Below the cliff the going is a little tougher. The area is open Access Land and you are free to wander, and wonder.
Approach: 10 minutes, distance 200m, ascent 30m.

Best time of year/day

An all year-round location. Combs Edge faces west to north west, with Castle Naze facing west and north. Depending on the time of year these edges receive late afternoon and evening sun. This escarpment is a very good sunset location for most of the year. In August the slopes below the edge are covered in vivid purple heather. Winter with a low sun and more contrast is also recommended, especially if there is changeable weather.

The pinnacle at Combs Edge (VP4). Sony A6000, 18–200
at 18mm, ISO 160, 1/200s at f/9. Aug. © MR

A minor road links Whaley Bridge/Horwich End in the north and Buxton in the south and traverses up Long Hill. This long ridge looks over Combs, Chapel-en-le-Frith and Kinder in the north east with Fernilee and Errwood Reservoir in the west. Just off this road are a series of worthwhile high viewpoints to explore and a more strenuous quest up onto Combs Moss with its fabulous views.

What to shoot and viewpoints

To the west of Combs Moss is the ridge of land known as Long Hill, topped at its northern end by Ladder Hill. The summit radio mast is visible from many places in the area. There is a lovely lane – Old Road – that climbs Long Hill from Whaley Bridge, crossing the summit ridge at Wainstones and ending at the White Hall Centre. Mileages along Old Road are from the A5004 Stalybridge to Buxton Road,

Viewpoint 1 – Ladder Hill
1.2 miles from the A5004 Stalybridge to Buxton Road.
Park in a small lay-by next to the Long Edge Plantation and follow the track along the wall into a beautiful old beech woodland with very dense characterful trees and a deep shade that illuminates beautifully in late evening light. You can access the summit of Ladder Hill from here by following the track leftwards, with great views down to the village of Combs and its reservoir.

Viewpoint 2 – Wythen Lache
2 miles from the A5004 Stalybridge to Buxton Road
Further along the road you can pull off the road and take the path by the farm of Wythen Lache through fields to a rocky hill, just below Ladder Hill. From the cliff top there are good late afternoon and evening compositions down to Combs and across to Combs Moss and Edge.

Viewpoint 3 – Wainstones
2.3 miles from the A5004 Stalybridge to Buxton Road
Beyond Wythen Lache the road goes through a rocky gap. Park before the gap and go through the gate and follow the path to the scattered rocks of the Wainstones. The composition to the west are tight here because of the telegraph wires, but it is a quick location if the light is good.

Viewpoint 4 – Round The Bend and Combs Moss
2.7 miles from the A5004 Stalybridge to Buxton Road
The south-western corner of Combs Moss overlooks the White Hall Outdoor Education Centre and parking can be found around the back of it at the end of Old Road from where public footpaths lead quickly to Access Land. This corner of the hill is actually Combs Moss's highest point at roughly 500m and the views northwards into valley of Combs and beyond that to the hills above and beyond Hayfield are spectacular. Below the crest line around SK 036 764 there are the remains of a long-abandoned quarry that is well on the way to being reclaimed nature. Fabulously runkled and lichened boulders abound here offering first class compositional counterpoints to the views behind them. The north to north westerly aspect means that you are best visiting on late summer evenings when the sun sidelights the whole area beautifully and when the heather is out.

Summer evening light in the woods near Wythen Lache (VP2). Canon 6D, 17-40 at 20mm, ISO 100, 1/2s at f/20, Grad. Aug. © CG

A passing raincloud showers Chapel-en-le-Frith, seen from Round The Bend quarries (VP4).
Canon 5D Mk 1, Canon 17-40 at 20mm, ISO 100, s at f/20, Grad. Jun. © CG

How to get here

All these locations are accessed from a minor road called Old Road above the A5004 Stalybridge to Buxton Road (Long Hill) which starts a third of a mile from Horwich End on the Chapel Road, it is initially called Elnor Road. At half-a-mile go left up Old Road.

Ladder Hill Parking Lat/Long:
53.305697, -1.968244
Parking Grid Ref: SK 022 787
Parking Postcode: SK23 7HD (0.7 km)

Wythen Lache Parking Lat/Long:
53.296284, -1.962107
Parking Grid Ref: SK 026 777
Parking Postcode: SK23 9XA (0.7 km)

Wainstones Parking Lat/Long:
53.290590, -1.959189
Parking Grid Ref: SK 028 770
Parking Postcode: SK23 9XA (0.5 km)

Round The Bend and Comb's Moss Parking Lat/Long:
53.285100, -1.953009
Parking Grid Ref: SK 032 764
Parking Postcode: SK17 6SX

Accessibility

These are mostly mellow walks along good paths, but with a stiff pull up from Round The Bend to Combs Edge. There are plenty of opportunities for good photography from the road for those who do not want to walk far.

Ladder Hill Approach: 20 minutes, distance 600m, ascent 64m
Wythen Lache Approach: 20 mins, distance 1km, ascent 12m
Wainstones Approach: 2 minutes, distance 100m, ascent 10m
Round The Bend Approach: 20 mins, distance 1km, ascent 70m

Best time of year/day

Most of these locations are good early and late, depending which way you are photographing.

Opposite bottom: The cliff beyond Wythen Lache (VP2).
Sony A6000, 18–200 at 18mm, ISO 100, 1/50s
at f/11. Aug. © MR

The ridge of Shining Tor stretches northwards with the Goyt Valley to the east and its undulating west slope eventually reaching the start of the Cheshire Plain south of Manchester. Windgather Rocks and Cats Tor are two west-facing gritstone outcroppings that sit on the ridge above Fernilee and Errwood reservoirs. These are convenient high crags when conditions are good especially for those who are accessing the Peak from the Manchester area. Close by is the Goyt Forest, great for intimate woodland portraits.

What to shoot and viewpoints

Viewpoint 1 – Windgather Rocks

Windgather Rocks often catch the afternoon and evening sun, and a good viewpoint of the edge itself is up the road to the south looking down on them – especially from the moorland east of the winding road. Also try from the road overlooking the drystone wall from the south. The small quarry just to the south, by a small lay-by, has some interesting subjects to photograph: steps, walls and the angular quarried rock.

The land here is sloping gently northward meaning that the best shooting positions face in that direction either from top of the cliff and or at its base. In the north west the valley descends to Kettleshulme while in the north east the views across the Goyt toward Chinley Churn and Lantern Pike and the Hayfield hills is wonderful.

There are interesting rock formations to anchor a composition and it's worth exploring the length of the cliff.

Up close the Chatsworth grit of the cliff is formed in layers, with quartz pebbles, and the buttresses lean back, or overhang, and make good close up studies especially when the heather flowers in August.

Viewpoint 2 – Cats Tor

From the car park at Pym Chair it is a short walk south up the hill to the summit of Cats Tor passing Old Gate Nick a protruding tilted buttress of gritstone. The eastern aspect of this ridge is across a broad, shallow shoulder into Shooters Clough, although the longer aspect is across the lovely hilltops toward Kinder Scout in the distance. The western aspect is mostly beyond a stone wall and barbed wire fence but occasionally the edge is sufficiently abrupt and close to the path to allow good compositions to the lovely views into the broad valley of Todd Brook and down toward Kettleshulme.

Viewpoint 3 – The Goyt Forest, Errwood and Fernilee Reservoirs

The pine forest to the east of Windgather is worth exploring especially in low light, when misty and especially in autumn. You can access the forest by a path behind Windgather Rocks and also on the west side of Errwood and Fernilee Reservoirs. Errwood Reservoir has an open and light feel to it and is home to Buxton Sailing Club. The woodlands around the public parking area here, although mainly pine trees have a number of good, large beech trees left over from when this was the parkland for Errwood Hall – whose ruins can still be visited. It is a characterful and moody place. Both Fernilee and Errwood collect autumnal mists on cool, moist and calm mornings.

Climbers on Windgather (VP1). Sony A6000, 18–200 at 18mm, ISO 100, 1/125s at f/11. Aug. © MR

A low bow near Windgather. Sony A6000, 18–200 at 80mm, ISO 100, 1/200s at f/7.1. Aug. © MR

Evening light on Windgather Rocks with Lantern Pike beyond (VP1).
Canon 6D, 17-40 at 20mm, ISO 200, 1/20s at f/13, Grad. Mar. © CG

How to get here

Pym's Chair and the parking for Windgather are on a minor road that can be accessed from the western end of the Cat and Fiddle Road, south from Kettleshulme; from the B5470 near Bollington and the A5004 from Buxton or Horwich End/Whaley Bridge. Plan your route before you leave as there is a potentially confusing network of small roads in this area. Pym's Chair is at the brow of a hill with a small car park. The parking for Windgather Rocks is in front of the cliff or at its southern end by a small quarry. Park well in as agricultural vehicles use this minor road and only access the cliff by the two stiles.

Pym's Chair for Cats Tor Parking Lat/Long:
53.287154, -2.010131
Parking Grid Ref: SJ 983 762
Parking Postcode: SK10 5XL

Wingather Rocks Parking Lat/Long:
53.299980, -2.009144
Parking Grid Ref: SJ 994 781
Parking Postcode: SK23 7RF (0.4km)

Accessibility

Both these locations are close to their parking spots and are accessed by good paths on moorland and through fields. You will encounter stiles to climb over.
Cats Tor Approach: 10 minutes, distance 800m, ascent 42m
Wingather Rocks Approach: 2 mins, distance 100m, ascent 8m

Best time of year/day

These are all-year round locations that face west and catch most of the afternoon sun and sunset all year. Some aspects lose sun near to sunset and will be in shade. August through autumn to early spring are the best times for photography at these locations. All these areas are busy at weekends and on Bank Holidays.

Middle: Sony A6000, 18–200mm at 18mm,
ISO 100, 1/160s at f/11. Aug. © MR

From the base of the cliff (VP1). Sony A6000, 18–200 at 18mm,
ISO 100, 1/100s at f/10. Aug. © MR

Winter on Shining Tor looking south toward Shutlingsloe and the Macclesfield Forest (VP4, p.216).
Canon 5D Mk 1, 17-40 at 20mm, Tripod, ISO 200, 1/100s at f/20, Grad. Dec. © CG

The Cat and Fiddle Road (A54/A537) links Buxton with Macclesfield and summits at 520m/1,690 feet at the Cat and Fiddle Inn – currently closed as of publication. This windy road, with some long straights (speed limit 50mph) traverses Goyt's Moss and Axe Edge Moor and has tremendous views along its entire length. Described are various locations near the road, the summit of Shining Tor – an attractive 559m hill with a short approach – and an escarpment close to the Cat and Fiddle Inn. This road is also one of the best places to photograph the attractive profile of Cheshire's Matterhorn, Shutlingsloe (506m).

What to shoot and viewpoints

Viewpoint 1 – Peak View Quarry (SJ 995 726)
There are only a few lay-bys on this busy road where it's possible to pull over and take photographs. If conditions are 'going off' it's good to be able to quickly pull over safely. One worthwhile spot is the quarry just down from the Peak View Tea Rooms a half a mile north (toward Macc) of the the Cat and Fiddle Inn. Above the quarry are views looking down and across to Shutlingsloe. Also try at the next bend near the Cat and Fiddle, parking is in a small quarry.

Other good places are the lay-bys near the turn off to Tegg's Nose at the Macclesfield end of the road. Care is needed getting back onto this busy road – double check each way. There are often footpaths leading off from the lay-bys for further exploration.

Viewpoint 2 – Cat and Fiddle Inn
Park in the lay-by across from the Cat and Fiddle Inn, or in the pub car park. Just north from the pub is a track that leads north east, follow this for 200m passing a building and along a fence to a high point (519m) with great views down over Goyt's Moss.

Viewpoint 3 – Cuckoo Rocks Escarpment
The main viewpoints are across the road from the pub on the Cuckoo Rocks Escarpment (SJ 995 713). Follow the wide path south, across a bridge over Clough Brook after 300m. Continue for another 700m to where the path starts to arc round. From here head west down a path that

follows Cumberland Brook. Almost immediately turn right and follow a wall to the edge of the Cuckoo Escarpment – the wall follows the brow of the slope. There are great views to the distinctive hill of Shutlingsloe with the Cheshire Plains in the distance and some useful foreground rocks on the slope.

Viewpoint 4 – Shining Tor (SJ 995 738)
Approach: 2km/1.2 miles, 154ft/47m elevation gain. The path to Shining Clough (559m/1,834ft) starts 250m north (toward Macc) of the Cat and Fiddle Inn. Park at the lay-by opposite the pub or at the start of the path if there is room. Follow the path and take the right fork staying high to a second cross path and turn left up the straight path to the summit of Shining Tor. There are many photographic opportunities on this approach across the moor. Go through the gate from the benches to the west-facing summit rocks and the summit cairn.

From the summit the view is impressive: farmland, Shutlingsloe, the Jodrell Bank radio telescope, the Clwydian Range in North Wales and the wide curve of the Cat and Fiddle Road. This is a prime sunset location at any time of year, or sunrise in the winter. Stormy mornings are also a favourite when the land in front is illuminated under an angry sky.

Other compositions: Walk down toward the south west to where scattered rocks litter the slope and provide some interesting compositions. Continue further down by drystone walls toward the lone Scots pine for a classic composition. The land adjacent to the pine is private, the rest is Access Land.

The Peak Quarry View to Shutlingsloe (VP1). Sony A6000, 18–200 at 25mm, ISO 160, 1/80s at f/8. Aug. © MR

Winter light on the moors to the east of Shining Tor. Canon 5D, 17-40 at 20mm, ISO 100, 1/20s at f/20, Grad. Dec. © CG

How to get here

From Buxton take the A53 north of the Opera House which travels south west up hill to a right turn on the A54 and along this to the A537 to the Cat and Fiddle Inn: 4.5 miles. From Macclesfield follow the Buxton Road/A537 west up the hill from the Silk Road to the Cat and Fiddle Inn: 7 miles.

Cat and Fiddle Inn Parking Lat/Long:
53.244108, -2.000223
Parking Grid Ref: SK 001 719
Parking Postcode: SK11 0AR (2km)

Accessibility

Take care on this road. Although the speed limit is 50mph there are many who speed, keep an eye out for bikers, there are blind bends and it is used by haulage lorries. It can be closed in winter although usually not for long. The walk to Shining Clough is the longest approach at 1.2 miles. Off the roadside locations there are well-travelled paths but for the adventurous there is nothing like following a trod across the moorland to some distant viewpoint. Wrap up well, take some food and Muck Boots or similar are recommended as this moor can be very wet and boggy.
Shining Tor: 40 minutes, distance 2km, ascent 38m.

Looking north west from shining Tor (VP1). Canon 6D, 17-40 at 20mm, ISO 100, 1/30s at f/10, Grad. Dec. © CG

Best time of year/day

High elevation moorland locations can be good anytime of year but it's best to visit when there is interesting light or weather conditions. Shining Tor faces west and towers over the landscape making it a great sunset location anytime of year. It is also good for sunrise in the winter months.

Teggs Nose Country Park is a compact hill occupying the end of a ridge above Macclesfield and overlooking a bowl of land formed by the western flank of the Shutlingsloe ridge, which also holds the Trentabank, Ridgegate, Bottoms and Teggs Nose Reservoirs. It is a popular walking area for people coming into the National Park from the west.

The views from here are predominantly looking toward the south west to south. Shutlingsloe does not present its best aspect from here but when the sun is in the west the views up to Sutton Common in the south are splendid and lend themselves to slightly longer focal lengths. For shorter focal lengths the old quarries, which are well-covered in heather these days, offer plenty of craggy foreground interest. This is a good spot if you are near and conditions are good, and whilst the views are fantastic it can be limited for good landscape photography.

What to shoot and viewpoints

The path starts at the car park entrance and carries on straight to two left turns, the second is good for wheelchair access. The path arcs round through heather to the old quarry – this area was quarried for millstone grit from the 16th century until 1955 – where there is a display of old equipment. There are viewpoints here of field patterns and up to the Macclesfield Forest and Shutlingsloe which are particularly good on misty mornings in the autumn.

Continue to the nose at the southernmost point to an official viewpoint looking down on the reservoirs across to Sutton Common, the BT Tower and lots of rolling, tree-covered hills.

If you venture around to the west the views open up to more of the Cheshire Plain and Manchester, with North Wales in the far distance. The more adventurous can scramble around the small heather-clad hillocks and rocks which provide good foreground subjects.

Around Tegg's Nose there are footpaths to explore which have good viewpoints. Also some of the roads in the west have good outlooks over Macclesfield which are worth seeking out especially when there is mist.

How to get here

At the Macclesfield end of the Cat and Fiddle Road turn south at Walker Barn down a minor road, signed Teggs Nose Country Park. The pay and display car park of Teggs Nose Country Park is on your left a half mile down this road.

Parking Lat/Long: 53.256151, -2.0759225
Parking Grid Ref: SJ 950 732
Parking Postcode: SK11 0AP (0.3km)

Accessibility

It is a pleasant walk on a well maintained path around Tegg's Nose. Wheelchair access is good on the main path all the way to the main viewpoints on the east side of the hill and just beyond the quarry. If you go off the main trail expect steep inclines over heather, with some drop offs. There is a visitor centre, cafe and toilets here.
Circuit: It is ten minutes to good views but give yourself an hour for the full circuit: total distance 2km, ascent 47m.

Best time of year/day

Afternoons to sunset for most of the year with sunrise good in the winter. August is a good time for heather and slightly earlier for other floral displays. This area is usually accessible after snow once the roads have been cleared and can be very special with some distinctive trees nearby.

Abobe: You may see this character on the way to Tegg's Nose. Canon 6D, 70-300 at 200mm, ISO 800, 1/1000s at f/5.6. Apr. © CG

From the far side Tegg's Nose, over Trentabank to Sutton Common.
Canon 6D, 17-40 at 20mm, ISO 100, 1/30s at f/13, Grad. Aug. © CG

Buxton is an old, old town with evidence of settlement stretching back 6,000 years to Stone Age times. The Romans discovered a warm spring and built a Roman bath here, establishing the settlement of Aquae Arnemetiae, the waters of the goddess of the sacred grove. In the 12th century the town was known as Buckstones.

The town was 'rediscovered' by the Victorians and, driven by the Dukes of Devonshire, it was developed based on Bath, as a spa town resort. You can still sample the healing waters of Buxton at St. Ann's Well by the Crescent.

The Victorian redevelopment masked much of the previous layers of architecture and while there are still traces of the old town to be seen, the flamboyance of the Victorian development compensates greatly for the absence of older layers. Fabulous stone buildings and cast-iron work typical of the period abound here.

What to shoot and viewpoints

GET A TOWN MAP AND EXPLORE

Highlights include the Cavendish Arcade, the Georgian Crescent, the Pavilion Gardens, the Opera House and the amazing Devonshire Dome at the University of Buxton Campus, which when it was built in 1880 was the largest unsupported dome in the world.

Buxton is a great town to wander around with a camera. The sharp-eyed will spot endless character and detail and not just Victoriana. Look, for example, at the walls of the Old Court House in George Street and you will see a set of fabulous little grotesques that pre-date the Victorian redevelopment. There are numerous listed buildings here. Photography within the Devonshire Dome is only permitted at times when there are no students around.

ON THE EDGE OF THE TOWN

Corbar Wood

To the north west of the town rises the hillside of Corbar Wood, which in spring at its western end is host to an extensive carpet of bluebells. The woods are walking

distance from the town, less than a kilometre, and are accessed off Manchester Road/A5004 that starts just north of the Park and the Pavilion Gardens, across from the junction with Park Road by the bus stop.

Grin Low Country Park, Solomon's Temple and Poole's Cavern

To the south of Buxton, high on a hill overlooking the town is Grin Low Country Park, a popular public space recovered from an area of old Lime Kiln working. At the top of this is Solomon's Temple, which because of its elevated position catches the morning and evening light well and is popular for photography. Although there are great views the tower's position makes it difficult to compose it against any meaningful background.

Below Grin Low is Poole's Cavern, one of the original 'Seven Wonders of the Peak' a natural limestone cave rich in detail and into which photographers can venture by prior arrangement with the owners. There is a charge for admission.

These locations can be accessed from the Visitor Centre, Green Lane, Buxton, SK17 9DH or if you just want to visit Solomon's Temple you can walk up from Grin Low Road.

How to get here

Buxton is approximately an hour's drive from the M1, M6, Manchester, Sheffield, Nottingham and Derby.

Parking Lat/Long: 53.260124, -1.914577
Parking Grid Ref: SK 057 736
Parking Postcode: SK17 6AH

Accessibility ♿

Most of these locations are accessible by all with rougher ground in the woods and a short climb up to Solomon's Temple.

Best time of year/day

Spring and autumn are the best times to visit. Buxton is 305m/1,000ft above sea level, in a hollow surrounded by hills and moorland. Buxton gets weather and is often the first place in the Peak to get snow. The town can be a good place to photograph when it is raining.

Opposite: a selection of photos from around Buxton. © CG

Of Three Shire Head strange tales are told
Of coiners, thieves and bandits bold.
Who long defied the country reeve
By hiding in some neighbouring greave;
Or, crossing o'er the border stream,
Which here with rapid waters teem,
His jurisdiction might defy
And nefarious burdens ply.
Walter Smith, 1923.

The headwaters of the River Dane gather on the moors to the south of the Cat and Fiddle and start to cut their way down through the soft rock. Geological weaknesses here mean the river is punctuated by tumbles and falls. At the confluence of the Dane and a minor tributary there is a compact sequence of cascades by two packhorse bridges.

Known as Three Shire Heads because of the convergence of the three shires of Derbyshire, Staffordshire and Cheshire. Photographers have been visiting this place since the invention of the Kodak Brownie in the early 20th century. In the 19th century counterfeiters, highwaymen and other ne'er-do-wells used this area as a base to evade capture as police could only act within their own county limits. The two packhorse bridges here probably date from Medieval times when packhorse ponies with pannier bags were used to transport goods – especially salt from Cheshire – over the moors.

As well as this famous bridge, the valleys and moorland, their water courses, the farms and drystone walls, and the views in this area provide a wealth of photographic opportunity.

What to shoot and viewpoints

Viewpoint 1 – Upper Dane Valley

The main destination, at least initially, will rightly be the Three Shire Heads. But as you traverse around Cut-thorn Hill or if you have approached from the south near the village of Gradbach, the valley below Three Shire Heads is a delight to photograph in the right conditions. The valley slopes down with rustic views down to Back Forest and over to the Roaches. This valley is particularly good in summer when the foxgloves flower and in autumn when the bracken turns bronze, and is better in the afternoon and evening with the sun at your side or behind you.

Viewpoint 2 – The Three Shire Heads Packhorse Bridge and Cascades

The ancient pack horse trail crosses the river over the old bridge. Below is Panniers Pool, into which one of the falls tumble. The water levels here vary tremendously but are pretty reliable in all but the driest weather. Care needs to be taken in spate conditions when this small, tight valley quickly fills up with storm water running off the hills.

There are three falls. The upper fall is split very pleasingly into two plumes by a prow of rock and is usually shot from southern edge of the pool below, which puts the pack horse bridge above and behind. Dynamic range can be an »

Three Shire Heads in summer. Sony A6000, 18–200 at 18mm, ISO 160, 1/80s at f/11. Jul. © MR

On the approach to Three Shire Heads (VP1). Sony A6000, 18–200 at 18mm, ISO 60, 1/60s at f/11. Jul. © MR

*Opposite: Cascades around Panniers Pool at Three Shire Heads (VP2).
Canon 5D, 17-40 at 20mm, ISO 50, 1s at f/20. Polariser. May. © CG*

issue here with bright sky and dark foreground. Choosing a dull day and carefully composing so that most of the sky is cut out will help.

A second fall comes into the valley from the west from the hills around Flash. This stream is less dramatic but a second packhorse bridge, a backdrop of lovely old trees and a deeper pool all build on the composition, compensating for the less dramatic nature of the water. This stream is also often discoloured.

A final cascade is formed below the confluence of the two streams where the water falls over a sequence of lovely rock steps.

Below the confluence the now larger River Dane continues to fall and tumble over shelves of varying size but there is one last and notable fall in this sequence at grid reference SK 009 683 where the water falls over a large shelf and has created a good sized pool, big enough for the water to rotate and create some long-exposure swirls.

Viewpoint 3 – Blackclough

Follow the path from the packhorse bridge at Three Shire Heads west, through a gate and uphill following a stream on your right. This remote feeling valley has a small packhorse bridge, some cascades and a great display of thistles in the summer.

Clulow Cross, an old barrow topped by a copse of beech can be photographed from the A54, just beyond where a road heads south to Wincle (SJ 952 674).

Viewpoint 4 – Flash and Quarnford

Sandwiched between the Dane Valley in the west and the A53 in the east is the parish of Quarnford, which is home to Flash, one of the highest villages in England at 463 metres (1,519 ft). Flash has an interesting history and it is worth investigating its connection to coal mining, cock-fighting, Flash money, a vegan brewery and Methodism.

The rolling moorlands of the parish reflect its altitude and in winter it can be very bleak. This section of the A53 is often one of the first roads in the Peak District to close when the snow falls. All landscapes have their qualities, however, and there is much to interest the photographer here. In terms of wildlife this is a very important area for migrating birds of prey, as evidenced by presence of Black Brook Nature Reserve (SK 018 643). Short-eared owls can be seen in this area quite regularly, particularly on Goldsitch Moss (SK 010 644) as can little owls and merlin.

Viewpoint 5 – Shutlingsloe From The South

One of the best views of Shutlingsloe (506m) is from the south and one of the best places to take a photograph of its profile with a foreground of fields and barns is from the A54 quite close to the parking for Three Shire Heads and just to the south west using footpaths near Berry Bank Farm that run down to the village of Wildboarclough or up to Birchenclough Hill.

How to get here

Three Shire Heads is situated a half-a-mile south of the A54 Congleton Road, starting at a lay-by 2.2 miles down the A54 where it leaves the Cat and Fiddle Road. There are four ways to reach the Three Shires Heads. Described is the approach around Cut-thorn Hill.

Park in a lay-by 2.2 miles from where the A54 leaves the Cat and Fiddle Road in the east or 2.2 miles from the excellent Rose and Crown pub on the A54 to the west. Walk along the narrow road to Cut-Thorn Farm where you go left through a gate and follow the sandstone-coloured path around the hill to reach the River Dane and up the valley to Three Shire Heads..

Parking Lat/Long: 53.215056, -2.001943
Parking Grid Ref: SK 999 686
Parking Postcode: SK11 0BQ (1 km)

Location Lat/Long: 53.213559, -1.9879804
Location Grid Ref: SK 009 685

Above: *Three Shires Heads side cascade and pool (VP2). Canon 450D, 17-40 at 20mm, ISO 100, 2s at f/13. Polariser. Apr. © CG*

Accessibility

The approach is initially on a good road then on an undulating footpath, but once off the paths the going is tough and often boggy, bring wellies. There are good paths to other locations described in this area.
Approach: 25 minutes, distance 1.5km, ascent 9m

Best time of year/day

The bridge and cascades are good anytime of year. They face south and if you are shooting from the south the light comes down from the north-west and can cause highlight over-exposure and flare. Cloudy days are good as long as it is not too grey. If the sun is shining the afternoons can be good but in the summer later in the day you will be shooting into the sun. Autumn and winter is best for colour when the vegetation changes, increased water flow and the sun is lower in the sky. If the area is covered in snow you will get a rare photograph as few will venture here.

Above: *One of many characterful barns on the Quarnford Moors (VP4). Canon 5D, 17-40 at 20mm, ISO 100, 1/2s at f/20. Grad. Aug. © CG*

Looking across Swythamley Park from near Hanging Stone toward The Roaches (VP3, p.228).
Canon 6D, 70-300 at 135mm, ISO 100, 1/60s at f/14. Oct. © CG

8 LUD'S CHURCH, BACK FOREST & HANGING ROCK

Lud's Church is a narrow gritstone canyon hidden deep in the trees of Back Forest near the hamlet of Gradbach. It is entirely natural and was caused by a large horizontal slip fault that has moved a large section of the hillside down toward Black Brook. This chasm is 100m long, 18m deep and sometimes only as wide as two body widths. In summer it is full of mosses, ferns and flowers with shafts of light illuminating its depths through the forest.

This area is steeped in myth and legend, having been used as a secret place of worship for persecuted faiths, a hiding place for Robin Hood and Bonnie Prince Charlie, and featuring in the tales of King Arthur.

From nearby Hanging Stone above Back Forest are tremendous compositions north to Shuttlinshoe and south east to the Roaches.

What to shoot and viewpoints

Viewpoint 1 – Back Forest
From the car park walk down the road to where the road splits. Go right here down to Gradbach Mill Outdoor Centre (left is to the Scout Camp). Follow the path beyond the centre following the River Dane and cross Black Brook by

Backlit sorrell and mosses in the chasm of Ludd's Church (VP2). Canon 6D, 70-300 at 150mm, ISO 400, 1/200s at f/8. Oct. © CG

a bridge. Head left following a path up into Back Forest and quickly turn right gradually climbing through the trees to a switchback left after 400m and on your right is a the narrow chasm entrance to the magical Lud's Church (signposted from the path).

The valley and the approach has a wealth of photographic opportunity including old buildings and farms, bridges, the River Dane, grassy glades, worn paths and stone stiles and the beautiful Back Forest.

Viewpoint 2 – Lud's Church
There are two major sections to the chasm. The lower section is deep and broad, and despite being an impressive place to witness it has few really good compositional components to work with on a wide angle. A longer lens, however, will pick out the impressive overhanging gardens of ferns that grow out of the moss and sorrel covered cliffs in the summer months which back-light very well from where you stand, down in the gloom at the bottom of the cleft. There is also a money tree here that visitor over the years have driven coins into for good luck and this is a curious and photogenic feature.

Higher up the gorge it becomes less deep and more narrow and the compositional figures become more obvious: narrow passages with steps, fabulous rock layers, huge shifted blocks of grit and glimpses of the woodland and sunlight above the gorge that can all be combined in a single frame, although the dynamic range may require the use of multi-frame techniques such as HDR and Exposure Blending to bring it all together.

Viewpoint 3 – Hanging Stone
Hanging Stone is a distinctive small gritstone outcrop sitting on a ridge (330m) above Hangingstone Farm. It can be reached by a steep footpath from the hamlet of Danebridge (a mile), from Roache End north of the Roaches (1.2 miles) or via Lud's Church (1.2 miles). At and above Hanging Stone are tremendous compositions north to Shuttlingshoe and south east to the Roaches that benefit from early morning and late afternoon light.

Opposite top: The Hanging Stone west to Bosley Cloud (VP3). Canon 6D, 17-40 at 20mm, ISO 100, 1/60s at f/14. Grad. Oct. © CG

Opposite bottom*: Deep in the chasm of Ludd's Church. Canon 6D, 17-40 at 20mm, Tripod, ISO 100, 1/2s at f/14. Grad. Jul. © CG*

How to get here

The hamlet and valley of Gradbach by the River Dane is hidden south of the A54 Buxton to Congleton road and north of the Roaches. It can be reached from the A53 Buxton-Leek road by going through the village of Flash or by turning down a minor road at the Rose and Crown Inn at Allgreave on the A54. Once in a dip go down a narrow road passing Manor Farm to a car park on the right.

Parking Lat/Long: 53.193906, -2.008305
Parking Grid Ref: SJ 995 663
Parking Postcode: SK17 0SU (0.5 km)

Lud's Church Grid Ref: SJ 986 656

Accessibility

It's less than a mile to Lud's Church from the car park on good paths, the latter half of the walk is uphill and can be slippery when wet. It is an uphill walk to Hanging Stone on paths and over moorland.
Lud's Church Approach from Gradbach:
40 minutes, distance 1.3km, ascent 42m.
Hanging Stone Approach from Danebridge:
60 minutes, distance 1.6km, ascent 143m.

Best time of year/day

This gorge is at its best in the summer months when the ferns and mosses are at their most colourful. At this time the gorge is less waterlogged. The bottom end of the gorge at the main entrance can become very muddy in wet weather. In summer the trees filter the high sun quite well and limit the dynamic range while in October the leaf colours of the deciduous trees of the woodland here add another exhilarating dimension. Autumn mornings after sunrise, and before sunset are best for compositions from Hanging Stone.

Parkhouse and Chrome Hills situated at the head of the Dove Valley are the remains of reef knolls from when a tropical sea covered the Peak District. There are many viewpoints of these distinctive knolls which are now all free to access courtesy of the CROW act. The views from Hitter Hill and on the hills themselves are all classic Peak District photographs. The surrounding countryside has a remote, ancient ambience and probably hasn't changed much since the surrounding farms were medieval monastic granges. Nearby are two more hills, High Wheeldon and and Hollins Hill, which are lesser known than Parkhouse and Chrome, but both worth visiting with great views and photographic potential.

To the north, at the head of the River Dove is a high limestone plateau, when the sun is low on an evening you will probably have this place to yourself amongst the limestone pavements, stands of trees and some magnificent views.

If you are in the area for sunset and fancy some real ale and real pork pies, step back in time by visiting Earl Sterndale's Quiet Woman pub. In the winter the fire will keep you warm in its simple beamed interior and plain furniture sat on quarry tiles. In the summer, you can share an outdoor table with budgies, hens, ducks and donkeys.

Maps

- OS Explorer Map OL241 (1:25 000)
  The Peak District: White Peak Area

On the concession path south of Stoop Farm at Tor Rock looking toward Chrome Hill (p.238). Canon 5D, 17-40 at 20mm, ISO 200, 1/50s at f/18. Grad. May. © CG

'Soft Words Turneth Away Wrath'. The Quiet Woman pub in Earl Sterndale. Recommended. © CG

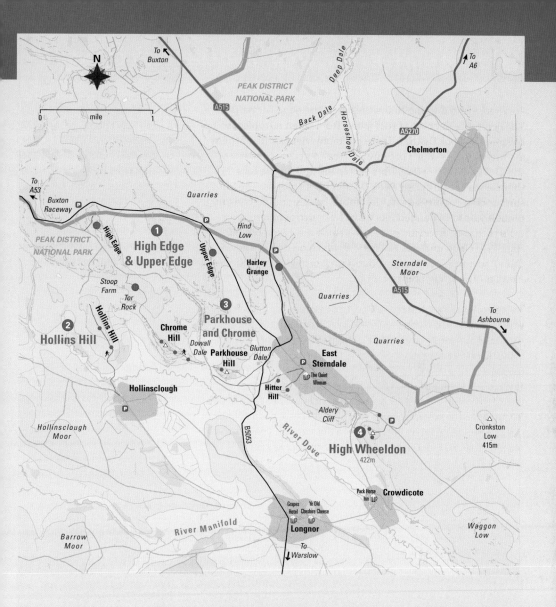

N

To
Buxton

PEAK DISTRICT
NATIONAL PARK

Deep Dale

To
A6

0   mile   1

A515

Back Dale

Horseshoe Dale

A5270

Chelmorton

To
A53

Buxton
Raceway

P

High Edge

PEAK DISTRICT
NATIONAL PARK

P

Quarries

Hind
Low

① High Edge
& Upper Edge

Upper Edge

P

Harley
Grange

Sterndale
Moor

A515

Stoop
Farm

Tor
Rock

② Hollins Hill

Hollins Hill

Chrome
Hill

Dowall
Dale

③ Parkhouse
and Chrome

Parkhouse
Hill

Glutton
Dale

Quarries

Quarries

East
Sterndale

P

The Quiet
Woman

Quarries

To
Ashbourne

Hollinsclough

P

Hitter
Hill

Aldery
Cliff

Cronkston
Low
415m

Hollinsclough
Moor

B5053

River Dove

④ High Wheeldon
422m

Pack Horse
Inn

Crowdicote

Barrow
Moor

River Manifold

Grapes   Ye Old
Hotel   Cheshire Cheese

Longnor

To
Warslow

Waggon
Low

North of Chrome and Parkhouse Hills, south of Buxton is a high limestone plateau that looks down on Upper Dove Dale. Whilst part of this area has an industrial element with quarries and a racetrack, it is nonetheless a beautiful area to explore with your camera with limestone pavements, stands of trees and some magnificent views.

What to shoot and viewpoints

Viewpoint 1 – High Edge

As its name suggests, at 462m High Edge is one of the highest parts of the Limestone Plateau (Only Eldon Hill and Starvehouse Moor are higher, both at 470m). During the Second World War two anti-aircraft batteries were sited here to protect the extensive Harpur Hill ammunition dump located just below the hill toward Buxton. The concrete gun emplacements are still present, as are the ammunition silos, which are now located within the perimeter fence of Buxton Raceway. Half of High Edge is Access Land, which means one of the two gun emplacements can be photographed and in among the grass on its flat summit there are also some very interesting limestone features that receive low sun late in the day. The saddle of land to the east holds some stands of trees that catch the light on summer evenings very nicely. Park near the raceway and a path traverses the low limestone cliff band of High Edge.

Viewpoint 2 – Upper Edge

Upper Edge is 1.2 miles from the junction at Earl Sterndale and 1.2 miles east of High Edge and also has quite a bit of photogenic limestone geology as well as a small number of characterful hawthorns. It also has a handy place to park a car, immediately adjacent to the footpath that accesses the hillside at SK 074 690.

Viewpoint 3 – Stoop Farm and Tor Rock

Go 0.8 miles down a minor road south of Buxton Raceway to the start of permissive footpath that heads toward Stoop Farm. Take the signed path south when close to the farm (turn left) passing Tor Rock (private) to access Chrome Hill. There are various viewpoints looking down to Dove Dale and this is also an alternative way to access Chrome Hill.

Viewpoint 4 - Harley Grange

The long ridge of land that slopes south from Hind Low is the final companion feature to High Edge and Upper Edge. This attractive, undulating spit descends gently toward Harley Grange and can be examined well with a long lens from the green lane that runs along the southern boundary of Sterndale Quarry and which can be accessed at the brow of the hill on the B5053 at SK086687 as you descend to Earl Sterndale.

There are opportunities here for longer focal length compositions and it can be particularly good as the sun sets with several trees silhouetted on the ridge to the west.

Limestone pavement on High Edge (VP2). Canon 30D, 17-40 at 20mm, ISO 100, 1/10s at f/18. Grad. Jul. © CG

How to get here

From the crossroads just north west of Earl Sterndale a minor road leaves Glutton Dale and traverses above the Upper Dove, passing Buxton Raceway, all the way to Axe Edge Moor joining the A515, 2.75 miles south of Buxton. Upper Edge and High Edge are right next to this minor road near the Buxton Raceway. The concession path near Stoop Farm/Tor Rock which leads to the summit of Chrome Hill is a short way off it. The Harley Grange viewpoints are on the B5053 just south of the A515 at Brierlow Bar.

High Edge Parking Lat/Long: 53.220415, -1.913267
Parking Grid Ref: SK 058 692
Parking Postcode: SK17 9NL (0.9 km)

Upper Edge Parking Lat/Long: 53.218848, -1.890565
Parking Grid Ref: SK 074 690
Parking Postcode: SK17 9PS (0.7 km)

Stoop Farm Parking Lat/Long: 53.212038, -1.904341
Parking Grid Ref: SK 064 683
Parking Postcode: SK17 0RP (1 km)

Harley Grange Parking Lat/Long: 53.215610, -1.873184
Parking Grid Ref: SK 085 687
Parking Postcode: SK17 0EL (0.4 km)

Accessibility ♿

Apart from the Stoop Farm concession path, all these locations are roadside or within 100m of the road.

Best time of year/day

These locations benefit from late afternoon sun and sunset at most times of year.

Above: *Great limestone scenery on Upper Edge (VP2). Canon 6D, 17-40 at 20mm, ISO 100, 1/60s at f/14, Grad. Sep. © CG*

On the west side of the Upper Dove Valley is the shapely Hollins Hill, the northern most point of the gritstone outlier that forms the western hills along this stretch of Dove Dale. Hollins Hill sits above the village of Hollinsclough, and offers an excellent aspect of Chrome Hill across the valley. Its ridge is followed by a drystone wall with many hawthorn trees on its eastern slope.

Hollinsclough is a remote and pretty village with some interesting buildings and is notable for the foxgloves that grow here. They are mostly found in the valley between the village and Hollins Hill by the described route.

What to shoot and viewpoints

Viewpoint 1 – The Walk

There is plenty to photograph on the way to Hollins Hill: foxgloves in the summer and lots of good views. Walk up the road passing Vicarage Farm on your right and a lovely

June foxgloves on the southern flank of Hollins Hill (VP2). Canon 5D Mk 1, 17-40 at 20mm, ISO 200, 1/640s at f/10, Grad. © CG

barn with a wall-mounted Victorian postbox on your left. Turn right at the next barn and follow the footpath down through the field and cross the River Dove by a bridge through a metal gate and turn left up the worn path through bracken to a track. Turn left and follow the track around and through the gate with the wooden sign saying 'Please Make Sure This Gate Is Closed'. On the right is a small gate and a concession footpath that leads up, often boggy, to the top of the walled field on your right where you turn left and then right and up to a gate. You are now on Hollins Hill Ridge.

Viewpoint 2 – Hollins Hill Ridge

A drystone wall follows the ridge all the way to the summit and tumulus of Hollins Hill 500m in the distance. Note the gritstone rock in contrast to the limestone in the east. The compositions open up as you traverse the ridge with the wall useful as a leading line with many shapely hawthorn trees, and foxgloves in the summer. On a summer's evening the ridges of Chrome Hill can look positively alpine, but get here early before the shadow of Hollins starts creeping up Chrome.

How to get here

Hollins Hill is accessed from village of Hollinsclough which is situated 5 miles south of Buxton between the A53 and the A515. Approach the village by one of several minor roads and park at the T-junction near the Methodist Chapel.

Parking Lat/Long: 53.195892, -1.904255
Parking Grid Ref: SK 064 665
Parking Postcode: SK17 0RH

Accessibility

This location involves a walk through fields then a short steep section to Hollins Hill ridge which can be boggy. Once on the ridge there is a good single track footpath.
Approach from Hollinsclough to Hollins Hill Ridge: 30 minutes, distance 1.5km, ascent 95m.

Best time of year/day

Very early midsummer mornings or late afternoon to sunset at other times of the year. The white blossom of the hawthorn flower in May/June bearing red berries in the autumn. There are lots of purple foxgloves throughout the summer months.

Opposite: The view across the Upper Dove valley from near Hollinsclough toward Chrome and Parkhouse Hills (VP1). Canon 5D, 17-40 at 20mm, ISO 400, 1/200s at f/10, Grad. Jul. © CG

Parkhouse and Chrome Hills in winter raiment, as seen from Hitter Hill (VP1).
Canon 5D, 17-40 at 20mm, ISO 100, 1/2s at f/20. Grad. Jan. © CG

A firm favourite with photographers of the Peak District, the beautiful and elegant twin peaks of Chrome (often pronounced 'Kroom') and Parkhouse Hills look lovely at any time of year and can be photographed from most directions, such is their appeal. These hills are the remains of a limestone reef knoll eroded by the ice sheet that covered this area.

South of Parkhouse Hill, accessed easily from the nearby village of Earl Sterndale, is Hitter Hill. This Access Land hill provides an outstanding view of Parkhouse and Chrome Hills. This is undoubtedly one of the 'must see' views of the Peak District.

What to shoot and viewpoints

The path to Hitter Hill from Earl Sterndale goes past the Quiet Woman Inn. In the fields behind you will often encounter a small and friendly group of donkeys. Chickens and ducks roam at will around the village green and pond of this lovely quiet Peak District village.

Go around the side of the Quiet Woman pub following a footpath sign. From here you can either go straight through two fields to the summit of Hitter Hill, or right following a path behind houses and through a field to the north west slope of Hitter Hill overlooking Chrome and Parkhouse Hills, above Glutton Bridge.

Viewpoint 1 – North West

Walk from the summit of Hitter Hill or traverse around to the north west slopes overlooking Parkhouse and Chrome. Also go lower down the slope where there are some trees. If you head to the west toward the wall that goes down to Glutton Dale there are viewpoints here where Glutton Grange farm is hidden by trees.

Viewpoint 2 – South

Around the other side Hitter Hill the view to the south along Dove Dale is seen, with beautiful lines of parallel walls that enclose buttercup-stuffed fields in summer, ruined barns and scrubby hawthorns. Best shot with the sun further 'round into the afternoon. The flank of the hill here is also a good place to find orchids and mountain pansies in late spring while the flat summit of the hill is a forest of thistles in midsummer.

Other Parkhouse and Chrome Hills viewpoints

Not only can these hills be photographed from a number of aspects from the surrounding hills (see from Hollins Hill on page 232 and Stoop Farm page 234) but such is their visual strength that there are many shots of each of the hills taken from the slopes of the companion peak.

Both hills are Access Land and can be accessed from footpaths near Glutton Grange farm at the bottom of Glutton Dale, from Hollinsclough and from Stoop Farm/Tor Rock by a concession footpath.

Late summer light over Parkhouse and Chrome from Hitter Hill (VP1). Canon 5D Mk 1, 17-40 at 20mm, ISO 100, 1/20s at f/16. Grad. Sept. © CG

Top: Parkhouse Hill from Dowel Dale between the two hills. Canon 5D Mk 1, 17-40 at 20mm, ISO 100, 1/25s at f/20. Grad. Feb. © CG

Above: Chrome Hill from Parkhouse Hill summit. Canon 5D Mk 1, Canon 17-40 at 20mm, ISO 100, 1/10s at f/20, Grad. Feb. © CG

Top: Parkhouse Hill from Chrome Hill. Canon 5D Mk 1, Canon 17-40 at 20mm, ISO 100, 1/5s at f/20, Grad. Dec. © CG

Above: Parkhouse Hill Hawthorn with Chrome Hill beyond. Canon 5D Mk 1, 17-40 at 20mm, ISO 100, 1/40s at f/20, Grad. Jun. © CG

From the flank of Chrome Hill, Parkhouse Hill makes a superb compositional figure against the retreating basin of the Dove Valley and Glutton Bridge behind. One great spot for this is halfway down from the summit of Chrome at a large sycamore tree looking towards Parkhouse.

June to August at this viewpoint sees the sun rise in the north east which illuminates the eastern flanks of Chrome and Parkhouse. When the sun rises in the south east later in the year they don't get the morning sun until later because of surrounding hills.

The complimentary view back from Parkhouse toward Chrome is equally appealing. To the west of the hills is the bowl of Dowel Dale into which the shadows of both hills are cast during the evening. The alignment of the hills is roughly NW-SE, which means that in midsummer a shot from Parkhouse to Chrome will be directly into the setting sun while in midwinter the complimentary shot from Chrome to Parkhouse is directly into the rising sun.

Evening light can be good with the west slopes of both hills illuminated, try north of the summit of both hills.

How to get here

Hitter Hill is a short walk from the village of Earl Sterndale, reached by going south for just shy of 2 miles on the B5053 from the Brierlow Brow junction on the A515, 3 miles from Buxton. or; if coming from the south, through the village of Longnor. There are various connecting roads from the A53 in the west and the A515 in the east to the village. Park near the Quiet Woman pub in Earl Sterndale.

Parking Lat/Long: 53.200561, -1.867392
Parking Grid Ref: SK 089 670
Parking Postcode: SK17 0BT
Map: OS Explorer Map 104 (1:25 000)
Redruth & St Agnes

Accessibility

It is a short stroll from the village through two fields to the viewpoints
Hitter Hill Approach: 5 minutes, distance 400m, ascent 20m.

Best time of year/day

The north west view from Hitter Hill to the twin peaks is great in the mid-afternoon at all times of year, with the caveat that in midsummer the sun gradually creeps around into the composition, throwing the hills into silhouette. The view down Dove Dale is best with sun further round in the late afternoon and evening.

South of Hitter Hill is High Wheeldon (422m/1,384ft) a very shapely conical hill and the highest peak in this section of Dovedale. With a wide lens it offers an excellent vantage point from which the features of the Upper Dove to the north west can be collected into a single composition – particularly excellent when accompanied by an early morning inversion. A longer lens will pick out Sheen Hill, the Ecton Hills and parallel walls around High Needham.

What to shoot and viewpoints

From the road follow the path down the hill, over a stile and follow the grassy steps to High Wheeldon's summit ridge and cairn. A short, sharp ascent.

Viewpoint 1 – The Road
You can get a very pleasing composition of the steep north west slope of High Wheeldon from the road, especially at sunset when the foreground and the view between High Wheeldon and Aldery Cliff may be illuminated.

Viewpoint 2 – The Summit
High Wheeldon's summit is a narrow and grassy ridge with fantastic views. The two main views are north west to include Parkhouse and Chrome Hills, and south west over Dovedale. If you venture down the ridge toward Earl Sterndale this is very good composition looking down to Abbotside Farm just below.

Parkhouse and Chrome Hills from the summit of High Wheeldon (VP2). Canon 6D, 70-300 at 236mm, ISO 400, 1/125s at f/10. Jul. © CG

High Wheeldon in late summer (VP1). Sony A6000, 18–200 at 18mm, ISO 200, 1/125s at f/8. Sep. © MR

How to get here

High Wheeldon is situated 0.8 miles south west of the village of Earl Sterndale. From the Quiet Woman drive south west and take the left fork at the junction and at 0.8 miles park next to the Wheeldon Trees Farm cottages near a footpath sign (coming from the south go through the villages of Longnor and Crowdicote)

Parking Lat/Long: 53.193103, -1.848180
Parking Grid Ref: SK102 662
Parking Postcode: SK17 0AA (100m)

Accessibility ♿

Whilst the approach is short it will take your breath away before you reach the summit, and again when you arrive at the summit when you see the view. VP1 is roadside.
Approach: 10 minutes, distance 250m, ascent 80m.

Best time of year/day

April to August when the sun rises in the north east, or early morning at other times of year. Late afternoon and sunset for most of the year.

'Ramshaw Edge, a grotesque succession of ghoulish faces, bovine and porcine heads, and half-finished monsters springing from parent rock. And beyond, where Hen Cloud extends its array of pinnacles, outlines that the camera may prove to less than vertical or only slightly overhanging, but to the eye appear like curving horns, their points overweighted with threatening tons of rock.

Then the Roaches, another peak of strange shape that appears to be a loose accumulation of boulders of all sizes and the most extravagant forms, gnarled, rifted, fantastically weathered, and often perched in positions that seem to defy the laws of mechanics.'

**– Moors, Crags and Caves of the High Peak, 1903.
Ernest A. Baker**

Maps

- OS Explorer Map OL241 (1:25 000)
  The Peak District: White Peak Area

The A53 Buxton-Leek road takes you over the highest main roads in this corner of the Peak District. At its southern end, near Leek, the land starts to fall away to the south west in a series of rocky layers topped by dramatic crags and pinnacles that interact wonderfully with the late afternoon light. Closest to the road is Ramshaw Rocks, whose dramatic ridge crest seems to almost overhang the road as you pass under it but with a gentler western flank making it completely accessible.

Beyond Ramshaw Rocks is the outline of Hen Cloud and The Roaches. They appear to be a pair of gentle hills but an approach from the south reveals them as a pair of rock ridges, like huge waves frozen into stone on the brink of breaking. They are threaded through with scores of interesting paths that explore their geography. Compositions from the summit ridges of these cliffs down to the surrounding countryside are classic Peak District photographs and a right of passage for any keen Peak District landscape photographer.

To the east of the Roaches is the small tarn of Blake Mere that overlooks Ramshaw and the Roaches and, to the east, acres of highly atmospheric, low, rolling moorlands dotted with villages and farm houses – perfect in atmospheric conditions. When in the area watch out for the wallabies, and don't fall into Doxey's Pool at the Roaches as Jenny Greenteeth will grab you by the feet and drag you down to join her in a watery grave.

Evening light illuminates some of the tooth-like pinnacles of Ramshaw Rocks (p.251). Canon 6D, 70-300 at 130mm, ISO 800, 1/80s at f/16. Mar. © CG

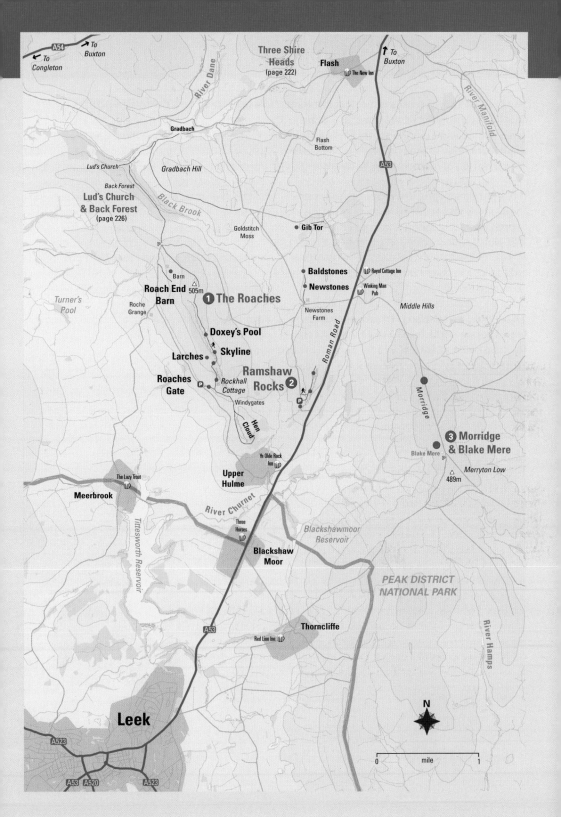

To Congleton
A54 → To Buxton

Three Shire Heads
(page 222)

Flash
↑ To Buxton

The New Inn

River Dane

Gradbach

Flash Bottom

A53

Lud's Church

Gradbach Hill

Back Forest

Lud's Church & Back Forest
(page 226)

Black Brook

Goldstitch Moss

Gib Tor

River Manifold

Barn

Roach End Barn

Turner's Pool

Roche Grange

505m

Baldstones

Newstones

Royal Cottage Inn

Winking Man Pub

1 The Roaches

Middle Hills

Newstones Farm

Roman Road

Doxey's Pool

Skyline

Larches

Roaches Gate

Rockhall Cottage

Windygates

Ramshaw Rocks **2**

Morridge

3 Morridge & Blake Mere

Blake Mere

Merryton Low 489m

Hen Cloud

Ye Olde Rock Inn

Upper Hulme

The Lazy Trout

Meerbrook

River Churnet

Tittesworth Reservoir

Three Horses

Blackshaw Moor

Blackshawmoor Reservoir

PEAK DISTRICT NATIONAL PARK

River Hamps

A53

Thorncliffe

Red Lion Inn

N

Leek

A523

A53 A520 A523

0 mile 1

Stuck out on the far south west corner like some final landscape hurrah is the Roaches – or hello if you are coming from the south. This splendid whale-back ridge of pink gritstone is one of the Peak District's great landscape locations.

The ridge aligns roughly NNW-SSE in a gentle curve and stretches from Roach End in the north all the way to Hen Cloud in the south, rising to just over 500 metres at its highest point. There is interest all the way along the ridge, which is almost entirely Access Land. Most activity is around the southern end of the main ridge, regarded as one of the foremost rock climbing cliffs in the UK. Huge buttresses of grit jut out over the Staffordshire countryside like a great fleet of dreadnoughts heading south to set sail on Tittesworth Reservoir below.

What to shoot and viewpoints

The Roaches rise to an elevation of 505m (1,657ft) starting at 338m (1,110ft) at the Roaches Gate. The walk from the car to Doxey's Pool on the Skyline is just over half a mile and takes around 25 minutes. From the road go through the Roaches Gate and follow the main path, then turn left up the rocky path to the rocks and Rockhall Cottage (a.k.a. The Don Whillans Memorial Hut).

Viewpoint 1 – Hen Cloud From The Path
Looking south to the towering crags of Hen Cloud, the path can be used as a leading line. This viewpoint is best in the afternoon and at sunset so that the west face of Hen Cloud is illuminated. Continue up to Rockhalll cottage at the base of the cliffs.

Stormy light over the southern buttresses of the Roaches with Hen Cloud beyond (VP5).
Canon 5D Mk 1, 17-40 at 20mm, ISO 100, 1/10s at f/20. Grad. Oct. © CG

Viewpoint 2 – Rockhall Cottage

Rockhall cottage, now known as the Don Whillans Memorial Hut and owned by the British Mountaineering Council, is an unusual but interesting photographic subject. It is built into the rocks and has a beautiful walled garden of boulders dotted with with bracken and foxgloves (July).

Viewpoint 3 – The Larches

At the base of the cliffs there is a lovely woodland consisting predominantly of colourful larch and in autumn they turn a lovely golden-orange with many different fungi flourishing here in among the dense mosses of the woodland floor. In the mist the evenly spaced trees offer some excellently moody compositions while the buttresses above also present themselves in a dramatic fashion when viewed from below.

Viewpoint 4 – The Steps and the Climbers

The cliffs around Rock Hall cottage are very popular with climbers and are home to many classic rock climbs. One of the best is the much sought after Valkyrie up the tallest buttress. Climbers are a friendly bunch and usually don't mind being photographed. Choose climbers who are dressed colourfully to give contrast from the brown and green rocks, and try to include all four limbs in your composition.

Carry on up the path passing a tall buttress with a big capping roof and turn right following steps to the next level.

Viewpoint 5 – Valkyrie View

At the top of the steps there is a wall and stone gate posts. This area provides a classic viewpoint looking south particularly at sunset when the buttresses by the steps in the foreground – Bengal Buttress and Raven Rock with »

its famous rock climb Valkyrie – catch the last of the sun. There are many compositional choices to make here: to include the gate and wall, to include Hen Cloud on the left, or Tittesworth Reservoir? Or a combination? Including the steps by a higher viewpoint up the path and left by the stone seat is also interesting.

Continue on the path under the tall buttresses, the one with the big capping roof has a climb called the Sloth that makes its way out of the central crack. Follow the path into the trees and follow it around right to rough steps which take you to The Skyline and arguably some of the best views in the Peak District.

Viewpoint 6 – The Skyline and Doxey's Pool

The path along the upper tier of the Roaches known as the Skyline has many great viewpoints to explore – go right, back on yourself, as well as left. Also look toward Ramshaw which are illuminated in evening light.

It is 350m north (turn left at the top of the steps) along the path to Doxeys Pool.

The principle landscape compositions here tend to focus on the view to the south west along the ridge toward the hill of Hen Cloud, which marks the southern end of the outcrop and there are many views all the way up the ridge to the pinnacle – a rock platform that juts out near Doxey's Pool, offers the longest view toward Hen Cloud. Beyond this the view bends away.

The role of Hen Cloud in these compositions is very important. There are very few places in the Peak District where there is a combination of leading line and distant feature toward which the view can be taken. In this respect

How to get here

The Roaches are situated off a minor road accessed from the A53 Buxton to Leek Road through the village of Upper Hulme. Upper Hulme Road is just short of 9 miles south of Buxton and 3 miles from Leek. If traveling from Buxton once at the Winking Man Pub drive 1.8 miles passing the jutting prows of Ramshaw Rocks down the hill to a right turn to Upper Hulme. If coming from Leek a half a mile after the village of Blackshaw Moor turn left at Upper Hulme to the Ye Olde Rock Inn.

Just after the Ye Olde Rock Inn take the sharp right through Upper Hulme village for 1.2 miles to the Roaches parking area passing the Tea Rooms and the Hen Cloud parking to the lay-by parking at the Roaches Gate.

Make sure you park inside the marked areas and don't block the road or any lanes, if you do you risk a fine from the police. Access is needed for local traffic, farm vehicles and emergency services. Leave no valuables in your car.

Parking Lat/Long: 53.156294, -1.995411
Parking Grid Ref: SK 004 621
Parking Postcode: ST13 8UA (0.5 km)

Accessibility ♿

The paths are well-maintained and broad, initially OK for wheelchairs up to Rockhall Cottage when the going gets rougher. There are two steep but short climbs up steps to the upper tiers.
Approach to Doxey's Pool: 25 mins, distance 1km, ascent 120m.

Best time of year/day

The Roaches face west and are best before and at the golden hour at any time of year with August through winter being the best times of year when the heather flowers and later when the bracken turns. Snow here is wonderful after the roads have been cleared, and of course when the weather is stormy with sun and showers. Misty mornings can be very special.

Above: The Roaches skyline from the Ramshaw parking (VP3. p.251). Sony A6000, 18–200 at 106mm, ISO 400, 1/3s at f/10. Sept. © MR

Hen Cloud performs the same compositional function as Lose Hill does in photographs along the Great Ridge from Mam Tor above the Hope Valley. Also available as a compositional figure to the photographer is Tittlesworth Reservoir to the south, which offers a great big mirror to the sky. Doxey's Pool offers great colour under the setting sun.

Roach End Barn

At the northern end of the Roaches Ridge at Roach End there is an old abandoned farm that is now elegantly tumbledown and very photogenic. By car drive north along the road from the Roaches Gate parking for 1.5 miles, the farm and its barn is in the field south of the junction. There is limited parking at the junction.

Roach End Barn is one of the most photographed Peak District locations and thankfully there is more than enough Access Land hereabouts to allow the photographer to explore. It is best at sunset at most times of the year.

At this junction a paved path ascends the ridge from Roach End toward the Roaches summit . The walker passes among huge, weathered gritstone pinnacles which offer a great foreground for compositions facing west and looking toward the cleft in the hills formed by the River Dane as it flows out of the Peak, past the sharp profile of Bosley Cloud and out to join the River Trent at Middlewich.

Below: Roach End Barn in midsummer. Canon 5D, 17-40 at 20mm, ISO 400, 1/500 at f/5. Grad. Jun. © CG

Bottom: The larch trees in the Roaches woodland (VP3). Canon 30D, 17-40 at 20mm, ISO 100, 1/20s at f/18. Nov. © CG

Below: Roaches summit ridge near Doxey Pool (VP6). Canon 6D, 17-40 at 20mm, ISO 100, 1/60s at f/14, Grad. Sep. © CG

Bottom: The view from the southern Skyline (VP6). Canon 5D Mk 1, Canon 17-40 at 20mm, ISO 100, 1/30s at f/20. Grad. Nov. © CG

The view south from the summit of Ramshaw Rocks on a misty late September day (VP2).
Canon 5D Mk 1, 17-40 at 20mm, ISO 320, 1/100s at f/18, Grad. Sep © CG

On midsummer evenings when the position of the setting sun does not compliment the alignment of the Roaches the photographer should head for Ramshaw Rocks, which are located only a couple of kilometres to the east.

A dramatic saw-tooth edge of pinnacles, Ramshaw Rocks aligns north-south and slope sharply from north to south meaning that for much of the year when the sun tends to be in the southern sky it is hard to photograph well. On summer evenings, however, the westerly aspect of the late sun matches perfectly the topography of the landscape here, illuminating the detail of the pinnacles well.

What to shoot and viewpoints

There are two paths to the rocks. The upper path at the top of the lay-by goes straight to the summit rocks at the northern end. The lower paths goes to the southern end of the rocks. A path traverses the full length of the rocks.

Viewpoint 1 – Southern Ramshaw
Take the path on the right at the bottom of the lay-by to the lower south end of Ramshaw to discover some good good viewpoints looking south with a clear view of Tittesworth Reservoir and Leek, and particularly to the north to the taller and bigger formations. Walking up the slabs gives access to some interesting eroded rock formations and the steep east side.

There is a gap in the rocks between the south and northern rocks, an ideal spot to frame the bigger and more featured summit rocks with the slopes of the hill on both sides.

Either follow the path from the southern rocks along the ridge or take the path from the top end of the lay-by to the summit of Ramshaw.

Viewpoint 2 – Northern Ramshaw
The path then climbs up to the summit passing a finger of rock which points skyward.

Hen Cloud to the south west reveals itself more along with the rest of the southern aspect and the higher you go the northern views starts to appear with Shutlingsloe's distinctive triangular profile in the north west. Compositions need to be explored here and the challenge is balance to create an image pleasing to the eye.

The ridge runs down creating a beautiful leading line toward the view with diagonal slopes leading off it, with more interest created by the beautiful rock formations. If you get it right foreground, mid-ground and background combine harmoniously. Almost in any direction and even at shorter focal lengths the '*ghoulish faces, bovine and porcine heads, and half-finished monsters springing from parent rock*' can be made use of to frame the landscape.

How to get here

Ramshaw Rocks lie immediately west and just above the A53 Buxton to Leek Road. They are 8 miles from Buxton and 4 miles from Leek. If approaching from Buxton take the A53 for 8 miles. You are nearly there when you have reached the Winking Man Pub, carry on by this pub for 1.2 miles, passing the rocks of Ramshaw to a small right turn at a stone building; if coming from Leek this right turn is 1.5 miles after the village of Blackshaw Moor. A tenth of a mile down this narrow lane is a lay-by on your left, the two paths up to Ramshaw Rocks are on your right at the top and bottom end of the lay-by.

Parking Lat/Long: 53.154679, -1.975198
Parking Grid Ref: SK 017 619
Parking Postcode: ST13 8UE (0.7 km)

Accessibility ♿

Roadside with a good path that goes uphill through rocks. Although the rocks may not be suitable for the less mobile, the road behind Ramshaw is and has many great viewpoints along its length. Care should be taken when it is windy as the drop off on the east side of the ridge is severe and when making some compositions the photographer might find themselves flirting with the drop. In dry weather the gritstone is grippy and trustworthy but in wet or ice caution is required.
Approach: 10 minutes, distance 0.5km, ascent 50m

Best time of year/day

This is a great sunrise location year round when the east side of the rocks are illuminated. It is best for sunset when the sun sets in the north west, and then in the winter when the sun sets in the south west. The summer heather here is spectacular and worth making a trip to photograph in August. Frosty or snowy winter mornings can be very worthwhile.

Looking north towards Ramshaw's summit. (VP1). Canon 6D, 17-40 at 20mm, ISO 100, 1/20s at f/14. Grad. Sep. © CG

South end of Ramshaw Rocks with Hen Cloud beyond (VP1). Canon 5D Mk 1, Canon 17-40 at 20mm, ISO 100, 1/30s at f/20. Grad. Aug. © CG

Viewpoint 3 – The Lay-By

The minor road behind Ramshaw has many good viewpoints especially if you are in a rush and is useful at sunset for a silhouette of the Roaches.

Baldstones

The continuation of the Roaches and Ramshaw Ridges to the north is worth exploring including **Newstones** (SK 018 638), **Baldstones** (SK 019 644) and **Gib Tor** (SK 018 648). Drive north of the Ramshaw parking to the T-junction at Tisha's Teas and park. A path leads north to Newstones, Baldstones with a detour around private land to Gib Tor.

The linear nature of Baldstones presents compositional challenges and lend themselves particularly to summer evenings when the light is in the west and the surrounding heather moorland is in bloom.

Also of interest is **Gradbach Hill** (SK 001 653) and over to the **Hanging Stone** (SJ 974 654) which also have some beautiful heather and some great rocky pinnacles. These locations are on Access Land and fully explorable (see p. 228).

A mention must be made here of barns, of which this area has many photogenic tumbledown examples. They are made of the same, pink grit from which the landscape is carved and they positively glow with warmth in the fading light of late afternoon.

Shutlingsloe from near Back Forest, the north of the Roaches. Canon 5D, Canon 17-40 at 40mm, ISO 100, 1/30s at f/20. Nov. © CG

Summer bilberry and the shapely outcrop of The Baldstones. Canon 6D, 17-40 at 20mm, ISO 100, 1/30s at f/14. Grad. May. © CG

The moorland and summit of Morridge sits on the western side of the very broad catchment of the River Manifold to the north west of Warslow. This area is low, rolling moorlands and dominates this corner of the Peak District, which is sparsely populated, highly atmospheric and otherwise relatively featureless. As well as the moorland its attraction for photographers are its views down to Leek and across to the Roaches, and the small tarn of Blake Mere.

What to shoot and viewpoints

At 489m, Merryton Low – the summit of Morridge – is the last significant part of the upland of the Peak District in the south west before the descent into Leek. The views from here are spectacular, particularly west to Ramshaw Rocks and the Roaches, which are presented very well in a long lens. Next to the summit is a small pool called Blake Mere in which the amazing sunsets that can be seen from here can be captured. The hill is prone to winds, however, and a getting a good reflection is a bit hit and miss. There are also a lot of midges here on summer evenings.

Blake Mere is sometimes also called Mermaid's Pool, after the legend of the ghost of a woman who was cast into the pool having been accused of being a witch by one Joshua Linnet, who's advances she had rebuffed. Linnet himself was found dead next to the pool three days later, his life having been claimed by the ghost of the woman he wronged. Doxey's Pool at the Roaches has a similar legend and there is another Mermaid's Pool just below Kinder Downfall.

The sparsely populated moorlands of both hills are very important for bird life with stand-out species awaiting the patient photographer in the form of short-eared owls, hen harriers and ring ouzels.

How to get here

Morridge is traversed by a high minor road, an impressive drive in itself. You can access this road from Leek by going through the village of Thorncliffe, by a minor road from Warslow or by taking the minor road just south of the Winking Man Pub on the A53.

Parking Lat/Long: 53.148649, -1.9410878
Parking Grid Ref: SK 040 612
Parking Postcode: ST13 8UL (0.6 km)

Accessibility ♿

These are roadside locations.

Best time of year/day

Sunset and heather season are fabulous at these locations, or anytime of year and day when there is atmospheric light.

The moorland east of Blake Mere is worth exploring. Canon 5D Mk 1, 17-40 at 19mm, ISO 100, 0.3s at f/20. Aug. © CG

Above: From Morridge to the silhouetted Ramshaw Rocks and Roaches. Canon 6D, Canon 70-300 at 230mm, ISO 100, 1/40s at f/10. Oct. © CG

Below: Blake Mere. Canon 5D Mk 1, 17-40 at 17mm, ISO 100, 0.8s at f/20. Nov. © CG

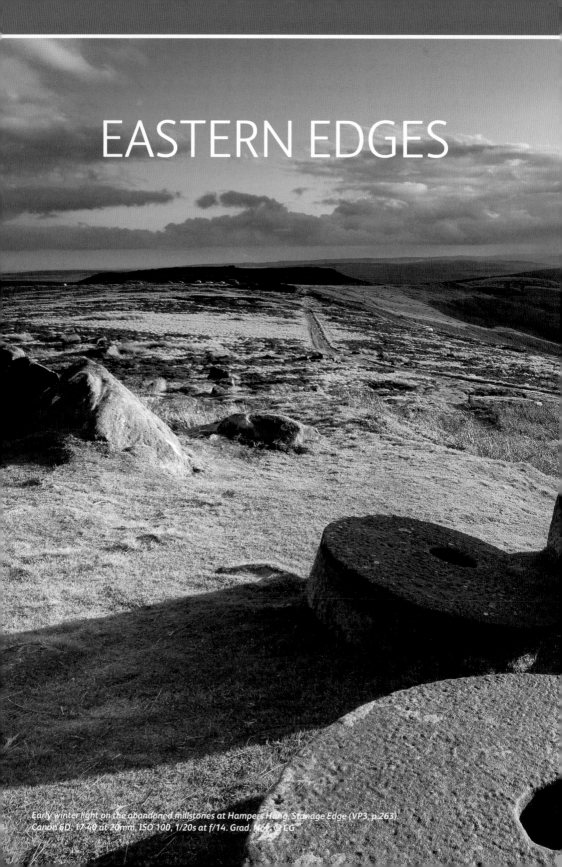

EASTERN EDGES

Early winter light on the abandoned millstones at Hampers Hang, Stanage Edge (VP3, p.263). Canon 6D, 17-40 at 20mm, ISO 100, 1/20s at f/14. Grad. Nd4. © LG

Being next door to Sheffield, the Hathersage area is one of the most popular places in the Peak, and one of the best areas for photography. Stanage Edge stretches for over a mile overlooking Hathersage and the Derwent Valley. It is the most extensive and continuous gritstone edge and a place for grand landscapes and intimate portraits of millstones strewn at its base. Nearby is another jewel of Peak photography, Higger Tor, with its distinctive rock formations and unusual for a gritstone edge as much of it faces the rising sun.

Surprise View is a place of contrasts, its high moorland plateau dotted with gritstone tors gives elevated views up and down the Derwent Valley which contrasts with the mysterious woodland of Bole Hill and Oxhay below the road. Lower down Burbage Brook, Padley Gorge is a popular autumn location with its stepped cascades flowing through beech and oak woodland – if it is too busy try Wyming Brook, a similar location north of Stanage.

If you want to view the whole of the Eastern Edges in all their glory there is no better place than the Eyam Moor, and for a view of Sheffield's skyline from the national park head to the edge of the Burbage Moor off Ringinglow Road.

Maps

- OS Explorer Map OL1 (1:25 000)
  The Peak District: Dark Peak Area
- OS Explorer Map OL241 (1:25 000)
  The Peak District: White Peak Area

Looking north above Stanage Plantation toward a distant High Neb (VP5, p.264).
Canon 5D, 17-40 at 20mm, ISO 200, 1/30s at f/20, Grad. Oct. © CG

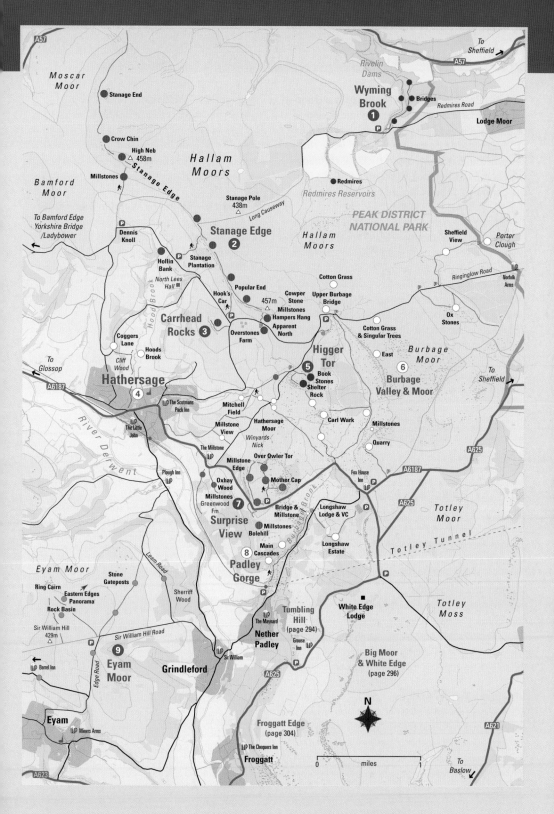

Wyming Brook cascades steeply down a wooded gorge from the Hallam Moors behind Stanage to the Rivelin Valley reservoirs on the A57 west of Sheffield. The gorge is a Wildlife Trust Nature Reserve and a narrow, often tricky path follows the course of the brook descending 100m from the car park to the valley below.

There is a good mixture of cascades and falls down the gorge and at all but the driest times there is always something to photograph. This location is at its superlative best in the autumn (October/early November) with the combined colours of the beech, silver birch and horse chestnut creating a golden ambience around the rushing brook. Nearby are the Redmires Reservoirs where a walk around their banks and on adjacent moorland yields many photographic possibilities, especially at sunset or on a stormy day.

What to shoot and viewpoints

Viewpoint 1 – Top of the Falls
From the car park don't take the bridleway but head down the steps to the brook and an open area that catches the sun for most of the day. Follow the path and cross the brook by the stepping stones following the path downstream and across a wooden bridge. Look out for white-chested dippers bobbing from rock to rock in the brook. You may also see small flocks of crossbill, an exotic-looking finch with a crossed bill – the males are red, the females green.

Viewpoint 2 – The Falls
After the bridge the path follows the brook on its left downhill and this is the main area for autumn shots. There are many cascades here first surrounded by birch trees then lower down where the ravine steepens, tall pine trees. There are ferns and moss-covered boulders.

Viewpoint 3 – The Bridges
After the pines the ravine levels out and there is an area with three attractive wooden bridges where the brook diverges and comes back on itself. You can use the leading lines of the stream and the bridges, with backlit leaves in autumn. Look also for worn stone steps, ferns and mossy boulders.

Viewpoint 4 – The Rivelin Dams
From the three bridges continue down the path crossing more bridges eventually moving away from the gorge into the woods then down to a gate and Wyming Brook Drive. If the light is good and the reservoirs mirror-calm they are worth exploring.

Viewpoint 4 – Return by Wyming Brook Drive
Wyming Brook Drive is the bridleway that runs by the reservoirs below the gorge. Turn left after the gate and follow the bridleway gently uphill through mixed woodland. Take the left turn up the hill back to the parking with views through the trees of the valley.

Redmires reservoirs
Within walking distance from the parking at Wyming Brook are Redmires reservoirs and Broadshaw plantation. The reservoirs in particular are worthy of attention if you walk out onto moors. They work well for reflections and as foreground in the summer when the sun sets in the north west. Bodies of open water are scarce in the Peak and this location is worth taking advantage of.

Opposite: Autumn at Wyming Brook. Canon 5D Mk 1, 17-40 at 20mm, ISO 50, 3s at f/20. ND, Polariser. Oct. © CG

How to get here
Wyming Brook nature reserve is 5 miles west from the centre of Sheffield situated just north of Stanage Edge and Hallam Moor. The approach to the top car park is along Redmires Road which changes to the Long Causeway with the parking on the right before the Redmires Reservoirs. Alternatively approach by the A57 Manchester road, to park by the Rivelin Dams and approach from below.

Parking Lat/Long: 53.368852, -1.596792
Parking Grid Ref: SK 269 858
Parking Postcode: S10 4QX

Accessibility &
The path down the gorge needs care to navigate. It is steep in parts with awkward steps and is very slippy when wet. Wear grippy-type wellingtons or stout boots. There is a bridleway that traverses above the gorge and this is suitable for wheelchairs with good views of the mixed woodland and the valley.

Best time of year/day
The best time here is autumn, early spring and when the snow falls in winter. The brook descends roughly south to north and the lower gorge can often be quite dark and dank. The most interesting part of the gorge is the top third near the car park especially later in the year when the low sun clips the tops of the trees.

From above the Stanage Plantation (V5, p.264). Canon 5D Mk 1, 17-40 at 17mm, ISO 50, 0.3s at f/20. Oct. © CG

Stanage Edge, the queen of the gritstone edges, stretches in an arc for four miles from the Cowper Stone in the east to Stanage End in the west. The cliff sits on heather moorland overlooking the verdant Derwent and Hope valleys with majestic views in all directions. The sweeping slope in front of the edge is covered with bracken, heather and moorland grasses which turn a burnished-brown in the winter and an almost fiery-red when the sun is low.

For photographers Stanage has much potential and variety. You can take images of the edge itself, often only a few metres from your car, and it provides a great vantage point to shoot grand landscapes of the surrounding dales and hills. Millstones, carved circular stones used for grinding barley, are particularly common at the base of Stanage Edge. This area is also grouse country with water-feeders carved in flat rocks on top of the edge.

Stanage is a large area and the viewpoints described are a selection of some the best spots for photography. There is a lot more to discover.

Stanage from Carrhead Rocks (VP1, p.266). Sony A6000, 18–200 at 18mm, ISO 125, 1/80s at f/8. Aug. © MR

What to shoot and viewpoints

Viewpoint 1 – Hooks Car
Approach: 25 minutes, distance 0.5km, ascent 60m. Park at Hooks Car. The flagged path to Stanage from Hooks Car parking provides a leading line through the bracken and moorland grasses up to the tallest sections of cliff. The vegetation changes through the seasons, with green bracken and purple foxgloves in the summer and golden and russet brown as the bracken dies back in the autumn and winter. Try mid-morning to evening for this shot as the sun will be behind you or will provide great side-lighting. Note, much of the bracken is being controlled in this area to stop it spreading.

Viewpoint 2 – Overstones Farm
Roadside. Overstones Farm is situated below Stanage near Hooks Car. These old stone buildings are a good subject from the road below across the fields looking up to Stanage or from the road above looking down to the Derwent Valley.

Viewpoint 3 – Millstones at Hamper's Hang
Approach: 20 minutes, distance 0.3km, ascent 20m Park at the Apparent North parking, a spacious lay-by where the road levels up the hill above Overstones Farm toward Burbage. Cross the road and take a major path

Early summer colours on top of Stanage (VP4). Canon 5D Mk 1, 17-40 at 20mm, ISO 100, 1s at f/20, Grad. Jun. © CG

toward the cliffs. If you head rightwards you will eventually get to a large detached boulder called the Cowper Stone and the start of Stanage Edge. Here the cliff faces east gets and the rising sun.

However the main viewpoint is to the southwest (left looking at Stanage) of the Cowper Stone underneath the main cliff edge; head directly to the cliff, slightly left on the path which leads up to several millstones scattered below the cliff face that climbers call Hamper's Hang. Early in the morning the millstones catch the first light especially in autumn and winter. You can shoot up toward the cliff, or in the opposite direction with Higgar Tor as the background. A great viewpoint with many possibilities.

Of note near the long lay-by parking of Apparent North is a short path with leads down to a great viewpoint overlooking Hathersage and the Derwent Valley.

Near Overstones Farm, looking across to Hathersage Moor (VP2). Canon 6D, 70-300 at 70mm, ISO 100, 1/50s at f/14. Nov. © CG

Hamper's Hang at a winter's sunset (VP3). Sony A6000, 10-18 at 16mm, ISO 160, 1/60s at f/10. Jan. © MR

Viewpoint 4 – Cliff Top Walk and Cliff Overlook
From the millstones (viewpoint 3) follow a path that weaves its way through low-lying rocks to the path on top of the cliff. Walk along the good path on the cliff edge. There are many viewpoints and photographic subjects along the top of Stanage. Good composition and atmospheric light conditions are the key here. Evening light bathes Stanage in a warm glow.

Viewpoint 5 – Stanage Plantation/Hollin Bank
Approach: 20 minutes, distance 0.7km, ascent 100m.
The Stanage Plantation is a grove of pine and deciduous >>

Win Hill, Lose Hill and Kinder from near High Neb (VP7). Sony A6000, 18–200 at 200mm, ISO 100, 1/320s at f/6.3. Mar. © MR

trees (some silver birch) below the cliff. It is about half-way along Stanage Edge. You can access the Plantation by parking at Hollin Bank car park (pay and display) which is 0.7 miles down the road from Hooks Car. Take the path through the trees to numerous boulders below the cliff. Once there head left up steps to the cliff top. There are multiple viewpoints here, the trees of the Plantation itself have many opportunities and there is an expansive vista to the west toward Win Hill with the cliff snaking along the skyline which is particularly good when the bracken turns in October.

Viewpoint 6 – High Neb and many millstones
High Neb is the summit of Stanage Edge marked by a trig point. You can reach High Neb by walking along the edge

from the Plantation. More conveniently there is parking at Dennis Knoll. From the parking area walk north along the Stanage Causeway, an old Roman road, toward the cliff. When just beyond the trees, cross a stile on the left and follow a climbers path through the bracken up to the cliff.

On the way to and below the cliff is the largest collection of millstones at Stanage. In summer the millstones are hidden in the bracken so it's best to visit from October to June. Sunset and sunrise both work well here, as do stormy days or clear sunny days in the autumn. There are grand views looking back from where you came to Hooks Car and in the opposite direction across to the Win Hill, Lose Hill, Mam Tor and Kinder Scout – a great sunset photograph.

The millstones at High Neb (V7). Canon 5D, 17-40 at 20mm, ISO 100, 1/8s at f/20, Grad. Dec. © CG

Viewpoint 7 – Crow Chin and Stanage End

The far north end has a remote feel and is definitely the quieter part of Stanage. It is accessed by a footpath starting at Moscar Lodge on the A57 or by walking across moor from Hordron Edge (p.132). Here there are grand views of Kinder and Bleaklow, with excellent compositional detail, including a quarry, pools, pinnacles and an old wall. The rocky prow of Crow Chin is here, which can be reached from High Neb. This is a midwinter location, when the low sun in the south and west highlights the immediate topography.

The rare ring ouzel, common at Stanage. Canon 6D, 400mm, ISO 640, 1/500 at f/8. Apr. © CG

How to get here

Stanage sits in the eastern Peak District above the village of Hathersage, an 8 mile drive from Sheffield. The most popular approaches are: from Sheffield by Ringinglow Road; from Hathersage by School Lane (aka The Dale) passing the Scotsman's Pack Inn; and by a minor road that passes Bamford Edge starting from the Yorkshire Bridge Inn near Ladybower reservoir.

There are four main parking spots: Apparent North near Burbage at the east end, Hook's Car near Overstone's Farm, the popular parking spot for climbers and walkers, Hollin Bank below Stanage Plantation in the middle, and Dennis Knoll near High Neb in the west.

Apparent North Parking Lat/Long: 53.339547, -1.6210842
Parking Grid Ref: SK 253 825
Parking Postcode: S32 1BR (1.4km)

Hook's Car Parking Lat/Long: 53.342444, -1.633635
Parking Grid Ref: SK 244 829
Parking Postcode: S32 1BR (0.7km)

Hollin Bank Parking Lat/Long: 53.350287,-1.6452643
Parking Grid Ref: SK 237 837
Parking Postcode: S32 1BR (1.2km)

Dennis Knoll Parking Lat/Long: 53.355534, -1.6602230
Parking Grid Ref: SK 227 843
Parking Postcode: S33 1BQ (1.4km)

Accessibility ♿

The paths up to and along the top of Stanage are well-traveled and maintained. There are several steep drop offs. Wear walking shoes or studied wellingtons when conditions are wet. For those in wheelchairs or of limited mobility the roadside locations around Stanage provide many great viewpoints. **Approach:** The easiest approach is from the Apparent North parking – 300m walk to the edge – the longest starts from High Neb at 1km. See individual viewpoints for more detail.

Best time of year/day

Most of Stanage faces south west, it is slow to get the sun in the morning. However its eastern end faces east getting early light. The northerly High Neb area arcs round to the northwest which means that in midsummer the sun shines directly along this section in the evening. The millstones – the High Neb ones are some of the best in the Peak District – are best photographed from autumn through to spring, in the summer they are hidden by tall bracken. Sunsets can be spectacular anytime of year.

Stanage can be good at anytime of the year. Heather flowers in August, light snow and frost add texture to the landscape and sunrise in winter hits more of the cliff. It is a location for all seasons.

Top right: Rock formations at Crow Chin (VP8). Canon 5D, Canon 17-40 at 20mm, ISO 200, 1/4s at f/20. Grad. Aug. © CG

Above: Carved, numbered grouse water bowls on the top of Stanage. Sony A6000, 18–200 at 18mm, ISO 400, 1/80s at f/11. Jul. © MR

Carrhead Rocks is a low gritstone edge hidden in front of Stanage and above North Lees Hall. The edge faces west south-west and lends itself to photography all year round, although the subtle nature of its features make it less appropriate for high sun positions.

The compositions that can be found in this gentle gritstone arc – just ten minutes walk from the road – are all similar in that they offer good foreground interest of textured rocks and moor backed-up by a grand vista or in the other direction looking up to Stanage. The knuckle stone is the obvious foreground object that wil help achieve some pleasing compositions. If there is low-lying fog in the valley this is a good vantage point looking down to Hathersage village using a long lens.

What to shoot and viewpoints

From Hook's Car walk to the junction and head down the road to Hathersage and over the cattle grid. After 100m there is a gate on your right (parking for two cars across from the gate). Go through the gate and follow the level grassy path through the heather passing two wooden posts to the south end of Carrhead Rocks. Go right at the second post. This edge is a jumble of small boulders and rocks with a few short rock faces; the whole edge is 350m long.

Viewpoint 1 – Approach Path

As you walk along the approach path there are good viewpoints of Overstones Farm behind you and Stanage with a foreground of heather. A great viewpoint in August when the heather flowers.

Viewpoint 2 – South End

The view is quiet impressive as soon as you arrive at the rocks; down left is Hathersage and its church spire, the cement works at Hope, and Win Hill in the far distance. In good light this is a great place for grand landscapes using foreground rocks as an anchor.

Viewpoint 3 – The Knuckle Stone

A short walk (75m) along the edge brings you to the knuckle stone, a small stone that sits on top of the edge. There are various compositions in several directions here that use this knuckle-looking rock as a subject. Also look out carved grouse water-feeders to include in your image.

Viewpoint 4 – North End

Beyond the knuckle stone the path and rocks descend to offer perhaps the most impressive views here. The prize is undoubtedly the views of Stanage Edge which sweeps away into the distance. This is either an early morning shot or evening, especially in the autumn when there is more colour in the landscape and the sun rises more in the south east and sets in the south west.

How to get here

Carrhead Rocks is in front of the road that follows the base of Stanage, it is a ten minute flat walk across heather moorland from the car park at Hook's Car near Overstone's Farm at the east end of Stanage.

Hook's Car Parking Lat/Long: 53.342444, -1.633635
Parking Grid Ref: SK 244 829
Parking Postcode: S32 1BR

Accessibility

Carrhead Rocks is ten minutes walk on a flat path through heather. Along the edge the path is rougher – watch your ankles – and there are short steep drop-offs.
Approach: 10 minutes, distance 0.4km, ascent 4m

Best time of year/day

Carrhead Rocks catches sun all day. Both sunset and sunrise are excellent and good side light is common. The rocks here are particularly characterful with lots of lovely weathered cracks and runkles, which pick up a low sun very well as it moves across them, revealing some great textures. Special times are in June when the the common cottongrass and hare's-tail cottongrass flower, August for heather flowers, and winter when the bracken is a bronzed-brown. Carrhead is a good vantage point if there is a storm or crepuscular rays in the Derwent and Hope valleys.

Opposite: Looking down over Dale Head to Eyam moor (VP2). Canon 6D, Canon 70-300 at 90mm, ISO 400, 1/200s at f/11. May. © CG

Looking back at Stanage (VP4). Sony A6000, 18–200 at 18mm, ISO 125, 1/80s at f/8. Aug. © MR

Night Photography at Carrhead Rocks

Carrhead is a great location for night photography. On some clear evenings well after sun down you will have a clear view of stars and the milky way relatively unpolluted by the urban lights of Sheffield due to the shield of Stanage Edge.

Top: The Knuckle Stone (VP3). Canon 6D, Canon 17-40 at 20mm, ISO 200, 1/200s at f/8, Grad. Dec. © CG

There is a network of footpaths around Hathersage that give good views of this ancient village. We describe three: one of St. Michael's Church and its spire, a view of the village in the context of its position in the Derwent Valley, and a convenient and delightful short walk up Hoods Brook starting from the centre of the village. These viewpoints benefit from mist in the valley or just a sunny morning most times of year.

What to shoot and viewpoints

Viewpoint 1 – Coggers Lane/Cliff Wood view of St. Michaels Church spire

From the main road in Hathersage village drive up Jaggers Lane, which is opposite and beyond Paul Bowyer's Butchers shop. At 0.2 miles up Jaggers turn right up Coggers Lane (signposted Stanage Moor) and travel another 0.2 miles to the last house. Pull over and you are at the viewpoint; either looking through the gate looking down on the church or go down the footpath to Cliff Wood. You can also walk to Cliff Wood from Hathersage by a track that starts between Jaggers Lane and the George Inn.

Carrhead Rocks (page 266) is also a good place to photograph St. Michaels Church spire and the footpaths below this small gritstone edge.

Viewpoint 2 – Hoods Brook

Starting on the main road opposite Paul Bowyer's Butchers, take the footpath that follows Hoods Brook to an area of parkland dotted by trees. The best viewpoints are up on the slopes above the main path looking down on Hathersage. Best early, but you will be shooting into the sun.

Viewpoint 3 – Mitchell Field view of Hathersage

These viewpoints give great close-up compositions of Hathersage and beyond up the Hope Valley to Mam Tor. Mitchell Field is accessed by The Dale, the road that runs by the Scotman's Pack Inn to Stanage. The footpath starts at the bend a mile up School Lane/The Dale from Hathersage. Parking is problematic and you are best walking from a nearby lay-by or from the car park at Hook's Car. Walk down the track and take a right, once just past Mitchell Field farm go right on a footpath through the trees and across a field to Access Land moorland. The viewpoints looking down over Hathersage up the Hope Valley to Win Hill and Mam Tor are on the right by the wall, the higher you get, the better it gets.

There are also equally good viewpoints on the footpath that goes left/east from Mitchell Field farm up towards Higger Tor. This path and its great view – from the road is good too – can also be accessed from the parking for Higger Tor. The footpath heads down to the south west.

Viewpoint 4 – Hathersage Moor

Down the road from Higger Tor, where the Mitchell's Field footpath joins the road there is an excellent view overlooking Mitchell Field and down to Hathersage. Also go east from here, following another footpath onto Hathersage Moor. Here you will find some distinctive trees that are worth visiting at either end of the day.

Opposite top: Looking down on Hathersage and in the distance the cement works (VP3). Sony A6000, 18–200 at 43mm, ISO 100, 1/100s at f/10. Oct. © MR

Opposite middle left: From Coggers Lane looking down on Hathersage chiurch (VP1). Sony A6000, 18–200 at 32mm, ISO 100, 1/200s at f/11. Sep. © MR

Opposite middle right: On Hathersage Moor (VP4). Canon 5D Mk 1, 17-40 at 17mm, ISO 50, 0.8s at f/20. Jul. © CG

Hoods Brook (VP2). Canon 5D Mk 1, 17-40 at 20mm, ISO 50, 1/13s at f/20. Oct. © CG

How to get here

Hathersage is situated in the Derwent Valley, 10 miles from Sheffield on the A6187. The viewpoints are within a mile of the village.

Mitchell Field Parking Lat/Long: 53.333180, -1.630390
Parking Grid Ref: SK 247 818
Parking Postcode: S32 1AY (1 km)

Coggers Lane Parking Lat/Long: 53.333846, -1.661461
Parking Grid Ref: SK 226 819
Parking Postcode: S32 1EQ (1 km)

Hathersage Moor Parking Lat/Long: 53.331193,-1.624054
Parking Grid Ref: SK 251 816
Parking Postcode: S32 1EQ (1.3 km)

Accessibility ♿

These viewpoints are accessible for most. Mitchell Field involves a short uphill walk. The Coggers Lane and Hathersage Moor viewpoints can be photographed from your car.
Mitchell Field Approach: 10 minutes, distance 580m, ascent 10m
Coggers Lane and Hathersage Moor Approach: Roadside.

Best time of year/day

Autumn mornings at times of radiation fog when there are thin wisps of most lining the valley floor. You need a cold clear night with calm winds and high pressure for radiation fog in the valley. The sun needs a good hour after sunrise for these viewpoints to be illuminated.

A frosty, misty winter dawn on Higger Tor, looking toward a shrouded Carl Wark (VP1, p.272).
Canon 6D, 17-40 at 20mm, ISO 100, 1/20s at f/16, Grad. Jan. © CG

Higger Tor is one of the classic locations for landscape photography in the UK. From its small flat summit – at 434m it is higher than its immediate surroundings – it offers great viewpoints of the edges and moorland of the eastern Dark Peak, and down to the Hope and Derwent Valleys.

The classic subjects here are gritstone rocks, purple heather with green ferns and sweeping moorland that reach down to faraway valleys below moody skys. Higger Tor is good all year round, sunrise and sunset being the best times. The short cliffs on its east side are rare for grit edges in that they catch light directly from the rising sun. This location's ease of access makes it a good destination if time is limited.

What to shoot and viewpoints

From the lay-bys go through the gate on the east side of the road and follow a short inclined path to the small plateau. For the first viewpoint follow the path leftwards to rocks overlooking Carl Wark, the gritstone promontory down and to the south-east.

Looking toward the Hope valley. (VP3). Canon 5D Mk 1, 17-40 at 20mm, ISO 200, 1s at f/20. Dec. © CG

Viewpoint 1 – East Side

The rocks on the east side of Higger face the rising sun directly whereas most of the gritstone edges face south to southwest and don't get morning sun until later in the morning. This gives the opportunity to feature gritstone illuminated by sunrise. There are many distinct boulders here – some are concave and hold water, some look like like stacked books, the **Book Stones** – to use as foreground with the moorland sweeping down to Carl Wark and beyond. Also look out for paths that serve as leading lines. This is a great sunrise location.

Viewpoint 2 – East Side – Shelter Rock

Walking down from the first viewpoint you will encounter Shelter Rock a huge layered rock that forms a cave that you can walk through. This is an interesting photographic subject from several angles; good at sunrise anytime or later in the day, especially when the heather flowers in August. It is also a useful shelter if it starts to rain.

Viewpoint 3 – South Side and the leaning boulder

The south edge of Higger Tor is littered with rocks and boulders that catch low evening light and sunset in the winter. Below the footpath is a huge boulder with a tilted front face. This face catches winter sunset and it is worth exploring the moorland below for a suitable composition.

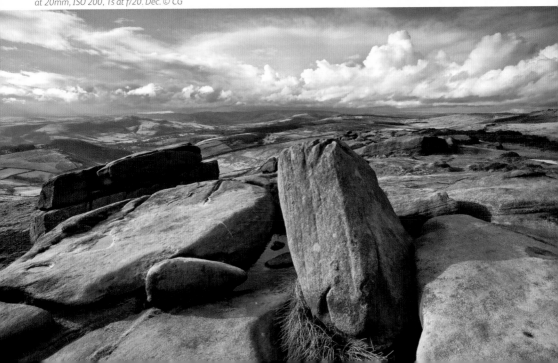

How to get here

Park in lay-bys either side of Ringinglow Road at the Higger Tor gate which is half-a-mile south of Upper Burbage Bridge or 1.5 miles up Ringinglow road from the A6187, the Hathersage to Sheffield road.

Higger Tor Gate, Ringinglow Road Parking Lat/Long: 53.337063, -1.616747
Parking Grid Ref: SK 256 823
Parking Postcode: S32 1BR)

Accessibility

Good paths and a short approach make this a very accessible location. It is wise to wrap up well in the autumn and winter. A good pair of walking shoes will suffice, or wellingtons if it has been raining – it can be very boggy on this moorland.
Approach: 10 minutes, distance 300m, ascent 10m.

Best time of year/day

The elevated cliff tops on Higger Tor which are the main viewpoints face east and south-west making this an ideal location for sunrise and sunset photography. Cotton grass and hare's-tail cottongrass arrive in June and July, purple heather, bilberries and green bracken in July and August and the rich colours of autumn in October and November. Winter can be drab but does bring dramatic skies and low celestial light which if combined with frost or snow is worth heading out for. In fact some say this is when Peak gritstone is at its best for photography as frost especially when combined with low winter light adds more texture and contrast to the land.

Above: *The Shelter Stone (VP2). Canon 5D Mk 1, 17-40 at 17mm, ISO 200, 0.5s at f/20. Sep. © CG*

Rock and pool at Higger. Canon 30D, 17-40 at 17mm, ISO 100, 2.5s at f/20. May. © CG

Gorgeous winter light on Hathersage Moor with the view from Carl Wark to Higger Tor (VP4, p.276).
Canon 6D, 17-40 at 20mm, ISO 100, 1/50s at f/14, Grad, Dec. © CG

6 BURBAGE VALLEY & MOOR

The Burbage Valley, lined by gritstone edges, runs from the north at Upper Burbage Bridge dropping 200ft to Lower Burbage Bridge in the south – which means it catches the low winter sun for most of the day. Subjects include the peaty-waters of Burbage Brook, the gritstone edge that lines the valley, Carl Wark – an old hill fort, views of Stanage and Higger Tor, an old bridge, scattered millstones and a quarry.

The area has recently undergone some thinning of its pine plantation and it is better for it; there are plans to plant deciduous trees here. On Burbage Moor, isolated gritstone tors and lonely trees provide photographic drama. Finally, just off Ringinglow Road is one of the best views of Sheffield's skyline from the Peak District.

What to shoot and viewpoints

Viewpoint 1 – Upper Burbage Bridge
Park at the main Burbage car park on the Stanage side. On the moor across the road from car park there is often an impressive display of cotton grass (June/July). This can work well at sunset shooting low at cotton grass level into the sun.

From here, and all along the Ringinglow Road, there are good viewpoints across the moorland to the rocky prominence of Stanage which is particular good when there is an impressive cloudscape.

This location is good just before sunset looking east to the west-facing gritstone edge of Burbage Rocks, then the

opposite at sunrise when the east facing cliff line in the west is lit up. This is a great stopping place to grab a shot if conditions are good.

Finally walk down to the old stone-arched bridge and the peaty-colored waters of Burbage Brook. This is the same brook that flows through Padley Gorge. A wide-angle lens and tripod are useful here to capture the small cascades, rocks and bridge.

Viewpoint 2 – Burbage Rocks East
On the eastern Sheffield side, by the smaller parking area is a path that follows the top of the edge. Walk along the top of the edge and look out for interesting rocks that look over dramatic views of moorland and a narrative that includes Higger Tor and Carl Wark; best either at midwinter dawn or a midsummer evening.

VP 3 – Packhorse Bridge & Burbage Brook
The valley is worth exploring using the green lane as an access point. The area is strewn with boulders and bracken and there is a network of paths. One subject is a single-arch stone packhorse bridge over Burbage Brook built around 1750 situated down from the elevated hill fort of Carl Wark. This area used to have a plantation of pine trees which were partially cleared in 2014.

Viewpoint 4 – Carl Wark
Carl Wark is a gritstone promontory possibly used as a hill fort in the Bronze or Iron Age sitting south east of Higgar Tor. There are two approach paths to Carl Wark, one from Higgar Tor and one from Lower Burbage Bridge in the south.

Looking at the Burbage Valley from the west path (VP1). Sony A6000, 10-18 at 10mm, ISO 100, 1/50s at f/9. Jan. © MR

A stone water trough below Carl Wark (VP4). Canon 6D, 17-40 at 20mm, ISO 200, 1/50s at f/14, Grad. Dec. © CG

The packhorse bridge (VP3). Canon 5D Mk 1, 17-40 at 20mm, ISO 100, 1/2s at f/20. Grad, Polariser. Jan. © CG

Walking to Carl Wark from either approach gives dramatic views and good compositions of Carl Wark in the surrounding landscape. If approaching from Higger in the north west, sunrise, early evening and sunset are the best times. If coming from Lower Burbage Bridge, sunrise and early morning are optimum. The summit plateau of Carl Wark is strewn with weather-eroded gritstone boulders which provide foreground subjects for landscape photographs of the surrounding land.

Viewpoint 5 – Burbage Quarry & Burbage East

Burbage Quarry is situated on the east side of the valley at its southern end and can be accessed by the green lane or by parking 200m up from the Fox House Inn on the Hathersage road toward Sheffield; take a path across moorland direct to the quarry if you park here. This is an elevated viewpoint with an interesting foreground – the quarry and natural rocks – with great views of the sweeping arc of the gritstone edge of the Burbage valley, >>

How to get here

At Upper Burbage Bridge on the Ringinglow Road there are two parking areas either side of the bridge and both are free. Approach along the A625 out of Sheffield and turn onto Ringinglow Road, Upper Burbage Bridge is 4 miles up this road . From Hathersage approach up The Dale road passing the Scotsman's Pack Inn or by going up the hill on the A6187 toward Surprise View/Millstone and taking a left at 1.2 miles from Hathersage, a 15 minute drive. At its southern end there is limited parking at Lower Burbage Bridge, and more extensive parking near the Fox House Inn.

Upper Burbage Bridge Parking Lat/Long: 53.342930, -1.611598
Parking Grid Ref: SK 259 829
Parking Postcode: S32 1BR

VP7 Sheffield View Parking Lat/Long: 53.354369, -1.573865
OS map co-ordinate: SK 284 842
Nearest Parking Postcode: S11 7TT

Accessibility

Some viewpoints are on or just off the road and are suitable for wheelchairs. Off the roadside the path running under the eastern edge, called the Green Lane, is well-maintained, wide but slightly inclined. On the moor the terrain is rocky, sometimes wet, with small drop offs. **Approach:** From roadside to a mile round trip.

Best time of year/day

Sunrise lights the eastern facing edge on the west side, sunset illuminates the western facing rocks on the east side. This area attracts stormy weather and good light can be experienced anytime on such days. Snow can hamper driving to Burbage, but if the roads are clear this location is worth a look. Burbage's best time is late afternoon in early winter when the sun shines straight into the valley.

Cotton grass along the Ringinglow Road (VP6). Sony A6000, 18–200 at 18mm, ISO 160, 1/160s at f/11. Jun. © MR

Viewpoint 6 – Cotton Grass and the Ox Stones on Burbage Moor

From Upper Burbage Bridge drive 1.2 miles toward Sheffield along Ringinglow Road – look out for cotton grass on the moors and solitary trees. Park in the lay-by on the left at the start of a plantation of pine trees. Opposite and south of the lay-by go through the gate and take the right hand path which after five minutes takes you to the Ox Stones, two wind-sculpted gritstone tors. A great sunrise/sunset location or on a winters afternoon when the sun is low.

Viewpoint 7 – A view of Sheffield

Close to the last viewpoint at the junction of Fulwood Lane and Greenhouse Lane, at the head of the Porter valley, there is a magnificent view of Sheffield and beyond including Ferrybridge and Drax power stations – if you look hard, with a spotter, you can also see York Minster in the distance. This location is marked by a toposcope (a marker showing points of the compass and notable landscape features that can be viewed from a vantage point).

To get here, go to the Norfolk Arms pub on Ringinglow Road and take Fulwood Road, a country lane, north for half-a-mile to the junction of Fulwood Lane and Greenhouse Lane where you can park by the toposcope. This is a great position to take a photograph of Sheffield's skyline on a moody or blustery day, or at night. You can walk here easily from the Ox Stones by crossing the road and walking across and down the moor on a footpath.

across to Carl Wark and Higger Tor which are presented as twin peaks, and in the south west, Over Owler Tor. There are a few scattered millstones below the quarry that are well worth looking for. Good at sunrise and sunset, but better on winter afternoons when the golden light can flood into the valley.

Down from the toposcope (VP6). Sony A6000, 18–200 at 32mm, ISO 100, 1/320s at f/10. Apr. © MR

Abandoned millstones below Burbage quarry (VP 5). Canon 5D Mk 1, 17-40 at 20mm, ISO 100, 1¼s at f/20, Grad, Dec. © CG

Stormy light and August heather near the top of Millstone Edge looking at Over Owler Tor (p.283).
Canon 5D Mk1, 17-40 at 20mm, ISO 200, 1/10s at f/20, Grad, Aug. © CG

If you were forced to choose only one Peak District photography location to visit then this is it. It has outstanding variety and easily identified subjects, great narratives, a short approach and is good all year.

Surprise View is the breathtaking view down the Hope and Derwent valleys as you turn the sharp corner down to Hathersage on the the A6187. This elevated moorland and its gritstone cliffs and tors has great photographic locations with views in all directions. Also, below the road, you have some of the most atmospheric woodlands in the Peak containing old millstones.

What to shoot and viewpoints

There are four footpaths that lead to the viewpoints from the Surprise View car park.

Viewpoint 1 – Surprise View

At the far end of the car park is a path signposted Surprise View. Go through the gate and follow the path (OK for wheelchairs) for 250m to a second gate and just beyond that is a bench and a fantastic view that encompasses the Hope Valley in the north west – including Kinder, Win Hill and Mam Tor – and the Derwent Valley in front of you stretching to the south west. This is a sunset or sunrise location using a wide angled lens with heather and rocks as foreground points, or zoom in for detail. Also consider a creative shot down by the road using its curve.

Viewpoint 2 – Millstone Edge

Millstone Edge or quarry has two main viewpoints to explore, the top of the quarry and the silver birches at the base of the quarry. Both are best accessed from the Surprise View viewpoint.

Silver Birches at the base of Millstone Edge

The approach to the quarry bottom is over the low wall and down a path from the Surprise View bench. Go right and along the old quarry track to the base of the quarry and stands of silver birch trees. This area is particularly good on a cold winters day with hoar frost.

The silver birch trees at Surprise View (VP5). Canon 5D Mk 1, 17-40 at 20mm, ISO 100, 1/20s at f/20, Grad. Jan. © CG

Stormy summer weather at Over Owler Tor looking at the Beehive and Mother Cap (VP4). Canon 6D, 17-40 at 20mm, ISO 200, 1/50s at f/13.Aug. © CG

Millstone Edge Top Path

The approach is the same as Surprise View but at the second gate go right and follow the path up the fence line to the highest point. There are several great compositions here. First shooting up the valley using the top of the quarry and purple heather as foreground subjects. Then looking over to jumble of rocks that is Over Owler Tor in the east with Stanage and Higger Tor to the north east in the background. These shots are best in August just before sunset or late afternoon in the winter. The following two viewpoints can be reached from the top of Millstone by a grassy path through the heather, or as described below direct from the car park.

Viewpoint 3 – Mother Cap

From the car park go through the gate just beyond the pay and display machine into the silver birches. Go steeply up the path over rocks then left at a path junction. Follow this path up to Mother Cap, the tallest solitary gritstone tor. In August there is purple heather as foreground but this is a good location year round, especially at sunset and sunrise.

How to get here

Surprise View is situated on the A6187 where Hathersage Road becomes Sheffield Road, 1.8 miles from Hathersage and 9 miles from Sheffield. Park in the Surprise View car park – charges from 10am until 6pm – near the sharp bend by the silver birch trees. Elevation here is 300m/1,000ft, Hathersage is at 140m/460ft.

Parking Lat/Long: 53.317417, -1.624215
Parking Grid Ref: SK 251 801
Parking Postcode: S32 2JA

Accessibility ♿

The approaches to the viewpoints are short (maximum 20 minutes). It is up hill to the top of Millstone Quarry and Mother Cap, and steeply downhill to Bolehill quarry and the base of Millstone. There is wheelchair access, although a bit rough, to the Surprise View viewpoint.

Best time of year/day

In July and August the heather's purple haze can be seen from miles around. The bell heather (Erica cinerea) flowers first in late July, followed by the common heather (Calluna vulgaris) and lasts usually into September, peaking in late August. Evenings are good for the top of Millstone Edge, sunrise and sunsets year round are best for the tors on the moorland and Surprise View. The woodlands, silver birch and ferns turn golden-brown in October. Winter frosts and misty mornings are a good time to visit Bolehill.

*Bolehill Quarry below Surprise View (VP6). Canon 5D Mk 1,
Canon 17-40 at 20mm, ISO 100, 1/4s at f/20. May. © CG*

Viewpoint 4 – Over Owler Tor and the Beehive

Continue past Mother Cap following the path up the hill.
On the left is a solitary beehive-looking low boulder which
receives side-lighting at sunrise in winter and warm
back-lighting at summer sunsets. The highest point at
Surprise View are the boulders and small cliffs of Over
Owler Tor (380m/1,250ft) just beyond the Beehive. One of
the best features is that Owler Tor has a double aspect,
offering views down both the Derwent Valley and up into
the Hope Valley, which gives excellent options for afternoon
and evenings all year. The views from here are expansive in
all directions and golden side light at sunset washes over
Carl Walk and Higger Tor in the northeast. In the early
morning walk 50m down from the rocks when Over Owler
Tor is lit up making a great composition looking back to
down to Millstone and the Hope Valley in the west.

Viewpoint 5 – Silver Birches

In autumn the silver birches with their oval golden leaves
near the Surprise View car park are worth exploring. Take
the path just beyond the pay and display machine and at
the path junction turn right and back down into the trees.
Below the moor and the road are two fine autumn
locations, Bolehill Quarry with its stand of silver birches and
millstones, and the more open Oxhay Wood that as well as
a fine selection of colourful trees, has great views up and
down the Derwent Valley.

Viewpoint 6 – Bolehill Quarry and Wood

Bolehill Quarry closed at the end of the first world war and
was rapidly colonised by white-stemmed silver birch trees
with their characteristic lenticellular bark. This stand of
graceful trees has a grass-covered old quarry track running
through it and a ruddish gritstone quarry with a pool at its
base. Old millstones are scattered throughout the area.

To get here walk out of the Surprise View car park
entrance, turn right and cross the road. Continue along the
narrow footpath by the road to just before the sharp right
bend. Take the footpath to your left, through a gate, then
right through another gate. Work your way down steeply
and leftwards (there are several paths) to the grass-
covered lane amongst the trees. This same spot can be
reached from below the sharp bend on the left at the start
of the old quarry track, a flatter approach.

Rather than pinpoint specific viewpoints this magical
location is left for self-exploration. It can be very special on
a cold autumn morning as the mist rises up from the valley,
or when the temperature dips below freezing. The first flush
of spring is also a great time to be here.

***Opposite top right**: Oxhay Wood (VP7) looking south. Sony
A6000, 10-18 at 18mm, ISO 200, !/125s at f/11. © MR*

Viewpoint 7 – Greenwood Farm & Oxhay Wood

At the bend in the road below Surprise View, just up the road from the Millstone Country Inn is a gated track that leads down to the 18th century Greenwood Farm and Oxhay Woods. There are various paths here. This is a great location in autumn for deciduous and pine tree photography, often with a base of bronzed ferns. Good views can be found here looking up and down the Derwent Valley, better first and last thing.

A Bolehill quarry and wood (VP6) selection. Autumn © CG

Burbage Brook drops steeply through Padley Gorge cascading over gritstone boulders forming peat-coloured pools making this oak and birch woodland one of the best locations to photograph waterfalls and cascades in the Peak District.

Autumn is quite magical here; orange and golden leaves litter the woodland floor and stream, moss-covered millstones lie next to Tolkienesque trees, paths lead up stone steps and over wooden bridges, fungi glisten in the dew as mist rises through the woods illuminated by the suns rays filtering down through the canopy.

What to shoot and viewpoints

Padley has a well maintained path that follows the brook. Photo viewpoints and subjects are many along this path and are described in general with one location pin-pointed.

Viewpoint 1 – The main cascades: Lower Padley

Park at Grindleford Railway Station and Cafe and walk down the road over the railway bridge to the footpath on the right and into the woods. The lower third of Padley has many accessible cascades and waterfalls to explore. Follow feint paths and keep low near the brook. A wide angle lens is useful and a tripod mandatory if you are taking photographs of the cascades. Take care with compositions to cut out distractions like stray twigs. A polarising filter will help reduce glare and enhance colour.

Viewpoint 2 – The Woods and millstones

Throughout the woods are old abandoned millstones which making intriguing subjects especially when covered with orange beech leaves. In early autumn, usually October, before the leaves fall the tree canopy is a kaleidoscope of autumn colours. The exact time this happens varies from year to year; use photographic social media to find out when the leaves are 'in'. Even after peak autumn, when the trees have shed their leaves, the colourful leaves that remain on the trees are more distinct. There is one particular millstone and tree that is worth searching out.

Viewpoint 3 – The Rock in the Tree

Either walk to the top of the gorge or park at the Granby Wood lay-by south of the National Trust's Longshaw and Eastern Moors visitor centre half-a-mile down the B6521 from the A6187.

Follow the path down into the woods passing a wooden bridge (itself a great photographic subject) and through the gate and just ahead of you is an abandoned millstone by an old beech tree with gnarled roots entwined around a gritstone boulder – a fitting photographic subject.

One of the most atmospheric photographs you can get in the woods is of early morning mist with shafts of light shining through the woods. If you have been out for a sunrise at a nearby location and there is mist about, head to Padley. Mist is common here in the autumn and rolls in from both higher and lower ground. Timing is crucial as the sun needs to be high enough to shine into the gorge of Padley.

The lower main cascades (VP1). Canon 6D, 17-40 at 20mm, ISO 100,3s at f/14. ND, Polariser. Nov. © CG

Above: A great sense of age in Padley Gorge (VP3). Canon 5D Mk 1, 17-40 at 20mm, ISO 100, 1/4s at f/20, Grad. Nov. © CG

Below: Misty early morning light in Padley Gorge (VP2). Canon 5D Mk 1, 17-40 at 20mm, ISO 100, 1/4s at f/20. Grad. Nov. © CG

Cotton grass on Totley Moss above Longshaw. Canon 5D Mk 1, Sigma 105mm, ISO 200, 1/1250s at f/3.2. Jun. © CG

Colours hanging on right into the early spring in Padley Gorge. Canon 6D, 17-40 at 20mm, ISO 50, 5s at f/14. Mar. © CG

Vibrant spring ferns in Padley Gorge. Canon 6D, 17-40 at 40mm, ISO 400, 1/125s at f/14. Jun. © CG

Tolkeinesque trees in Padley. Canon 5D Mk 1, 17-40 at 30mm, ISO 100, 1/4s at f/20. Grad. Nov. © CG

Longshaw Estate

Padley can be popular. A nearby alternative is to go for a walk around Longshaw Estate. Park at the Longshaw Lodge and National Trust visitor centre situated just off the A625 near The Fox House Inn. The few acres around the lodge are gently sloping and face west. Although not developed as parkland, this area has network of paths that explore moorland, fields and Granby Woods, a mainly deciduous woodland that offers some wonderful autumn colour.

Mist and beech trees at Longshaw Estate. Canon 5D Mk 1, 17-40 at 20mm, ISO 100, 1/4s at f/20. Grad. Nov. © CG

How to get here

Padley Gorge is situated off the B6521 just north of Grindleford and down from the Fox House Pub on the A6187 Hathersage to Sheffield road. Park at Grindelford station and cafe if you want to walk up Padley Gorge to the main cascade area. Or, if you want to walk down the gorge park at the Granby Wood lay-by south of the National Trusts Longshaw Visitor Centre half-a-mile down the B6521 from the A6187.

Grindelford Station and Cafe Parking Lat/Long: 53.306148, -1.626318
Parking Grid Ref: SK251789
Parking Postcode: S32 2HY (150m)

Accessibility

Most of the viewpoints of Padley Brook are less than fifteen minutes walk from either parking spot. Padley trail follows the Burbage Brook crossing it several times by wooden bridges. This is quite rough terrain in parts, with steep drop offs and is very slippy when wet. A good pair of stout shoes or boots are advisable and wellingtons can be very useful. Down by the water's edge, particularly on the east bank, there are many faint paths. Some of these are actually quite precipitous and need to be approached with caution. **Approach:** 5 minutes, distance 300m, undulating terrain.

Best time of year/day

Overcast days, misty days and sunny mornings in autumn (usually October and November) are the best times to visit. In the summer browns and greens dominate which is one reason why autumn is so important to Padley when the beech in particular adds nuggets of brilliant red to the beautiful water. Also, although shooting moving water on a sunny day is not usually good practice, with Padley it is a good thing to try because the reflection of a blue sky in the water brings the other end of the colour gradient into play. There are enough trees and twists in the gorge to create the required shadows for long exposures even when the sky is clear. Peak autumn is spectacular, but also later in autumn (late November) is very worthwhile when there are less leaves on the trees. Take a look when frosty or when snow covered and if you have caught sunrise nearby, head to Padley afterwards. Spring is also worthwhile when new leaves and flowers start to appear.

Panoramic views of the Eastern Edges from the summit of William Hill. Five image stitch. © CG

Above Grindleford, Sir William Hill Road leaves the B6001 Hathersage Road at the The Sir William Pub and gives access to several country lane, woodland and moorland locations that are worth exploring anytime of year. There are also great landscape compositions here looking at Surprise View and its tors, and more intimate views of Froggatt and Curbar Edges and the woodlands below.

What to shoot and viewpoints

Viewpoint 1 – Sir William Hill Road
The section of Sir William Hill Road near the described parking (it turns into Edge Road here) gives good viewpoints of Froggatt in the east and down the Derwent Valley which is illuminated after sunrise in autumn and the winter, and in the afternoon and at sunset for most of the year.

Viewpoint 2 – Eyam Moor
The best access point for Eyam Moor is at the described parking spot up the track at the sharp bend 1.2 miles up Sir Richard Hill Road from Grindleford. You can also access the moor from near Leam Farm on Leam Road, that approach is uphill, but is the easiest way to a small woodland rich with silver birch that abut the heather

moorland. There are two main footpaths that start from the unpaved road at the junction of Sir William Hill Road and Edge Road. One path diagonals down across the moor with great views to the east. Lower down there are some old stone gateposts and some mountain ash that bare red fruit in August. The heather is particularly beautiful here in August and is mixed with bilberry, bracken and mosses.

Eastern Edges Panorama
The other path traverses up across the moor for 600m to Rock Basin just below the radio tower at the summit of Sir William Hill (this point can be approached from that summit too). Here there are solitary trees, old shooting butts, walls and rocky outcrops and importantly, a complete panorama of the Eastern Edges.

Viewpoint 3 – Leam Road
Leam Road is a quiet country lane at the base of Eyam Moor accessed from Sir William Hill Road just after the bend after leaving Grindelford, or from just outside Hathersage on the B6001after the Plough Inn. This is a lovely lane to explore especially in autumn when the sun is filtering through the trees or even in low light.

On lower Eyam Moor (VP2). August. Sony A6000, 10-18 at 18mm, ISO 200, 1/200s at f/8. Jul. © MR

From Leam Road to the hills above Hathersage (VP3). Canon 6D, 17-40 at 20mm, ISO 100, 1/10s at f/14, Grad. May. © CG

How to get here

Sir William Hill Road can be accessed from Grindelford by taking the B6001 Hathersage Road and turning left up the hill at the The Sir William pub, or from Eyam by the steep minor road north out of the village; or by the Barrell Inn from Great Hucklow or Foolow. Parking can be found up the track at the sharp bend 1.2 miles from Grindelford next to the footpath for Eyam Moor.

Parking Lat/Long: 53.298594, -1.6646433
Parking Grid Ref: SK 224 780
Parking Postcode: S32 5QT (0.7km)

Accessibility ♿

Many of the viewpoints described here are roadside. If you venture onto Eyam Moor there is a short walk on good, but often wet, paths.

Best time of year/day

Heather time in August, autumn, spring and after snow are all great times to be here. The wider landscape compositions are better in October when there is more contrast with the emergence of autumn colours

Top: *Midsummer colours on Eyam Moor (VP2). Canon 5D Mk 1, 17-40 at 20mm, ISO 100, 1/10s at f/20, Grad. Aug. © CG*

Middle: *Stone gateposts on Eyam Moor (VP2). August. Canon 5D, 17-40 at 17mm, ISO 100, 1/30s at f/20, Grad. Sep. © CG*

Bottom: *Early morning on Eyam Moor (VP2). Canon 5D Mk 1, 17-40 at 20mm, ISO 100, 1/50s at f/20, Sep. © CG*

The eastern boundary of the national park follows a broad sweeping arc of millstone grit topped by flat moorlands and along its edge are steep cliffs that overlook the Derwent Valley with the rolling green hills of the limestone dales beyond.

It is hard to overstate the importance of this corner of the Peak District, both as a place to visit for a wander and as a source of inspiration for the photographer. Some of the vistas offered by this grand shelf of rock are among the best known and best loved Peak District views.

Footpaths course its length from Longshaw in the north to Baslow Edge and Chatsworth in the south. At Curbar Gap the path north along Curbar Edge and south along Baslow Edge has been upgraded and is quite accessible for people with limited mobility. Access Land and countless informal footpaths give the photographer access to all of the nooks, crannies, pinnacles and views here whose character changes constantly throughout the seasons.

There are bare, rugged cliffs and intimate copses, standing stones, millstones and characterful broken down walls. The trees sparkle with air frosts in the winter and then surrender to green as spring approaches. Summer heather splashes the moors with colour then the many warm hues of autumn are carried by the woodlands in the valleys below and the bracken that grows within them. The influence of the river Derwent is considerable. Throughout autumn, winter and spring it is possible to get superb dawn temperature inversions as the valley collects the cool, damp air along the river channel. Below the gritstone ramparts along the Derwent we describe a delightful river walk between Calver and Froggatt villages.

And it's not just the views. The gritstone edges are a post-industrial landscape and carry the scars of hundreds of years of quarrying. Now reclaimed and softened by nature these are some of the most important rock climbing locations in the world. On warm summer afternoons the light is in just the right position in the sky for sports photography.

Beyond the edges themselves the moors here are host to some great wildlife. Big Moor and Leash Fen in particular will interest the wildlife photographer with resident herds of red deer and regular visits by short-eared owls and barn owls.

Maps

- OS Explorer Map OL241 (1:25 000) The Peak District: White Peak Area

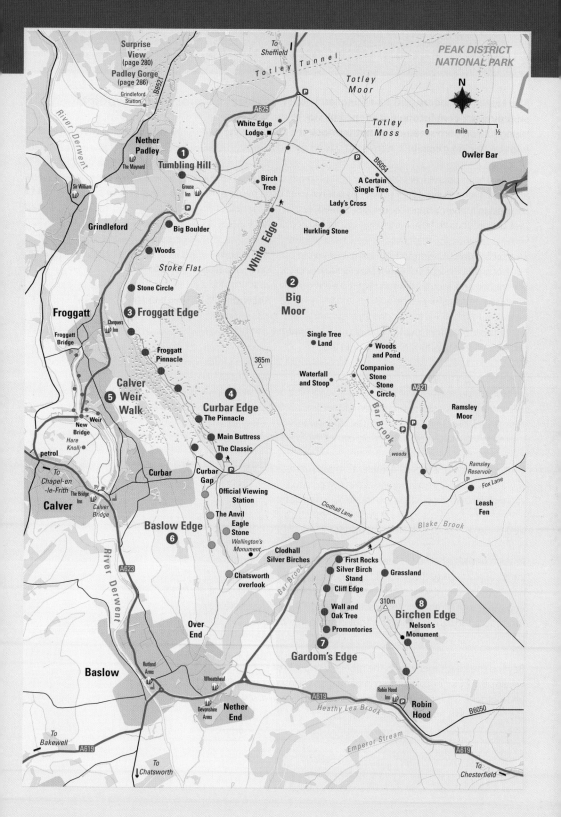

Surprise
View
(page 280)
Padley Gorge
(page 286)

Grindleford
Station

To
Sheffield

PEAK DISTRICT
NATIONAL PARK

N

Totley
Moor

Totley
Moss

Owler Bar

River Derwent

B6621

A625

White Edge
Lodge

B6054

0   mile   ½

Nether
Padley

The Maynard

1 Tumbling Hill

Grouse
Inn

Birch
Tree

A Certain
Single Tree

Sir William

Grindleford

Big Boulder

Lady's Cross

Hurkling Stone

Woods

White Edge

Stoke Flat

Stone Circle

2

Big
Moor

Froggatt

3 Froggatt Edge

Chequers
Inn

Single Tree
Land

Woods
and Pond

Froggatt
Bridge

Froggatt
Pinnacle

365m
△

Waterfall
and Stoop

Companion
Stone
Stone
Circle

A621

Ramsley
Moor

Calver
Weir
Walk

5

4

Bar Brook

Weir

New
Bridge

Curbar Edge

The Pinnacle

woods

Ramsley
Reservoir

Hare
Knoll

Main Buttress

Fox Lane

petrol

Curbar

The Classic

Leash
Fen

To
Chapel-en
-le-Frith

Curbar
Gap

Clodhall Lane

The Bridge
Inn

Calver

Calver
Bridge

Official Viewing
Station

Blake Brook

Baslow Edge

6

The Anvil
Eagle
Stone

Wellington's
Monument

Clodhall
Silver Birches

First Rocks

310m
△

8 Birchen Edge

Grassland

Silver Birch
Stand

Nelson's
Monument

River Derwent

A623

Over
End

Chatsworth
overlook

Cliff Edge

Wall and
Oak Tree

Bar Brook

Promontories

7

Baslow

Rutland
Arms

Wheatsheaf

Gardom's Edge

Robin Hood
Inn

Robin
Hood

B6050

Devonshire
Arms

Nether
End

A619

Heathy Lea Brook

To
Bakewell

A619

To
↓Chatsworth

Emperor Stream

A619

To
Chesterfield

Also known Jubilee Beacon, Tumbling Hill sits proudly on its own jutting out of the hillside looking down on the village of Nether Padley and the Derwent Valley.

Tumbling Hill's easily accessible summit is the top of an old quarry that has yet to be fully softened by the gradually encroaching countryside. The view to the north east up the Derwent Valley to the Hope Valley is spectacular. It is a similar view to that from the northern end of Froggatt but even more open. The encroaching slopes of Eyam Moor lose their dominance and summer evening light sweeps down the Derwent Valley here.

The approach to Tumbling Hill passes through some birch woodland; beautiful in the evening light.

From Tumbling Hill into the Hope Valley to the north. Canon 6D, 17-40 at 40mm, ISO 100, 1/4s at f/18. Dec. © CG

What to shoot and viewpoints

Walk 150m north of the Grouse Inn to a gate on the left just after a stone wall. Go through the gate and trend left through another gate by a National Trust sign (Jubilee Beacon). Follow the grass lane by the wall to Hay Wood. At the end of the wall continue straight on into the trees.

Viewpoint 1 – Hay Wood
This grove of birches catches the evening sun and its tightly packed trunks make interesting subjects at most times of year.

Viewpoint 2 – Tumbling Hill
Continue through the woodland onto open moorland and just beyond is Tumbling Hill, progress being stopped by the quarried cliff face. This is a great open viewpoint for landscape photography especially looking to the north west up the Derwent Valley and also north east toward Millstone Quarry, Surprise View and Higger Tor. Convenient and spectacular when the light is dramatic, even in midday sun in autumn or late spring.

How to get here
Tumbling Hill is situated 600m off the A625 north of Froggatt Edge near the Grouse Inn. Park just south of the Grouse Inn at the National Trust's Haywood car park. There is a spacious lay-bay on the A625 below the Grouse Inn from where Tumbling Hill is an easy walk. This road is very busy at times, take care.

National Trust's Haywood Parking Lat/Long: 53.296074, -1.6179299
Parking Grid Ref: SK 255 777
Parking Postcode: S32 2HX (0.7km)

Accessibility
The path to Tumbling Hill is flat but rough in parts.
Approach: 15 minutes, 600m, level

Best time of year/day
Because of its accessibility Tumbling Hill is worth a visit anytime of year when the light is good. Evening in the summer sees the light from the setting sun light up the valley below and the woodlands on the approach. Autumn is good when the bracken changes colour, and August when the heather flowers.

Above: *Dramatic summer light near the summit of Tumbling Hill. Canon 5D Mk 1, 17-40 at 20mm, ISO 100, 1/20s at f/20, Grad. Jul. © CG*

Below: *Frosty light in the old quarry below Tumbling Hill. Canon 6D, 17-40 at 20mm, ISO 100, 1/2s at f/14. Grad. Dec. © CG*

Leash Fen is at its best in autumn (p.303). Canon 6D, 70-300 at 300mm, ISO 100, 1/15s at f/14. Sep. © CG

The Eastern Moors is an area of 3,000 acres of moorland just outside of Sheffield. It is managed by the National Trust and the Royal Society For The Protection of Birds (RSPB) – the Eastern Moors Partnership. At an elevation of a thousand feet above sea level, Big Moor is an undulating area of acid grassland, heather, bracken, trees, and gritstone outcrops, with an attractive brook running through it. White Edge is a gritstone edge in the west where Big Moor slopes down to Froggatt and the Derwent Valley.

This area has a rich history. There is evidence of Bronze Age field systems, stone buildings, burial chambers and the remains of four stone circles. In the 13th century the area was used primarily as a route for packhorse trains carrying salt from the mines of Cheshire to towns east of the moor. In the 18th century an act of parliament decreed that routes over open countryside be marked with guide stones or guide stoops and there are many on Big Moor. These passage ways can still seen by linear depressions or 'hollow ways' across the moor.

Around this time the moor was used for millstone manufacture, lead smelting and corn milling using the power of Bar Brook and later a reservoir. In the 19th century, following the Parliamentary Enclosure Acts the area became part of the Duke of Rutland's grouse shooting estate. Today Big Moor can be enjoyed by all (visit-eastern-moors.org.uk).

What to shoot and viewpoints

WHITE EDGE

Viewpoint 1 – White Edge Lodge

The National Trust managed White Edge Lodge, an old gamekeeper's cottage, reminds some of the Burrow, the Weasley's house in Harry Potter, or to others, the Local Shop from the League of Gentlemen. It makes a great photograph on a stormy day or when the sun sets in the south west. From the lay-bys go through the white gate and down the lodge track to good viewpoints some distance from the house. You can continue on a footpath by the house to a junction of paths where you can turn left up a gully to a gate and the path that traverses White Edge.

The Lady Stone, an 11th century boundary stone (VP3). Canon 5D Mk 1, 17-40 at 20mm, ISO 100, 1/8s at f/20. Grad. Aug. © CG

The silver birch and White Edge (VP3). Sony A6000, 18–200 at 21mm, ISO 100, 1/60s at f/10. Oct. © MR

Viewpoint 2 – Walk along White Edge

From the lay-by, don't go through the white gate but through the adjacent kissing gate to a path that goes south across the moor above a pine plantation. Follow this path to breaks in the pines where there are good compositions across to Higger Tor. Better, is further along at a gate where the views open up down the Hope Valley to Mam Tor in the north west. If you go through the gate and turn left there are good viewpoints at the edge of the slope. There are many viewpoints on the edge and on the moor here.

Carry on along the moorland path toward White Edge until you come to an opening in a drystone wall.

Viewpoint 3 – The Birch

If you go right and follow the path down to the Grouse Inn (another access point to the moor) there are good viewpoints down to the valley below. Over to the right across the moor is a beautiful solitary silver birch and compositions close up in good light are worth exploring.

Viewpoint 3 – Hurkling Stone and Lady's Cross

This area is perfect for compositions showing the vastness of the moor perhaps using drystone walls, the Hurkling Stone and Lady's Cross, as subjects.

How to get here

Big Moor is situated east of Froggat Edge and just 5 miles drive west from Sheffield. It is enclosed by the Owler Bar Road/B6054/A625 in the west and the A625 in the east, with several lay-bys giving immediate road-side access.

White Edge: Park at the junction of Owler Bar Road/B6054/A625 at the start of the track to White Edge Lodge. There are several lay-bys here.

White Edge Parking Lat/Long: 53.306733, -1.598659
Parking Grid Ref: SK 268 789
Parking Postcode: S11 7TZ (1km)

Bar Brook: Park at one of two lay-bys on the A621 by a white gate 0.8 miles north of the junction of Clodhall Lane and the A621 Sheffield-Baslow road which is 2 miles south of Owler Bar. A concessionary bridleway starts on the west side of the road by a lay-by. This is a lay-by for Ramsley Moor opposite as well.

Bar Brook Parking Lat/Long: 53.272512, -1.579862
Parking Grid Ref: SK 281 751
Parking Postcode: DE45 1PR (2km)

Accessibility

You can venture just a few metres onto Big Moor or go for an all day walk covering several kilometres. This is a flat area with few inclines and good paths, although as this is Access Land you can go where you like. Once you venture off the paths the going gets tougher with thick bracken (wear over-trousers if it has been raining) and tussocky heather and grass. Wellingtons boots are recommended when the area is wet.

If you turn left along the broken drystone wall to its end there is a low gritstone rock, the Hurkling Stone. This rock is good for sitting on to eat sandwiches, sip tea and enjoy the view. Hurkling means crouching in Old Norse and this stone has no doubt been used to sit on since the Bronze Age people lived on the moor and later by shepherds whilst they were tending their flocks. The stone has many old carvings and stands at the junction of the present day parish and district boundaries.

Another, lower, drystone wall trails off to the north, if you go north west from the Hurkling Stone you will pick up a wheeled-track which is followed for around 500m and on your left is Lady's Cross on a mound. Lady's Cross is thought to be ancient boundary stone dating back to the eleventh century.

Viewpoint 4 – Further along White Edge

If you continue along the path from the drystone wall that runs along White Edge there several outcroppings that can be used as anchors in a composition looking westwards. These viewpoints lack the narrative of the lower gritstone edges being far from the Derwent Valley. They are at their best when there is a dramatic sky.

The path can be followed to White Edge summit (3.3km from the described parking) and onwards to Curbar Gap, a further 1.5km.

Viewpoint 5 – A Certain Silver Birch

There is a certain silver birch tree that is popular to photograph on Big Moor. It is situated south of the B6054 near Barbook Bridge.

BAR BROOK

Go through the white gate and follow the bridleway. On your left there is access to a grove of trees – oak, ash, alder, beech and birch – that runs down to Bar Brook. An ideal place for photographic studies of trees especially in autumn. Continue along the bridleway and 500m from the lay-by is one of the best preserved Bronze Age stone circles in the Peak District. Called Barbrook I it is just off the path with 12 or so stones with the most prominent in the south west.

A little further along the track is one of several companion stones in the Peak, modern stone sculptures with poetic inscriptions set next to old guide stoops. (www.companionstones.org.uk).

Continue on to a small Victorian reservoir surrounded by trees. This a delightful area in the autumn and spring or on a still summer day for reflections.

Continue a short way beyond the reservoir and cross a small stone bridge. Turn left and back by the reservoir and continue past it. On the horizon to the south west are numerous solitary and grouped trees, mainly silver birch; autumn and winter is the best time for photography.

Looking south west walking along White Edge (VP4). Sony A6000, 18–200 at 43mm, ISO 125, 1/320s at f/9. Nov. © MR

Walking to the Hurkling Stone (VP3). Sony A6000, 18–200 at 55mm, ISO 100, 1/250s at f/5.6. Nov. © MR

Above: *White Edge Lodge (VP1). Sony A6000, 18–200 at 86mm, ISO 200, 1/100s at f/10. Oct. © MR*

Below: *The track down to the Grouse Inn (VP3). Sony A6000, 18–200 at 24mm, ISO 100, 1/60s at f/11. Nov. © MR*

A red deer stag and hinds on Big Moor. Sony A6000, 18–200 at 179mm, ISO 400, 1/320s at f/8. Oct. © MR

Wildlife and Red Deer

Big Moor is home to a diverse community of animals and is a treat for those interested in wildlife photography. Key species include adders, grass snakes, lizards, curlew, buzzard, merlin, snipe, the elusive short-eared owl, woodpeckers and golden ringed dragonflies. It is best known however for its herd of red deer. Red deer are native to the Peak District and were common in Medieval times when they were hunted by nobility. They became extinct as a wild species in the 17th century due to deforestation, extreme winters and the enclosure act. There has however been a substantial herd at Chatsworth House since the early 15th century and escapees from this deer park now make up the wild population in the Peak.

As of 2015 there were 263 red deer on Big Moor. Controversially the herd will be managed to keep the numbers under 200 to prevent habitat damage. A healthy population of deer helps the ecology of the area, but with no predators, the numbers must be kept in check by periodic culling – the meat will be sold as it is at Chatsworth. The viewing of red deer is encouraged by the National Trust and RSPB who manage the area.

The deer can be photographed year round, but the best time is from late September until November when the stags rut for the attention of the hinds. Some say the roaring and grunting of the stags can be heard as far as way as Sheffield. As well as this primitive sound the stags display their dominance, often next to a group of hinds, by parallel walks as they assess each others size. A battle may then ensue with a clashing of antlers. These battles are dangerous and occasionally result in the death of one or even both stags.

The best times to photograph red deer on Big Moor is in the autumn rutting season at either end of the day. This is when the deer are at their most active with the added bonus of a low sun – good for silhouettes – and often morning mist. A lens with a focal length of 200mm or more is best and although a tripod is useful it is not essential (crank up that ISO). Wear brownish clothing, no perfume and don your wellingtons – it will be wet. You have a choice of routes to take across the moor – there are no guarantees as to where the deer will be and sometimes several visits are needed to get close. They are active all day long at this time of year.

Traversing along the path that runs along White Edge can be productive, either from the junction of Owler Bar Road/B6054/A625 or from Curbar Gap, or by following Bar Brook to the Victorian reservoir. A note of warning, don't get too close, the stags can be aggressive. If you are after silhouettes, the White Edge path is best in the morning shooting to the east, and approach anywhere from the east for sunset silhouettes. If you want to get close be prepared to crawl or find a spot and wait. The deer are very attentive and they will see you.

Leash Fen and Ramsley Moor

Leash Fen occupies a shallow basin of land in the hinterland of Big Moor, behind White Edge, and is bounded by Ramsley Moor in the north and Gardoms and Birchins Edges in the south. As the name implies it is a fairly damp place. Its swathes of long grass are dotted with silver birch trees. It is at its best in autumn when the cooling air collects in gentle drifts of mist that interact beautifully with the dawn light, creating some very atmospheric scenes.

Recommending a particular spot to aim for in the predawn gloom is problematic because the conditions will of course vary but Fox Lane in the area of SK288746 offers a good vantage point over the fen from which a quick assessment can be made. There are some nice solitary trees along here within close shooting distance of the road which can be incorporated in a composition. Similarly with Ramsley Moor, an opportunistic wander, the area is Access Land, can pay dividends.

A certain silver birch (VP5). Sony A6000, 18–200 at 110mm, ISO 200, 1/100s at f/10. Dec. © MR

Maples on Ramsley Moor, near Shillito Wood. Canon 5D Mk 1, 17-40 at 20mm, ISO 100, 1/10s at f/20. Grad. May. © CG

Leash Fen. Canon 6D, 70-300 at 140mm, ISO 100, 1/8s at f/14. Sep. © CG

Dawn light and late summer colours over Froggatt Edge (VP4). Canon 6D, 17-40 at 20mm, ISO 100, 1/20s at f/13. Sep. © CG

Froggatt Edge juts its gritstone nose out into the Derwent Valley above Grindelford and Froggatt villages. Although contiguous with its neighbour Curbar Edge, Froggatt presents the photographer with some compositional conundrums. The Derwent Valley here is quite narrow and the vistas are cramped by the edge of Eyam Moor, which rises steeply to the west. There is also currently active quarrying on the edge of Eyam Moor that the photographer will want to avoid. Without the big vista to resort to Froggatt's secrets lie in the views along it.

What to shoot and viewpoints

From the lay-by on the A625 walk with care down the road (narrow path on left) and through the white gate on the left.

Viewpoint 1 – Big Boulder

Just after the gate and around the corner there is a low boulder on your right. For the agile the top of this boulder gives a great view looking over trees up the Derwent Valley.

Viewpoint 2 – The Woods

The first half a mile is through silver birch woodland following the path. Autumn with its low light and the golden leaves of the silver birch are a great time to visit, as is later in the autumn and the winter when the white trunks and red branches are at their most distinctive.

Viewpoint 3 – The Stone Circle and Stoke Flat

Once through a gate and over a stream, at the edge of the wood as you enter open moorland on the left is an ancient circle of 11 stones. Whilst not particularly photogenic, in good light the creative can make something of this. Look out for isolated groups of silver birch on the heath of Stoke Flat which stand out in stormy 'sunny' weather.

Viewpoint 4 – Cliff Top

Even though Froggatt is at an elevation of 300m it has restricted vistas because of the narrowness of the Derwent Valley at this point. As you walk along the cliff top path a number of interesting subjects are encountered that can be focussed on or included in a composition running along the cliff top. Look out for sculpted boulders that sit at the top of the cliff and water pools formed in depressions in the rock. Parts of the cliff jut out and these are good vantage points to take photographs of the cliff as it is warmly lit by the evening sun. This area is popular with climbers and there are over 200 named rock climbs here, one to look out for is Froggatt Pinnacle, a free-standing pinnacle of rock, and a very popular climb. When taking photographs of climbers look out for interesting body positions and choose the most colourful climbers to contrast with the grey rock.

The remains of a stone circle in morning frost (VP3). Canon 5D Mk 1, 17-40 at 20mm, ISO 100, 1/6s at f/20. Grad. Feb. © CG

How to get here

Froggatt Edge can be accessed from Curbar Gap with a walk north of just over a mile along Curbar's summit path. More conveniently, park at the National Trust's Hay Wood car park on the A625 below the Grouse Inn or at the lay-by on the bend by the entrance to Froggatt. The white gate to the path along the top of Froggatt is on the bend below the lay-by.

National Trust's Hay Wood Parking Lat/Long:
53.296074, -1.6179299
Parking Grid Ref: SK 255 777
Parking Postcode: S32 3ZJ

Accessibility ♿

The path along the top of Froggatt is level and broad and is suitable for wheelchairs. To take in all the edge it is a 2 mile round trip if you retrace your steps.
Approach to Froggatt Pinnacle: 30 minutes, 1.25km, ascent 17m

Best time of year/day

Froggatt Edge faces west and south west so it gets sun for most of the day, apart from sunrise in the summer. Morning and evening are best in the summer .

Top: Looking south. Canon 6D, 17-40 at 17mm, ISO 100, 1/6s at f/14. Sep. © CG

Middle: Looking north to Froggatt pinnacle (VP4). Canon 6D, 17-40 at 20mm, ISO 100, 1/6s at f/14. Grad. Sep. © CG

Bottom: The cliff bottom path. Canon 5D Mk 1, 17-40 at 17mm, ISO 800, 1/25s at f/20. Grad. Jul. © CG

Curbar Edge's proximity to a good car park make it a first choice destination for many photographers. Its popularity is due to more than just ease of access however. It is a fine viewpoint with lots of classic Peak District compositions, it is good for both morning and evening photography and a great place from which to witness the many Derwent Valley misty temperature inversions that characterise spring and autumn. If you're lucky and early enough you may encounter some of the red deer that roam Big Moor behind the cliff edge.

The gentle south-facing inclination of the first section of cliff top and the open aspect of the Derwent Valley it looks onto offer the easiest compositions but exploration to the north of this point yields its own rewards. Like Baslow Edge, large stretches of Curbar Edge have been made accessible and with some assistance a wheelchair user can gain access to the initial viewpoints.

What to shoot and viewpoints

From Curbar Gap car park, follow the path behind the car park; this path is joined by another path that starts opposite the Baslow path. They join at a gate where there is a short ramped incline for wheelchair users. Once through the gate you are on the main path that follows the cliff top of Curbar all the way to Froggatt Edge.

Viewpoint 1 – The Classic

Almost immediately when you are through the gate head left on a small path to the cliff edge and slope. The cliff is here is small and intermittent. Looking back toward Baslow Edge there is a lovely composition of a gate, drystone wall, two trees and a bench. Once at the cliff edge the view is impressive, there are three narratives: up and down the Derwent valley and the village of Baslow; and out west to the rolling fields and dales of the White Peak. The initial cliff top offers you boulders and platforms of rock that extend like fingers out to the valley. This is a great location at sunrise and especially when the valley is filled with mist. Just below the cliff top, at a depression there are some millstones, this is also a great autumn spot to include the birches below the steep buttress in the distance.

Viewpoint 2 – Main Buttress

Continue along the cliff edge to a prominent buttress that protrudes outwards; it has a profile from this angle that looks like a lizards mouth. The top of this buttress, which is the highest part of the cliff at Curbar, is a large flat platform. Compositions here include both to the south, west and as the valley opens up, to the north.

Looking south toward Baslow Edge (VP1). Canon 6D, 17-40 at 40mm, ISO 100, 1/4s at f/20. Grad. Nov. © CG

Above: *A Peak District and Curbar classic (VP1). Canon 5D, 17-40 at 20mm, ISO 100, 1/4s at f/20. Grad. Nov. © CG*

Below: *Sundown at the Main Buttress (VP2). Sony A6000, 18–200 at 105mm, ISO 100, 1/200s at f/9. Jun. © MR*

Viewpoint 3 – The Pinnacle and Millstones

Walk a little further north from the main buttress. Whilst you won't want for foreground subject matter here, just beyond the main buttress are two striking foreground subjects, a small detached pinnacle and some millstones that lend themselves to a composition looking to the south especially around sunset when they are often illuminated by golden side light. Better in autumn and winter.

Viewpoint 4 – Cliff Faces and Big Moor

If you walk beyond the pinnacle and look south (from where you came) there are sections of the cliff that you can view that provide side-foreground subjects to a grand landscape composition. Also from the main path here look east over moorland grasses and heather to White Edge. Also you can descend here to the base of the cliff for different perspectives.

Viewpoint 5 – A Bit Further

If you continue another ten minutes beyond the pinnacle there are more pinnacles, boulders and cliff that juts out, to explore. Once the path starts to descend you start to approach Froggatt Edge.

Viewpoint 6 – Below The Edge

There is a climbers path that traverses the base of the cliff and this is worth exploring for compositions and for close up shots of the highly textured rock. The main buttress (viewpoint 2) of Curbar is illuminated at sunset most of the year and can be photographed from the boulder-covered slope below it or from road, best in autumn when the bracken and silver birches change colour.

More formations along the Edge (VP5). Canon 5D Mk 1, 17-40 at 17mm, ISO 50, 1.6s at f/20. Grad. Jul. © CG

How to get here

Curbar Edge is situated above the villages of Calver and Curbar. Parking is at a National Trust pay and display car park at Curbar Gap (the same parking as for Baslow Edge) accessed via a minor road above the village of Curbar, and a mile west of the A621 Sheffield Road. Curbar is 13 miles from Sheffield centre, 6 miles from Hathersage and 35 miles from Manchester. As well as the pay and display car park there is also limited free parking in lay-bys down the hill toward Curbar village.

Parking Lat/Long: 53.268654, -1.6101252
Parking Grid Ref: SK 261 747
Parking Postcode: S32 3YR (0.4km)

Accessibility ♿

The main path is level, but once off this path the going is a little rougher. There are steep drop offs, careful when near the cliff edge. Wear walking shoes or studied wellingtons when conditions are wet. The first half-a-mile of the main path is suitable for wheelchair users, with a short ramped incline at the first gate.
Approach: 20 minutes, distance 1km, ascent 19m.

Best time of year/day

This is a location for any season; August provides vibrant purple heather, in autumn the ferns and trees turn golden brown, winter can shroud the area in snow and spring brings new life and greenery. Both sunset and sunset are the prime times to visit Curbar. From autumn to early spring morning radiation fog is common in the valley below Curbar; watch out for clear, still nights with rapidly decreasing temperatures to catch these 'cloud inversions' which can be spectacular.

Rock striations (VP2). Canon 5D Mk 1,17-40 at 20mm, ISO 100, 1/6s at f/20. Grad. Nov. © CG

Above: *Along the Edge are millstones and a pinnacle (VP3). Canon 5D Mk 1, 17-40 at 20mm, ISO 100, 1/4s at f/20. Grad. Nov. © CG*

Below: *Under the cliff (VP6). Canon 6D, 17-40 at 20mm, ISO 100, 1/13s at f/14. Grad. © CG*

Froggatt Bridge from the west bank. Sony A6000, 10-18 at 10mm, ISO 125, 1/50s at f/6.3. Oct. © MR

Between Calver and Froggatt villages is a beautiful walk by the river Derwent. Surrounded by a variety of trees, when the Derwent slows and the wind drops this location is perfect for reflections. Along the way there is an old mill, a grade II listed weir, three bridges, a wetland habitat, all with good views up to Curbar Edge; perfect for an autumn or spring morning stroll with your camera.

What to shoot and viewpoints

You can park at either of the three bridges and just take a brief walk if conditions are favourable or, described are a short and a long circular walk.

New Bridge to Froggatt Bridge Loop (1 mile/1.6k)

Park at New Bridge on the A625. Nip down to the weir on the east bank for reflections in the weir pool, especially of Shuttle House on the opposite bank. Compositions can be good from the bridge itself in both directions but especially up to Curbar Edge over the weir.

Take the path north of the road on the east bank, here there are gaps in the trees to take photographs of reflections and waterfowl. This path takes you to Froggatt bridge and village. At Froggatt cross the bridge and go through a gate, here you can get below the 17th century bridge with its two different arches. Return on the west bank path which is more overgrown and is ideal for studies of trees and shrubs. As you approach New Bridge and go over a small wooden bridge you are in the midst of Stoke Brook marsh which is home to the rare brook lamprey, a primitive fish that looks like a small eel. They are best seen at breeding time between March and June when they gather on gravel beds in large numbers to build nests and lay eggs.

Just beyond the marsh there are good viewpoints for photographs of New Bridge with Curbar Edge and its woods in the background. This walk is the best option for interesting photography.

From the east bank walking toward Froggatt Bridge. Sony A6000, 10-18 at 10mm, ISO 100, 1/25 at f/9. Oct. © MR

How to get here

The village of Calver is at the junction of the A623, A635 and the B6001, 4 miles south of Hathersage. Either park at New Bridge on the A625 for the short walk (the road that goes below Froggatt Edge to Sheffield) or near Calver Bridge in Calver village for a longer walk.

New Bridge Parking Lat/Long: 53.274709, -1.6355467
Parking Grid Ref: SK 244 753
Parking Postcode: S32 3XT

Calver Bridge Parking Lat/Long: 53.266849, -1.6322958
Parking Grid Ref: SK2 467 44
Parking Postcode: S32 3XA (40m)

Accessibility &

This a riverside walk on good paths. North of New Bridge on the east side is suitable for wheelchairs.
Approach: Roadside, short walk 1.6k, longer walk 3.6k

Best time of year/day

The river flows from north to south and is in shade at sunrise due to the escarpment to the east. The best times are a couple of hours after sunrise at most times of year, and a couple of hours before sunset. Autumn is particularly beautiful. Steaming river mist (evaporation fog) first thing is common here, especially at the weir.

*Opposite left: Shuttle House near Calver Weir.
Canon 6D, 70-300 at 70mm, ISO 100,
1/50s at f/11. Oct. © CG*

Calver Bridge to Froggat Bridge Loop (2.2 mile/3.6k)

Park at Calver Bridge and take the small road that leads to Calver Mill (the mill is private). Go to the end of the road and into a field to the farm and through the gate. Head right to the river and the goit, an artificial channel, and views of the river. One diversion here is to ascend Hare Knoll by a path up the green fields to the west where there are good compositions up to Curbar Edge. The river path takes you down a delightful wooded path to the Shuttle House and New Bridge. From here you can continue up the shorter loop to Froggatt Bridge. Return by the weir on the east bank by a path that stays close to the river until it emerges on Dukes Road where there is a good view of Calver Mill across the river and back to Calver Bridge where there is a cafe.

Opposite right: Looking over Calver Weir from Calver Bridge toward Curbar Edge. Canon 6D, 70-300 at 120mm, ISO 100, 1/2s at f/14. Oct. © CG

Baslow Edge is separated from its bigger and more popular neighbour Curbar Edge by Curbar Gap. The view to the north toward Curbar is outstanding with characterful rock structures for foreground and colourful heather in August. Further to the south is the Eagle Stone and an attractive silver birch woodland. Baslow Edge is noteworthy for its ease of access, the southern viewpoint that looks down to Chatsworth is accessible by wheelchair. Look out for the Highland Cattle here.

What to shoot and viewpoints

From the pay and display car park at Curbar Gap cross the road and take the broad path westward toward a gate and two trees. Go through the gate and take the path that follows the wall (wheelchair accessible). At 400m take a right fork to an official viewing station (viewpoint 1) with an interpretive sign overlooking the cliff with the whole of the northern Derbyshire Dales stretching out before you. This broad path continues along the wall to the Eagle Stone.

Viewpoint 1 – Official Viewing Station

The official viewing station and locations beyond it provide great viewpoints for panoramic images looking across to Curbar Edge in the north and the limestone dales and hills in front of you. Good at anytime of year, autumn is very special when the bracken and leaves turn to gold. Early winter mornings when valley fog starts to lift are also special as our summer evenings at sunset. This is a place for a quick hit if conditions are good and you are nearby.

From the official viewing station follow a rocky path along the cliff edge.

Viewpoint 2 – The Anvil and other formations

After around ten minutes walking along the cliff edge – just beyond a rock free patch of cliff top – you will arrive at an area with many small boulders on the cliff top. The most distinct is a head-height tall boulder shaped like an anvil which is perched right on the edge of the cliff, a bit further along. In this area there is also a rock that from some angles looks like a turtle. At sunrise and sunset these rocks catch the light, as do most of the cliff top rocks. Look out for man-made water troughs or sheep feeds that are carved into boulders, there are at least two of them here. Most of these features can be used as foreground subjects.

The Anvil (VP2). Canon 6D, 17-40 at 17mm, ISO 400, 1/125s at f/14. Apr. © CG

*Opposite: Very close to the viewing station (VP1). Canon 5D Mk1,
17-40 at 20mm, ISO 100, 1/2s at f/20. Grad. Aug. © CG.*

Higland cow in the Clodhall silver birches (VP5). Sony A6000, 18–200 at 22mm, ISO 400, 1/100s at f/9. Apr. © MR

***Opposite**: The last glow at the end of Baslow Edge (VP2). Canon 5D Mk 1, 17-40 at 20mm, ISO 100, 1/20s at f/20. Grad. Mar. © CG*

Viewpoint 3 – Chatsworth House Overlook

Walk along the cliff edge to its end – to the Loaf Stone – and head left to the main path where it splits (there is a stone cross, Wellington's Monument, on the left fork). Head down right to a bench and magnificent views down the Derwent Valley to Chatsworth House and its Capability Brown designed estate. Late summer and autumn morning mists are best here. Also go down the lane to near a gate for more tremendous viewpoints.

Viewpoint 4 – Eagle Stone

The large boulder by the main path on the moorland is known as the Eagle Stone, a popular rock climbing boulder. In days gone by the bachelors of Baslow village had to climb this rock before they got married. This boulder makes an interesting subject especially if combined with the foreground grasses and heather.

Highland Cattle

This area is used for grazing by Highland cattle and they make a unique subject to photograph with their golden coats and large horns. Approach them slowly and you may get lucky with a unique portrait of these wonderful beasts. It is not a good idea to have a dog with you as the cattle may get aggressive.

Viewpoint 5 – The Clodhall Lane Silver Birches

At the southern end of Baslow Edge is a dense wood of silver birches which are well worth a visit for their twisted silver trunks and branches contrasting with bracken and moss-covered rocks. You can approach them from Baslow Edge by following the path by the Wellington's Monument (the stone cross), the woods will be on your right.

Alternatively; from the pay and display car park at Curbar Gap drive east toward Sheffield down Clodhall Lane to just before A621 (Sheffield Road). There is limited free parking by a gate, don't block the gateway. Go through the gate and follow the furrowed track, eventually along a stone wall and passing an old stone sign and a small modern sculpture to the birches.

Opposite middle: Down toward Chatsworth Estate (VP 3). Sony A6000, 18–200mm at 20mm, ISO 100, 1/100s at f/9. Sep. © MR

How to get here

Baslow Edge is situated above the villages of Baslow and Curbar, and is accessed from a National Trust pay and display car park at Curbar Gap situated off a minor road above the village of Curbar, a mile west of the A621 Sheffield Road. There is also limited free parking in lay-bys down the hill toward Curbar.

National Trust's Haywood Car Park Lat/Long: 53.269436, -1.608036
Parking Grid Ref: SK 262 747
Parking Postcode: S32 3YR

Accessibility ♿

There is wheelchair access at this location on the level path that parallels Baslow Edge back from the cliff top and along a side path that leads to the first viewpoint.
Approach (to end of the edge): 20 mins, distance 1km, ascent 0m

Best time of year/day

Baslow faces due west and the setting sun can pour glorious golden light on the cliff all year round. It gets early light in the winter when the sun rises in the south east. If there is snow or a storm this is a great place to be. First thing in August when the heather blooms is the best time in the summer. Autumn through to spring can bring valley fog. When overcast or misty, especially just after sunrise, try the Clodhall Lane silver birches.

Fields near Baslow from VP3. Canon 6D, 70-300 at 277mm, ISO 400, 1/30 at f/16. Oct. © CG

Until recently Gardom's Edge was difficult to access before the CROW act of 2000 opened up its viewpoints and now its features are easy to access. Along the edge itself there are many rocky subjects including pinnacles, standing stones and erratics. There is a silver birch woodland that blends with large areas of heather, dotted with large, speckled rocks and lime green drifts of moss. One of its strengths is the impressive view across the valley to the birch woodland of Jack Flat and Clodhall.

The view from the north end is somewhat cut-off by southern end of Baslow Edge but at its southern end the views open out over Baslow to Chatsworth and beyond. Needless to say there is something to shoot here at any time of year and at any time of day.

What to shoot and viewpoints

Park in lay-bys near the junction of Clodhall Lane/Sheffield Road/A621. At the road junction go through the gate on the south side of Clodhall Lane. The path forks immediately, left goes to Birchen Edge, head right following a path across the moorland to Gardom's Edge toward some rocks on the edge of the valley slope.

Viewpoint 1 – First Rocks

Walk across the moorland to a jumble of boulders that sit above the road. Viewpoints from here include looking back in the direction you came to the curve of the Sheffield road and also looking across the wooded valley. The first jumble of rocks is worth exploring in the autumn as it is rich in colour and contrast, and has some lovely trees on its rocks.

Viewpoint 2 – Silver Birch Woodland

After the rocks go through a gate to a delightful stand of silver birch trees. The woodland floor has a colourful mix of small moss-covered boulders and heather. These trees are backlit at and near sunset. This is a great spot to visit when it is very misty.

Viewpoint 3 – Valley Sides and the Cliff Edge

As you continue along the path you begin to follow the edge of the cliff. Below the cliff and on the other side of the valley toward Baslow Edge are thick stands of silver birch and oak trees that obscure the road. This ancient woodland, known as Jack's Flat, provides many great compositions in the autumn, winter and spring. The cliff top is useful to position a tripod.

Viewpoint 4 – Drystone Wall and Old Oak Tree

As you continue you pass a drystone wall and an old oak, fitting subjects.

Viewpoint 5 – Rock Promontories

The cliff curves around and the views into the Derwent Valley open up. There are some rock promontories that extend from the main rock face and make good viewpoints down to the village of Baslow and the rural valley below.

Opposite top: The tors at the northern end of Gardoms Edge (VP1). Canon 6D, 17-40 at 20mm, ISO 100, 1/20s at f/14. Sep. © CG

The southern end of Gardoms Edge (VP5). Canon 30D, 17-40 at 20mm, ISO 200, 1/4s at f/13. Grad. Aug. © CG

Approaching Gardom's (VP1). Sony A6000, 18–200 at 20mm, ISO 100, 1/100s at f/9. Oct. © MR

How to get here

Gardom's Edge sits in front of Birchen Edge above the village of Baslow. Park in lay-bys near the junction of Clod Hall Lane/Sheffield Road/A621 (2 miles up the Sheffield Road from Baslow village) as for the northern approach for Birchen. You can easily combine a visit to Gardom's and Birchen by walking between the two across the moorland to the north of Birchen.

Clod Hall Lane/Sheffield road/A621 Parking Lat/Long: 53.262544, -1.585419
Parking Grid Ref: SK 277 740
Parking Postcode: DE45 1PR (1.2km)

Above: The oak tree (VP4). Canon 5D Mk 1, Canon 17-40 at 20mm, ISO 100, 1/60s at f/20, Grad. Mar. © CG

Accessibility

The path to Gardom's crosses sometimes boggy moorland to a good path along the top of the cliff top. It is half a mile to the top of the edge. **Approach:** 15 minutes, distance 0.7km, ascent 7m.

Best time of year/day

Facing west Gardom's is lit up by the setting sun for most of the year. Until late autumn morning sun shines down the wooded valley of Bar Brook below the crag. Autumn is the best time for the silver birches and colourful bracken, and also coincides when morning mist fills the valley.

Above: The back of Gardoms Edge adjacent to Leash Fen. Canon 6D, 17-40 at 20mm, ISO 100, 1/20s at f/14. Grad. Sep. © CG

Birchen Edge looks westward toward the north end of Chatsworth Park and to the south is the expanse of East Moor. This cliff features Nelson's Monument, an attractive slender column placed to commemorate the Royal Navy's and Admiral Lord Nelson's victory at Trafalgar (1805), while three large rocks sitting just back from the edge have the names of three of Nelson's ships - Victory, Defiance and Royal Soverin (sic) carved into them.

The Three Ships have limited photographic potential but the position of the column toward the front of the edge mean that it presents itself as a good compositional figure at both ends of the day. Below the edge there is a beautiful stand of silver birch trees, which offer superb autumn colour. Approaching from the north (Clodhall Lane/Sheffield Road) you pass through through an old field system that is now thick with moorland grass with singular and groves of trees.

What to shoot and viewpoints

Two approaches are described as they both have good photographic potential.

Viewpoint 1 – The Grassland from Clodhall Lane/Sheffield road/A621

Park in lay-bys near the junction of Clodhall Lane/Sheffield road/A621. At the road junction go through the gate on the south side of Clodhall Lane. The path forks immediately, right goes to Gardom's Edge, head left following a path across the moorland toward Birchen Edge. This moorland grassland location is good when the weather is changeable or at anytime when there is a moody sky which can be combined with stands of birches or individual trees. Follow the path through the trees in the distance to the base of Birchen Edge where you can access the cliff top by a diagonal path up the slope.

How to get here

Birchen Edge has a commanding position at an elevation of 300m between the A619 and the A621 above Baslow. There are two approaches, both just over half a mile from car to the top of the cliff. For an approach through the trees park at the pay and display car park just above the Robin Hood Inn off the A619 Chesterfield Road 1.8 miles from Baslow (please don't use the pub car park). To approach through the moorland grassland to the north, park in lay-bys near the junction of Clodhall Lane/Sheffield Road/A621.

Clod Hall Lane/Sheffield road/A621 Parking Lat/Long: 53.262544, -1.585419
Parking Grid Ref: SK 277 740
Parking Postcode: DE45 1PR

Robin Hood Inn/A619 Parking Lat/Long: 53.245804, -1.580784
Parking Grid Ref: SK 280 721
Parking Postcode: DE45 1PU

Accessibility

The paths are well maintained but rocky and rough in parts with some short inclines. After rain the terrain can get very boggy.
Clodhall Lane Approach to Nelson's Monument: 30 minutes, distance 0.7km, ascent 43m
Robin Hood Inn Approach to Nelson's Monument: 30 minutes, distance 1km, ascent 71m

Best time of year/day

Late evening and sunset is a favourite time to visit Birchen Edge when it can be awash with golden side light. Late summer, autumn and spring are the best seasons.

The silver birch below Nelson's monument (VP3). Canon 5D Mk 1, 17-40 at 20mm, ISO 100, 1/4s at f/20. Grad. Apr. © CG

Hood Inn off the A619 Chesterfield Road 1.8 miles from Baslow. Walk out the car park and turn left and just beyond the Robin Hood Farm B&B go through the gate and follow the path up steps along the wall into the woodland (good in autumn). Further along the path are good views up the bracken slope through the trees to the cliff.

You have two choices to reach the top of the edge. Two hundred metres from the gate is a steep path that leads to moorland on the cliff top, or continue on the main path to below Nelson's Monument at the main cliff. There are two paths that lead through rocks to the cliff top.

Viewpoint 3 – The Cliff Top

The top of Birchen Edge provides commanding views looking down onto drystone walls and a farm. In the distance East Moor gets the best light in the evening. Then there is Nelson's Monument itself a 2m high slender stone monument topped by an orb. The monument makes a striking subject both in the morning and at sunset. North of the monument is a trig point, the actual summit of Birchen, from here there are interesting compositions that include the moorland and the snaking line of Sheffield road.

Opposite: *Nelson's Monument (V3). Canon 5D Mk 1, 17-40 at 25mm, ISO 100, 1/10s at f/20. Grad. Apr. © CG*

The grassland on the approach (VP1). Sony A6000, 18–200 at 20mm, ISO 100, 1/100s at f/9. Sep. © MR

Below Birchen Edge. Canon 5DMk 1, 17-40 at 20mm, ISO 100, 1/10s at f/20. Grad. Apr. © CG

Evening light in Tideswell Dale (page 348).
Canon 6D, 17-40 at 20mm, ISO 100, 1/40s at f/13. Sep. © CG

DERBYSHIRE DALES

Wrapped in the arms of the embracing grit of the Dark Peak is the White Peak – the remains of a great anticline of limestone scraped flat by the ice sheets of the last ice age and later scoured into a complex, fascinating landscape by the melt waters from the same. The most northerly section of the White Peak, to the south of the Hope Valley, is soft rurality with villages, farms, field barns and meadows and a high plateau cut through by dales rich with flowers and wildlife.

The limestone here, like most Peak District rock, was deposited in the Carboniferous period over 320 million years ago when a warm sea covered the area. It is composed of the remains of lime-rich small plants and animals including corals, crinoids, brachiopods, bivalves and algae that formed a carbonate sand and mud that in time formed limestone rock. To the north and west limestone reefs sometimes formed and which erosion has now revealed. There are very good examples in Winnats Pass and in the Upper Dove valley. This area is also rich in mineral deposits such as galena (lead sulphide) and blue-john (fluorspar). There is a long history of mining, with even the Romans coming here to extract the lead while Blue John seems to have gained popularity as a semi-precious material some time in the middle ages. The mineralogy and geology of the area is crucial in drawing people to the White Peak, in describing the history of their habitation and the ways in which they have shaped and used the land.

There are a number of great vantage points in the area, with the escarpments of Eyam Ridge and Longstone Edge in particular providing impressive outlooks over the network drystone-walled fields and villages below; from which the frequent temperature inversions that form low-lying valley mists can be photographed. The river Wye and its tributaries, along with glacial melt water a long time ago, have formed narrow rock-lined gorges like Chee Dale that provide excellent fishing for wild brown, rainbow trout and grayling; and impressive bluffs of limestone provide climbers with many interesting and tricky challenges. Some of the Wye's limestone dales – Cressbrook, Hay and Monk's Dale – make up part of the Derbyshire Dales National Nature Reserve and have a tremendous diversity of habitats including limestone grassland, scrub and valley woodlands. If you enjoy woodland and flower photography these habitats are amongst the most flower-rich places in Britain.

With settlements reaching back to Medieval times, this area is the place to explore some of the cultural history of the Peak, home to stone circles, old mines and beautiful villages such as Tideswell, Litton and Ashford-in-the-Water.

Maps

- OS Explorer Map OL241 (1:25 000) The Peak District: White Peak Area

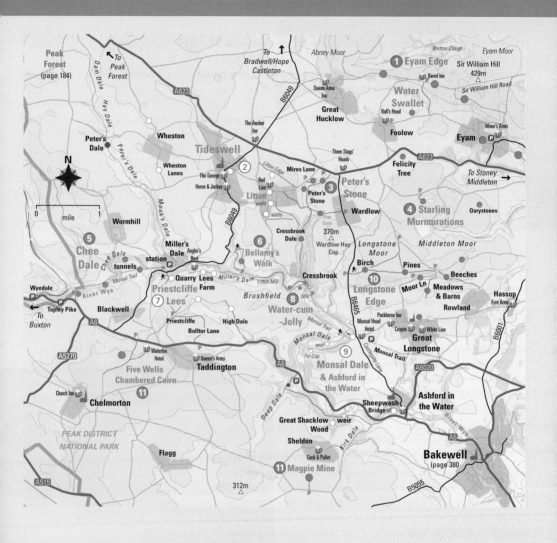

Peak Forest (page 184)

To Peak Forest

To Bradwell/Hope Castleton

Abney Moor

Bretton Clough

Eyam Moor

1 Eyam Edge

Sir William Hill 429m

Barrel Inn

Sir William Hill Road

Water Swallet

Queen Anne Inn

Bull's Head

Great Hucklow

Foolow

Miner's Arms

Eyam

Peter's Dale

Wheston

Tideswell

Wheston Lanes

The Anchor Inn

Mires Lane

Three Stags' Heads

Felicity Tree

To Stoney Middleton

2

Litton Edge

Red Lion

Peter's Stone

3

Peter's Stone

Wardlow

4 Starling Murmurations

Oarystones

The George

Horse & Jockey

Litton

walls

walls

Star Gate

370m

Wardlow Hay Cop

Longstone Moor

Middleton Moor

Wormhill

Cressbrook Dale

Birch

Pines

Beeches

5

Chee Dale

Chee Dale

tunnels

Miller's Dale

station

Angler's Rest

6

Bellamy's Walk

Cressbrook

Longstone Moor

10

Longstone Edge

Moor Ln

Meadows & Barns

Hassop

Eyre Arms

Wyedale

Quarry Lees

Farm

Miller's Dale

Litton Mill

8

Water-cum -Jolly

Rowland

Topley Pike

7

Priestcliffe Lees

Brushfield

Mill

Packhorse Inn

Monsal Head Hotel

Crispin

White Lion

Great Longstone

To Buxton

Blackwell

Priestcliffe

High Dale

Bulltor Lane

Monsal Dale

weir

Fin Cop

Monsal Trail

Waterloo Hotel

Queen's Arms

Taddington

9

Monsal Dale & Ashford in the Water

Ashford in the Water

Five Wells Chambered Cairn

Deep Dale

Sheepwash Bridge

Church Inn

Chelmorton

11

Great Shacklow Wood

weir

Kirk Dale

Bakewell (page 380)

PEAK DISTRICT NATIONAL PARK

Flagg

Sheldon

Cock & Pullet

11 Magpie Mine

312m

Eyam Edge, near The Barrel at Bretton (VP1). Canon 6D, 17-40at 20mm, ISO 100, f1/10s at f/14. Grad. Feb. © CG

Eyam Edge on the southern slope of Abney Moor overlooks the northern limestone dales and its patchwork of fields, drystone walls and small villages. This is a convenient roadside location, especially good at sunrise and sunset, when there is mist and anytime when there is changeable weather. Just below, near the village of Foolow, is a magical waterfall hidden in a limestone cavern surrounded by trees. Then, near Stoney Dale, is the plague village of Eyam.

What to shoot and viewpoints

Two of the locations described are on Sir William Hill Road above Eyam, one just outside Eyam, and the waterfall a spit from the village of Foolow.

Viewpoint 1 – Barrel Inn

When the light is favourable the Sir William Hill Road near the Barrel Inn provides a perfect vantage point for looking down on the limestone fields and dales in the south, and toward the acidic moorland of Bretton and Abney Moors and their cloughs in the north. It's an easy place to get to quickly if conditions are 'going off'. A wide angle lens will give classic landscape compositions, although foreground interest is limited. A longer focal length will allow you to pick off interesting details in the landscape. Try up the road from the Barrel Inn and also below on the footpath that leads down through fields.

Viewpoint 2 – Eyam and Stoney Middleton Overlook

From the Barrel Inn head toward the village of Eyam along the Sir William Hill Road and round two bends a view opens up down to villages of Eyam and Stoney Middleton with the Eastern Edges in the background. This is a good composition when the midground and background are lit up.

Viewpoint 3 – Eyam village

Eyam is a village rich in history with much to photograph especially the graves, the church and houses of the plague years of 1665/66 when 260 villagers out of a population of 350 died. Visit the National Trust's Eyam Hall and Craft Centre for more information. Just outside the village is a viewpoint overlooking the village of Stoney Middleton with Froggatt and Curbar Edges in the background. From the market place in Eyam go to Lydgate Lane near the telephone box. Follow this to a junction, over the stile and follow the path through fields to a small gritstone boundary stone that was used by villagers to leave vinegar soaked money in exchange for food at the time of the

Stoney Middleton from the Sir William Hill Road (VP2). Sony A6000, 18–200 at 32mm, ISO 250, 1/160s at f/11. Sept. © MR

plague. The land drops down here and on the left are a group of distinctive trees. This is a great sunrise spot at most times of year especially when there is mist around.

Viewpoint 4 – Waterfall Swallet

Waterfall Swallet is situated just off a minor road 0.5 miles east from Foolow toward Eyam by Waterfall Farm. Parking is problematic at the moment, try up the road. Opposite

the farm walk down the lane opposite and turn left over the stone stile and down the steep slope to the waterfall. This limestone sink hole is home to a beautiful waterfall that cascades steeply for 40ft over a limestone cliff. Although surrounded by trees it does get reflected light, but a tripod will be very useful, especially in winter. If it freezes in winter, and in autumn, it is very much worth a visit. It works well both close up and from a distance.

How to get here

The Barrel Inn is a good place to head for on Sir William Hill Road that traverses Eyam Edge. It can be approached by minor roads from Eyam or Grindleford in the east or from Great Hucklow and Foolow in the west and south.

The Barrel Inn Parking Lat/Long: 53.297927, -1.7005688
Parking Grid Ref: SK 200 779
Parking Postcode: S32 5QD (200m)

Eyam and Stoney Middleton Overlook Lat/Long: 53.290110, -1.7035407
Parking Grid Ref: SK 210 774
Parking Postcode: S32 5QT (300m)

Waterfall Swallet Lat/Long: 53.290110, -1.7035407
Parking Grid Ref: SK 198 770
Parking Postcode: S32 5QA (600m)

Accessibility ♿

The Eyam Edge locations are roadside accessible to all. The Eyam village location involves a short walk along a good path. The path down to Waterfall Swallet is steep and awkward and requires care.

Best time of year/day

The limestone dales below Eyam Edge are often enveloped in wispy mist at sunrise in the autumn through to spring. At most times of year, apart from high summer the fields are lit with light from the setting sun. If there is sun and showers in the afternoon this is a great chance of rainbows and shafts of light. Waterfall Swallet is best after times of heavy rain – it can dry up – and is especially good in autumn and after a hard freeze in winter.

Opposite: *Winter conditions in Swallet, near Eyam (VP4). Canon 6D, 70-300 at 150mm, ISO 50, 2s at f/30. Jan. © CG*

Viewpoint 5: The Felicity Tree

During 2015 one of the authors (Mick Ryan) photographed this ash tree every month. He christened it after his daughter, Felicity. The tree is situated near the Foolow turn off on the A623 before the road descends into Stoney Dale.

The Felicity Tree © MR

Tideswell and its smaller neighbour Litton, a mile away, are two well preserved villages in the heart of limestone country. Tideswell has its roots as a market town in the Middle Ages, though both grew because of the local lead mining.

A walk around them provides the photographer with a glimpse to the past, both retain traditional village buildings and features. Tideswell is home to a 14th-century parish church, the Church of St John the Baptist, also known as the Cathedral of the Peak. All around Litton, Tideswell and Wheston are some of the best ancient fields and closely packed dry stone walls in the Peak.

What to shoot and viewpoints

Viewpoint 1 – Tideswell and the Cathedral of the Peak

A wander around Tideswell's alleys, lanes and several squares will yield great images of its limestone-built cottages, houses and shops; and detail shots of mouldings, mullions, decorated gables and facades. Spring and early summer are best when the village flowers start to bloom.

The Church of St John the Baptist, also know as the Cathedral of The Peak, is the most important photographic feature of Tideswell. It has a very pleasant spacious interior and some excellent stained glass. Permission should be sought out of politeness but photography inside the church is usually permitted.

To photograph the whole of the church in its context, walk up Church Lane opposite Markovitz builders merchants to the first bend where there is an elevated viewpoint looking down on the church – also try down the footpath here. This aspect is tight, beware of barrel distortion when using a wide-angle lens. This composition is good in the mornings when the south side of church is lit by sun, at sunset whWhestonen its steeple and spires make a great silhouette, and at dark when the outside of the church is lit up

Tideswell has one of the grander of the summer well dressings (last week of June) and it is well worth a visit to record. Also venture out on the minor roads that go west from Tideswell toward Wheston and Monks Dale. These lanes offer beautiful vistas over the surrounding countryside.

A summer evening in fields near Tideswell. Canon 5D Mk 1, 17-40 at 20mm, ISO 100, 1/5s at f/20. Grad. Jul. © CG

Above: *The Cathedral of the Peak in Tideswell from Church Lane (VP1). Sony A6000, 18–200 at 63mm, ISO 250, 1/160s at f/5.6. Jun. © MR*

Below: *Great winter conditions on Lunch Lane near Cressbrook Dale. Canon 5D, 17-40 at 20mm, ISO 200, 1/10s at f/20. Grad. Feb. © CG*

Viewpoint 2 – Litton Village, Fields and Walls

Like all beautiful Peak District villages Litton has a bit of a parking problem and this inevitably affects its photographic potential. On the village green there is an old market cross and a old pair of stocks, which offer interest. In spring the Green is an absolute riot of daffodils and is worth visiting in early afternoon during the week when the angle of the sun is at its best and there are fewer cars around. The 17th century Red Lion Pub, as well as serving great food and beer, is good to photograph.

Field Systems and Drystone Walls

Just south of Litton are many drystone walls and narrow fields. The long, narrow nature of these wall-enclosed fields is the result of the Enclosure Act of the 18th century when land was subdivided. Some are S-shaped, created by 'ridge and furrow' horse ploughing as far back as Medieval times. These rows and patchworks of fields and walls – which have been the subject of a Phd thesis – make great photographic studies and are a classic image of the Peak District.

For an overview overlooking the fields and walls, a short walk up a path at the west end of the village leads you to Litton Edge. The elevated aspect here is to the south-west which is better later in the year for morning light and good anytime of year for afternoon and sunset.

For more intimate views travel down Hall Lane, a minor road that leaves the village heading south between the Methodist church and the post office/community shop/ cafe. You don't have to go far, immediately to your right are parallel rows of drystone walls.

A little further and around two bends Hall Lane offers a beautiful prospect – and more walls – out over the upper reaches of Tansley Dale toward Wardlow Hey Cop in the east, an excellent midwinter dawn shot. Photographing walls and fields is challenging and fun, and requires thought and experimentation to get appealing compositions.

Footpaths from Litton, and a green lane heading east from Hall Lane 500m from Litton offer more intimate portraits of walls, meadows and trees.

Viewpoint 3 – Wheston

A narrow road heads west from Tideswell to the hamlet of Wheston, along this country road and south of Wheston on the Pennine Bridleway are many rural photographic subjects including stands of trees, grassy lanes and walled fields. Beautiful in both spring and summer, this area is also worth exploring after snow.

A detail from the interior of Tideswell Church. Canon 6D, 70-300 at 150mm, ISO 800, 1/200s at f/5.6 © CG

__Opposite bottom__: Tideswell Well Dressing in July. Canon 6D, 17-40 at 40mm, ISO 400, 1/80s at f/8. Jul. © CG

Winter on The White Peak Way north of Wheston. Canon 5D Mk 1, 17-40 at 20mm, ISO 100, 1/20s at f/20. Grad. Dec. © CG

How to get here

Tideswell is a third of a mile south of the A623, the Peak Forest to Calver road, turn at the Anchor Pub. Litton can be accessed from Tideswell by several minor roads or along Mires Lane just east of Wardlow Mires on the A623.

Tideswell village Parking Lat/Long: 53.278487, -1.772914
Parking Grid Ref: SK 152 757
Parking Postcode: SK17 8LF

Litton village Parking Lat/Long: 53.273269, -1.7562246
Parking Grid Ref: SK 163 751
Parking Postcode: SK17 8QY

Accessibility ♿

These locations are roadside and accessible to all with some short country walks suggested around Litton to get the best viewpoints of the drystone walls and field systems.

Best time of year/day

Spring, summer and snowy times in winter with early morning and close to sunset being the best times of day.

Above: Walls and fields in Tansely Dale in summer and winter. Accessed by a footpath from Litton. Canon 5D, 17-40 © CG

Peter's Stone is a distinctive knoll that sits at the head of the narrow limestone valley of Cressbrook Dale. Geologists think this limestone pinnacle slid downhill on a layer of clay from the main formation millions of years ago. It has a grisly human history. It is reputed to have been a 'gibbet rock' where the body of a convicted murderer Antony Liggard was displayed in 1815, the last public displaying of gibbeting.

The dale is rich in wild flowers especially orchids. A worthwhile photo-walk is to follow Cressbrook Dale down passing Tansley Dale toward Ravensdale Cottages and eventually the small village of Cressbrook at the junction with Monsal Dale.

What to shoot and viewpoints

The area around Peter's Stone is all Access Land and on a good evening it is worth exploring the entire vicinity of Peter's Stone, including the high, eastern edge of the dale. All aspects offer opportunities here when the light is favourable. More convenient is the western rim 100 metres either side of the gate into the dale from Mires Lane and along the bottom of the dale on the approach to Peter's Stone from Wardlow Mires.

Viewpoint 1 – Dale Bottom and Eastern Slope

At the head of the dale near the A623 there are various viewpoints looking south on both sides of the path, some up the slope. These viewpoints are at their optimum in late May and June when the early purple and spotted orchids bloom on the slopes, and field buttercups and cowslip line the dale bottom. Also try close up to Peter's Stone for a more intimate perspective.

Viewpoint 2 – West Rim

From the lay-by on Mires Lane follow the path in either direction that traverses the west rim of the valley looking down onto Peter's Stone. There are many viewpoints here along the rim path to compose your shot. The slope down to Peter's Stone has several hawthorn bushes – they flower in May – and a wall to use as foreground interest. Depending on the time of year this can be a midday shot (winter) or late afternoon (4pm in July), don't leave it too late because a shadow line soon appears as the sun dips and the whole scene is in shadow two hours before sunset. Sunrise can also work in May and July when the sun rises in the north east.

Opposite: Early purple orchids flower in May and June (VP2). Canon 5D Mk 1, 17-40 at 20mm, ISO 200, 1/100s at f/11. Jun. © CG

Peter's Stone from the west side near the road (VP2). Canon 5D, 17-40 at 20mm, ISO 100, 1/40s at f/20. May. © CG

Viewpoint 3 – Tansley Dale and lower Cressbrook Dale

If you walk down the dale from Peter's Stone around the bend you will reach Tansley Dale which comes in from the west. Here there is usually an excellent display of orchids throughout the spring and early summer including early purple, heath-spotted, fragrant, pyramidal and bee orchids as well as the best patch of globeflower in the Peak. From here you can follow the dale south into the wooded Cressbrook Dale SSSI with its rich diversity of flowers in spring including bluebells, violets, orchids, bugle, cowslips, water avens and moschatel. Continue on to the isolated Ravensdale Cottages before meeting Monsal Dale at the now-restored Cressbrook Mill.

Tansley and Cressbrook Dale from Star Gate (VP4). Sony A6000, 10-18mm at 18mm, ISO 100, 1/125s at f/11. May. © MR

Viewpoint 4 – Star Gate and a high level walk

If you walk down the dale around the bend beyond Tansley Dale there is another bend. A path climbs the eastern slopes here to a junction of paths known locally as Star Gate. Star Gate is named as this is the place where miners used to see the stars when walking back to the local lead mines. This elevated position gives good compositions across to Tansley Dale. The path to the west leads to the hamlet of Wardlow Mires and is worth following to narrow meadows that are flower filled in spring. From Star Gate Access Land can be followed along the eastern flank of the valley to a new gate in the wall at SK173740 that provides access to the summit of Wardlow Hey Cop, around which there are many pretty little character hawthorn trees. While keeping to the dale side of the wall the walker traverses the upper pinnacles of Ravensdale Crag, best illuminated on midsummer evenings when the sun gets 'round into the northwestern sky. Eventually you reach Bull Tor, from which the prospects down over Cressbrook and into Water-cum-Jolly are superb.

Opposite: Winter at Peter's Stone (VP2) Canon 5D Mk 1, 17-40 at 25mm, ISO 50, 1/8s at f/20. Dec. © CG

How to get here

Park in a lay-by a quarter of a mile up Mires Lane (road to Litton) off the A623. The turn for Mires Lane is 0.3 miles west along the A623 from Wardlow Mires and the Three Stags' Heads pub. The footpath down into the dale starts at the lay-by.

Parking Lat/Long: 53.275591, -1.742168
Parking Grid Ref: SK 172 754
Parking Postcode: SK17 8RW (0.8km)

Accessibility

This is a roadside attraction on good level paths a few minutes from the road. Care is needed after rain on the steep slopes. A wheelchair would be able to negotiate the top part of the path from Mires Lane. If you go on the east side of the dale the slope is steep. The walk down to Cressbrook village is on a good path and is a 6km round trip from Mires Lane. **Walk from Peter's Stone to Cressbrook village:** 1hr, distance 3km, descent 64m.

Best time of year/day

The north end of Cressbrook Dale near Peter's Stone takes a roughly NNE to SSW alignment and its best prospects are the southerly views. This means that as long as you avoid the midday sun there is always some aspect that can photographed well here. By far the best time is May when the late afternoon and early evening light rakes across the western flank of the valley where a lot of the orchids flower at this time. Along with the white froth of the hawthorn blooms they act as an excellent counterpoint to the backdrop of Peter's Stone, which is well-illuminated at this time.

In early autumn, when the afternoon sun returns to this aspect the orchids are replaced by a number of different varieties of thistle, with the pretty musk thistle being dominant. Misty autumn mornings and drab winter days can add a different atmosphere, as can snow of course. Sunlight is limited in the winter. The dale gets sunlight just after sunrise in May and July.

One of the most dramatic wildlife spectacles between October and March each year is the starling murmuration. Amongst those that occur in the Peak District, one of the best can be seen on Middleton Moor, a marshy area above the village of Stoney Middleton.

From a distance this synchronised display looks like a moving black cloud; an ever-changing aerial sculpture. Up close it is one of the most incredible and breathtaking natural sights to witness in the UK, especially if you can hear the murmuration as well as see it. The noise of thousands of rippling wings, murmuration actually means 'the utterance of low continuous sounds.'

The common starling (Sturnus vulgaris) is a bit smaller than a blackbird and a frequent visitor to gardens in the summer searching for insects, or fruit in the autumn. Up close the birds have a beautiful iridescent plumage of purples, greens and blacks with white spots when they moult in autumn.

Starlings are highly social and are often seen in small flocks. They breed in the summer but when the days shorten in late autumn their flocking behaviour increases. During the day flocks of up to several hundred individuals scavenge fields and moorlands for food. Starlings eat plant matter as well as insects in the winter. A couple of hours before sunset these flocks fly to a nearby communal roosting site – often a reed bed, a woodland or a building/structure such as a pier or bridge.

Before they roost for the night the separate flocks, who have often flown in from over 20 miles away, coalesce in one huge shape-shifting mass of birds – called a murmuration – and the aerial dance begins. The murmuration, often numbering 100,000+ starlings swoop, glide and flutter around the roost site morphing into mesmerising moving shapes for up to half-an-hour before they filter down to their roost.

For my father. Taken at the time he died. Sony A6000, 18–200 at 52mm, ISO 250, 1/1000s at f/7.1. 18th November 2015. © MR

A grey wet evening on Middleton Moor. Sony A6000, 18–200 at 50mm, ISO 800, 1/500s at f/7.1. Dec. © MR

How to get here

This murmuration currently occurs on a marshy reed-bed on Middleton Moor, next to Cavendish Mill which is accessed by a minor road above Stoney Middleton. From the middle of Stoney Middleton by the Moon Pub follow Middleton Lane up the hill for 1.8 miles and just beyond Cavendish Mill on the left is a gate by a woodland, park carefully here. If coming from the west, 0.7 miles beyond Wardlow Mires on the A623 turn right along the minor road then first left for half a mile to the gate and parking.

Parking Lat/Long: 53.272627, -1.699789
Parking Grid Ref: SK 201 751
Parking Postcode: S32 4TH (350m)

Accessibility &

It is 100m up a grassy path to the viewing place for the murmuration, and a further 200m to the bird hide. Wellington boots are a good idea as the ground is often boggy.

Best time of year/day

Starling murmurations usually begin in October with the numbers of birds increasing as the winter progresses. By December to February the numbers and display is at its peak with the birds dispersing in March. Numbers vary, often dependent on the severity of the winters in northern Europe.

Get here at least an hour before the sun sets to witness the whole show. The best displays are on clear evenings so check the forecast or keep your eye on the weather during the day. Early in the season the birds can go straight to roost, especially if it is cloudy, raining or very windy. Be prepared for some disappointment.

Departure from the roost at sunrise can be impressive, although they do not murmurate but usually fly off as several flocks in different directions.

There have been over 100,000 starlings at Middleton Moor in recent times: 2013/14, but in 2014/15 after a build up in numbers to late December, the flock re-located to another location after a particular hard freeze over the Christmas period.

What to shoot and viewpoints

Go through the gate and up the grass track to the top of the slope and into the field. A popular spot to view the starlings is on the raised bank in front of you from where you will be looking to the east. To get to the hide turn left and follow the grass track at the edge of the reed bed to a bird hide sign. Enter the marsh and at the end of a usually boggy path is a small bird hide that faces south.

What usually happens is that the sky will be clear of birds then one or two flocks fly in and join together, then more and more. Sometimes a very large flock will be murmurating then another large flock will fly in and double the size.

Photographing Murmurations

You don't need a special camera to photograph a murmuration; a mobile phone camera, compact or DSLR will all do. But, as murmurations happen at sunset as the light levels decrease, it is useful to have a camera that allows you to change the sensor sensitivity to low light (high ISO) so that you can freeze the swirling flight patterns of the birds; unless you want the opposite, an artistic blurry movement of the flock.

Keep an eye on the weather and try and choose an evening promising a clear sky as a backdrop.

Exposure Settings

As the murmuration will move quite considerably, tripod shots are problematic unless you are skilled at using your tripod when panning your camera. A monopod can work but with the speed the murmuration moves hand-held is best. Camera settings normally revolve around freezing the bird's movement and reducing blurry images. The most dramatic displays tend to occur close to roosting time which means it will be getting quite dark. You will typically need a high ISO (1000+) to allow shutter speeds of 1/125 and higher to capture sharp images with no movement. Apertures should be set at the widest (smallest number e.g. f/2.8) to allow the fastest shutter speeds and lowest ISO.

Lens

Generally the sought after image is a distinct pattern in the sky showing the incredible numbers and beautiful shapes the flock forms. For this a wide angle lens is useful. Better to go too wide then crop in later than to miss some aspect of the pattern. A standard (mid) zoom will be best so that you can vary the focal length from wide to close up.

A longer lens (200-300mm) will allow you to capture the incredible density of birds flying in such close proximity. Try a slower shutter speed to add some creative blur.

Light and Composition

Shooting toward the sun will get great silhouettes of murmuration shapes against a colourful sunset. Your camera should focus lock on the murmuration producing a pin sharp image.

Try compositions of sky and murmuration only and then also including some of the landscape to add scale and foreground. If shooting with the sun to your back it will light up the murmuration and the ground-level landscape.

Pick your spot; the best photographs are taken of the murmuration against the sky rather than against the land where they will be lost against the dark background.

Starling close up. Nikon D4, 300mm + 2x converter at 600mm, ISO 1000, 1/1600s at f/13. © Andrew Marshall

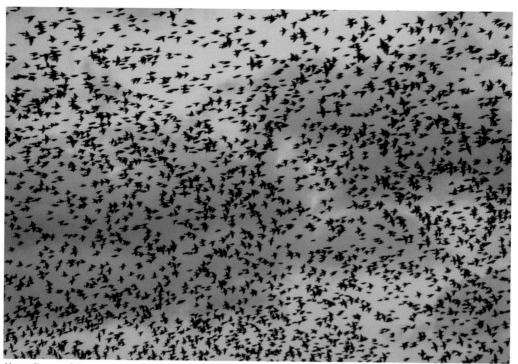

Above: *Close up of the murmuration, the sound and spectacle is mesmerising. Sony A6000, 18–200 at 200mm, ISO 1000, 1/200s at f/6.3. Jan. © MR*

Below: *Sunset on Middleton Moor. Sony A6000, 18–200 at 200mm, ISO 1000, 1/200s at f/6.3. Jan. © MR*

The River Wye, a tributary of the River Derwent, begins its journey west of Buxton on Axe Edge Moor. East of Buxton the Wye Valley begins and the section below the villages of Wormhill and Blackwell is known as Chee Dale, a dramatic 300ft deep limestone gorge. Old railway tracks from Buxton to Matlock follow the Wye Valley and part of it is now the Monsal Trail, a flat, broad footpath and cycleway starting at Blackwell Mill and ending 8.5miles/13.7km later just short of Bakewell. The Monsal Trail is a good access point for several places in Chee Dale and the upper Wye Valley.

For the photographer Chee Dale offers views into the gorge and many subjects within it; wild flowers, stepping stones, old railway tunnels, the river, limestone cliffs, many species of birds, large patches of the rhubarb-like butterbur and steep sided woodland.

What to shoot and viewpoints

For the first two viewpoints use the Topley Pike lay-by.

Viewpoint 1 – Topley Pike

From the lay-by walk up the road to the footpath that goes down the ravine to the river and the Blackwell Halt cottages. Follow this footpath a short way down then head right to the ridge (with drystone wall) above the ravine.

The compositions here from various spots look down to the cottages surrounded by trees and may include Great Rocks Dale that leads off to the north west. Late afternoons

and sunsets, especially with some cloud are the best times here throughout the year.

For compositions looking from the west to the east up Chee Dale, on the ridge follow the footpath, through the gate eastwards into fields where you can access the edge of the dale and look for a clear viewpoint where you can see the cliffs, the Monsal Trail and a tunnel entrance. The edge of the dale is 'free-to-roam' Access Land, but beware of very steep drops. This viewpoint is best when the sun is in the west at most times of year.

Viewpoint 2 – Stepping stones, tunnels and deep in the dale

The Monsal Trail is an interesting walk accessible to all, you can also venture off this broad path down to the riverside footpath. There is much to photograph by the river including two sets of stepping stones and large patches of butterbur – a rhubarb-like plant that flowers in late March and April, but is at its densest in August.

From Topley Pike lay-by take the footpath down the hill to the river and turn right along the broad Monsal Trail or use the flat approach from Wyedale car park. The verges of the old railway are rich with orchids in the spring. Follow the trail for 600m, passing some impressive limestone cliffs, to Rusher Cutting Tunnel. At the entrance to the tunnel go right down a stony path down to the river. There is a popular climbing cliff on your left just above the river and just beyond that the stepping stones (SK 122 729. If the river is high the stepping stones will be submerged. »

Top right: Chee Dale from the edge of Millersdale Quarry. Canon 5D, 17-40 at 40mm, ISO 100, 1/40s at f/20. Grad. Oct. © CG

At the edge of Chee Dale (VP1). Canon 6D, 17-40 at 20mm, ISO 100, 1/40s at f/13. Grad. Jun. © CG

The stepping stones in Chee Dale (VP2). Canon 6D, 17-40 at 20mm, ISO 100, 1/4s at f/13. Oct. © CG

Stormy evening light at Topley Pike in Wye Dale (VP1). Canon 6D,
17-40 at 20mm, ISO 100, 1/40s at f/13, Grad. Jun. © CG

You can continue to follow this riverside path, look out for dippers, which goes under a bridge on the Monsal Trail and does a loop to the north. There is another set of stepping stones again under a steep cliff. The riverside path is followed and emerges at another bridge on the Monsal Trail which can be followed through Chee Tor tunnels 1 and 2, which are popular for photography, to retrace your steps to Topley Pike (3miles/5km round trip). For the following two viewpoints park at Millers Dale station (pay and display).

Viewpoint 3 – The Monsal Trail and the Tunnels

The walk along the riverside path is an adventure and can be tricky under foot. Easier is to walk the Monsal Trail starting at Millers Dale station. You will be amongst the trees and there will be lots of flowers in the spring. You will pass some old lime kilns and it is just 0.5miles/0.8km to Chee Tor tunnels 1 and 2. At the station you can also explore the old railway station and the bridge over the River Wye and the B6049.

Viewpoint 4 – Peter's Dale

Peter's Dale's principle value is to those interested in wildflowers, butterflies, birds and brown hares. It is part of the Derbyshire Dales National Nature Reserve.

This long dale starts high in the north-west at the village of Peak Forest. First it is Dam Dale, then Hay Dale and Peter's Dale before it becomes Monk's Dale and joins the Wye Valley at Miller's Dale.

Park at Millers Dale station then walk up the road toward Wormhill. At the first bend and the cottages take the path on the right down into Monk's Dale. Turn left up a path that can be followed to Peak Forest. At first this dale is tree-choked with some open meadows, higher in Peter's Dale it begins to open up. Orchids flower here beginning in spring but continue well into the summer because of the damp and cool nature of parts of the dale.

The all-weather Monsal Trail tunnels make for an unusual image. (VP3) Canon 5D, 17-40 at 40mm, ISO 100, 1s at f/11. © CG

How to get here

We recommend three access points for Chee Dale: Topley Pike lay-by east of Buxton along the A6 for views into the gorge and also the quickest way to the stepping stones; Wyedale car park which is down in the dale and the start of the Monsal Trail for those who want a flat approach into Chee Dale; and from Millers Dale station at the bottom of Blackwell Dale for the tunnels and access to Monk's Dale.

Wyedale car park is at the bottom of the Topley Pike hill opposite a quarry entrance 2.8 miles from the roundabout by Morrisons supermarket in Buxton.

Parking Lat/Long: 53.249907, -1.845880
Parking Grid Ref: SK 103 725
Parking Postcode: SK17 9TE (200m)

The Topley Pike lay-by on the A6 is at the top of the hill on the north 3.2 miles from the roundabout by Morrisons supermarket in Buxton.

Parking Lat/Long: 53.249019, -1.832652
Parking Grid Ref: SK 112 724
Parking Postcode: SK17 9TF(300m)

Millers Dale Station is situated just up from the bridge over the Wye at the hamlet of Millers Dale, off the road to Wormhill village.

Parking Lat/Long: 53.256190, -1.7938077
Parking Grid Ref: SK 138 732
Parking Postcode: SK17 8SN (300m)

Accessibility ♿

These are varied locations but all require short walks sometimes over rough and vegetated ground. The Monsal Trail is accessible by wheelchairs. The path in Chee Dale by the river is rocky and extremely slippy when wet.

Best time of year/day

The locations in Chee Dale and Monks Dale are best for wild flowers from May to August, with the orchids at their peak in late May and June. Some species flower later. The butterbur flowers from late March and reaches full height in August. For views into Chee Dale from Topley Pike late afternoon to sunset sees the dale illuminated. Autumn is stunning here with the dale's rich canopy of trees.

Opposite: Down by the river Wye in Chee Dale (VP2). Sony A6000, 18–200 at 26mm, ISO 200, 1/160s at f/5.6. Oct. © MR

David Bellamy is a well-known botanist who used to appear on TV in the 1980s and 1990s. His lifelong passion for flowers, wildlife and ecology – he's now in his 80s – was ignited by trips as a youth to Miller's Dale especially around Ravenstor. Just down from Ravenstor YHA, an old mill owner's mansion, is Bellamy's Bank which is rich in orchids in the spring and has a plaque commemorating the great botanist.

What to shoot and viewpoints

This short walk, it is just over a mile with 300ft of height gain, is good anytime in the spring starting in early May (May is the best time for the orchids here) through to July and takes in riverside locations, a beautiful limestone dale, a volcanic quarry, an open limestone hillside covered with orchids, and woodland.

Viewpoint 1 –Tideswell Dale

From the parking spot walk up the dale on a broad track. Almost immediately there are butterburs next to the stream. As you progress up the path and come to a bridge the dale opens up a little and there are usually an array of flowers here. The stream provides a backdrop for flower photography and often a leading line. Look near limestone rock outcroppings and small caves for orchids. Continue up the dale around a bend then another bend, the stream here is usually lined either side by blue forget-me-nots.

Forget-me-nots in Tideswell Dale (VP1). Sony A6000, 18–200 at 200mm, ISO 250, 1/160s at f/7.1. May. © MR

THE DAY THAT DR. BELLAMY RANG
by Stephen 'Mid' Middleton

As a passionate 'floraphile' I was visiting Miller's Dale during the spring of 2014 searching for the season's first wild flowers when I chanced upon a small commemorative plaque near the top of the sloping footpath that leads to Ravenstor Youth Hostel. It read: 'This limestone bank is dedicated to Dr. David Bellamy, International Botanist & T.V. Personality. It was here in 1954 that he was first inspired by wild flowers.'

But, was it true? After a little internet detective work I tracked down his agent's address and dispatched a letter asking if Dr. Bellamy could confirm or deny the astonishing claim. I never expected to receive a reply, but sure enough I got one: "Dear Stephen, please send me your telephone number so we can have a chat."

That phone call came at 9 pm. on Friday 11th April 2014: "Hello. Am I speaking to Stephen Middleton?", inquired a lady's voice, senior and well-spoken. "It's Rosemary Bellamy. David would like a word with you. You'll have to speak up, his hearing is not as good as it used to be."

So, then. Was it true that David Bellamy became a legendary botanist because of the flowers he found in Miller's Dale? "Absolutely", he said. How do I know? Because he told me.

The full account of David's experience is contained in his autobiography The Jolly Green Giant (2002). Incidentally, the image on the front cover was taken by another Peak District photographer, John Beatty of Bamford.

Red campion in Tideswell Dale (VP1). Sony A6000, 18–200 at 121mm, ISO 400, 1/80s at f/5.6. May. © MR

Early purple orchids on Hammerton Hill (VP3). Sony A6000, 18–200 at 18mm, ISO 160, 1/80s at f/9. May. © MR

Viewpoint 2 – The Volcanic Quarry

Once past the second bend look right and a path leads up the slope and leads to an old quarry and a flat area that is usually rich with orchids. In the quarry dolerite is exposed formed from volcanic explosions in the area over 300 million years ago.

Viewpoint 3 – Hammerton Hill

From the quarry walk along the path southwards through a gate and then through another gate to a permissive path at the base of Hammerton Hill. Some of this area is Access Land. Ascend the hill to its nose where a solitary hawthorn grows. Take care not to stand on any flowers. There is a feint path which contours just below the top of the hill. The nose of Hammerton Hill is best photographed in May in the evening and hopefully you will get light that illuminates the carpet of orchids on the slope and the dales below.

Red campion by the river Wye (VP6). Sony A6000, 18–200 at 24mm, ISO 400, 1/160s at f/5.6. May. © MR

Butterburs in Tideswell Dale (VP1). Sony A6000, 18–200 at 18mm, ISO 400, 1/80s at f6.3. May. © MR

Viewpoint 4 – Woodlands

Follow the contour path around the hill where there are hawthorns on the hillside and usually even more orchids and limestone flowers.

Contour down the slope to woodland and a gate which leads down through the woods, bluebells in April to early June, to a path that leads by the field study centre and back to the small car park.

Viewpoint 5 – Bellamy's bank

Bellamy's Bank can be reached from the car park by a path to the west that leads to the YHA. Go up a slope and steps and you are there. Bellamy's plaque is half-way along the ridge. As well as orchids this ridge is a good vantage point down the dale when the light is good or in autumn.

Viewpoint 6 – Riverside

The minor road by the river provides a great viewpoint for photographing flowers and moss-covered trees on the river bank (look out for water voles here). Try using a tripod and slow shutter speed (using an ND filter) to give the river a milky effect with the flowers in sharp focus.

Viewpoint 7 – Ravenstor YHA woodlands

Back down the road a short way is a stone gate and a sign for the YHA. The track leads up into woodlands that skirt the edge of the hostel and in April and May this woodland is filled with bluebells and wild garlic.

Viewpoint 8 – Litton Mill

It is worth driving to the end of the road at Litton Mill, an old textile mill now converted to apartments. This is a beautiful spot on a spring or summer day with trout in the river, a small bridge and cottages. It is ironic that the mill was notorious for the abuse of children in the 19th century. The walk following the river toward Cressbrook is very worthwhile for woodland stream photography – good when the light filters through the trees and especially in the autumn.

Opposite top: *Early purple orchids on Hammerton Hill (VP3). Sony A6000, 18–200 at 90mm, ISO 400, 1/160s at f/5.6. May. © MR*

Hawthorn on the slopes of upper Tideswell Dale. Sony A6000, 18–200 at 29mm, ISO 125, 1/100s at f/7. May. © MR

How to get here

This walk starts by the River Wye in Miller's Dale near the Field Study Centre before you get to the end of the road at Litton Mill. From the hamlet of Miller's Dale on the B6049 between the A6 and Tideswell, follow a minor road passing the Angler's Rest pub. Drive slowly down this narrow road by the river for one mile passing the overhanging Raven's Tor cliff on your left, around the corner and just before you get to the hamlet of Litton Mill, is a small car park on your left.

Field Study Centre Car Park Parking Lat/Long:
53.254899, -1.767035
Parking Grid Ref: SK 156 731
Parking Postcode: SK17 8SR (300m)

Accessibility

The first part of this walk is good for wheelchair users and those with limited mobility as it follows a broad level track of compacted limestone and the river bank is right next to the road. Higher up the dale the path steepens a little, then this walk branches out onto rougher paths with one steep, but short ascent to the top of Hammerton Hill.
Total Loop: 1/2 hours, distance 2km, ascent 100mm..

Best time of year/day

To get the best of this walk botanically do it from the second week of May through June. The orchids on Hammerton Hill are relatively short lived – two weeks or so – and are usually at their best at the end of May. Evening light is best for Hammerton Hill, the other locations are not time of day dependent. The bluebells and ramsons (wild garlic) in the woodlands usually start to flower in April but can last until June.

When flowers are at their peak is dependent on the vagaries of the weather, especially temperature and rain.

The all-white form of the early purple orchid. Sony A6000, 18–200 at 160mm, ISO 200, 1/80s at f/9. May. © MR

Down the River Wye from Chee Dale, high on the south rim above Miller's Dale is Priestcliffe Lees, a rolling plateau of fields and small dales. From the quarry here and along the edge of the dale the views down to the river and beyond over limestone meadows and dales are tremendous.

Priestcliffe quarry is a National Nature Reserve managed by the Derbyshire Wildlife Trust, a sanctuary for wildlife and orchids on its lead spoil heaps. It is home to the common spotted orchid, dark green fritillary and wych elm. Further east toward Lees Farm (a holiday cottage) high meadows are carpeted with cowslips and early purple orchids in early June with clear views down to a tree-shrouded Raven Tor and Water-cum-Jolly Dale. Late summer sees the rare Grass-of-Parnassus flower. South of the edge of the dale are a network of green lanes and footpaths, the old ways around limestone meadows near the village of Priestcliffe.

What to shoot and viewpoints

Viewpoint 1 – Priestcliffe Lees Nature Reserve and the Quarry

For the steep approach park in Miller's Dale Station or just up from the bridge over the Wye in Miller's Dale at the bottom of Blackwell Dale. Locate the footpath sign just up from the bridge and follow the stepped path south up the hillside and through the trees. Eventually on your left is a grassed-over quarry road. Follow this into Priestcliffe quarry.

Grass-of-Parnassus or bog star, a flower not a grass, is found at Priestcliffe Lees, on boggy ground. Canon 5D Mk 1, !05, ISO 400, 1/125s at f/14. Sep. © CG

The quarry road can also be reached from above from Priestcliffe village by walking along the left-hand track from Lydgate farm then following a footpath across fields. The base of the quarry is open and has lead spoil mounds which are rich with flowers in the spring. For the more adventurous you can also traverse a path along the top of the quarry which gives magnificent landscape compositions up, down and across Miller's Dale – approach from either end of the quarry. If you continue east along the top path you will reach Lee's Farm (0.5km).

Viewpoint 2 – Priestcliffe Lees – Lees Farm

Lees Farm is a desirable residence (now a holiday cottage) that overlooks Miller's Dale. You can walk here from the quarry or park in Priestcliffe village and from Lydgate Farm follow Broadway Lane to its end. The dale top here has less trees and the grassland is rich with wild flowers in late May and June. The orchids and cowslips provide a compelling foreground to expansive landscape compositions to the west,

How to get here

The most direct route to Priestcliffe Lees is by a steep stepped path through woodland from Miller's Dale. Park at Miller's Dale station or by the bridge in Miller's Dale. If you want a more leisurely but slightly longer approach, park at Priestcliffe village accessed from the A6 or from the Blackwell Dale road.

Miller's Dale Station Parking Lat/Long: 53.256190, -1.7938077
Parking Grid Ref: SK 138 732
Parking Postcode: SK17 8SN (300m)

Prestcliffe VillageParking Lat/Long: 53.245501, -1.792462
Parking Grid Ref: SK 139 720
Parking Postcode: SK17 9TN (130m)

Accessibility

The walk from Miller's Dale up the south slope of the dale to Priestcliffe quarry is very steep but on a good stepped path. Your calves will burn and you will be out of breath. The approach from Priestcliffe village is a pleasant country walk along a track and footpath through fields.
Miller's Dale Approach: 20 minutes, distance 400m, ascent 86m
Priestcliffe village Approach: 30 mins, distance 1km, ascent 0m

Best time of year/day

These locations are best from spring to autumn. The orchids start to flower in May, the Grass-of-Parnassus July to September. June and July with their fresh summer growth are best for the green lanes around Priestcliffe village. Summer evenings are best for the views down into Miller's Dale along with any time of the day when the leaves turn in autumn.

Opposite middle: Near Bulltor Lane (VP3). Sony A6000, 18–200 at 24mm, ISO 400, 1/160s at f/5.6. May. © MR

Limestone fields (VP3). Sony A6000, 18–200 at 107mm, ISO 200, 1/160s at f/6.3. Jun. © MR

south and east. Sunrise and sunset in the middle of summer are good, and when the sun is in the south. The best spot is west of the house and accessed by a footpath near the house, with a good view down to the Raven's Tor cliff. From the house a footpath leads down the dale side. This slope is known as Brushfield and is Access Land so you can explore various viewpoints looking down to Litton Mill and beyond to Water-cum-Jolly Dale.

Viewpoint 3 – The Old Ways: Bulltor Lane and High Dale

East of the village of Priestcliffe is a network of green lanes and footpaths. These 'old ways' or ancient routes, as described by Robert Macfarlane in his book of the same name, give access to narrow fields, old barns and a secluded dale. Those interested in photographing flowers, trees, meadows, fleeting foxes and a time gone by will enjoy a summer evening, or early morning, following these tracks. As a starting point park either in Priestcliffe village and head east, or in Taddington and follow footpaths that start on the north side of the A6. High Dale is worth searching out, especially when the hawthorn flowers in May.

Near Lees Farm (VP2) Sony A6000, 18–200 at 24mm, ISO 400, 1/160s at f/5.6. May. © MR

Below Miller's Dale and beyond Litton Mill the Wye Valley closes in and becomes more gorge-like with towering buttress of limestone overlooking the river. It opens out again at Water-cum-Jolly a small dale by the village of Cressbrook. The Wye is dammed here by a weir forming a small waterfall and a large millpond which on a calm day is mirror-like and perfect for reflections of trees and small limestone cliffs. Swans and their cygnets are usually found on the river. There is access above the dale and along a path by the Wye offering further photographic opportunities, and along the river is perfect for woodland studies.

What to shoot and viewpoints

Viewpoint 1 – The Weir and Pool

From the road walk down the path by the car park of Cressbrook Mill by the castle-like house toward the river around the corner and over a small bridge to the pool.

The footbridge and Cressbrook Weir is on your left. A popular composition is of the weir's waterfall across the pool from or before/on the bridge with the blue-grey and white cliffs in the background. There are various viewpoints on the bank by the pool and often there are swans here.

Mallards on the pool (VP1). Canon 6D, 70-300mm at 300mm, ISO 250, 1/400s at f/5.6. Sep. © CG

Where did the name Water-cum-Jolly come from?

The appearance of the name Water-cum-Jolly in texts is coincident with the period when Matthew Dickie Ltd. owned and operated Cressbrook Mill. It was probably christened by Mr. and Mrs. William Mallison, who lived in Cressbrook Hall in the 1920s. William Mallison was one of the partners in Matthew Dickie Ltd.

Mr. and Mrs. Mallison built a pair of boathouses on the pool, one on the side of Cressbrook Hall at the bottom of what is now known as the 'Nun's Steps,' a name acquired from another period of Cressbrook Hall's history, and another on the side of the mill, next to the weir. The Mallisons then bought a pair of 'Jolly' Boats with which they would entertain guests at the hall by boating on the pool.

Jolly boats were small boats of a certain design used in the 18th/19th centuries for ferrying people to and from ships, and for other short journeys. The word jolle is the German and Swedish word for a small boat or dingy.

Ordnance Survey maps from the 1940s show the two boathouses clearly. The Mallisons moved out of Cressbrook Hall just before World War II consequent to the mills first bankruptcy but by then the name of the pool – Water-cum-Jolly – had become well-established in the local vernacular and its name had started appearing in tour books. The Ordnance Survey started using the name on maps in the mid 1970s and it has been widely known by this name ever since. Boats were still being used on the mill pool up until the mill's eventual closure in 1975. They were used to maintain the pool and since the maintenance has ceased the pool has been steadily silting up and becoming reclaimed by nature. It remains one of the Peak District's best beauty spots.

The weir outlet (VP1). Sony A6000, 18–200mm at 28mm, ISO 100, 1/5s at f/8. Oct. © MR

Honeysuckle flowering near the mill pool in Cressbrook Dale (VP1).
Canon 6D, 70-300L at 200mm, ISO 800, 1/800s at f/5.6. Jun. © CG

Viewpoint 2 – Riverside Path

Water-cum-Jolly is rich with bird life and flowers and a good way to enjoy them is to follow the concessionary path along the Wye on its north bank going underneath the cliffs – very popular with climbers. This path floods after heavy rain. A great composition can had of the pool just beyond the cliffs. The sun streams in from the south through the trees that sometimes overhanging the river, and if mist is rising off the water this can make a very atmospheric and mysterious photograph.

Viewpoint 3 – Far Bank Path and the Monsal Trail

Brushfield is the southern slope of the Wye Valley here that ends with steep cliffs then the river. The Monsal Trail travels along this slope sometimes bored through the rock with passageway through tunnels. This now popular trail can be reached by going across the footbridge in front of weir and heading left up the hill following a stepped path. The tunnels themselves are fun to photograph and the trail also gives unique views down to Water-cum-Jolly and Cressbrook Mill and village.

If you don't mind walking along a airy path for good views of Cressbrook Hall, situated high in Cramside Wood, cross the footbridge but this time go right and follow a narrow track above the river. This is a particularly good viewpoint on autumn mornings.

How to get here

Park by Cressbrook Mill at the bottom of the road below Cressbrook village, or approach from the minor road from Monsal Head.

Cressbrook Mill Parking Lat/Long: 53.251394, -1.741586
Parking Grid Ref: SK 173 727
Parking Postcode: SK17 8SA (80m)

Accessibility   ♿

The path into Water-cum-Jolly dale is flat but a little uneven in places, but is ok for adventurous wheelchair users. It is 200m to the pool on the Wye from the road. However the riverside path here is prone to flooding and it is a good idea to bring wellingtons. On the far bank the path along the river is single-track with steep drops close by and steep if you go up to the Monsal Trail.

Best time of year/day

Spring through autumn are the best seasons to visit, with early mornings and early evening being the best times of the day. Because of the deep nature of the dale it starts to receive sun an hour or so after sunrise, and loses light well before sunset. River mist is common on autumn mornings and is a special time to be here for photography with ethereal light passing through the russet and gold canopy.

Opposite top: The mill pond and cliff of Water-cum-Jolly (VP1). Canon 6D, 17-40 at 24mm, ISO 50, 0.5s at f/13. Jul. © CG

Opposite bottom left: Riverside path detail (V2). Canon 6D, 70-300 at 200mm, ISO 400, 1/250s at f/5.6. Nov. © CG

Opposite bottom right: Summer in Water-cum-Jolly, below Litton Mill (V2). Canon 6D, 70-300 at 140mm, ISO 400, 1/200s at f/7.1. Jul. © CG

High on Brushfield above Water-cum-Jolly Dale (VP3). Canon 5D Mk 1, 17-40 at 20mm, ISO 100, 1/20s at f/20. Grad. Jun. © CG

Old sluice gate mechanism (VP1). Sony A6000, 18–200mm at 45mm, ISO 100, 1/13s at f/8. Oct. © MR

The view from Monsal Head down to the River Wye and up to Cressbrook is one of the most spectacular in the Peak District; it is also roadside and has a great pub, the Monsal Head Hotel. If you are passing it is always worth a look and a photograph. Monsal Dale below, and following the Wye as it makes its way to the River Derwent, is a beautiful area and has several locations to visit and photograph. We describe some highlights including the Sheepwash bridge at Ashford in the Water.

What to shoot and viewpoints

Viewpoint 1 – Monsal Head

A classic view from the car park. The dale up to Cressbrook runs to the north west and the sun shines down the valley at and near sunset from April to August – this is also a good time of the year for a foreground with flowers. Early mornings especially in autumn may see wispy mist or even thick fog in the dale and after snow this view can be magical. With a wide angle lens you can include both forks of the dale and the Headstone railway viaduct.

Viewpoint 2 – Doctor's Rocks

If you walk north up the road from Monsal Head toward Wardlow, on the left you will come to a gate in the wall which gives access to the dale side at Doctor's Rocks (Access Land). This viewpoint is particularly good for midsummer sunsets as it allows you to compose to the west and north with a more manageable dynamic range. It is also quite different to the traditional view from Monsal Head. (SK 182 719).

Viewpoint 3 – Monsal Weir

On the river below Monsal Head is Dale Head Farm where there are often chickens running around, cows in the meadows, and beyond that a pretty footbridge over the river. 750m downstream from here is a beautiful weir that once drove a corn mill. The weir can be reached from Monsal Head by taking the footpath west down through the trees. The weir is good for close ups and abstracts as well as the whole of the waterfall. It is great in summer when the water levels drop slightly, but is always worth a visit. Dippers and water voles are common here while jackdaws, ravens and kestrels soar on the updraughts at Monsal Head. (SK 177 713).

Monsal Head, as seen from Cressbrook. Canon 6D, 70-300 at 250mm, ISO 100, 1/20s at f/14. Dec. © CG

How to get here

Monsal Head car park is a 3 mile drive from the town of Bakewell up the A6 to Ashford in the Water then through the village and up the B6465 – the Roman road of Castlegate – to Monsal Head and the Monsal Head Hotel. From the north, on the A623, turn south on the B6465 passing Wardlow for 2.5 miles to Monsal Head. There is a pay and display car park at Monsal Head.

Parking Lat/Long: 53.240840, -1.725364
Parking Grid Ref: SK 184 715
Parking Postcode: DE45 1NL (100m)

Accessibility   ♿

The view from Monsal Head is roadside, as is Sheepwash Bridge at Ashford in the Water. The other viewpoints are on good paths that can be slippy when wet.

Best time of year/day

Before and at sunset is a great time to photograph the view down into Monsal Dale, but in mid-summer you will be shooting directly toward the sun. Early mornings are good although it takes a couple of hours for the sun rays to reach all of the dale below. Spring and early summer is the best time for flowers. Monsal Weir can be good at anytime with cloudy but light days being best. Sheepwash Bridge is best on autumn or spring mornings.

Avove: *The classic view of Monsal Head (VP1). Canon 5D, 17-40 at 20mm, ISO 100, 1/60s at f/20. Grad. May. © CG*

Monsal Dale as seen from Putwell Hill (VP4). Canon 5D Mk 1, Canon 17-40 at 40mm, ISO 100, 1/40s at f/20. Grad. Jul. © CG

Viewpoint 4 – Northern Side

For different views of the dale, but requiring some effort to reach, is the north side above the Headstone Viaduct that carries the Monsal Trail. From north side of the viaduct take a stony path up the slope to its crest. Access Land here gives you the freedom to explore. (SK 174 717).

Viewpoint 5 – Southern Side and Fin Cop

To explore the south flank of the dale from Monsal Head take the footpath west along the edge of the dale. Where the footpath doglegs south through fields a concession path continues west to the dramatically positioned ancient settlement at Fin Cop, near the rocky outcrops of Hobbs House, from which the spectacular views continue. (SK 180 711)

Viewpoint 6 – A Weir & Great Shacklow Wood

North west of Bakewell and Ashford in the Water along the A6 are two worthwhile locations. One mile north west along the A6 from Ashford in the Water by the Wye there is footpath that follows a track to an an old, derelict mill with a lovely curving weir. From here you can access Great Shacklow Wood, perfect for bluebells and wild garlic in May. Then a mile further on along the A6 where Monsal Dale meets Deep Dale there is a car park (SK 170 706). From here you can access Deep Dale, an excellent place to photograph wild flowers.

Viewpoint 7 – Ashford in the Water and Sheepwash Bridge

The River Wye flows through the pretty village of Ashford in the Water, famous for its black marble. The village was once owned by the Cavendish family (of Chatsworth) and retains much of its original rustic charm. The highlight seen from the A6 is Sheepwash Bridge, a three-arch low packhorse bridge with an adjacent stone sheepwash, used to wash sheep before shearing. There is access on the A6 side of the river and composing up to the bridge makes a classic Peak District photograph. Early morning is best in from spring to autumn.

A dipper at Monsal Weir (VP3), Canon 6D, 70-300 at 300mm, ISO 2000, 1/1250s f/5.6. Jul. © CG

Monsal Weir (VP3). Canon 5D Mk 1, Canon 17-40 at 20mm, ISO 100, 10s at f/20. Polariser, ND. Oct. © CG

Wild garlic in Great Shacklow Wood (VP6). Canon 6D, 17-40 at 21mm, ISO 200, 1/50s at f/13. May. © CG

Top: *Monsal Weir (VP3). Canon 30D, 17-40 at 20mm, ISO 100, 2s at f/20. Polariser, ND. May. © CG*

Middle left: *The weir near Great Shacklow Wood (VP6), Canon 6D, 17-40 at 21mm, ISO 200, 2s at f/13. Polariser. Jul. © CG*

Middle right: *Sheepwash bridge at Ashford in the Water (VP7) Canon 30D, 17-40 at 20mm, ISO 100, 1/50s at f/20. May. © CG*

Waves of grain near Monsal Head (VP1). Canon 6D, 17-40 at 20mm, ISO 200, 1/40s at f/14. Grad. Jul. © CG

Standing on Moor Lane below Longstone Edge on an autumn morning looking down toward the village of Great Longstone and south over the limestone dales with layers of hilltops and trees emerging from the mist is one of the great experiences in the Peak District.

Up on the moor there are dramatic views in all directions with groves of distinctive trees to study with your camera. Access is either roadside, or by short walks, in good conditions this is one of the greats of Peak District photography.

What to shoot and viewpoints

Moor Lane is a specific viewpoint which also gives access to the fields below the edge as well as higher viewpoints east of the bend in the road near High Rake. Longstone Moor, accessible from Castlegate Lane or from the road that splits the moor, has many places to photograph including some beautiful distinctive trees.

Viewpoint 1 – Moor Lane
This is certainly one of the easiest places to witness and photograph a misty temperature inversion and good access means that you can venture, above or below the road, depending on the height of the mist.

Higher up, at the bend in the road, footpaths access further east below High Rake and quarry workings where there is an attractive stand of beech trees.

Viewpoint 2 – Hardrake Lane and Fields
Just before the road turns near its highpoint there is a footpath down the slope across a field which is worth exploring. The path joins up with Hardrake Lane then by the mound of trees and Hacksall Dale. There are several barns and attractive coppices in the meadows below.

Viewpoint 3 – Longstone Moor and Edge
This moor is a limestone heath where acidic wind-blown loess soils mask the underlying limestone. Heather, bilberry and cotton-grass normally at home on gritstone moors merge with limestone grassland in a mosaic.

Three access points are described for Longstone Moor. A short, but steep approach from Castlegate Lane takes

you direct through fields to a very photogenic group of trees near the summit of Longstone moor with great views to the west. This area is best at sunset all year round.

The quickest and least strenuous approach however is from the top of Moor Lane at the bend. Follow a broad path west which takes you by hawthorns and also quickly to a small group of attractive pine trees. This is best at sunrise especially in the winter when the sun rises in the south east.

The other approach from the Longstone Moor lay-by gives you the option of several paths across the moor and also is the best approach for viewpoints looking from the moor down to the limestone fields of Wardlow and is good in the summer especially when the cotton-grass flowers in June/July or when there is snow.

Viewpoint 4 – Great Longstone village
After early morning up high, descend to the pretty village of Great Longstone for rural village photography of its church, cottages, pubs and village green.

St. Giles church in the village of Great Longstone. Sony A6000, 10-18 at 11mm, ISO 200, 1/100s at f/6.3. Oct. © MR

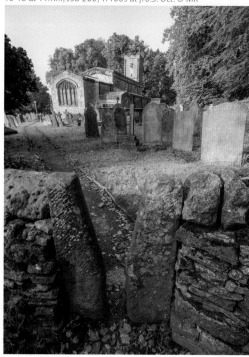

Top: Looking down from just above Moor Road (VP1). Sony A6000, 10-18 at 10mm, ISO 100, 1/250s at f/11. Oct. © MR

Above: Maple trees in buttercups and yellow rattle in fields south of Great Longstone. Canon 5D Mk 1, 17-40 at 20mm, ISO 100, 1/40s at f/20. Grad. Jun. © CG

Top The south east edge of Longstone Moor (VP3). Sony A6000, 18–200 at 34mm, ISO 160, 1/3200s at f/9. Dec. © MR.

Above: Trees on the south west edge of Longstone Moor (VP3). Canon 5D Mk 1, 17-40 at 20mm, ISO 100, 1/2s at f/20. Grad. Jan. © CG

Below: A frosty, misty sunrise on Longstone Moor (VP3). Canon 5D Mk 1, 17-40 at 20mm, ISO 100, 1/2s at f/20. Grad. Feb. © CG

Hacksall Dale (VP2). Sony A6000, 18–200 at 18mm,
ISO 160, 1/100s at f/6.3. Oct. © MR

How to get here

Longstone Edge is a high ridge of land (summit 400m) that runs east-west to the north of the village of Great Longstone.

Castlegate Lane Lay-By

Access to the west end of the ridge is by Castlegate Lane, the B6465, that runs from the A623 at Wardlow south to Monsal Head. The parking on this road is at a small lay-by at the top of the hill 1.5 miles from Wardlow/A623 or a mile north of Monsal Head. Take care, this road can be busy and cars travel fast along it. The path starts by a gate on the east of the road.

Parking Lat/Long: 53.255496, -1.7271597
Parking Grid Ref: SK 183 732
Parking Postcode: DE45 1NL (1.6km)

Moor Road

For Moor Lane just below the edge you can approach from the A623 at Wardlow, or more simply by heading north from Great Longstone village and follow Moor Lane up the hill where the view opens up where the road traverses up the edge; there are several lay-bys here. At the bend at the top of the hill there are more lay-bys and footpaths start from here on both sides of the road.

Parking Lat/Long: 53.254244, -1.697898
Parking Grid Ref: SK 202 730
Parking Postcode: DE45 1TR (1km)

Opposite top: *Barns by Hardrake Lane (VP2). Sony A6000, 18–200 at 18mm, ISO 160, 1/100s at f/8. Oct. © MR*

Opposite left: *The path to Hacksall Dale. (VP2). Sony A6000, 18–200 at 18mm, ISO 400, 1/160s at f/9. Oct. © MR*

Longstone Moor Lay-By

The back road that gives access to Longstone Moor from the north is accessed either by driving up Moor Road or by taking the minor road between Wardlow and the Foolow turn off on the A623, just by the small reservoir, and taking the second left to a plantation of trees where there is a lay-by and footpaths that lead up on to the moor.

Parking Lat/Long: 53.260900, -1.7056167
Parking Grid Ref: SK 197 738
Parking Postcode: S32 4TH (1.6km)

Accessibility ♿

The views south from Longstone Edge on Moor Road are roadside and accessible to all. The other viewpoints are on paths, some with inclines, over moorland and are all less than a kilometre/0.6 miles to reach. Wrap up well, this an exposed spot.

Best time of year/day

The views south from Moor Lane and higher up on the edge and moor are best near sunrise and sunset later in the year. When there is a temperature inversion and mist this is one of the top places to visit in the Peak. Inversions can occur all year round but are most common September to late November, and February to April. After snow, especially if there is high pressure and few clouds, sunrise and sunsets can be incredible here. Bare in mind that in midsummer the sun sets in the north-west and casts the south-facing slopes into shadow.

Above: *Hacksall Dale from Moor Road (VP1). Sony A6000, 18–200 at 32mm, ISO 200, 1/200s at f/9. Sep. © MR*

Our history is evident in the Peak District landscape from Stone Age flint arrowheads buried in peat on the Kinder plateau to the splendours of Chatsworth House by the River Derwent. Stone circles and burial mounds are some of the oldest signs dating back to the Neolithic and Bronze Age over 4000 years ago.

Five Wells Chambered Cairn on a limestone plateau west of Taddington are the remains of a Neolithic burial chamber. Originally more extensive and probably buried to form a barrow or tumuli; 17 sets of human bones along with pottery, flint arrowheads and animal teeth were found here during excavations in the 19th century.

Mining has existed in the Peak District since before Roman times, the landscape is littered with spoil heaps, mine shafts and quarries. One of the most striking of these sites is Magpie Mine, an 18/19th century lead mine south of Sheldon. Restored and managed by the Peak District Mines Historical Society, Magpie Mine is extensive with several buildings and wooden horse gins. It very much resembles a Cornish tin mine.

What to shoot and viewpoints

Five Wells Chambered Cairn

The cairn consists of half a dozen slabs which do not rise much above the surrounding fields. Be aware that in summer the site can become overgrown with cow parsley and it might be difficult to actually make it out. Midsummer dawn and sunset is a good time to be here, when the outlook beyond as well as the cairn are lit well. The cairn itself is not particularly photogenic and is best presented with good illumination and a good sky.

Magpie Mine

The Peak District has long been an important location for the extraction of lead ore but there are few places where there are obvious post-industrial remains. Magpie Mine is a notable and very photogenic exception. The most obvious features are the pit-head lifting gear and the pump engine house, which was built in the 1860s by Cornishmen in an attempt to contain the flooding that impeded work. The Cornish miners have left a lasting legacy on the map, there is a Wheal Farm and Wheal Lane nearby – Wheal being the Cornish word for a mine. The pleasing collision of blocks, circles and girders along with the exposed and sometimes bleak position makes for good photography, looking like a mine out of Poldark. Off to one side are the restored remains of the old horse gin and an ore-crushing device. The timber construction of some of the remains offers up a soft, organic juxtaposition to the hard edges of the Magpie Mine buildings.

Left: *Nature is gradually reclaiming the site at Magpie Mine. Canon 6D, 70-300 at 200mm, ISO 800, 1/800s at f/5.6. Jun. © CG*

Sunset at Five Wells Chambered Cairn. Canon 5D MK 1, 17-40 at 20mm, ISO 100, 1/8s at f/20. Grad. Jun. © CG

A passing snow shower at Magpie Mine. Canon 5D Mk 1, 17-40 at 20mm, ISO 100, 1/4s at f/20. Grad. Dec. © CG

Magpie Mine and night time photography (thanks to James Mills). Canon 6D, 17-40 at 20mm, ISO 800, 20s at f/8. Mar. © CG

How to get here

Five Wells Chambered Cairn is 500m south of the A6 a mile west of Taddington. Park near the second track west of the The Waterloo Hotel and follow this track to a gate just before Fivewells farm at the junction of several walls. Turn left and through two fields is Five Wells Chambered Cairn. You can also approach the cairn from the village of Chelmorton by the Pennine Bridleway.

Parking Lat/Long: 53.236263, -1.8158984
Parking Grid Ref: SK 123 710
The Waterloo Hotel Postcode: SK17 9TJ

Magpie Mine is near the village of Sheldon just south of the A6 near Ashford in the Water. The best approach is to take the minor road south from the A6 at Ashford in the Water signposted Sheldon but continue past the right turn to the village to a second right turn and at 0.4 miles along this road park up by a gate. The Mine is 300m down the track from the gate..

Parking Lat/Long: 53.206642, -1.743474
Parking Grid Ref: SK 172 677
Parking Postcode: DE45 1QU (300m)

Accessibility

Magpie Mine has a level short approach on a good track and is suitable for wheelchair users. The approach to Five Wells Chambered Cairn includes walking across fields.
Five Wells Chambered Cairn Approach: 30 minutes, distance 1km, ascent 83m
Magpie Mine Approach: 10 minutes, distance 300m, ascent 0m.

Best time of year/day

Five Wells Chambered Cairn is on a high limestone moorland with an elevation of 400m. The cairn gets sun all day but is best at sunset in the summer or under a stormy sky. The land around Magpie Mine is generally flat with an elevation of 300m and gets sun all day. Sunsets are a good time, and the spring sees lots of limestone flowers. The mine is also great for night photography and light painting. In winter if it snows this is a great location.

CHATSWORTH & BAKEWELL – INTRODUCTION

Bakewell and its surrounding area is the rural heart of the Peak District. Three rivers confluence here, the Wye, Lathkill and the mighty Derwent, and several warm springs allowed early settlers to harvest several crops a year from fields near Bakewell. There have been permanent settlements here since the late stone age period (Mesolithic) and the market town of Bakewell was mentioned in the Anglo-Saxon chronicle as Badecanwylla or Baedeca's springs. The three river valleys here are lush and verdant in the summer and are not surprisingly home to the Peak District's two main stately homes, Chatsworth House and Haddon Hall with their extensive gardens, farm estates and deer parks. Nearby is Rowsley Mill, a flour mill on the river Wye which we describe, one of many that were once in the area. This area was the bread basket of the Peak District.

The rocky canyon of Lathkill Dale, south east of Bakewell, is part of the Derbyshire Dales National Nature Reserve where a walk with a camera gives many opportunities; it is home to the Jacob's Ladder, the county flower of Derbyshire, old mines and beautiful views – make sure you explore the surrounding fields and lanes in summer.

There is gritstone here as well as limestone, the area being close to the Eastern Edges of Beeley Moor and Stanton Moor. Both of these stand high above the river Derwent, giving a grandstand view into the valley, and are special on misty mornings in autumn and in August when the heather flowers.

Maps

- OS Explorer Map OL241 (1:25 000) The Peak District: White Peak Area

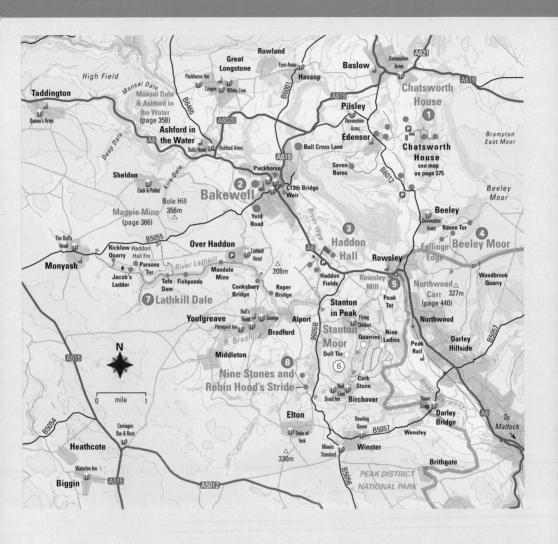

High Field

Taddington
Queen's Arms

Monsal Dale & Ashford in the Water (page 358)

Deep Dale

Rowland

Great Longstone

Packhorse Inn
Crispin White Lion

Eyre Arms Hassop

Baslow

Devonshire Arms A621

A619

Chatsworth House ①

Kirk Dale

A6 Ashford in the Water

Bulls Head Ashford Arms

A6020

A619

Pilsley

Devonshire Arms

Edensor

Ball Cross Lane

Chatsworth House
see map on page 375

Brampton East Moor

Sheldon
Cock & Pullet

Packhorse

Bole Hill
356m
△

Bakewell ②

C13th Bridge
Weir

Seven Barns

River Wye

B6012

Beeley Moor

Magpie Mine
(page 366)

Yeld Road

Beeley

Raven Tor

Devonshire Arms

④

The Bull's Head

B5055

Over Haddon

Ricklow Haddon
Quarry Hall Fm

Parsons
Tor

Lathkill
Hotel

Haddon Hall ③

A6

Rowsley

Fallinge
Edge

Beeley Moor

Monyash

River Lathkill

Mandale
Mine

208m
△

Haddon
Fields

Rowsley
Mill ⑤

Northwood
Carr 327m △
(page 440)

Woodbrook
Quarry

Jacob's
Ladder

Tufa Fishponds
Dam

Conksbury
Bridge

Raper
Bridge

Peak
Tor

⑦ Lathkill Dale

Youlgreave

Bull's
Head George

Alport

Stanton
in Peak

Flying
Childers

Northwood

Farmyard Inn

Bradford

Stanton
Moor

Quarries

Nine
Ladies

Peak
Rail

Darley
Hillside

N

R. Bradford

Middleton

B5056

Doll Tor

Nine Stones and
Robin Hood's Stride ⑧

⑥

Cork
Stone

Peak
Rail

A515

0 mile 1

Red
Lion
Druid Inn

Birchover

Three
Stags

Darley
Bridge

A6

Elton

Bowling
Green B5057

Wensley

To
Matlock

B5054

Duke of
York

Carriages
Bar & Rest

Miners
Standard

Winster

Heathcote

330m
△

Brithgate

Waterloo Inn

PEAK DISTRICT
NATIONAL PARK

Biggin A515

A5012

B5056

Opposite: *Under the three-arch bridge at Chatsworth (p.376). Sony
A6000, 18–200 at 18mm, ISO 250, 1/60s at f/10. Jun. © MR*

Chatsworth House and the river Derwent (VP6). Sony A6000, 18–200 at 26mm, ISO 100, 1/100s at f/9. Sep. © MR

Chatsworth House is a remarkable sight as you approach through the surrounding parkland. The grandeur, history and position bring a mix of feelings, but overwhelmingly the sense is one of romanticism. Specimen oaks, some well over 200 years old, reach back to a time of Elizabethan deer hunting parties, with hounds barking and arrows slicing through the air. Royal visits, parties and balls, scandal, the estate to manage, game to look after, constant improvements to the house and park, wealth, industry and titles; a rich history set in the beautiful landscape of the Peak District. Chatsworth is very special.

Chatsworth has been the seat of the Dukes of Devonshire since 1549 and 16 generations of the Cavendish family have cared for this place which is now in trust for the benefit of the public. It is the home of Peregrine Cavendish, the 12th Duke of Devonshire and his wife Amanda Cavendish, the Duchess of Devonshire.

The house has 26 rooms open to the public filled with antique furniture, paintings and neo-classical sculptures. The gardens are a delight with fountains, specimen trees, sculptures, modern art installations, lawns and several themed gardens. Photography is allowed in both the house and gardens.

It is however Chatsworth Park that we concentrate on photographically. Chatsworth Park occupies a thousand acres of parkland around the house designed by Lancelot 'Capability' Brown, it is open to the public and free of charge all year-round. Walking around Chatsworth Park with a camera early on an autumn or spring morning is one of the greatest joys in the Peak District. Herds of red and fallow deer roam amongst the trees whilst a morning mist rises from the river Derwent where flighty herons watch for rising trout by the weir. A nye of pheasants crow to each other on the lane above Edensor village. Down by James Paine's three- arch bridge the Derwent is still, a coot draws a ripple across the water as the golden windows of the house shimmer as the morning sun breaks through.

Chatsworth is steeped in the past, harking back to a rural idyll and lifestyle that we all may admire. In the present its history is there for us to witness with our eyes, our emotions and our cameras.

The three-arch bridge completed in 1761. (VP7). Sony A6000, 18–200 at 19mm, ISO 160, 1/125s at f/10. Jul. © MR

How to get here

Chatsworth House is on the B6012 situated just south of the village Baslow and 8 miles north of the small town of Matlock. From the M1 take Junction 29, Chesterfield, and follow the brown Chatsworth signs for 16 miles.

Parking: The house car park is open every day until 7pm, £4 per car (£10 at Christmas market weekends in November). Calton Lees car park at the southern end of the park is open every day until 7pm, £2 per car Monday – Friday, £3 per car Saturday, Sunday and bank holidays. Do not park by the side of the road anywhere.

Parking Lat/Long: 53.229005, -1.612281
Parking Grid Ref: SK 259 702
Parking Postcode: DE45 1PP

Accessibility &

Photography at Chatsworth is suitable for all including wheelchair users and for those with limited mobility. You are free to wander as far as you like on the network of paths in the public part of Chatsworth Park. It is steep uphill walk on paths to Viewpoint 14: The Aqueduct and Viewpoint 15: Emperor and Swiss Lakes with a round trip around 2 miles with 400ft of elevation gain. Both the house and gardens require a fee for admission, but not the park. Please use the official car parks and don't stay after dark.

Special Concerns

Chatsworth House is the home of the 12th Duke and Duchess of Cavendish and their family. Please respect their privacy and the land.

- Avoid long lenses pointing at the house, especially close-up, this is intrusive. If you look suspicious you may be approached by security.

- Photography is allowed but only for personal use. Contact Chatsworth House estate for commercial use permits.
- Park only at Calton Lees car park or at Chatsworth House car park
- Don't stalk deer, walk quietly around the park and you will see them.
- Stay within the public part of the park and stick to paths.
- Drop no litter.
- Only take photos between sunrise or sunset unless at a Chatsworth event. At night you may be mistaken for a poacher. This is a working estate.

Best time of year/day

Nearly a million people visit Chatsworth House and Park each year and unless you like taking photographs of people, or one of the many events held here, it is best to avoid peak holiday times and busy weekends. However, even during summer holidays if you visit very early or late, you will find solitude. The best times of year for photography are spring, late summer, autumn and when it snows. Early morning and evenings are the best times, however Chatsworth House itself rarely gets direct sunrise because of its aspect and hills that block the rising sun – you have to wait an hour or so after sunrise. The house and the estate faces west so late afternoon to sunset is often perfect, but the sun does drop behind the surrounding hills before sunset. If there is a chance of a temperature inversion and valley mist, head for Chatsworth early and spend several hours here, it will be worth it.

Above: *A summer evening at Chatsworth.. (VP6). Sony A6000, 18–200 at 19mm, ISO 100, 1/125s at f/9. Jul. © MR*

What to shoot and viewpoints

Whilst the viewpoints are described from the south starting at Calton Lees car park then northward, each viewpoint can be visited individually. Chatsworth Park has many excellent viewpoints and subjects to photograph, those described will give you a good starting point.

Viewpoint 1 – One Arch Bridge

At the south of the park near to Calton Lees car park is the beautiful One Arch Bridge built by James Paine and completed in 1760. The bridge, constructed from finely cut local sandstone is reflected in the river Derwent when calm. It can be photographed from the park or from the road.

Viewpoint 2 – The Mill

On the path to Chatsworth House from Carlton Lees down by the river is an ornamented working mill. It was built for aesthetic reasons by James Paine 1762 to enhance the south end of the park. It was damaged by falling trees in a storm in 1961 and Duchess Deborah made it safe as a ruin so preserving this beautiful building which is a treat to photograph in the autumn with its adjacent beech trees.

Viewpoint 3 – The Weir

Beyond the the mill along the path is a beautiful six-step weir, the first of two weirs on the Derwent at Chatsworth. This weir is best photographed at sunrise and early morning in autumn/winter when illuminated by the sun or surrounded by mist.

Viewpoint 4 – The Second Weir

About 500m further toward the house is a second weir. The view is restricted by trees but if you are lucky you will witness one of Chatsworth's herons fishing in the pool above the weir. You will need a long lens and need to be very stealthy in your approach.

Viewpoint 5 – Chatsworth House and River Derwent View

Just beyond the second weir the ground slopes down and this elevated position allows an uninterrupted view following the broad River Derwent to Chatsworth House. This is a classic view, especially when there are deer in the foreground. Good from early morning onwards but quite special near or at sunset for most of the year. There is a bench under some trees to the north west which makes a beautiful foreground subject.

St. Peter's and Edensor from Park Wood Hill (VP8). Sony A6000, 10-18 at 11mm, ISO 640, 1/160s at f/9. Jun. © MR

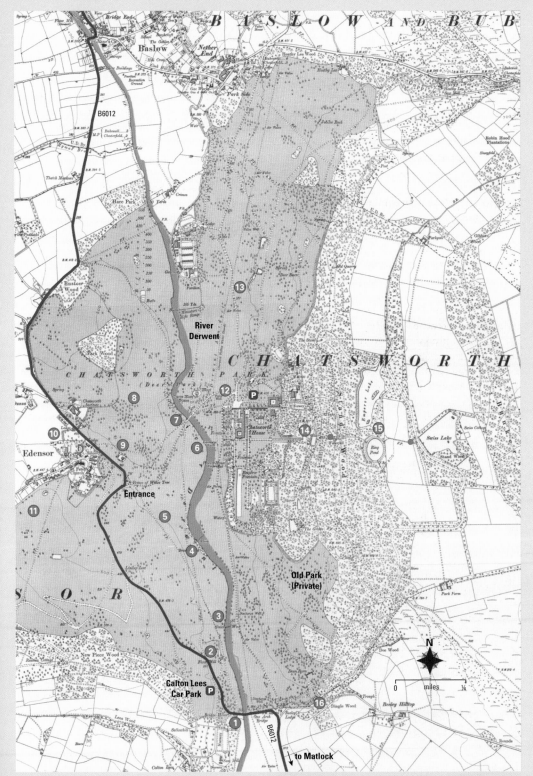

An OS map of Chatsworth. Revised: 1919 to 1920. Published: 1923. With numbered viewpoints marked.

Viewpoint 6 – Chatsworth House Reflection

Just by the Three Arch Bridge on Chatsworth's main driveway the river bends and flows leisurely, coots and other water fowl are often seen here. If there is little wind the gold-gilded window frames shimmer in the river lit by the evening sun, or visit early on a misty morning.

Viewpoint 7 – Three Arch Bridge

James Paine was a prolific architect who designed many grand buildings and structures in the 18th century. His Three Arch Bridge was based on the Ponte di Tiberio, Rimini, Italy and completed in 1761. The bridge was purposely positioned to provide a view of the house and from several points around the bridge there are excellent compositions, not just with house in view, and also detail shots.

Close by, on the house side of the river, is Queen Mary's Bower, a 16th century building that was once part of a water garden by the river and it is thought that it was used as a place of repose for Mary Queen of Scots when she was held captive at Chatsworth in the 1570s.

Viewpoint 8 – Park Wood Hill

Both slopes and the summit of Park Wood Hill, between the house and the village of Edensor, can be accessed from the village or from Three Arch Bridge. Here you will find many beautiful singular trees and groups of trees, and often fallow and red deer. It is also a great viewpoint for both the church spire of St.Michael's Church at Ednsor on the west slope and, by the riverside, compositions of Chatsworth House to the east. In the winter the slope down to Endensor is a great sledging hill.

Viewpoint 9 – The Gardeners Cottage

Opposite Edensor is the Gardener's Cottage, a grade II listed building built in the early 19th century. This is a beautiful study especially early in the morning. Also of note, and perhaps better, are the Tudor-style cottages either side of the entrance gate which both have delightful colourful gardens in the summer. There are maples nearby which produce wonderful colours in early autumn.

Viewpoint 10 – Edensor

Edensor is a village built and owned by the Dukes of Devonshire, often mentioned as one of the most beautiful villages in England. There has been a village here since the first century but the original site was in direct view of Chatsworth. The 6th Duke of Devonshire moved the village to its present position with current houses built by Joseph Paxton in 1839 based on illustrations in a book entitled *The Encyclopaedia of Cottage, Farm and Villa Architecture* by *John Claudius Loudon*. Each house has a different style of chimney pot. The residents of Edensor either work for Chatsworth or are retired from service.

Edensor is at its best in late spring and in the autumn, and is usually accessible after snow. The gardens are immaculate and the village green has rows of crab apple trees – they blossom in spring and bare fruit in autumn – beautiful pines, a weeping beech and colourful maple trees. St. Peter's Church is worth a visit both inside for its many antiquities and outside, watch for the sheep grazing

The Weeping Rock above Chatsworth House (VP14). Canon 6D, 70-300 at 84mm, ISO 50, 1s at f/20. Feb. © CG.

in the graveyard. The Dukes of Devonshire are buried in the graveyard as are Debra Mitford, the Dowager Duchess of Devonshire who died in 2014 and Kathleen Kennedy, the sister of President John F Kennedy. Up the lane behind Edensor provides a great viewpoint back down to the church and further up hill are usually lots of pheasants.

Viewpoint 11 – The Seven Barns of Edensor

Behind the village of Edensor the park rises up to New Piece Wood and Calton Pasture. Below the wood are seven barns situated in a shallow valley. Walk up the lane above Edensor or take a footpath from Edensor to reach these barns. This photographic walk has lots of subjects: the view down to Edensor and the church spire, the barns themselves, deer and pheasants, solitary trees and, if you go up high near the New Piece Wood, great compositions of Chatsworth House and the Hunting Tower in Stand Wood. In autumn the best time is mid-afternoon to an hour before sunset, earlier in the winter.

Viewpoint 12 – View of the Hunting Tower

If you park at Chatsworth House there is a great view up to the Hunting Tower which was completed around 1582 for Bess of Hardwick, the ancestress of the Dukes of Devonshire. There are paths that pass by the tower for more intimate portraits. If you walk west, south of the river from the Three Arch Bridge, there are good views of the Hunting Tower.

The Tudor gatehouse (VP9). Sony A6000, 18–200 at 24mm, ISO 100, 1/200s at f/8. Aug. © MR

Park Wood Hill sledging slope and Edensor (VP8). Sony A6000, 18–200 at 18mm, ISO 200, 1/100s at f/8. Jan. © MR

Viewpoint 13 – The Deer Park

To the north of the house there is no one stand-out subject to visit but this tree-studded parkland and its river present many photographic opportunities including avenues of trees, a cricket green, riverside walks and in the autumn, rutting deer. Again autumn mornings are rather special. See Big Moor (page 296) for more on photographing deer.

Viewpoint 14 – The Aqueduct /15: Emperor and Swiss Lakes

This is a round trip of around 2 miles with 400ft of elevation gain from Chatsworth House car park.

Behind Chatsworth House is Stand Wood. Whilst not the original medieval woodland this mixed-deciduous woodland provides a texture and an often colourful backdrop to the house. It has a network of footpaths and highlights here are part of the extensive waterworks designed by Joseph Paxton that provide Chatsworth's ponds, gardens and fountains with a reliable source of water. The four-arched stone Aqueduct behind the gardens funnels water and creates a single-drop waterfall as well as providing unusual views of the house and park. Above is the Souter Stone where you will find another waterfall. These waterfalls are fed by four small lakes, especially Emperor and Swiss Lakes which should be high on your visit list for autumn.

Viewpoint 16 – Old Park View

If you walk up the steep lane that leaves the B6102, beyond the One Arch Bridge passing Beeley Lodge you can peer over the fence and wall into the private Old Park where there are several ancient specimen oak, often deer and a stone deer barn.

Fallow deer in Chatsworth Park. Canon 450D, 400, ISO 800, 1/200s at f/5.6. Oct. © CG

The six-step weir at the south end off the park (VP3). Sony A6000, 18–200 at 18mm, ISO 200, 1/125s at f/9. Sep. © MR

Chatsworth House garden detail. Sony A6000, 18–200 at 183mm, ISO 160, 1/500s at f/10. Jul. © MR

Opposite: *Looking down on three arch bridge by the river. Sony A6000, 18–200 at 39mm, ISO 200, 1/160s at f/10. Oct. © MR*

Top: A winter wander (VP12). Sony A6000, 18–200 at 25mm, ISO 200, 1/160s at f/6.3. Jan. © MR

Above: A view of the hunting tower (VP12). Sony A6000, 18–200 at 57mm, ISO 200, 1/100s at f/9. Oct. © MR

Top: In late September the leaves start to change colour. Sony A6000, 18–200 at 18mm, ISO 100, 1/160s at f/9. Sep. © MR

Above: Three of the seven barns of Edensor (V11). Sony A6000, 18–200 at 38mm, ISO 100, 1/100s at f/11. Oct. © MR

The origins of Bakewell can be traced back to Anglo-Saxon times with its parish church, All Saints, founded in the 9th century. Whilst still a market town and a centre for agriculture, it is now one of the most popular towns for tourism in the Peak District – if you visit you must try the local confection, Bakewell Pudding.

The river Wye meanders slowly through the town and its river walks are a delight. The town's famous five-arch bridge dates from the 13th century, one of oldest structures in the area. In July or early August the busy Bakewell Show, established in 1819, provides ample photo-opportunities of prize-winning livestock, horticulture, rural crafts and local characters.

What to shoot and viewpoints

Viewpoint 1 – The Church from Yeld Road

There is a particularly good shot of the parish church from Yeld Road. Walk up the Monyash Road (B5055) from the roundabout at the town centre for 0.2 miles and go left on Yeld Road where the view opens up. This viewpoint is best on an autumn afternoon when the sun lights up the church and the countryside behind it.

Viewpoint 2 – All Saints Church and the Saxon Carvings

All Saints Church is host to an amazing collection of Saxon carvings. The collection is located in the western portico at the rear of this medieval church. There is also a beautiful Saxon Cross in the churchyard just next to the east face of the church. The carvings in the portico are best shot at midday in summer when the sun reflects off the stone floor and illuminates the interior with lovely warm light.

Viewpoint 3 – The 13th Century Bridge

This beautiful five-arch bridge carries the Baslow Road across the River Wye. It can be photographed from all sides but the most sympathetic angle is from the riverside walkway upstream of the bridge on the northern bank.

Viewpoint 4 – The Packhorse Bridge

Upstream from the main bridge a riverside footpath takes you through meadows where you will often see people fly fishing for the abundant trout. 500m walk upstream of the main bridge is an old packhorse bridge. This is best lit in the afternoon when the sun is in the west.

Opposite: The Medieval bridge (VP3). Sony A6000, 18–200 at 18mm, ISO 400, 1/80s at f/11. Jun. © MR

Vernon Chapel in All Saints Church (VP2). Canon 6D, 70-300 at 70mm, ISO 2000, 1/1000s at f/5.6. © CG

Bakewell show, worth a visit. Sony A6000, 18–200 at 80mm, ISO 400, 1/125s at f/5.6. Aug. © MR

A showman and prize bull at Bakewell Show. Canon 30D, 70-300 at 140mm ISO 400, f5.6, 1/200s. Aug. © CG

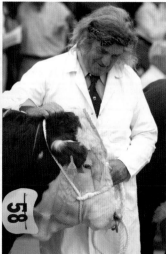

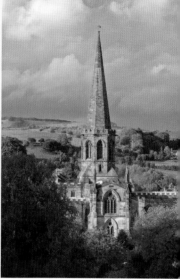

Mmmm, Bakewell Pudding … © CG

Above right: All Saints Church from Yeld Road (VP1). Canon 5D, 70-300 at 120mm, ISO 100, 1/30s at f/14. Sep. © CG

Viewpoint 5 – The Weir

Just downstream from the bridge there is a small weir which is a focus for all sorts of animal life; ducks, gulls, geese and trout all flock around the weir especially when there are people there to feed them. Get here early or stay later for compositions across the weir when the light will be better and there will be fewer people.

Viewpoint 6 – The Bakewell Show

Bakewell Show is one of the largest agricultural and country shows in the Peak District. There are competitions for best livestock, pets, flowers and vegetables, various equestrian competitions, and the show features rural arts and crafts. It is well-attended, with much of the local farming community attending and offers a fantastic mix of photo-opportunities. The show is usually held in the last week of July or first week of August. See **www.bakewellshow.org** for more information.

Viewpoint 7 – Ball Cross Lane

There is a lovely view over Bakewell from Ball Cross Lane, which crosses the hills to the east of the town to Chatsworth. Ball Cross Lane branches off Station Road and passes the golf club before zig-zagging its way through the woods. There is a wide point in the lane at the first zig-zag where you can park a car. This position is particularly good on late spring mornings when the dawn light bathes the town and the mists linger in the valley below you. A longer lens suits the position best as there is little foreground on offer.

How to get here

Bakewell is on the A6, 12 miles east of Buxton and 9 miles north west of Matlock. There is plenty of parking in several pay-and-display car parks.

Parking Lat/Long: 53.211803,-1.670746
Parking Grid Ref: SK 220 684
Parking Postcode: DE45 1EZ (100m)

Accessibility ♿

Bakewell town centre is fairly level and has drop kerbs. Outside the immediate town centre the roads and paths get quite steep so although the path surfaces are all good some uphill walking is required to see the entire town.

Best time of year/day

Bakewell sits in a bowl formed by the surrounding hills and can lose the sun quite quickly on winter afternoons. Spring and autumn in Bakewell are both lovely. Because of the river, the town often gets morning mist from autumn through to spring and if you are up high, its church spire can be seen popping out of the valley mist.

Top left: Trout from the bridge near the weir (VP5). Sony A6000, 18–200mm at 40mm, ISO 400, 1/125s at f/5.6. Aug. © MR

Haddon Hall from Haddon Fields, autumn is the time (VP6)
Sony A6000, 18–200 at 44mm, ISO 250, 1/125s at f/9. Oct. © MR

The origins of Haddon Hall date back to 1066 and William the Conqueror, whose illegitimate son William Peverell the Elder first held the manor. The hall passed to the Avenell family and then by marriage to Sir Richard Vernon, and eventually to the Manners family when it became one of the seats of the Duke of Rutland. Haddon is now the home of Lord Edward Manners, brother of David Manners, 11th Duke of Rutland.

The Hall is unique, in that it has retained most of its 16th century architecture and decor as it was left untouched for 200 years while the Dukes of Rutland resided at Belvoir Castle. In the 1920s John Manners, the 9th Duke of Rutland, realising the importance of the hall being frozen in time, set to work restoring it so that now we can enjoy a step back to Medieval and Tudor times.

Visit Haddon in July for its gardens. Sony A6000, 18–200 at 120mm, ISO 200, 1/100s at f/8. Jul. © MR

Inside the Banqueting Hall at Haddon Hall. Canon 5D Mk 1, 17-40 at 20mm, ISO 100, 2s at f/20. Jan. © CG

Photography is welcomed at Haddon by Lord Edward, both in the hall and in its beautiful walled gardens and a visit will not be disappointing. The Hall is set in mixed woodland of Haddon Estate Parkland on a south west slope next to the river Wye.

What to shoot and viewpoints

Viewpoint 1: The Courtyard
The immediate view from the entrance gate into the courtyard takes in the superb front aspect of the hall.

Viewpoint 2: Architectural Details and the Gardens
A walk around the outside of the hall will reveal many architectural details to photograph, especially carved stonework (patinations) and leaded-windows, often shrouded with flowers. Look up at the eaves of the buildings and the crenellations. The hall is covered in fabulous stone detail that evokes its age and history. A photographic walk around the Elizabethan terraced gardens – there is a lower and upper garden – is best in late spring and early summer.

Viewpoint 3: The Bridge from the Garden
One corner of the terrace looks out over the river Wye, down to a pretty stone footbridge that crosses the river. This composes well with the tree-shrouded river beyond it. A path leads down to the bridge and from here are compositions looking back at Haddon with the river Wye in the foreground.

INSIDE THE HALL
The house has two courtyards surrounded by many rooms, all have photographic interests but highlights include:

Viewpoint 4: The Banqueting Hall
Immediately inside the front door to the hall is the Banqueting Hall. In the afternoon the light streams into here from the large south-facing windows.

Viewpoint 5: The Long Gallery
Up some stairs at the back of the hall is the Long Gallery. A wonderful room, well lit from windows on both sides. Fabulously photogenic.

The courtyard of Haddon Hall from the entrance. Canon 5D Mk 1, 17-40 at 20mm, ISO 100, 1/20s at f/20. Grad. Jan. © CG

FROM AFAR

Viewpoint 6: The Hall from Haddon Fields

Opposite the hall entrance driveway between a house and the car park two footpaths lead up hill through the fields, know as Haddon Fields. One path follows a wall up by some dew ponds, the other traverses across the field by a field barn. Both footpaths have great viewpoints looking back at the hall. The best time is late autumn, usually in November, when, with the sun rising in the south east and setting in the south west, the hall will be illuminated for most of the day surrounded by a kaleidoscope of autumn hues. For the golden hours, get here just before sunrise (sunrise 7am) or at least two hours before sunset (sunset is 4.30pm in November).

Note: Sometimes the car park by the hall will be closed and there is no good parking close-by. In these circumstances drive toward Rowsley and turn right on the B5056 toward Alport and park at the first junction (53.180131, -1.655357) there is a footpath that leads by Shining Bank quarry to the north and then right over the hill passing a plantation to Haddon Fields in front of the hall.

How to get here

Haddon Hall is located on the A6 a mile and a half south of Bakewell. Parking is in a large private car park on the A6 opposite the hall.

Parking Lat/Long: 53.191786,-1.652251
Parking Grid Ref: SK 233 661
Parking Postcode: DE45 1LA

Accessibility ♿

Access from the car park to the hall is via a gravel drive. The hall is slightly uphill from the drive. The paths around the gardens are also gravel. Within the hall itself the floor is a mixture of old, undulating and uneven gritstone slabs and floorboards with rugs in places.

Best time of year/day

Haddon opens daily from May to October and is best in the early summer when the gardens are at their most beautiful. You are likely to get fewer people in your photographs if you visit during the week outside the holiday periods. There is an entrance charge, check **www.haddonhall.co.uk** for details.

Private Viewings

Photographers and clubs wishing to get the place to themselves can attend outside normal opening times, during which time they are also free to use a tripod with rubber feet. This is quite useful given the fact that many of the rooms are kept deliberately darkened to help preserve the fragile furniture and fittings in the house. Rates for commercial photography and individuals wanting to visit outside opening times are subject to negotiation and depend on the use to which the resulting pictures will be put.

Beeley Moor and Fallinge Edge is the high moorland east of the A6 between Beeley in the north and Darley Dale in the south. The moor sits above the Derwent Valley and various points on the skyline here provide very good viewpoints on autumn mornings looking down into a mist-filled valley. On the moor there are ancient remains including a triple-ring cairn and a tooth-shaped standing stone near Raven Tor. Below Raven Tor the land falls down to manicured trees and fields that in a low-sun cast wonderful shadows.

South of Chesterfield Road, which crosses the moor above Rowsley Bar, the character changes with heather and lone silver birches dominating offering opportunities for minimalist compositions during the heather bloom in August. At Woodbrook Quarry there is one of the most colourful patches of rhododendron in the Peak District. This section of the moor is also good for cotton grass in late spring.

What to shoot and viewpoints

Viewpoint 1 – Raven Tor Standing Stone and Derwent Views

From the parking on Bent Lane walk north onto the moor following an old quarry track and across the moor trending west to Fallinge Edge. At roughly SK 280 669 there is a tooth-shaped standing stone with a superb view behind it giving a great early morning autumn shot. There are many viewpoints here looking down to the Derwent Valley.

Viewpoint 2 – Fallinge Edge Heather and Silver Birches

From the parking spot walk east down Chesterfield Road toward Rowsley to enter Little Bumper Piece by a gate (SK 276 659) that leads to the southern part of Fallinge Edge. The rich heather moorland here has several singular silver birches, best photographed in August.

Viewpoint 3 – Woodbrook Quarry Rhododendrons

Just east of the junction along Chesterfield Road is a stile (SK 282 662). Through this and south takes you across Access Land to the disused Woodbrook Quarry. Immediately after the quarry the land descends and a big stand of rhododendron occupies the damp ground around the head of a brook. Unlike most feral Rhododendron ponticum, which tends to be relentlessly purple, this stand is riot of different colours. In summer, bees abound, cuckoos call and the air is heady with scent. On a calm, late spring evening when the sun is low in the western sky this is a magical place to be.

Beeley Hilltop isolated in the morning mists (VP1). Canon 5D Mk 1, 70-300 at 120mm, ISO 100, f1/10s at f/14. Oct. © CG

How to get here

Fallinge Edge and Beeley Moor can be accessed from Chesterfield Road, which goes west from the village of Rowsley up the steep Rowsley Bar. Follow the A6 east from Bakewell for 2.5 miles to Rowsley. Turn left onto the B6012 toward Beeley and Chatsworth and then after a tenth of a mile turn right onto Chesterfield Road. Follow the lane upwards, though the bends of Rowsley Bar and onto the moor. Turn right onto Bent Lane and park immediately on the left, where there is space for a several cars.

Parking Lat/Long: 53.191671,-1.580351
Parking Grid Ref: SK 281 661
Parking Postcode: DE4 2NN (1 mile)

Accessibility

Although this is Access Land it is rarely visited country and for the most part passage is via rough paths and sheep tracks through often deep heather.

Best time of year/day

In spring (June) there can be a lot of cotton grass here while in August the heather is superb. The aspect is quite flat and combined with its high elevation the area receives light well in both the morning and the evening. There may be morning mist in the adjacent Derwent Valley from autumn through spring.

Top: From Fallinge Edge, looking north (VP1). Canon 5D Mk 1, 17-40 at 20mm, ISO 100, 1/20s at f/20. Grad. Oct. © CG

Heather on Fallinge Edge punctuated by lone silver birch trees. Canon 30D, 17-40 at 20mm, ISO 100, 1/20s at f/20. Aug. © CG

Rhodedendrons at Woodbrook Quarry. Canon 6D, 17-40 at 20mm, ISO 100, 1/20s at f/14. Grad. Jun. © CG

Looking down on Rowsley from Peak Tor (p. 392, VP5). Canon 6D, 70-300 at 140mm, ISO 100, 1/6 at f/20. Dec. © CG

By the river Wye in the village of Rowsley is Rowsley Mill, or to give its proper name, Caudwell's Mill. Built in 1874 by John Caudwell, replacing two previous mills on the same site, initially it used eight gritstone millstones powered by the fast-flowing river Wye to mill grain to produce flour for bread making.

In 1885, after a visit to an international milling exhibition, Caudwell reconfigured the mill to use electric-powered cast-iron rollers, with the water wheels being replaced by a water-powered turbine. The mill operated full-time in this mode for over 100 years before becoming the historic, listed building that it now is. The successive layers of technology have created an extraordinary interior. An almost steam-punk-like mash-up of history colliding with hardware that is full of detail and interest. Band hoists sit comfortably next to modern hydraulics while the stained and beautifully patinated wood is annotated in knife and pen by the workers who toiled here. The visitor-access walkways bring you into close proximity with the details.

What to shoot and viewpoints

Viewpoint 1 – The Leat

The leat, or goit, is a water channel that feeds the mill. It runs off the river Wye just upstream of the mill. There is footpath that runs alongside it from the mill that offers compositions of the mill, mill weir and the pretty cottages alongside it. You will often find ducks swimming in the leat. It is best later in the day when the sun illuminates this side of the mill complex.

Viewpoint 2 – External machinery

Immediately around the environs of the mill there is a lot of exposed machinery and engineering paraphernalia that offers good detail.

Viewpoint 3 – Inside the mill

A whole host of photogenic detail, from individual components, traces of social/historical comment left by the workers to impressive engineering set pieces. The Roller Room in particular makes for a superb HDR/Exposure blend

opportunity. An opportunity worthy of many visits. The interior of the mill is best photographed in the late afternoon or early evening when the sun enters through the many windows on that side of the building.

The makers badge on one of the roller presses at Caudwell Mill.© CG

How to get here

Situated in the village of Rowsley, Rowsley Mill is 2.5 miles east of Bakewell and 4.3 miles north of Matlock. Passing through Rowsley take Woodhouse Lane immediately opposite the Peacock Hotel. The Rowsley Mill car park is on your right.

Parking Lat/Long: 53.187833,-1.617712
Parking Grid Ref: SK 256 657
Parking Postcode: DE4 2EE

Photographer Visits

Photographers are welcome at Caudwell's Mill during normal opening hours as regular paying guests but the use of tripods is not allowed at this time as they create a trip hazard in the public access areas. The Trust, who operate the mill, welcome groups and visitors outside the usual opening times by special arrangement for a couple of hours after the mill has closed to the public for the day when tripods can be used. There is a small fee. Please contact the mill well in advance of your visit so that staff cover can be arranged to accompany you. We recommend that you visit in the summer months when the evening light will be at is most advantageous to photography. There are also craft shops and an excellent cafe here. For more information see **www.caudwellsmill.co.uk**
Telephone: 01629 734374
Email: enquiries@caudwellsmill.co.uk

Accessibility ♿

The approach to the mill is a level, gravel track. Within the courtyard is a mixture of level surfaces. Inside the mill is wooden flooring with a mixture of stone and wooden steps. Those with limited mobility will find moving around the inside of the mill tricky.

Best time of year/day

If visiting out of hours then late on the long days of midsummer are best. The evening sun washes into the interior of the mill through the west-facing windows. Dynamic range might be an issue but the subject lends itself well to HDR techniques. Externally autumn is good as the area has many colourful deciduous trees.

Above: *The cottage next to the leat at Caudwell's Mill (VP1). Canon 5D Mk 1, 17-40 at 20mm, ISO 100, 1/4s at f/20. Grad. Oct. © CG*

Below: *The roller press room at Caudwell's Mill (VP3). Canon 6D, 17-40 at 20mm, ISO 100, 2s at f/14 © CG*

Situated above the Wye and Derwent valleys, Stanton Moor has been frequented by humans for thousands of years and dominates the skyline above Darley Dale in the east. Among its heather and stands of silver birch are barrows, stone circles, ancient enclosures, quarries, gritstone blocks and standing stones.

The best-known feature of the moor is the Nine Ladies Stone Circle which, whilst not particularly impressive, has a powerful draw. Stanton Moor is a beautiful, haunting and bewitching location with, for the photographer, both the natural and man-made features contributing to its charm. The whole area is a scheduled ancient monument.

What to shoot and viewpoints

Viewpoint 1 – The Cork Stone

The Cork Stone is located east of the parking area, a hundred metres from the road. It is a natural gritstone pinnacle that has had foot holes cut into it to allow people to climb to its top. It is a bit of an ugly brute but it is intricately carved with hundreds of years of graffiti, making it an interesting subject.

Viewpoint 2 – Nine Ladies Stone Circle

Nine Ladies Stone Circle (SK 249 634) is three-quarters of a mile following paths north east from the parking on the edge of the moor. Thought to have been built in the early Bronze Age, local tradition believes it to depict nine ladies turned to stone as a penalty for dancing on Sunday. The eastern side of the circle is sheltered by a stand of trees which shades it at sunrise all year round.

Viewpoint 3 – Doll Tor Stone Circle

The Doll Tor Stone Circle (SK 238 628) is a low circle of six stones tucked into the north eastern edge of the woods. It is best visited on midsummer evenings when the sun illuminates this part of the wood. Access is informal but there is a proper pedestrian access gate in the wall at SK 241 628 on the Birchover Road and you will have to route-find your way to it.

Viewpoint 4 – The Old Quarries

On Stanton Moor quarrying is mainly confined to the western edge of the moor. Nature has intervened favourably here and silver birch and heather abound, softening the hard edges of industry. This area is worth exploring as views suddenly open up and evening light dapples beautifully through the silver birch trees.

Viewpoint 5 – Peak Tor

On the north-eastern corner of Stanton Moor is Peak Tor (SK 252 652), a shapely tree-covered knoll that dominates the skyline above Rowsley and can be photographed from all angles in the area. In spring the areas between the trees are full of bluebells and the lovely crown of trees is a mixture of russet hues in autumn. There is a footpath that runs below the tor.

Across the fields toward Peak Tor, taken near Rowsley (VP5). Canon 6D, 70-300 at 120mm, ISO 100, 1/40s at f/14. May. © CG

The Cork Stone (VP1). Canon 6D, 17-40 at 20mm, ISO 100, f/14 at 1/30s. Grad. Aug. © CG

Nine Ladies Stone Circle (VP2). Go early or late. Canon 5D Mk 1, 17-40 at 20mm, ISO 100, 1/100s at f/20. Grad. Apr. © CG

Rhododendron floating on heather on Stanton Moor. Canon 5D Mk 1, 17-40 at 20mm, ISO 100, 1/40s at f/20. Grad. Aug. © CG

How to get here

Access to the moor is easiest from the minor road (Birchover Road) between the villages of Stanton in Peak and Birchover. Both villages are usually approached from the A6. The parking spot is 0.8 miles south of Stanton in Peak and half-a-mile north of Birchover on Birchover Road near the summit trig point and cairn of the moor (elevation 323m).

Parking Lat/Long: 53.161959,-1.639554
Parking Grid Ref: SK 241 628
Parking Postcode: DE4 2BN (1km)

Accessibility

The moorland paths here are sandy and well-drained. It is possible to enjoy the moor without too much exertion however it is challenging for wheel-chair users.

Best time of year/day

Stanton Moor stands above the surrounding countryside and is not overshadowed. It illuminates well at all times of day and throughout the year. The heather here is very good in August, the autumn colours superb and the many bare trees in winter offer endless possibilities. It is a very good all-year-round location.

"the purest and most transparent stream that I ever yet saw … and breeds, it is said, the reddest and the best trouts in England."
Charles Cotton, The Compleat Angler.

The river Lathkill rises in a bowl of land at the heart of the White Peak plateau below the village of Monyash. The river, a six and a half mile tributary of the river Wye, flows intermittently down Lathkill Dale. Over 150ft deep in places, this dale is an impressive rocky canyon at its west end with limestone crags and pinnacles with woodland taking over further east. The dale is a national nature reserve and an ancient monument for its lead mining which can be traced back to the 16th century.

Lathkill Dale has much diversity, offering close up studies of flowers, woodland, geology, river, waterfalls and wildlife as well as wider, limestone country landscape compositions. Both Monyash with its village pond and church, and the village of Over Haddon, give details of Peak District village life and architecture and are surrounded by flower-filled hay meadows in summer.

What to shoot and viewpoints

Through a kissing-gate a grassy footpath leads down to the dale from the lay-by near Monyash and onto Ricklow Quarry on your left.

Viewpoint 1 – Around Ricklow Quarry

As you walk down to the dale wildlife can be abundant near this old marble quarry and this is a good place to stake out at dawn or just before sunset. With luck, and stealth, you will encounter little owls, barn owls and stoats. It's a steep walk from the dale up to the quarry.

Lathkill Dale from the promontory of Parsons Tor (VP3). Canon 5D Mk 1, 17-40 at 20mm, ISO 100, 1/40s at f/20. Nov. © CG

One of several weirs on the fishponds (VP5). Canon 5D, Canon 17-40 at 20mm, ISO 100, 4s at f/20. Polariser, ND. Jun. © CG

Viewpoint 2 – Below Ricklow Quarry and Jacob's Ladder

The dale closes in as you walk beyond the quarry with limestone cliffs on both sides. Early summer (June/July) sees purple clumps of the rare Jacob's Ladder (the county flower of Derbyshire) in this stretch of the dale. This area can be good at sunset for wide shots of the dale.

Viewpoint 3 – Parsons Tor

On the north rim of the dale 500m east of Ricklow Quarry is a prominent nose of limestone called Parsons Tor. This is one of the best viewpoints looking down into the dale and can be accessed by a path that follows the rim from Ricklow Quarry to the rocky promontory (it can also be accessed below by walking up the sub-dale by it). Care is needed here, the tor is named after the vicar of Monyash who fell into the gorge to his death after a late night in Bakewell. The rocky pinnacle and the scoop of the dale sides provide foreground to the receding dale. Early and late light from September to March illuminates this scene well.

Below Parsons Tor is a large hole, Lathkill Head Cave (SK 170 658) this is a resurgence where the River Lathkill gushes when the water table is high enough. Below this point the river starts to emerge in wet weather and where Cales Dale joins Lathkill Dale the grassy dale slopes become covered by trees.

Viewpoint 4 – The Tufa Dam

Just over a a kilometre from Parsons Tor and below Haddon Grove Farm at SK 183 657 there is an exceptionally photogenic tufa dam or weir that usually has water flowing over it. Tufa is a porous limestone formed by deposition of calcium carbonate from the water and here the mineral has been deposited on algae, mosses and liverworts, and it is still growing. The water plunges in segments and is surrounded grasses and watercress. Best to use a polarising filter to reduce glare and pull out detail for your composition, and using an ND filter to slow shutter speed to several seconds will give you that milky effect.

Viewpoint 5 – The Fishponds and Mandale Mine

Below the Tufa Dam the river is interrupted by a sequence of beautiful fishponds, each one with a different weir. They are all immensely photogenic and the crystal clear waters utterly compelling. As you walk eastwards you will encounter first an old corn mill, now just a pool and two old millstones, then below the village of Over Haddon are the remains of Mandale Mine: an old lead mine, including an engine house, aqueduct and sough (drainage tunnel).

Viewpoint 6 – Conksbury Bridge and Raper Lodge Packhorse Bridge

Between the villages of Over Haddon and Alport, just before the river Lathkill joins the Wye is a lovely old bridge with low arches. Conksbury Bridge is not the easiest thing to photograph because the vantage points are restricted but there is a footpath upstream from the bridge.

Follow a path downstream on the south bank of the river for 400m to Raper Lodge Packhorse Bridge, a pretty little packhorse bridge that joins Raper Lodge to the now disused Raper Mine. Immediately above the bridge there is an elegant curving weir which photographs well with the river Lathkill leading the eye away and up to a small cascade above the weir pool. The pool is often rich with water lilies in summer.

Below right: The Tufa Dam in Lathkill Dale (VP4). Canon 5D Mk 1, 17-40 at 20mm, ISO 100, 2s at f/20. CPL. Jun. © CG

The beautiful, curving weir at Raper Lodge Bridge (VP6). Canon 6D, 17-40 at 20mm, ISO 100, 1/2s at f/14. Polariser. Jul. © CG

There are many dippers in Lathkill Dale. Canon 6D, 70-300 at 300mm, ISO 2000, 1/80s at f/5.6. Feb. © CG

How to get here

Lathkill Dale has a number of access points points but for a good exploration of its charms (or if heading straight to its Tufa Dam or Parsons Tor) start at the lay-by on Bakewell Road, just east of Monyash. If coming from the town of Bakewell take the B5055 (Kings Street) leaving the A6 immediately before the Matlock side of the Rutland Square roundabout. Head uphill where it becomes Monyash Road and continue for 3.5 miles. Just before Monyash there are some public toilets on your left, park just after them in a lay-by on your right.

Parking Lat/Long: 53.194948,-1.765757
Parking Grid Ref: SK 157 664
Parking Postcode: DE45 1JH (500m)

There is a pay and display car park in Over Haddon village. The walk down into the dale from here is via a short steep lane and then around half-a-mile along a good path to the Tufa waterfall by several weirs and mine workings.

Parking Lat/Long: 53.194464, -1.6969800
Parking Grid Ref: SK 203 664
Parking Postcode: DE45 1HZ

Between the villages of Over Haddon and Alport you will find Conksbury Bridge and Raper Lodge Packhorse Bridge.

Parking Lat/Long: 53.187822,-1.684833
Parking Grid Ref: SK 211 656
Parking Postcode: DE45 1JW (250m)

Above: *The view into Lathkill Dale from near Haddon Grove Farm. Canon 6D, 17-40 at 20mm, ISO 100, 1/40s at f/14, Jun. © CG*

Right: *Jacob's Ladder—the county flower of Derbyshire (VP2). © MR*

Accessibility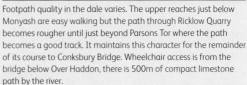

Footpath quality in the dale varies. The upper reaches just below Monyash are easy walking but the path through Ricklow Quarry becomes rougher until just beyond Parsons Tor where the path becomes a good track. It maintains this character for the remainder of its course to Conksbury Bridge. Wheelchair access is from the bridge below Over Haddon, there is 500m of compact limestone path by the river.

Best time of year/day

There is something to photograph in Lathkill Dale at all times of the year. The river can dry up in the summer – old mine workings drain it in several places – but most times it is usually flowing. Spring and autumn or anytime after heavy rain are the best times to photograph the tufa dam. Parson's Nose is best when the sun rises in the south east (March to Sept). The hawthorn blooms white in May/June, Jacob's Ladder flowers in June/July, in winter the trees frost up beautifully. Note that the dale runs east-west and is quite deep. The middle section does not illuminate well in the winter.

Robin Hood's Stride is shapely double-summited pinnacle of gritstone between the villages of Birchover and Youlgreave. Popular with climbers and other visitors, this tor has also been used as a location for The Return of Sherlock Holmes and the 1987 film The Princess Bride. Portraits of the sculpted rocks from below and views over the surrounding countryside from its summit are worthy of a couple of hours photographic meditation; in good light you will be rewarded with exquisite drama.

Just across the fields from Robin Hood's Stride, and clearly visible from it to the north, is a group of Bronze Age standing stones known as Nine Stones Close or The Grey Ladies. Although there are now only four stones, when complete they would have been one of the best stone circles in the Peak District, and even with only four stones remaining they are still impressive.

What to shoot and viewpoints

Viewpoint 1 – From the Copse

Immediately to the west of the Stride are some trees through which the tor composes well in afternoon and early evening light throughout the year. There are also some additional stones in the foreground that can be used as a counterpoint.

Viewpoint 2 – Up Close

Up closer to the rocks there are many compositions that can be made looking up and through the crags from below. This is particularly good in rain showers when stormy skies are punctuated with bursts of good light.

Viewpoint 3 – Around the Pinnacles

Those with a head for heights can scramble up the tor's southern aspect. The summit is reasonably level and the two pinnacles can be shot as separate compositions. A low sun helps here to pick out the foreground detail. Also look out for studies of rock textures and old carvings in the rock. Using a long lens (200mm) you can compose an image of the four standing stones of Nine Stones Close to the north – best on a misty autumn morning.

How to get here

The formal parking for Robin Hood's Stride is on the B5056 near Birchover. If approaching from Matlock drive north along the A6 for 1.8 miles. At Darley Dale turn left onto the B5057. Continue through Darley Bridge, Wensley and Winster and after 3.7 miles you will reach a crossroads with the B5056. Turn right. Follow the bends for just over half-a-mile and park in a large lay-by on the right. Walk up a farm track on the opposite side of the road marked Limestone Way. Robin Hoods Stride is reached after 600m.

Parking Lat/Long: 53.153567,-1.659229
Parking Grid Ref: SK 228 618
Parking Postcode: DE4 2HX (750m)

An alternative, level approach is offered from Cliff Road, which is a small lane that links Elton to Alport. Immediately adjacent the track at SK 222 624 there is enough room to park two cars. Access to the Stride from here is via public footpaths, which in wet weather can be quite muddy.

Accessibility

The track leading up to Robin Hoods Stride is level but unsurfaced. The grass apron around the Stride is pleasant enough to walk on. Access to the upper parts of the tor require scrambling.

Please Note: the Nine Stones are on private land and do not have a formal right of way leading to them. Access is entirely at the discretion of the landowner. Do not interfere with or damage walls or gates when walking to and from the field where they are found.

Best time of year/day

Robin Hood's Stride occupies an elevated position and is one of the highest points in the immediate area and catches the light well at all times of year. The tree colour is best in autumn when the nearby ferns will be reddish-orange.

The northern pinnacle on Robin Hood's Stride (VP2). Canon 6D, 17-40 at 20mm, ISO 100, 1/60s at f/14. Grad. Apr. © CG

Above: Nine Stones Close. Private land, access at the discretion of the landowner. *Canon 30D, 17-40 at 20mm, ISO 100, 1/20s at f/20. Grad. Jun. © CG*

Below: The summit of Robin Hood's Stride (VP3). *Canon 5D Mk 1, 17-40 at 20mm, ISO 100, 1/10s at f/20. Grad. Nov. © CG*

The drama of the Lower Dove begins in Beresford Dale south of the village of Hartington. Charles Cotton, a 17th century poet, writer and keen fisherman lived at Beresford Hall and was a close friend of Izaak Walton, author of *The Compleat Angler*, published in 1653. Cotton built a fishing house by the Dove, the Temple, with *Piscatoribus Sacrum* carved above its door, it means sacred to anglers. Charles Cotton's Temple Beat in Berseford Dale is one of the best wild fisheries in the UK with no stocked fish and catch-and-release only. His friends book, a celebration of the art and spirit of fishing in prose and verse, is one of the most important books written in the English language. If you are after images of fly fishing this is the place to be. Described are a walk around Beresford Dale, the very pretty village of Hartington, and north to Pilsbury Castle, a stronghold location favoured by the Celts, Saxons and Normans.

South of Beresford Dale the sculpted gorge of the Dove deepens as it changes to Wolfscote Dale, arguably some of the most dramatic landscape in the Peak District. The steep sides of the dale fall over 400 feet down to the sparking waters of the Dove. A walk down side dales reveal slopes covered with orchids and other wild flowers in the spring, and the views from several high viewpoints for landscape compositions take the breath away. It isn't with whimsy that we have called this the Grand Canyon of the Peak District.

You may want to avoid the busy Dovedale near its famous stepping stones at weekends and holiday times. Close by however there is much to explore around Ilam, and other beautiful villages such as Tissington and Parwich, or venture to the hidden Peak in the Hamps and Manifold valleys. Finally, salmon are trying to make their way back to the Peak District – Charles Cotton and Izaak Walton would be pleased – they have been sighted at Duffield on the Derwent near Derby. If you want to photograph them even closer head down to the weir at Norbury, south of Ashbourne, the furthest inland migration of any salmon in the UK.

Maps

- OS Explorer Map OL241 (1:25 000) The Peak District: White Peak Area
- OS Explorer Map OL259 (1:25 000) Derby

Minninglow from Moat Low (p.416). Sony A6000, 18–200 at 38mm, ISO 320, 1/60s at f/10. Sep. © MR

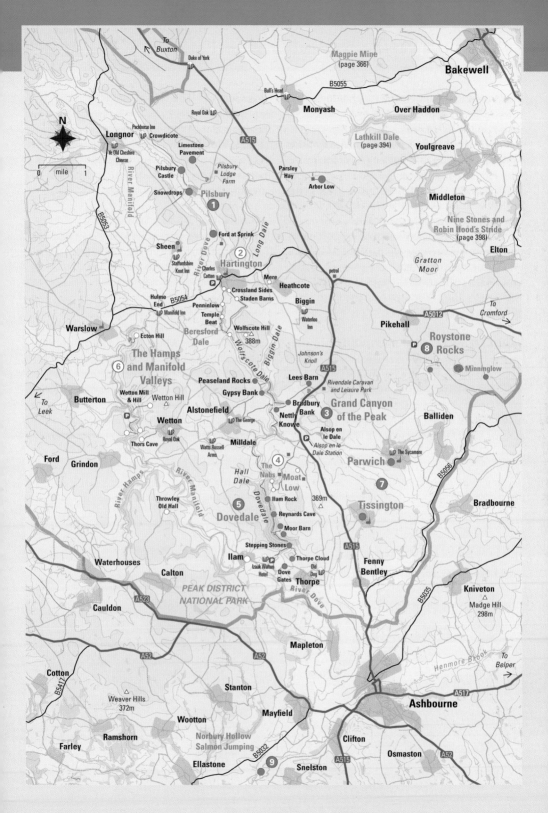

"Pilsbury Castle, guarding the valley of the Upper Dove, is one of the most evocative places in the White Peak."
From *The Peak, A Park for All Seasons* by Brian Redhead with photographs by Ray Manley.

North of the village of Hartington and below Earl Sterndale the river Dove flows through gentle rolling limestone country where compositions are not obvious. This is a rural area of drystone walls, fields dotted with trees, remote farms, hamlets, lime kilns, lead rakes and ancient remains of times gone by. Described is a short tour of places to visit and photograph. This isn't a busy area and there is a good chance you will be alone in this small dale.

What to shoot and viewpoints

From the village square in Hartington head north by the village duckpond following Dig Street and head right at the fork where the village ends. The locations are along this minor track. The left fork leads to the former manor house of the de la Pole family, now known as Moat Hall.

Viewpoint 1 – The Ford at Sprink

Just beyond Bank Top Farm, 0.8 miles from the fork there is a minor track on the left signposted Sprink. There is room to park the car here. Immediately down the minor track is a beautiful ford in the river, surrounded by trees that reflect very prettily in the stream above the ford. Water tumbles pleasingly through the foreground rocks.

Viewpoint 2 – Pilsbury Snowdrops

Just over a mile along the lane from the ford is Pilsbury, no more than a farm, it is host in February to one of the best displays of snowdrops in the Peak. Park carefully on the bend immediately beyond the farm.

Viewpoint 3 – Pilsbury Castle

Along a track beyond Pilsbury, Pilsbury Castle sits on high ground above the river Dove next to a small limestone outcrop, surrounded by sheep-cropped grass. This was a stronghold location favoured by Celts, Saxons and Normans, all that remains are the Norman motte and bailey earthworks associated with the long-disappeared structures. This location is atmospheric and is best visited on summer evenings close to sunset when the light is

Looking into the Upper Dove across the meadows north of Hartington. Canon 5D, Canon 17-40 at 20mm, ISO 100, 1/100s at f/20. Grad. Jul. © CG

How to get here

Pilsbury is in the Dove Valley, west of the A515, north of the village of Hartington. Access is by a minor track that starts in Hartington. Hartington is 2 miles west of the A515, 13 miles south of Buxton and 13 miles north of Ashbourne.

Hartington Parking Lat/Long: 53.139138, -1.811643
Parking Grid Ref: SK 126 602
Parking Postcode: SK17 0BE

Arbor Low is 10 miles south of Buxton, south of the village of Monyash, just off the A515. If travelling from Buxton head south on the A515 to Parsley Hay and turn left onto The Rake, signposted Monyash, after a tenth of a mile turn right on Long Rake and after half-a-mile turn right to park at Upper Oldhams Farm (£1 charge). Arbor Low is in the field next to the farm.

Arbor Low Parking Lat/Long: 53.169785, -1.764642
Parking Grid Ref: SK 158 636
Parking Postcode: DE45 1JR

Accessibility ♿

These locations are very accessible being either roadside or involving short walks on good paths.

Best time of year/day

These are all-year round locations with the best times described in each viewpoint. Arbor Low is five minutes walk across two flat fields and through two gates.

sympathetic to the gentle topography and the one large tree on the site is in leaf. Looking north west receding in the distance are Chrome and Parkhouse hills. This location is also illuminated at sunrise in winter.

Viewpoint 4 – Limestone Pavement

Despite having a limestone basement the Peak District is not blessed with the extensive limestone pavement featuring the clints and grikes of the Yorkshire Dales. But here in the middle of the Dove Valley and just above Pilsbury Castle is probably the best example to be found in the region.

Continue on the road through, around and above Pilsbury, passing some farm buildings and round a bend to park carefully by the road by a circular dew pond at SK 124 636 (before Pilsbury Lodge Farm). »

Opposite: If you explore the Upper Dove north of Hartington you will be rewarded with many beautiful views. Canon 6D, 70-300 at 93mm, ISO 125, 1/25 at f/20. May. © CG

Follow a broad farm track west (this is Access Land), by the dew pond and small ruins to where limestone pavement about the size of a couple of tennis courts can be found. Occasional scrub hawthorns offer compositional punctuation here. They present well in late afternoon light during the winter months. The views from here over Carder Low to the south and to Hartington beyond are splendid and isolated copses of trees crown the skyline.

The ford at Sprink on the River Dove (VP1). Canon 5D, 17-40 at 20mm, ISO 100, 1s at f/20. Polariser. Sep. © CG

Viewpoint 5 – Arbor Low

Five miles from Pilsbury Castle on the other side of the A515 is Arbor Low, the Peak District's best known Neolithic monument. A circle of 50 or so limestone blocks that lay flat here rather than upright, with several central stones that form a 'cove'. Know as a recumbent henge this is one of the most well preserved henge monuments in the UK. Arbor Low is managed by English Heritage and there is no entry fee, however access is across private land

and there is a charge of £1 per person payable at the adjacent farm. Whilst slightly elevated above the surrounding farmland, the views are not dramatic, but it still has photographic potential and of course great historical significance.

The topography of the site is subtle so it benefits from a low sun. The north east aspect makes it much more favourable for early morning photography rather than late afternoon and anytime of year is good to visit.

Nearby Location – Sheen

Sheen is a small Staffordshire hamlet north west of Harrington surrounded by pasture that runs down to the river Manifold. The village is best approached from Hulme End. As well its rural photographic subjects, it is worth a visit for its medieval church, rebuilt in the 19th century, but home to some original medieval gargoyles.

One of the medieval gargoyles in the churchyard at Sheen. Canon 6D, 70-300 at 120mm, ISO 100, 1/40s at f/8. Mar. © CG

Pilsbury Castle between Hartington and Crowdecote (VP3). Canon 6D, 17-40 at 40mm, ISO 100, 1/30s at f/14. Grad. Jul. © CG

The Staden barns (VP3) a short walk from Hartington. Sony A6000, 18–200 at 18mm, ISO 125, 1/100s at f/11. May. © MR

A tour of Hartington is a must for those who love rural life. The village is home to a 13th century church, an old hall, cottages and gardens, pubs, an old school house and village duck pond. Many of the buildings are constructed from sandstone although the village is firmly in limestone country and it is this which makes the area outside of the village so attractive for rural landscape photography. If you are interested in trout fishing, nearby in Beresford Dale is Charles Cotton's Temple Beat immortalised by Izaak Walton in his book *The Complete Angler*.

Described are several locations that can be visited individually or together as a photographic walk.

What to shoot and viewpoints

Viewpoint 1 – The Village and St. Giles' Church

A wander around the village with a camera is a must in late spring and summer when the gardens are in full flower and the ducks are swimming on the village pond. However if you want to stretch your legs the photographic tour starts at the footpath between the Charles Cotton Pub and the pay and display car park between the public toilet and the cafe. Take this path marked Footpath 31 to Dove Dale via Beresford and Wolfscote Dales.

The path heads right (viewpoint of house and hill) and almost immediately turn around for a viewpoint of the St. Giles' Church through the trees. Continue on the path to a gate. After the gate head left up the wheeled track to a gate opening.

Viewpoint 2 – Crossland Sides (SK 129 599)

On the right is a small hill, this is a significant viewpoint from which to take interesting compositions of wall patterns and barns – and if you shoot wide, St. Giles' Church tower popping out from trees – and sweeping vistas of the surrounding countryside. This area is known as Crossland Sides.

Go through the stone stile and cross the field toward a barn (more opportunities) to turn right down Renyards Lane.

Viewpoint 3 – Staden Barns (SK 132 593)

When past a barn turn right down another lane toward the two Staden Barns and an excellent composition of the barns from the lane.

Continue to the junction with another road – significant distinctive trees on the hillside – and turn right. Follow this lane down the hill ignoring any footpath signs on the right until you come to a narrow foot lane on your right.

Head down this lane to the River Dove and the junction of Beresford and Wolfscote Dales (see viewpoint 5).

Viewpoint 4 – Wolfscote Hill (SK 136 583)

Wolfscote Hill (388m) is a high viewpoint topped by limestone pavement with expansive views south down the river Dove and the hills beyond. Evening light bathes these summit rocks for a southerly composition, and sunrise for the northerly aspect. To reach the summit don't head down to Wolfscote Dale but continue down the road to Wolfscote Grange, the farm on the right, on the left is a footpath that traverses steeply up the hill to the summit.

Warm evening light on St. Giles' Church. Canon 6D, 70-400 at 200mm, ISO 400, 1/200s at f/8. Jul. © CG

A stone stile at Crossland Sides (VP2). Sony A6000,
18–200 at 24mm, ISO 125, 1/100s at f/11. May. © MR

Viewpoint 5: Wolfscote Dale

SK 130 584

(Continued from viewpoint 3) In May the wall sides of the lane down to the dales are dense with red campion. Once near the river there is a lovely composition looking into Wolfscote Dale and two cliffs, called the Celestial Twins.

Viewpoint 6 – Beresford Dale

Stay on this side of the river, turn right toward Hartington and through the stile passing a bridge into open meadow and the meandering river; you may see ducks and dippers, and rising trout in the spring and summer. Look right for a floral hillside and Scots pines. Continue and cross two little wooden bridges, turn sharp right and follow the river into the woods by Beresford Hall following the river by several weirs and the Pike Pool, a distinctive small limestone tower right in the river. This section of river is known as the Temple Beat, named after Charles Cotton of Beresford Hall who built a fishing cabin here called the Fishing Temple (hard to see). Cotton's friend Izaak Walton was inspired to write the book *The Compleat Angler* here.

This is woodland and river photography with dappled light and the dale here is narrow with dense with foliage.

Viewpoint 7 – Penninlow

Cross a bridge from Staffordshire back in to Derbyshire and continue through the Morson Wood through a stile to open meadow. The hill on the right is Penninlow and this makes a beautiful composition in the spring when a cascade of field buttercups cascade down from its summit. Continue on the broad path back to Hartington. Look left for an excellent view of snaking drystone walls and barns.

An English country garden in Hartington. Sony A6000, 18–200 at 18mm, ISO 160, 1/25s at f/10. Oct. © MR

How to get here

All the viewpoints are described starting from Hartington village which is situated two miles west of the A515, 13 miles south of Buxton and 13 miles north of Ashbourne. Park in the pay and display car park and walk up to the cafe down from the Charles Cotton Pub.

Parking Lat/Long: 53.139138, -1.811643
Parking Grid Ref: SK17 0BE
Parking Postcode: SK 126 602

Accessibility ♿

Most of these locations are very accessible involving short walks on good paths. The photographic walk taking in all the viewpoints but without Wolfscote Hill is a 3 mile round-trip. To reach the summit of Wolfscote Hill involves a stiff uphill walk for 30 minutes.

Best time of year/day

Good light and the weather are more important here than time of year. In May and June the meadows start to flower creating contrast in the land and late in the day with a low sun breaking through stormy clouds can yield spectacular photographs. Later in the summer, the hedgerow flowers will be at their peak. Autumn by the river is very colourful and if it snows, freezing days with clear skies are not to be missed.

Above: The small hill viewpoint at Crossland Sides (VP2). Sony A6000, 18–200 at 18mm, ISO 125, 1/100s at f/11. May. © MR

Fly fishing on the river Dove. Sony A6000, 18–200 at 29mm, ISO 100, 1/90s at f/6.7. Jun. © MR

Wolfscote Hill and its limestone pavement (VP4). Sony A6000, 18–200 at 18mm, ISO 400, 1/640s at f/8. Jun. © MR

The steep gorge cut by the River Dove where Wolfscote Dale ends and Dove Dale begins is 400ft deep. This is the Peak District's Grand Canyon with footpaths and Access Land on the rim giving access to spectacular views up and down the dale.

Quieter, more remote and wilder than southern Dove Dale at Thorpe with its coach-loads of visitors, this area offers a lot for the photographer. As well as the breathtaking vistas, on the steep slopes of these dales are limestone crags and pinnacles and beautiful displays of wild flowers. The clear waters of the Dove, home to trout and a variety of birds, is crossed by stepping stones, bridges and damned by weirs.

What to shoot and viewpoints

The viewpoints are described starting from the lay-by on the A515 next to Rivendale, with the alternative approach from Alstonfield described in the Peaseland Rocks viewpoint.

Viewpoint 1 – Lees Farm

Walk down Liffs Road toward Biggin and under the old railway bridge for a beautiful composition of Lees Farm and its pines with Johnson's Knoll, the wooded hill, in the background. By the bridge is a path up to the Tissington trail for an elevated viewpoint. Good at most times of the day, it is best early or late.

Viewpoint 2 – Bradbury Bank

Continue down the road to Lees Farm and just before the farm is a footpath on your left that leads down a dale. Follow this footpath by a wall to where there is a steep slope on your left, this initial slope has the most amazing display of yellow cowslip and a few orchids in May – best in the afternoon and evening when the slope is illuminated. Continue down the path to a gate and a National Trust sign, Bradbury Bank (0.6 miles from the lay-by) – the path splits here, continue straight down into Dove Dale and Coldeaton bridge or up and left following track up the slope. In May there is one of the best displays of early purple orchids in the Peak here; thousands of them pop their heads up on the grass slope and around the rocks. »

How to get here

The approach is either from the A515 from a lay-by 7 miles north of Ashbourne or from the village of Alstonfield in the west. For the east approach from the A515, which is recommended, park in a lay-by just down from the Rivendale Caravan and Leisure Park next to a minor road (Liffs Road) to Biggin. Just down this road is a bridge that carries the Tissington trail.

Rivendale Lay-by (A515) Lat/Long: 53.106396, -1.763346
Parking Grid Ref: SK 159 566
Parking Postcode: DE6 1QU

Alstonfield Parking Lat/Long: 53.097567, -1.8055987
Parking Grid Ref: SK 131 556
Parking Postcode: DE6 2FY

Accessibility

Whilst not far from the road and generally on good grass paths, some of these locations do involve sometimes walking up or down steep slopes and there are steep drop offs. Take care if it is wet as the limestone can be very slippy.
Rivendale Lay-by (A515) Round-Trip to Nettly Knowe: 2 hours, distance 3.5km, ascent 93m.
Rivendale Lay-by (A515) to Gypsy Bank/Peaseland Rocks: 2 hours, 3.5km, ascent 100m
Alstonfield to Gypsy Bank/Peaseland Rocks:
40 minutes, distance 2km, ascent 38m

Best time of year/day

Wolfscote Dale and Dove Dale run north to south illuminated by direct sunlight at midday and receiving side light at most other times. The topography is complex as the dale twists and turns with several side dales, including Biggin Dale, adding to the complexity. Generally late afternoon to sunset in the spring and summer is best, with midday in the winter offering low light that illuminates the rim of the gorge. It is recommended to study a map and use the Photographer's Ephemeris in preparation of your visit to calculate where the light falls. Late April and May is the best time for orchids, cowslips and mayflower. If it snows, although the going may be tough, it is worth it. If you are an early bird, these locations are very special at sunrise especially on misty mornings.

Above: *The View (VP4) looking down to Wolfscote and Biggin Dale. Canon 5D Mk 1, 17-40 at 28mm, ISO 100, 1/20s at f/13. Grad.*

Opposite: *On the flanks of Wolfscote Hill looking across the Dove to Peaseland Rocks.(VP5). Canon 5D Mk 1, 17-40 at 20mm, ISO 100, 1/30s at f/20. Grad. May. © CG Jun. © CG*

If you enjoy photographing flowers in a beautiful dale, this is a place to linger. Take extreme care not to trample any flowers as you take close up and overview photographs of this wonderful floral spectacle. Timing is important as in May/June the sun will drop behind the hills around 6pm leaving the slope in shadow. Best is early to late afternoon, from around 1pm until 5pm.

Viewpoint 3 – Nettly Knowe

Follow the track that diagonals up the slope of Bradbury Bank then at the top arch right keeping this side of the wall. Continue along the edge of the dale by a feint path, by rocks, and eventually following a wall, all the way to an overlook down into Dove Dale. There are numerous viewpoints on this walk looking down into the dale of Bradbury Bank with the grand finale as you reach Dove Dale looking down onto Coldeaton bridge. This is a magnificent viewpoint looking north to where Wolfscote Dale and Biggin Dale split, best both at sunrise in late summer and autumn, and at late afternoon most times. To return, retrace your steps but head right on a footpath that takes you by Nettly Knowe, a hard to see Bronze Age Barrow, to the Tissington Trail and back to the lay-by with plenty of opportunities for compositions across fields and walls to Johnson's Knoll, the tree-covered hill in the distance. This is a a 2.2 mile round trip.

Viewpoint 4 – The View

If you walk by Lees Barn on Liffs Road toward Biggin, a left turn down a track takes you to Coldeaton and Dove Top Farm. There is a great viewpoint here, but you must ask for permission to visit it at Dove Top Farm as access is on private land and because of livestock please leave dogs at home. This location is not marked on the map.

Viewpoint 5 – The River Dove, Peaseland Rocks and Gipsy Bank

Peaseland Rocks is a group of limestone pinnacles on the west slope of Wolfscote Dale where Biggin Dale joins it. You can access Peaseland Rocks by a footpath up Gipsy Bank, a very steep slope, either by walking down to Coldeaton Bridge from Bradbury Bank, or from the west from Alstonfield by walking down Lode Lane from the village to a track on the left, Gratton Lane, then a right and by a farm to the top of Gipsy Bank. Peaseland Rocks are at the junction above where Biggin Dale joins the end of Wolfscote Dale. The pinnacles are north facing but do get direct sun at summer sunsets and are backlit for most of the day. There many compositions here depending on the light and also consider descending and ascending the nose between the two dales for an elevated viewpoint looking across to the pinnacles

Opposite top: Lees Barn near Bradbury Bank (VP1). Canon 6D, 17-40 at 40mm, ISO 200, 1/100s at f/20. Grad. May. © CG

Bradbury Bank and its impressive orchid display (VP2). Sony A6000, 10-18 at 10mm, ISO 125, 1/80s at f/8. May. © MR

From the path above Bradbury Bank toward Nettly Knowe. VP3.Sony A6000, 10-18 at 13mm, ISO 100, 1/200s at f/9.5. May. © MR

Barrows or tumuli are ancient burial sites, usually formed of a mound of earth and stones over a grave. There are many in the Peak District including the prominent Minninglow. Moat Low is a hilltop bowl barrow (it looks like an upturned bowl) and was excavated in 1845 by Thomas Bateman who found a rock-cut grave containing two skeletons, accompanied by burnt bones, a bronze flat axe and the jaw of a pig. The axe indicates a Bronze Age date for the barrow, perhaps created 3000 years ago. It is of interest to photographers because of its distinctive group of attractive sycamore trees that crown the barrow. Nearby is another impressive viewpoint down into Dovedale from two small hills, the Nabs and Bailey Hill.

What to shoot and viewpoints

Viewpoint 1 – Moat Low

The crown of wind-distorted sycamore trees on the tumulus of Moat Low (340m) can be seen from several high places around Dovedale. But such is the beauty of its distinctive group of trees it is worth a close inspection both from the south and the north, especially at sunset. Moat Low can be reached by following the footpath across the field opposite the car park passing a dew pond and a barn, across the country lane and after New Hanson Grange

farm and just before Hanson Grange farm take the footpath on the left up the fields to Moat Low. You can also approach from Gag Lane half a mile south of the car park and take the footpath from Moatlow farm through the field to the tumulus. From the south is best for silhouettes at sunset, and from the north the trees are illuminated by golden light in the evening. Great photographs have been taken of Moat Low in the mist from a distance, but this has eluded us so far.

Viewpoint 2 – The Nabs and Bailey Hill

From Alsop en le Dale Station cross the road from the car park and follow the footpath across the field passing a dew pond and a barn, follow the lane passing New Hanson Grange farm to Hanson Grange farm. Just before the farm take a footpath to the left which by-passes the farm to a footpath junction, go right as for Dove Holes but then turn sharp right up hill rather than down into Dovedale.

There are various places along this ridge that give great views down into Dovedale and across to Hall Dale. Limestone rocks and trees on the steep slope can provide foreground subjects. At the northern end of the Bailey Hill, opposite Raven Tor on the other side of the gorge, are good views down to Milldale, and back south down Dovedale.

Opposite top left: Dovedale below The Nab. Canon 6D, 17-40 at 30mm, ISO 100, 1/20s at f/14. Grad. Jun. © CG
***Opposite top right**: Moat Low from near Hanson Grange Farm (VP1). Sony A6000, 18–200 at 29mm, ISO 100, 1/90s at f/11. May. © MR*

Moat Low from the south (VP1). Sony A6000, 18–200mm at 18mm, ISO 100, 1/60s at f/9. Sep. © MR

How to get here

Park at Alsop en le Dale Station on the A515 for both Moat Low and the Nabs. Alsop en le Dale Station is 5.6 miles north of Ashbourne next to the village of Alsop en le Dale and by the minor road to village of Milldale.

Alsop en le Dale Station on the A515 Parking Lat/Long: 53.091131, -1.7685199
Parking Grid Ref: SK 156 549
Parking Postcode: DE6 1QP

Accessibility

Easy walking on good paths and through fields. There is a steep uphill section to get to the Nabs.
Moat Low Approach: 25 minutes, distance 1.5km, ascent 64m.
The Nabs Approach: 40 minutes, distance 2.3km, ascent 52m.

Best time of year/day

Moat Low is good all year round, especially before and at sunset, but better in the summer when the sun sets in the north west. A misty sunrise would be good from a distance if you can find a suitable spot. For the views into Dovedale from the Nabs, as Dove dale runs south to north the best times to photograph here are early morning, late evening and sunset. Try May and June with the first flush of spring and October when the leaves change.

Above middle left: Winter sunset at Moat Low from the north. Canon 5D, 17-40 at 20mm, ISO 100, 1/10s at f/20. Grad. Feb. © CG
Above middle right: A Virgin balloon floats above the Dovedale Hills. Canon 6D, 70-300 at 300mm, ISO 400, 1/200s at f/8. Jun. © CG

Dovedale from the flanks of Hall Dale, near Raven Tor. Canon 5D, 17-40 at 20mm, ISO 100, 1/20s at f/20. Grad. Jun. © CG

"What's here, the sign of a bridge?
Do you travel in wheelbarrows in this country?
This bridge was made for nothing else – why a mouse
can hardly go over it, tis not two fingers broad!"
Izaak Walton, the Viator (Latin for traveller) in *The Compleat Angler*

Viator's Bridge (aka Wheelbarrow Bridge) at Milldale, the northern entrance to lower Dovedale (p.423).
Canon 6D, 17-40 at 37mm, ISO 50, 1/8s at f/13. Jun. © CG

Between the hamlets of Milldale and Thorpe the River Dove has cut a narrow canyon filled with limestone caves, ridges and pinnacles, the gorge's steep sides covered in dense woodland. This three mile section of the River Dove, known as Dovedale, is dramatic. It is also a popular 'beauty spot' receiving over a million visitors a year, mainly in the summer months, and most congregating around its famous stepping stones, a half mile walk from the National Trust car park at Thorpe.

For the photographer there are many attractions in Dovedale; the prominent peak of Thorpe Cloud, near where the Dove joins the river Manifold, has tremendous vistas overlooking the southern Peak and down into the dale. There are many impressive limestone rock formations to study, and in autumn this is an excellent place to visit to record the years most colourful season. The dale is abundant with flowers in the spring and early summer, and the river itself can always be photographed.

Dovedale from Thorpe Cloud summit (VP2). Canon 5D, 17-40 at 20mm, ISO 200, 1/60s at f/20. Jan. © CG

What to shoot and viewpoints

From the National Trust car park a footpath follows the Dove into the canyon. The stepping stones are half a mile (700m) away at the first big bend in the river.

Viewpoint 1 – The Stepping Stones

Dovedale Stepping Stones are legendary and have been since Victorian times when they featured in early Peak District travel guides. They are best photographed from the northern bank of the river just beyond a gate. From here the view back towards them includes a reflection of Thorpe Cloud in the calm waters of the small weir in front of you. This is one of the busiest parts of Dovedale and on weekends you are unlikely to get it to yourself. It is best visited in the afternoon when Thorpe Cloud is illuminated.

Opposite: Looking across the Dove and up to Thorpe Cloud (VP1). Canon 6D, Canon 17-40 at 20mm, ISO 100, 1/2s at f/14. Jun. © CG

How to get here

Dovedale is 4 miles from the town of Ashbourne and 20 miles from Buxton, accessed by minor roads heading west that leave the A515 near the villages of Tissington and Fenny Bentley. All of the locations described are best accessed from the National Trust car park at the southern end of Dovedale next to the village of Thorpe.

Thorpe Parking Lat/Long: 53.055105, -1.7833471
Parking Grid Ref: SK 146 508
Parking Postcode: TR5 0NS (nearby Chapel Porth)

Accessibility ♿

Significant efforts have been made to make Dovedale as accessible as possible. Most of the paths are level but the nature of the terrain means that there are some steps and gradients, including the stepping stones, although these can be avoided by taking the bridge across the river immediately north of the car park and proceeding along the rough eastern bank of the river. Access to some of the viewpoints is steep and often over rough ground.

Best time of year/day

The deep nature and north-south alignment of the dale make sympathetic illumination difficult. By the time the sun is high enough in the sky to illuminate the features at the bottom of the dale the light is harsh and white. The vantage points higher up the valley sides receive much more favourable light but require more effort to reach. It is highly probable that you will want to come back here many times. In doing so each visit will help you make more sense of what you see. Thorpe Cloud is best at winter sunrise and sunset, or anytime of the year when the weather is a mix of sun and rain, or stormy. Avoid summer weekends and bank holidays when the sun is out, you'll be lucky to get a parking spot.

Viewpoint 2 – Thorpe Cloud

Two hills dominate the southern end of Dove Dale where the River Dove emerges. On the western bank is the craggy flank of Bunster Hill but offering better photographic potential is Thorpe Cloud on the eastern bank. From Thorpe's lofty summit there are superb views down into Dovedale as it wraps around the base of Bunster Hill and south over limestone fields. Timing is important as for much of the year the late afternoon summit view is into the setting sun. Winter afternoons are particularly good, especially if you can time it so that the sun is still illuminating the south east facing flank of Bunster Hill immediately in front you. If you want colour in the sky winter sunrise is best when the sun rises in the south east. Access Thorpe Cloud's summit by a path that starts from the stepping stones or from an informal path that starts from the bridge (SK 147 510) just above the NT car park. Either approach is just short of a mile.

Viewpoint 3 – Moor Barn high viewpoint

The next viewpoints take you out of Dovedale to a high viewpoint on the rim of the gorge, below Moor Barn, that look down on the rock pinnacles of Tissington Spires and wooded slopes to the north, and to the south, Thorpe Cloud.

Tissington Spires

Continue up the dale from the stepping stones for about 600m, on your right is a sub-dale across from the tree-shrouded pinnacles of the Twelve Apostles. Follow this path which leads to the rocky promontory of Lovers Leap (itself a good viewpoint especially in autumn looking down onto the trees) take a right turn off the main path and up the hill (this is Access Land) until you can see a barn, follow the path left through a gate then slightly down to the top of the spires. Care should be taken here as there are steep drops. You will have a great vantage point looking down onto the spires from here and also a little further on at the top of Sharplow Dale.

Looking out of Reynards Arch (VP4). Sony A6000, 18–200 at 18mm, ISO 200, 1/40s at f/11. Jul. © MR

Ilam Rock, best revealed when the trees are not in leaf (V5). Canon 6D, 17-40 at 20mm, ISO 100, 1/40s at f/14. Grad. Mar. © CG

*Thorpe Cloud (left) and Dovedale. The Moor Barn viewpoint (VP3) gives great views up and down the dale.
Canon 5D Mk 1, 17-40 at 20mm, ISO 100, 1/20s at f/20. Grad. Sep. © CG*

Thorpe Cloud from Above

At the top of the sub dale and before the barn, this time go right and up. Contour around to hawthorn trees on a south-facing slope where there are great compositions looking across to Thorpe Cloud and down to the stepping stones.

Viewpoint 4 – Reynards Cave Natural Arch

About 800m up the path by the river north of the Twelve Apostles/Lovers Leap is a clear path that branches off right uphill toward a huge, natural stone arch. It is possible to climb through this. Like many of the valley floor features it illuminates poorly much of the year, but gets good light from midday for most of the year, especially in summer. There is a pleasing composition through the arch from above, looking back down to the valley below.

Viewpoint 5 – Ilam Rock and Pickering Tor

A further 500m beyond Reynards Cave is Ilam Rock (on the left across a footbridge) and its close neighbour Pickering Tor. Ilam Rock is a huge blade of free-standing limestone,

a true pinnacle, while Pickering Tor on the opposite bank is a set of equally impressive pinnacles. This section of the dale is deep and narrow and only illuminates properly when the sun is quite high in the sky. It is also quite wooded here, meaning that the topography of the rock is best revealed in winter, when the trees are bare and the sun is still quite low in the sky even at midday.

Milldale

If you carry on up the dale and over bridge, you will eventually reach the Viator's Bridge (photo p.418) and the pretty village of Milldale.

Viewpoint 6 – Dove Gates

The River Dove exits the hills through a dramatic cleft between Bunster Hill and Thorpe Cloud. This feature is viewed well from the side of the road that descends from Thorpe to the river (SK 150 506). Mid-afternoon is particularly good for this when the light sweeps down and across the landscape here.

The River Manifold rises on the gentle moorlands below the village of Longnor and flows south, cutting through the same range of limestone hills as Dove Dale to the east but in a less dramatic fashion, though nonetheless still beautiful. The River Hamps begins to the west and flows south, then north, meeting the south-flowing Manifold at Beeston Tor south of Wetton, forming a curious inverted Y shaped arrangement of pretty valleys. The Manifold emerges from the hills at Ilam where it joins the River Dove.

The two valleys have very similar characteristics and while not quite as craggy as Dovedale still offer tremendous photographic opportunities. There is deciduous woodland here so spring and autumn colours are reliably wonderful. At the bottoms of both dales there were narrow gauge railway tracks that served the quarrying operations. These tracks have been converted into cycle routes and quiet roads that give excellent access to the countryside here, which are ideal for photographers with less mobility.

Five diverse locations are described running from Ecton House and Hill in the north to Ilam Hall and Ilam Park in the south. A mix of the natural and the man-made, including the magnificent Thors Cave.

A country lane on the walk from Wetton to Thors Cave. Canon 6D, 17-40 at 20mm, ISO 100, 1/40s at f/14. Grad. Jun. © CG

ECTON HOUSE AND ECTON HILL

In the 18th century Ecton Hill was the site of a profitable copper mine owned by the fourth and fifth Dukes of Devonshire. Much of that copper was used to plate the hulls of British warships to protect them from rot, and the profit made from this industry funded the building of Buxton Crescent and work on the Chatsworth House Estate. Below the hill is the small hamlet of Ecton, and Ecton House (now a field studies centre), built by Arthur Ratcliffe MP in 1932 and modelled on a medieval castle complete with battlements and a distinctive copper spire. The view and compositions from Ecton Hill of Ecton and the sweeping bend of the River Hamps are worth exploring.

Looking down on Ecton House

You can walk direct up Ecton Hill, or contour more gently to its summit up good paths although this is Access Land and you are free to wander. On late autumn afternoons the woods looking down to Ecton House are very colourful. The footpath to the top of Ecton offers a superb aspect back northwards to the ridge of wooded land on which Ecton House sits.

How to get here

Ecton is five miles west of the A515 best approached through the village of Hartington to Hulme End and a left at the the Manifold Valley Inn, then the first right down to Ecton. Park by the road below Ecton Hill at the bend of the valley.

Parking Lat/Long: 53.121222,-1.857171
Parking Grid Ref: SK 096 582
Parking Postcode: ST13 7SS (1km)

Accessibility

It is a steep walk up Ecton Hill.

Best time of year/day

Spring (hawthorn and orchids) and autumn (woodland) are both very good here. Late afternoons when the sun is in the west present the landscape well.

The spectacular view into the Manifold valley from Ecton Hill. 6D, 17-40 at 24mm, ISO 100, 1/40s at f/14. Grad. Sep. © CG

THE WETTON HILLS

The Wetton Hills, a beautiful cluster of rolling green hills, give great elevated views down into the Manifold Valley. Close by is the Staffordshire village of Wetton and Wetton Mill next to the River Manifold.

Viewpoint 1 – The Wetton Hills

Park at the NTs Wetton Mill car park (cafe) and take the footpath at the rear which leads up a grassy ridge above the hawthorns toward rocky outcrops. The best viewpoints down into the valley are toward the summit.

Viewpoint 2 – Around Wetton Mill and Wetton

The old bridge at Wetton Mill is very photogenic and the village of Wetton (1.5 miles away) has many stone-built properties including an inn, and a 14th century church with an external staircase to its belfry. There is a footpath that leads north from the village to the summit of Wetton Hill.

How to get here

From the A515 approach from either Alstonfield or Hulme End, the National Trust's Wetton Mill is the best place to access the hills. Wetton village is a mile and a half away from Wetton Mill on the east side of the valley.

Parking Lat/Long: 53.102061,-1.860311
Parking Grid Ref: SK 094 561
Parking Postcode: DE6 2AG (200m)

Accessibility

Wetton, and Wetton Mill are roadside locations. In the Wetton Hills you will require a good level of fitness, be prepared for steep ground often off the main footpaths (the area is Access Land) to get the best viewpoints.

Best time of year/day

The Wetton Hills mostly face west, making evenings the best time of day. The slopes are dotted with hawthorns that flower in May while the valley floor has many deciduous trees making autumn spectacular here.

THOR'S CAVE

Thor's Cave is an impressive elevated cave entrance in the limestone walls of the Manifold Valley, from which there are excellent views. The cave entrance forms an arch 7.5 metres wide and 10 metres high. This cave has been popular since the Stone Age as a shelter and also as a burial site. Since Victorian times it has been a popular visitor attraction – thousands of feet have polished the limestone to glass, so care is needed inside the cave.

Viewpoint 1 – Thors Cave Summit

On the approach path described head straight to the summit – you will need a head for heights but this elevated position gives a majestic view of the Manifold Valley. This is best in autumn either early morning or late afternoon.

Viewpoint 2 – Inside the Cave

This is a much sought after photograph. The main cave window faces north west and if you want the sun in your shot it is best late on a summers afternoon (check the sun position). Either exposure blending or HDR techniques work best if you want some cave detail in your composition as well as detail in the sky and the slope opposite. Exposing for the outside gives a good silhouette-type shot with cave's window contours in darkness. Even better if you have a willing subject to pose for you in the cave entrance.

Viewpoint 3 – Thor's Cave from Outside

There are several viewpoints from afar to take photographs of the cave entrance, usually in the afternoon. One is on the first bend of the Leek Road as it descends down into the Manifold Vally. The other is on the west slope of the valley opposite the cave in a meadow approached up a path that goes through Ladyside wood.

How to get here

Park on School Lane in the village of Wetton and walk down the Leek Road and turn left down a narrow bridleway/green lane. Follow this lane to where it ends and head right on a footpath that takes you to the summit of Thors Cave, or head up right and down and around to the window of the cave. You can also reach the cave from the Manifold Valley by a steep concession footpath.

Parking Lat/Long: 53.096202, -1.8390727
Parking Grid Ref: SK 108 554
Parking Postcode: DE6 2AF

Accessibility

All these locations are reached on good footpaths but there are slopes, steep inclines, drop offs, and the paths are muddy after rain.

Best time of year/day

Generally autumn is the best time but for sun shining in the cave summer evenings are best. Check the position of the sun using the sun compass, the sun needs to be in the north west.

Thors Cave from the Leek Road (VP3). Canon 6D, 17-40 at 20mm, ISO 100, 1/40s at f/14. Grad. Jun. © CG

The grand view from the interior of Thors Cave toward the Wetton Hills.
Canon 6D, 17-40 at 40mm, ISO 100 at f/14, 1/20s. Jun. © CG

THROWLEY OLD HALL ♿

Throwley Old Hall (origins 1208) is what is left of a large, medieval manor house with architectural and historical interest. Very photogenic it occupies a fine position high up on the western flank of the Manifold Valley.

You can access the ruins by good paths and the structure is well illuminated at all times with the exception of late afternoons in winter, when the sun dips below the hill immediately to the west. Overview shots are challenging but are best from the south. This is a place for close-up detail shots of this beautiful ruin.

How to get here

Throwley Old Hall is on a minor road between the villages of Calton and Ilam, best approached from Ilam. Descend to Ilam and cross the bridge into the village. Keep left at the cross and pass through the village, avoiding the entrance to Ilam Hall. After a third of a mile turn left onto Lodge Lane, signposted Calton and Throwley. Pass through Rushley and after 1.2 miles reach the remains of Throwley Old Hall. Park carefully on the verge in front of the hall where there is enough room for one car.

Parking Lat/Long: 53.069310,-1.835941
Parking Grid Ref: SK 110 524
Parking Postcode: DE6 2BB (600m)

The great architectural details of Throwley Old Hall. Canon 6D, 17-40 at 40mm, ISO 100, 1/40s at f/14. Jun. © CG

ILAM HALL AND ILAM PARK

Ilam Hall and Park is a beautiful, archetypal English country house and parkland, with many excellent specimen trees laid out with space and balance. It is a great place to walk around with a camera on a sunny afternoon in either spring or autumn.

Viewpoint 1 – The Hall

Built in the 16th century and although redeveloped considerably in the 19th century Ilam Hall oozes character. Its slightly elevated position with respect to much of the park makes it slightly awkward to shoot but the side lawn, adjacent to the cafe offers a very good perspective. The gateway hosts some superb detail.

Viewpoint 2 – Ilam Church

The Church of the Holy Cross is actually Saxon in origin and its dimensions are quite awkward in comparison to the neighbouring Hall. There is much interesting detail here.

Viewpoint 3 – The Park

A photo-walk around the park in autumn, when the trees are at their best, is a lovely experience.

Viewpoint 4 – The Village

Ilam village is very picturesque, with its Swiss chalet style houses and matching school house. Also worth a photograph is the recently restored the Grade II* listed Mary Watts-Russell Memorial Cross (built in 1841).

How to get here

Ilam is is just west of Thorpe at the south end of Dovedale accessed by minor roads three miles from the A515. Exit the A515 opposite Tissington and pass through Thorpe to Ilam, park on the left hand side of the road near the cross and walk into the grounds of the Hall. There is a great cafe here.

Parking Lat/Long: 53.054791,-1.800085
Parking Grid Ref: SK 134 508
Parking Postcode: DE6 2AZ

Accessibility ♿

The hall is a National Trust property and operated in conjunction with the YHA. Access is good and well maintained.

Best time of year/day

Being principally deciduous, the parkland is at its best in autumn but the house has much architectural interest and can be photographed at any time of year.

The restored Mary Watts-Russell Memorial Cross (built in 1841). Canon 6D, 17-40 at 40mm, ISO 100, 1/60s at f/14. Jul. © CG

Ilam Hall built in the early 1800s, now a youth hostel. Canon 6D, 70-300 at 70mm, ISO 125, 1/50 at f/14. Jul. © CG

Tissington is one of the most beautiful villages in the Peak District. Built around Tissington Hall this estate village is unspoilt with broad green spaces between the cottages, beautiful gardens, a traditional butcher, a sweet shop, duck pond and a Norman church. It is also the spiritual home of the Derbyshire tradition of well dressing. Tissington escaped the Black Death (plague) of the 14th century and villagers attributed this to the purity of the water in their wells. They gave thanks for this by dressing the wells with flowers pressed in clay designed into Biblical themes. This is celebrated each year in May on Ascension Sunday and Tissington's seven dressed wells are the most visited in the Peak District. Tissington is the part of the Tissington Trail, a 13 mile path that runs from Ashbourne to Parsley Hay. Don't forget to visit Herbert's Fine English Tearooms in the village.

What to shoot and viewpoints

Viewpoint 1 – Well Dressing
In May Tissington is the first of the Derbyshire well dressings to take place. The village has up to seven different wells dressed with the most impressive being opposite the Hall. You can buy a guide to the location of each of the wells from one of the stewards at the car park. Use a zoom or macro lens to photograph the intricate floral designs as well as taking overview compositions.

Fields near Parwich. Sony A6000, 10-18 at 14mm, ISO 100, 1/200s at f/9.5. May. © MR

Viewpoint 2 – The Hall
Sir Richard FitzHerbert and Lady Fiona FitzHerbert are the present custodians of Tissington Hall. The hall was built in 1609 by their ancestor Francis FitzHerbert to replace the moated fortification that guarded the Norman Church of St Mary's in the centre of the village. For over 400 years the Hall has presided over this picturesque Estate Village. The Hall has a curious, squat character rather than the flamboyance more characteristic of the time. It faces slightly north east so is best lit in the mornings and benefits from having a dramatic sky behind it. When shooting from the entrance gate you look slightly uphill at it.

Viewpoint 3 – The Village
A wander with a camera around the village will reward the photographer with many pleasant village subjects and details. The cottages, the church, the old school, wells and the duckpond are all within easy reach of each other. St Mary's Church is Norman and was established in 1227 and sits on a mound almost opposite the hall.

As with most village photography it is best to arrive early, just after sunrise, when the village will be quiet. Spring and autumn are the best seasons, although in the summer the cottage gardens will be at their best.

Parwich
Three miles north of Tissington, just east of Alsop en le Dale, is another beautiful village that was named by the Sunday Times as one of the best places to live in Britain. Parwich is off the beaten track but is worth a visit if you enjoy photographing unspoilt rural life. This White Peak village has a stream running through it and a duck pond, a village green and a beautiful Anglican church. Many houses have mullioned windows and the village is very well looked after. Its history reaches back to the Domesday Book of 1086, although most of the buildings are 18/19th century. If driving from the A515 along Dam Lane to Parwhich look out for a tree-lined avenue on your left that leads to Peakway house. The network of country lanes around the village are worth exploring in the spring when the hawthorns flower and the hedgerows burst into life.

St Peter's Church in Parwich dates back to Norman times. Sony A6000, 10-18 at 14mm, ISO 100, 1/200s at f/8. May. © MR

Above left: *Tissington Well Dressing. Canon 5D Mk 1, 17-40 at 25mm, ISO 400, 1/200s at f/13. May. © CG*

How to get here

Tissington is 5 miles north of the market town of Ashbourne, half a mile east of the A515 down a beautiful avenue of lime trees. Parking is at the far (eastern) end of the village. Because of the popularity of the well dressing in May the village adopts a temporary one-way system to accommodate the number of visitors and access to the village is by the minor road of Rakes Lane just to the north. Care is needed at all times at both junctions to Tissington as the A515 is a fast, busy road.

Parking Lat/Long: 53.066046,-1.735759
Parking Grid Ref: SK 178 521
Parking Postcode: DE6 1RA (200m)

Accessibility ♿

Pathways and roads in the village are level and well maintained.

Best time of year/day

The rural nature of the setting makes late spring and autumn the best times to visit, early morning being the best part of the day. The well dressing is very popular so expect it to be busy at this time.

Tissington Hall (VP2). Canon 5D Mk 1, 17-40 at 26mm, ISO 400, 1/500s at f/13. May. © CG

Although the rolling greens fields and deep dales of the White Peak plateau don't have the immediate drama of the Dark Peak, unless you are on the edge of Dove Dale, the area contains many gems that are worth seeking out. Roystone Rocks is one of those places. It is an extensive outcrop of weathered dolomitic limestone hoodoos (rocky spires) with a wonderfully spooky atmosphere. The area has some limestone pavement with stunted trees. Nearby is Minninglow, a round barrow containing Neolithic burial chambers topped by a distinctive crown of trees. This makes a fine backdrop to landscape photographs in this area.

What to shoot and viewpoints

Leave the car park and walk back to and continue down (south) Parwich Lane. After 400m turn left into Minninglow Lane and then after 500m turn right toward Roystone Grange. At Roystone Cottages go through a gate and continue along the track. After a further 200m the ground starts to rise up on your right hand side. Enter through the metal pedestrian gate onto Access Land and climb the hill. Most of the hoodoos are found on the western flank of this hill and cannot be seen from the track so you will have to cross the hill to the other side.

Viewpoints

This is a location that rewards exploration and has many options. At different times of year different aspects of the hill, hoodoos, and the character scrub trees illuminate. The southern aspect of the hill enjoys the best outlook with the craggy dales above Ballidon combining well with the weird shapes of the foreground rocks. To the west the distinctive outline of Minninglow offers an excellent background figure to compose against.

Minninglow

Minninglow isn't on Access Land, although the Pennine bridleway skirts close by. A concessionary seasonal path sometimes leads to it but google it to find out the current situation before visiting. It is however better to photograph it from afar rather from within or right by it.

Opposite: Minninglow often features in the back of compositions, this from near Roystone Rocks. Canon 5D Mk 1, 17-40 at 20mm, ISO 100, 1/10s at f/20. Grad. Jan. © CG

Minninglow, as seen from the High Peak Trail near Pikehall. Canon 5D Mk 1, 70-300 at 100mm, ISO 200, 1/200s at f/8. Jan. © CG

How to get here

Roystone Rocks is located south of the villages of Youlgreave and north of Tissington, three miles from the A515, a mile south of the A5012 from the village of Pikehall. Park at the High Peak Trail car park which is 0.6 miles south of Pikehall down Parwich Lane and left on Mouldredge Lane.

Parking Lat/Long: 53.120414, -1.710971
Parking Grid Ref: SK 196 575
Parking Postcode: DE4 2PR (750m)

Accessibility

The walk to Roystone Rocks is on good tracks and paths. The hill where the rocks are has no paths and is rough pasture but is not particularly arduous walking. This area is Access Land meaning you are allowed to wander around.

Best time of year/day

Morning all year round is very good here, with the low light working well. Winter afternoons work similarly well. A high sun at any time of year will flatten the potential drama. A stormy sky would increase the drama for any compositions and in changeable weather experienced in April/May would be a good time to visit.

Limestone hoodoos and scrub trees at Roystone Rocks. Canon 5D Mk 1, 17-40 at 20mm, ISO 100, 1/60s at f/20. Grad. Jan. © CG

Salmon have been missing from the Peak District for over 200 years, victims of pollution and barriers such as weirs blocking their passage upstream. When Izaac Walton wrote *The Compleat Angler* published in 1653, the river Dove would have been teeming with salmon. They are now making a comeback. For over a decade the Trent Rivers Trust have released nearly a million salmon char into the Dove (and in the rivers Trent and Churnet) and the salmon are slowly returning. One of the places to see them is at a weir close to Norbury near Ashbourne.

What to shoot and viewpoints

From the bridge walk east along a footpath through fields for quarter of a mile to the weir. The sloping weir is a challenge for the salmon, sea trout and brown trout to swim up, being shallow, fast flowing and a steep gradient. A platform by the weir provides a good viewing point to photograph the fish jumping in the bottom pool and then attempting to thrash their way up the weir.

To capture the fast moving fish it best to use a zoom lens 100 – 400mm – the fish may be 15m or so away, a high ISO of 400+, a medium aperture of around f/8, and a fast shutter speed of 1/250s or more. Focussing is problematic, try spot focus and also manual by pre-focussing where you think the fish will jump – best of luck with that. At this location hand holding your camera is easiest as the fish will jump at various places, although panning with a tripod works too but it is essential is to have your shutter on continuous. You may have to play around with exposure to retain detail as you will be shooting a dark fish on a bright background – for this reason overcast days are best.

You have to be patient, and it is a waiting game with the occasional burst of fish jumping and running up the weir. But it is worth it for the amazing spectacle. The hours can soon pass.

Salmon attempting to get past the weir at Norbury. Few succeed, a fish ladder is needed. Sony A6000, 18–200 at 65mm, ISO 400, 1/400s at f/5.6. Nov. © MR

Sony A6000, 18–200 at 27mm, ISO 400, 1/250s at f/5.0. Nov. © MR

***Opposite right**: The salmon can swim up the face of the weir, but cannot pass the lip. They have difficulty swimming against the speed of flow on the face of the weir. Sony A6000, 18–200 at 38mm, ISO 400, 1/400s at f/5.6. Nov. © MR*

How to get here

The village of Norbury is 7 miles drive south west of Ashbourne.
Follow the A52 to Mayfield then south west along the B5032 to
Ellastone. Drive through the small village of Ellastone and take a
left on the B5033 toward Norbury and park at the first bridge
over the river Dove.

Parking Lat/Long: 52.978711, -1.822640
Parking Grid Ref: SK 120 423
Parking Postcode: DE6 2ED

Accessibility

It is a flat quarter of a mile (0.4km) walk through fields to the weir.

Best time of year/day

Anytime of day around mid-October. The salmon run usually lasts
for 3 to 4 weeks. After or during rain is a good time to visit when
there is a decent flow of water. Overcast days are best.

When the boundaries of the Peak District National Park were set in 1951 their extent down the Derwent Valley stopped at Rowsley, in part because of complications of adding undesirable planning restrictions to one of the area's largest conurbations in the Matlock area but also the southern part of the Derwent valley at this time was in significant industrial decline and was simply not 'picturesque'. In the intervening years, however, the extraordinary industrial heritage of the area has become a significant cultural and tourism asset, with the area to the south of Matlock Bath being designated in 2001 by UNESCO as a World Heritage Site. The combination of the careful preservation of selected aspects of the industry and the steady reclamation by nature of the remainder has delivered a fabulously photogenic legacy which we describe.

This is a diverse and accessible area. As well as the Derwent mills, the remains of older mills at the autumn hot spots of Lumsdale and Sydnope Brook, and heritage railways, the Matlock area is a place for flowers and is home to some of the best bluebell woods, and drifts of snowdrops in the Peak District. Both limestone and gritstone rocks also feature with the best being the impressive limestone cliff of High Tor towering above the inland seaside town of Matlock Bath, and magnificent landscape compositions from the gritstone ramparts of the Black Rocks of Cromford.

Barley at Holestone, as seen from Round Plantation (p.448). Canon 6D, 17-40 at 20mm, ISO 100, 1/40s at f/14. Grad. Jul. © CG

Maps

- OS Explorer Map OL241 (1:25 000) The Peak District: White Peak Area
- OS Explorer Map 269 (1:25 000) Chesterfield & Alfreton

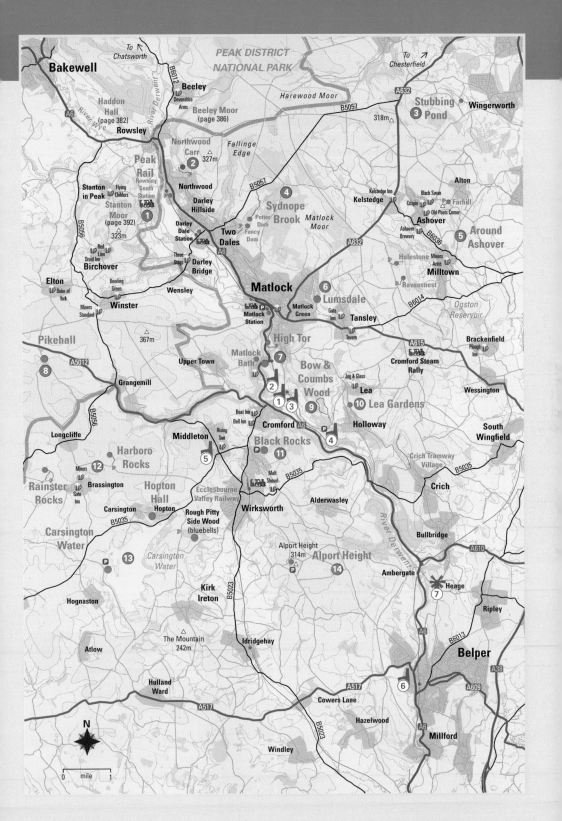

Peak Rail runs steam and diesel locomotives on a four mile stretch of dual line between Rowsley South Station and Matlock Sation. This is the perfect place to photograph and experience the romance of steam trains, both whilst traveling on the trains, and from the stations and surrounding countryside.

Headquartered at Rowsley South station, Peak Rail runs regular services at weekends throughout the year and selected weekdays during the summer season. As well as owning both steam and diesel locomotives they also regularly host guest heritage locomotives. Exactly what is running and when, is listed in detail at – *peakrail.co.uk.*

The countryside the line passes through has a number of vantage points to photograph the trains and photographers are welcome on the station

At Rowsley South Station. Canon 6D, 70-300 at 70mm, ISO 400, 1/400s at f/7.1. Aug. © CG

platforms. These offer more close-up opportunities but please be aware that they are subject to all of the usual by-laws that control pedestrian access to railways and these should be observed.

What to shoot and viewpoints

Viewpoint 1 – Rowsley South Station and Marshalling Yard

There are many engines, carriages and stock vehicles in the marshalling yard and viewing access is generally very good. The working engines also wait at the platforms in steam between runs offering very good close-up opportunities.

Viewpoint 2 – Darley Dale Station

Darley Dale station, located on the B5056 at 3 Station Rd, Darley Dale, DE4 2EQ, is a particular favourite with photographers because it has platform buildings on both sides of the track and the trains often cross here. Parking is tricky, there is limited space available roadside on the B5056 immediately adjacent to the station.

Viewpoint 3 – Matlock Station

Peak Rail enters Matlock station at Platform 2, which is the opposite side of the station to the main car park, which itself is just off the A6 (postcode DE4 3NA). Access is over the station footbridge via steps and a sloping ramp. The train enters the station slowly and on a long curve so offers itself up to the camera very well indeed. It is possible to photograph the footplate in detail from the platform while the train waits. The car park is pay and display.

In the marshalling yard at Rowsley South Station. Canon 6D, 70-300 at 70, ISO 400, 1/400s at f/7.1. Aug. © CG

How to get here

There is ample free parking at Rowsley South Station, which is 4.5 miles north of Matlock just off the A6. From Matlock pass through Darley Dale and Northwood. Just after entering open country look for a turning on the left in to Harrison Way. At the roundabout at the bottom of Harrison Way turn left. The track deteriorates somewhat as you enter Rowsley South station yard.

Parking Lat/Long: 53.175509,-1.609518
Parking Grid Ref: SK 261 643
Parking Postcode: DE4 2HX (400m)

Accessibility &

The car park is rough and not surfaced but it is level. The station platforms are accessed by either steps or by a ramp.

Best time of year/day

Peak Rail runs all year and is good at most times of year. For private visits by groups to the headquarters at Rowsley South Station, Peak Rail recommend the longer evenings of spring and summer when there is more time to explore the yards, the stations and the engines and when there is time to operate, for example, the turntable which is a very interesting feature. They are also happy to open the buffet bar for refreshments.

Photographers are welcome to visit at any time of year, as long as the site is open. Colder weather will enhance the steam that the engines produce, if that is the effect you wish to photograph.

Above: Trackside access at Rowsley South Station. Canon 6D, 70-300 at 70mm, ISO 400, 1/400s at f/7.1. Aug. © CG

Engine detail at Matlock Station. Canon 6D, 70-300 at 70mm, ISO 800, 1/400s at f/7.1. Aug. © CG

On the flanks of Fallinge Edge above the settlement of Northwood is Tinkersley Woods and Northwood Carr, one of the best places in the Peak District to photograph bluebells. The drifts of colour in spring are stunning and there are enough paths in and around the woods to allow access without trampling.

What to shoot and viewpoints

Viewpoint 1 – Main Bridleway

On entering the woods the views of the blubells appear, with the drifts building up steadily. There are very good views diagonally down from here, across the flank of the hill that concentrates colour well.

Viewpoint 2 – Bridleway north

The north end of the bridleway heads out toward Tinkersley. On the way the leaf canopy breaks up a bit, introducing more flower varieties, particularly stitchwort and campion. There are some larger trees here and a lovely old wall offering some excellent compositions.

Viewpoint 3 – Diagonal pathway

Running diagonally downhill from the north end of the bridleway there is another path which offers excellent views up through the crown of the bluebells, compressing the colour really well. The view down this path when the light crosses it from the west is fabulous.

At Northwood Carr, from the main bridleway (VP1). Canon 6D, 70-300 at 200mm, ISO 100, 1/150s at f/10. May. © CG

How to get here

Northwood Car is above Northwood, on the eastern side of the A6, 4 miles north of Matlock. From Matlock drive northwards along the A6 through Darley Dale. After Darley Dale pass a large engineering works on your left and then in 200 yards look for Northwood Lane on your right (this is 1.3 miles after Rowsley if coming from the north). Ascend Northwood Lane steeply, through bends and at the top turning onto Whitworth Lane. Park carefully and considerately along Whitworth Lane. On foot follow Lumb Lane for 75m before taking a bridleway left. After a further 150m enter Northwood Carr and be amazed.

Parking Lat/Long: 53.177717, -1.5987307
Parking Grid Ref: SK 269 645
Parking Postcode: DE4 2HS (200m)

Accessibility ♿

Once off the tarmac of Lumb Lane are typical woodland pathways, good when dry but muddy when wet. The main bridleway through the woods is level and easy to walk along. Other paths that leave this are steep in places..

Best time of year/day

Bluebells usually flower in May into June. Northwood Carr is best in the mid to late afternoon when the light filters down through the trees, illuminating the bluebells in a heart-stoppingly beautiful way.

Other bluebell woods

Bow and Coumbs Wood, page 458
Bellamy's Walk, page 348
Rough Pitty Side wood, see map on page 437

Above: *Spring colours at Northwood Carr. Canon 6D, 70-300 at 150mm, ISO 100, 1/200s at f/10. May. © CG*

Below: *At Northwood Carr, from the diagonal footpath (VP3). Canon 6D, 70-300 at 100mm, ISO 100, 1/200s at f/10. May. © CG*

Olave St. Clair Baden Powell, the wife of Lord Robert Baden-Powell, was born on 22 February 1889 at Stubbing Court, a Georgian country house near Chesterfield. The house is surrounded by parkland, unfortunately not open for public use, However roads traverse partly around the Great Pond of Stubbing and its boat house which makes a very attractive photograph.

What to shoot and viewpoints

The old stone boat house is in a state of romantic decay and it nestles in its backdrop of pretty trees while ducks may paddle around its opening. The variety of trees surrounding mean that autumn can be particularly rewarding, especially with a morning mist on the water.

How to get here

The Boat House at the Great Pond of Stubbing is located a mile from the village of Wingerworth and 3 miles south west of the town of Chesterfield. From Chesterfield go south on the A61, Derby Road for 1.5 miles and turn left into Wingerworth. Follow Lodge Drive then right onto Longedge Lane for 0.8 miles to crossroads. Go straight across Hillhouses Lane and a first right along Pearce Lane for half-a-mile to a left and the Great Pond of Stubbing – park by the side of the road – the Boat House is right in front of you.

Parking Lat/Long: 53.201001, -1.458294
Parking Grid Ref: SK 362 672
Parking Postcode: S42 6QR

Accessibility ♿

The Boat House viewpoint is roadside and suitable for all.

Best time of year/day

The position of the Boat House, tucked into the south eastern corner of the lake and backed by a stand of trees, makes this location good for evenings, particularly autumn evenings when the colours are good. Calm weather will also render some beautiful reflections here.

Romantic dilapidation; the Boat House by the Great Pond of Stubbing. Canon 6D, 17-40 at 40mm, ISO 50, 1/5s at f/16. Polariser, Grad. Sep. © CG

Sydnope Brook breaks into the Derwent Valley through the hills above Two Dales and for the most part remains hidden in the dale below Sydnope Hall. In the woodlands below the hall, however, it is collected by Potter Dam and Fancy Dam. The dams, which were built to provide power to flax and flour mills, are in a quite poor condition but this only adds interest to the scene adding a random quality to the way the waters tumble through them. There are several small cascades and waterfalls here, as well as the two small reservoirs and in the autumn the mixed woodland shows off its colours.

Sydnope Brook can be combined with nearby Lumsdale (page 450) for a real October-November photographic treat of woodland, fast-flowing water and industrial remains.

What to shoot and viewpoints

A track leads down to the brook and joins a path which follows the brook by the dams.

Viewpoint 1 – Fancy Dam

Fancy Dam is the more broken down of the two accessible dams. The water flows very pleasingly over the tumble and random gritstone blocks that have been dislodged by years of wear and tear.

Viewpoint 2 – Potter Dam

The old beech trees hem Potter Dam in tightly. It is a sheltered location so offers colourful reflections in autumn very easily. You can follow the brook beyond the dams then take a path up through the fields below Sydnope Hall and its parkland, with great views over the Derwent Valley.

How to get here

Sydnope Brook is located immediately adjacent to the hamlet of Two Dales, 3 miles north of Matlock up the A6. At the crossroads in Darley Dale drive up the Chesterfield Road/B5057 toward Two Dales for half-a-mile and turn right down Ladygrove Road. After 0.2 miles fork right into the industrial estate and park considerately at the far end. A footpath follows the right hand bank of the stream uphill into Ladygrove Wood alongside the brook.

Parking Lat/Long: 53.162364,-1.571887
Parking Grid Ref: SK 287 628
Parking Postcode: DE4 2FJ

Accessibility &

Parking is on a surface road but the footpaths through the woods are unsurfaced. It is a gentle climb through the woods that can be slippery when wet.

Best time of year/day

The woods and brook are best in autumn on still clear days after there has been some rain.

Opposite: Horse chestnut avenue on the driveway to Sydnope House. Canon 6D, 17-40 at 40mm, ISO 100, 1/60s at f/14. Sep. © CG

Reflections in Potter Dam (VP2). Canon 6D, 17-40 at 40mm, ISO 50, 1/5s at f/16. Polariser. Apr. © CG

The tumbledown blocks of Fancy Dam (VP1). Canon 30D, 17-40 at 20mm, ISO 100, 2s at f/20. Sep. © CG

Ripening barley at Holestone (page 448). Canon 5D Mk 1, 17-40 at 20mm, ISO 100, 1/40s at f/20. Grad. Jul. © CG

The Amber Valley runs parallel to the Derwent Valley through the hills to the west of Chesterfield. The upper reaches of this valley are gentle but south of the A632 around Ashover the valley takes on a different character with some great photographic potential.

The hills on the western flank of the valley here form a lovely north east facing escarpment with the fields along its crest often planted with barley, which in July offer a lovely compliment to the bleak rockiness of the hills and moorlands in the north of the Peak District. Holstone and Ravensnest in particular are great locations for this.

On the eastern side of the valley above Farhill there is a prominent rocky tor known as the Fabrick. The views from here down into the valley around Ashover are tremendous. There is also nothing higher than this point to the east as far as the Lincolnshire coast. On a very clear day it is possible to see Lincoln Cathedral, it's worth bringing a pair of binoculars.

What to shoot and viewpoints

Viewpoint 1 – Holestone
Follow a clearly marked footpath from Holestone to Round Plantation. Here you pass through beautiful fields of ripening barley in late July and can photograph their interaction with the woodland, particularly that of Round Plantation. You can explore further into the fields and visit Cocking Tor and Gregory Mine.

Viewpoint 2 – Ravensnest
As for Holestone for the barley fields but also explore Ravensnest Woods.

Viewpoint 3 – Farhill
A short walk on good footpaths brings you to Farhill and the rocky promontory of The Fabrick, a brutal tor that offers an excellent counterpoint to the softness of the location, particularly in August when the heather here is in bloom. There are also very good views from here to Ashover down below, which lights up beautifully in the late summer evening sun.

Barley at Holestone (VP1). Canon 5D Mk 1, 17-40 at 20mm, ISO 100, 1/40s at f/20. Grad. Jul. © CG

Opposite left: Below Ashover at Milltown, wild garlic and the river Amber. Canon 6D, 17-40 at 30mm, ISO 100, 1/2s at f/14. Polariser. May. © CG

Opposite middle: The east rim of the Amber Valley at The Fabrick (VP3). 5D, 17-40 at 30mm, ISO 100, 1/10s at f/20. Aug. © CG

Opposite right: Wild garlic near the river Amber at Milltown. Canon 6D, 17-40 at 30mm, ISO 100, 1/2s at f/14. May. © CG

Winter snows at Round Plantation, Holestone (VP1). Canon 5D Mk 1, 17-40 at 20mm, ISO 100, 1/20s at f/20. Jan. © CG

How to get here

Ashover is located 4.5 miles north east of Matlock on the B6036, which is off the A632 Matlock to Chesterfield Road. Holestone is located on the Matlock side of the Amber Valley a mile and a half outside Matlock, look for a right hand turn onto Holestone Gate Road, this is at the crest of the very steep Slack Hill. Holestone is half-a-mile along Holestone Gate Road. Look for an obvious copse in the fields on your left. Ravensnest is a further half-a-mile along Holestone Gate Road where it makes a sharp right turn. Turn left at this point onto a minor track. There is very limited parking opportunities for Holestone Copse. It is often better to proceed to Ravensnest where there is parking on the minor track.

Farhill is on the opposite side of the valley to Holestone. Proceed down Slack Hill from Matlock and up through Kelstedge. Half-a-mile after Kelstedge look for a right turn into Hut Lane. At the end of Hut Lane turn right into Bath Lane and then after a quarter-of-a-mile turn left into Hilltop Road. Follow Hilltop Road for a mile and after it changes to Bassettbarn Lane it turns into Alton Lane where there is parking for several cars just after the junction with Brownhills Lane.

Top: Passing storms and cut barley at Ravensnest (VP2). Canon 5D Mk 1, 17-40 at 30mm, ISO 100, 1/20s at f/20. Grad. Aug. © CG

Holestone Parking Lat/Long: 53.152059,-1.495116
Parking Grid Ref: SK 338 617
Parking Postcode: S45 0JS

Ravensnest Parking Lat/Long: 53.145791,-1.490225
Parking Grid Ref: SK 341 610
Parking Postcode: S45 0JT

Farhill Parking Lat/Long: 53.169876,-1.464554
Parking Grid Ref: SK 358 637
Parking Postcode: S45 0BB (400m)

Accessibility

Although all of these locations are close to parking with reasonably level walking they are on unsurfaced footpaths.

Best time of year/day

For Holestone Copse and Ravensnest it is best to visit when the barley is out and ripening or has just been harvested, which means July or August. For Farhill August is best, when the heather is in bloom. They are all late afternoon/early evening locations.

Lumsdale Valley is one of the most accessible and most-visited locations in Derbyshire for photographing waterfalls. It is situated just outside Matlock on the course of Bentley Brook, which drains water from Matlock Moor.

There have been mills on this section of Bentley Brook since the 1600s but it was most developed as an industrial site by Richard Arkwright consequent to his successes at Cromford and in response to his need for more locations in the vicinity. The falls that the water flowing down the valley create are not on the natural line of drainage but are rather a product of human intervention in redirecting the water flow to suit the needs of the mills.

The location is managed by the Arkwright Society and is one of the best examples of a water-powered industrial archaeology site in the UK. As well as waterfalls the main subjects are old mill ruins, beech woodland, a mill pond, and birds such as dippers.

What to shoot and viewpoints

Walk up the road for 50m to a path entrance on the right between a wall and a fence, marked by a Arkwright Society plaque. The viewpoints are described from this point.

Viewpoint 1 – Mill Ruins

The ivy-covered mill ruins make an interesting study amongst the trees. Ferns sprout from the leaf litter and the stone walls and arches. Light will be low here so a tripod is recommended.

Viewpoint 2 – First Waterfall

Walk up the path and up two sets of steps to the first waterfall. Wide-angled compositions are good from both the path and also from various places actually in and down by the stream – wellington boots are recommended. Leaves usually spread out on a rock platform at the base of the cascade providing a good foreground. Slow shutter speeds of 1–3 seconds with a tripod and ND filter work to blur the water.

Opposite: The tallest waterfall at Lumsdale (VP3). Sony A6000, 10-18 at 10mm, ISO 100, 4s at f/8. Oct. © MR

Viewpoint 3 – Water Wheel Waterfall

Continue up the next step of steps to an old mill building and water wheel pit. This waterfall is the tallest here and has a clean drop. Wide-angle compositions can capture the buildings with the fall and the stream below which add contrast to the red of the beech leaves littering the floor.

Viewpoint 4 – Stone Wall Waterfall

Continue up the path to another old building which makes an interesting study. Various spots on the path also allow you to look amongst the tree canopy for detail studies of leaves. Beyond the building a series of cascades run by a lovely featured stone wall. Low compositions, excluding the highlights of the sky, are best here.

Viewpoint 5 – The Mill Pond

The final cascade pours over the dam wall and again because of back-light a low composition is a good option. Follow the path around to the left and you are greeted with a delightful mill pond bordered by trees which is great for reflections on calm days. Later in autumn is best as there will be more colour.

How to get here

Lumsdale Valley is situated 1.5 miles east of Matlock, north of the A615. From Matlock drive east toward Alfreton on the A615 and turn left before the village of Tansley, a half-a-mile after leaving Matlock. Go down this narrow road, by the mills and up the hill. The parking is just after a bend on the right in a large lay-by across from some abandoned mill houses.

Parking Lat/Long: 53.140756,-1.533907
Parking Grid Ref: SK 312 605
Parking Postcode: DE4 5EX

Accessibility

This shaded valley can be damp, muddy and slippery at all times of year. Care should be taken when walking around the site, particularly when close to the brook. Parts of the site are also very steep.

Best time of year/day

This is primarily an autumn location and one of the best from October through November. Earlier in autumn you will get a mix of green with autumn colours. Later, fewer leaves on the trees give a more minimalist look. Water flow isn't usually an issue in autumn. Bright overcast days are the best for both photographing the leaf-strewn cascades and reflections in the mill pond, as on sunny days there will be glare and low contrast.

Above: *The top waterfall (VP4). Canon 5D Mk 1, 17-40 at 17mm,*
ISO 50, 4s at f/22. Polariser. Nov. © CG

Above: *Mill building (VP3). Canon 5D Mk 1, 17-40 at 17mm, ISO*
50, 0.4s at f/20. Nov. © CG

Such was the energy of the post-glacial meltwaters 12,000 years ago that in their route south along the Derwent Valley they cut a great gap in the limestone hills to the south of Matlock. The gorge here is at its deepest where the river squeezes between Masson Hill and High Tor. Much of the Masson side of the valley is both wooded and private but the rock face and summit of High Tor has been a public attraction since Victorian times. The summit offers a superb views and if you have a head for heights try a walk along Giddy Ledge, a path that traverses just below the cliff's summit.

Matlock Bath is nearly 100 miles from the sea yet is lined with amusement arcades and fish and chip shops. The town was established as a resort for visitors by the Victorians and it is still a very popular destination. The Heights of Abraham Cable Car departs from the valley floor next to the station and takes visitors to an attraction at the top of Masson Hill (**www.heightsofabraham.com**).

What to shoot and viewpoints

HIGH TOR

High Tor is impressive enough to photograph from the valley floor, but looking down 250 vertical feet from its grassy summit plateau to the river Derwent and Matlock Bath is one of the wonders of the Peak District. The cliff faces west and the valley runs north-south so the cliff face and the narrow valley doesn't get sun until midday. It does get glimmers of light when the sun is in the south east (winter sunrise). If you are an early bird and there is a chance of low-lying mist, this is a good place to be, especially with autumn colours in the woodlands below.

Approach from High Tor Road to the grassy plateau which ends at the precipice.

Viewpoint 1 – High Tor Viewpoint

There is good access to the cliff edge at various spots. Be very careful here, don't get too close and pay attention if using a tripod.

From the edge a wider lens will give you a very good sense of location but also be prepared to use a long lens to pick out detail such as the Heights of Abraham cable car and the beautiful woodlands that cover this flank of Masson Hill. Also look down to the River Derwent that can be seen snaking its way through the woodland. Temperature inversions can fill the valley below with dawn mists.

Viewpoint 2 – The Precipice Path: Giddy Edge

Those with a good head for heights can venture along Giddy Edge that crosses the face of the cliff immediately below the summit. The start is signposted and at various spots is equipped with a solid iron hand-rail (like an Italian Via Ferrata) to help confidence. Good viewpoints are restricted but the experience is exhilarating and this is an impressive place to photograph a friend above the drop. Of additional interest here are old lead mines, known as Fern and Roman Caves, which are by the paths that lead down through the woods to Matlock Baths.

The Heights of Abraham Cable Car from High Tor (VP1). Canon 6D, 70-300 at 280mm, ISO 400, 1/200s at f/8. Jun. © CG

Above: *Matlock from the top of High Tor (VP1). Sony A6000, 18–200 at 70mm, ISO 400, 1/200s at f/10. Oct. © MR*

Below: *The river Derwent from High Tor (VP1). Sony A6000, 18–200 at 85mm, ISO 200, 1/80s at f/10. Oct. © MR*

MATLOCK BATH

Viewpoint 3 – Matlock Bath Visitors

Matlock Bath is a very popular tourist destination, particularly with motorcyclists. On any given Sunday it is possible to photograph just about any make of motorbike that you might care to think of.

Viewpoint 4 – Matlock Bath Illuminations

On evenings in September and October the local council run the Matlock Bath illuminations, where colourfully lit craft float down the river and fireworks are set off from the cliffs above. See website for details, times and costs **www.derbyshiredales.gov.uk/leisure-a-culture/ matlock-bath-illuminations**

Viewpoint 5 – St John The Baptist Chapel

The wonderful St John The Baptist Chapel is located at SK 294 594 (53.130957, -1.5620509) on St John's Road, half-a-mile north of Matlock Bath and high on the flanks of Masson Hill. This wonderful Arts and Crafts building is a subject worthy of photographic study.

Viewpoint 6 – Above Matlock Bath

There are a network of very steep and narrow roads accessed from Matlock Bath opposite the railway station. It is not advised that you drive up these narrow roads but walk up Holme Road to Upperwood Road for various impressive views looking down on Matlock Bath.

High Tor and Riber Castle from Mason Hill. Canon 6D, 70-300 at 180mm, ISO 200, 1/200s at f/8 Jul. © CG

How to get here

Matlock Bath is located 1.5m due south of Matlock on the A6. There is plenty of pay and display parking at the railway station which is signposted on the left on entering the town from Matlock.

Parking Lat/Long: 53.121339,-1.557322
Parking Grid Ref: SSK 297 583
Parking Postcode: DE4 3NT

High Tor is most easily accessed from the Matlock Green (just east of Matlock) to Starkholmes road. Head away from Matlock town centre on the A615 Alfreton Road. After a third of a mile at Matlock Green turn right immediately before the filling station up Starkholmes Road. After half-a-mile look for somewhere to park on the right hand side of the road. Locate and walk along High Tor Road on the right hand side and enter the parkland through a gate. Follow the track and reach the edge of the cliff after 250m. Follow the paths upward and to right to reach the summit, a flat grassy area.

Parking Lat/Long: 53.126896,-1.557713
Parking Grid Ref: SK 296 589
Parking Postcode: DE4 3DD

Accessibility ♿

The footpaths around the main thoroughfare at Matlock Bath are fully accessible. The side roads, however, are very steep. The footpaths in and around High Tor are unsurfaced but they have been designed to be as accessible as this steep location will allow. The views from the top of cliffs can be accessed by an almost level approach.

Best time of year/day

The bottom of the valley where Matlock Bath sits can be quite dark in winter so it is best visited outside this time. High Tor faces west and the subjects that can be photographed from here are best revealed by a mid-morning light, which illuminates from the south east and the south.

Above: Giddy Edge, VP2. Sony A6000, 18–200 at 58mm, ISO 200, 1/125s at f/10. Oct. © MR

Below: The grand vista south of High Tor (VP1). Canon 6D, 17-40 at 30mm, ISO 100, 1/100s at f/14. Grad. Jun. © CG

8 PIKEHALL HARNESS RACING

Harness Racing or Trotting, is a type of horses racing where the jockey is pulled along in a two-wheeled cart or sulky, and the horse trots rather than gallops.

Harness Racing started in the Peak at Pikehall in 1998 and there are now two meets a year in June and July. Each meeting comprises of a race card of 6 or 8 preliminary races and a final race-off for the winners of the preliminaries. A race consist of one speed-controlled warm-up lap around the oval grass track and then two full speed laps. There is an entrance fee but the entertainment is excellent and there are also usually refreshments available.

See **pikehallharnessracing.co.uk** for more details.

Being close to a group of thundering horses at high speed is very exciting and the photographer needs to have their wits about them to get the best shots.

If you are not used to photographing fast moving horses it can take a bit of practice. A mid-zoom lens is ideal. Use a highish shutter speed of 1/250s or above, and depending on the light you may need to increase the ISO. Go for a mid-aperture or wide aperture (smaller number) to isolate the action. Ditch the tripod and also try panning around with the moving horses and carts – reduce your shutter speed to 1/60s or 1/30s and pan your camera to track the horse and rider. The result is a relatively sharp subject but a blurred background that gives a feeling of movement and speed.

What to shoot and viewpoints

Viewpoint 1 – The Starting Gate
The horses will gather behind the control car before the start of the warm-up lap. If you stand near the starting gate you will get some good close-up detail.

Viewpoint 2 – The Second Bend
The spectators position is to the south of the track, looking north, meaning that the light on the course is usually good. The best shooting position is on the second bend where the horses compress together well in the viewfinder and the action is at its most intense. A mid-range zoom will be useful.

Viewpoint 3 – Behind the Race Line
Look behind the race line for local characters, particularly the bookies.

Exciting action at Pikehall Harness Racing. You need to have your wits about. Canon 6D, 70-300 at 180mm, ISO 400, 1/400s at f/8. Jul. © CG

How to get here

Pikehall is located on the A5012, 11 miles west of Matlock. From the west Pikehall is best approached from Cromford. At the traffic lights on the A6 in Cromford turn into the village on the B5036 signposted Wirksworth and then after a tenth of a mile turn right onto the A5012. Follow the road for 7 miles and just before reaching Pikehall turn left onto Mouldrige Lane, the entrance to the parking area is on your right.

Pikehall can also be approached from the west from A515, the Buxton-Ashbourne road. Turn onto the A5012 at Newhaven and it is 2 miles to Pikehall.

Parking Lat/Long: 53.126829,-1.704482
Parking Grid Ref: SK 198 588
Parking Postcode: DE4 2PG (250m

Accessibility ♿

The race field is level and grassy. There are no access problems.

Best time of year/day

The race meeting is restricted to particular dates and times.

These superb bluebell woods are in the hills to the east of the Cromford Canal, two miles south of Cromford. Bow Wood has more canopy than Coumbs and is slightly easier to access being at the base of the hill. The bluebells in Bow Wood are also more interspersed with other flower types, particularly stitchwort and campion and offer a wonderful tapestry of colour. At a higher elevation – and a longer walk – the bluebells at Coumbs are more drift-like and there are more silver birch trees.

What to shoot and viewpoints

From the car park at High Peak Junction walk up Lea Road to a stile just before Smedley's Works. The left fork beyond the stile traverses around Bow Wood, the right fork goes behind Smedley's Works then up and round to Coumbs Wood. You can do a circular walk visiting both woods. There is both dense woodland here and more open spaces, including the woodland edges, and all three types of location are good for bluebell photography

Rather than describe specific viewpoints, self-exploration is far better here, here are some tips for photographing bluebells to consider.

How to get here

For both Bow Wood and Coumbs Wood park at the pay and display car park at High Peak Junction just off the A6, 1.3 miles south of Cromford. It is also possible to park carefully and considerately adjacent to Smedley's Works on Lea Road close to where the footpath starts into the woods.

Parking Lat/Long: 53.103307,-1.531429
Parking Grid Ref: SK 314 563
Parking Postcode: DE4 5AA (200m)

Accessibility

The pay and display car park at High Peak Junction is surfaced. The tracks around the woods are unsurfaced and there is some up hill walking. Wear some good walking shoes or if wet, wellington boots.

Best time of year/day

These woods are best visited in April when the bluebells will be at their best. Coumbs Wood is a better morning location and Bow Wood is a better afternoon location so they can be combined comfortably in a single visit.

Coumbs Wood. Canon 5D, 17-40 at 40mm, ISO 100, 1/40s at f/20. May. © CG

Mottled light in Coumbs Wood. Canon 6D, 17-40 at 40mm, ISO 100, 1/10s at f/14. May. © CG

Bluebell shooting tips

- **A low shooting position** – In this way you gather the blooms together in a compressed line of sight, increasing the colour density.
- **A longer focal length** – wide-angle will cause the blooms closest to the camera to separate, meaning that you will see predominantly green in the foreground and reduce the impact of the deeper blue, which will be starting in the middle ground. A longer focal length (a zoom) will maintain the packing density of the blooms that the low shooting angle delivers.
- **A gently convex slope** – This is a hard one to get but a slope will cause the blooms to all hang in the same direction. By positioning yourself at the bottom of the slope you will be shooting upwards into the face of the blooms, maximising colour. If the slope is gently convex – bulges out – then even better because the bend of the slope will maximise colour density across the crown.

- **Nicely spaced, thin, bare tree trunks** – The nature of bluebell woodland means that you are likely to get this anyway but the trunks can be used to break up the texture and add interest, particularly in the presence of the next ingredient …
- **Low, raking backlight** – The final ingredient is probably best found toward the edges of the wood. As the trees stop they create a lovely void into which the sun can be placed. Position the camera so that a convenient tree trunk cuts through the brightest part of the shot and you will dramatically reduce the dynamic range. The backlighting will cause the blues and greens of the bluebells to glow, it emphasises the texture gradient and the dramatic raking shadows of the trees introduces a lovely and highly desirable acceleration.

Lea Gardens are located above the village of Lea to the south of Matlock, on the east side of the Derwent valley. This secluded and peaceful garden specialises in azaleas and rhododendrons, that flower all the way from Easter to June and are at their best around late April and early May. The garden also hosts many other plant species which flower outside these times.

The immediate proximity of such a large number of beautiful plants makes it an ideal location for garden flower photography, particularly for those of limited mobility. It is very easy to while away a peaceful couple of hours with the camera here.

Lea Gardens welcomes photographers, either as casual visitors during normal opening times or as organised groups by special arrangement outside these times. When visiting during normal opening times please show consideration for other garden users, particularly if using a tripod, and be aware that on a nice day the garden is likely to be very busy. Please contact the Gardens to arrange for group visits; parking is free and dogs on a lead are allowed. The garden has an excellent tea room.

Because of the absolute riot of colour available at the garden you might find your camera produces a better colour response when the weather is slightly duller. The dynamic range will be lower and over saturation less likely.

www.leagarden.co.uk   t: 01629 534 380

What to shoot and viewpoints

The lovely network of intimate gravel paths wind their way around the hillside among a stunning variety of blooms, most of which are immediately adjacent to the paths and can be photographed in considerable detail.

Excellent close-ups are available pathside all over at Lea Gardens. Canon 6D, 17-40 at 40mm, ISO 200, 1/40s at f/8. Jun. © CG

Beautiful detail, easily captured at Lea Gardens. Canon 6D, 70-400 at 100mm, ISO 400, 1/100s at f/10. Jun. © CG

How to get here

From Matlock take the A6 south through Matlock Bath to Cromford. At the traffic lights in Cromford turn left onto Lea Road, past Cromford Mill. After2 miles you reach Lea and turn left, uphill past John Smedley's factory. Turn sharp right into Long Lane (not Church Street, which is immediately before). Lea Gardens is on the right hand side after 400 metres. Parking is on Long Lane, adjacent to the gardens.

Parking Lat/Long: 53.110128,-1.517551
Parking Grid Ref: SK 323 571
Parking Postcode: DE4 5NX

Accessibility ♿

The paths in the garden, some of which are narrow, are finished mainly in pea gravel. Some are level but some slope significantly. Access is generally easy and there is plenty to see and photograph from the most accessible paths.

Best time of year/day

From late spring through to mid-summer. The gardens have a westerly aspect meaning they are best lit in the afternoon.

Above: *Flowering azaleas. Canon 6D, 70-400 at 100mm, ISO 400, 1/100s at f/10. Jun. © CG*

Azaleas. Canon 6D, 17-40 at 40mm, ISO 200, 1/40s at f/8. Jun. © CG

On the western side of the Derwent Valley high above Cromford is Black Rocks, a majestic gritstone cliff of tall rounded buttresses set on the edge of Cromford Moor. From the rocky promontory at the top of the rocks there are superb views to the north up the Derwent to Matlock and beyond. Set in a country park, made popular in Victorian times, there are pleasant walks and photographic studies amongst the oak and birch woodland. This is popular place for walkers and rock climbers, if you visit at weekends when the weather is good it will likely be busy.

What to shoot and viewpoints

Viewpoint 1 – Below Black Rocks

From the top car park walk along the High Peak Trail through woodland to the base of the rocks. There is a steep open rocky slope that leads up to the cliffs that provides good studies of trees next to the rocks, especially in the autumn.

Opposite top: Looking down on Cromford (VP2). A6000, 18–200 at 18mm, ISO 100, 1/160s at f/10. Oct. © MR

The narrow valleys and history around Cromford and Matlock (VP2). Sony A6000, 18–200 at 49mm, ISO 100, 1/30s at f/11. Oct. © MR

Viewpoint 2 – Summit Pinnacles

A path leads up the side of the steep open rocky slope, and follows close to the base of the cliffs, up into woods where a path on the left over easy-angled rock slabs, leads to a promontory at the top of the pinnacles. The pinnacles jut out like fingers over the drop and care must be exercised if you are close to the edge of the drop, especially if setting up a tripod.

The views are always dramatic here, although to the west there are old quarry workings which aren't particularly attractive. The views to the north west and north are best, looking up the Derwent toward Masson Mills and Matlock. Sunrise is problematic here as Matlock Moor rises behind you and blocks early light. When there is a temperature inversion after sunrise is best, especially in the autumn and spring, or at sunset in late June and July. The rocky fingers and cliff faces provide foreground subjects, the challenge is to position them well in a composition that includes the distant view.

Of interest is the old graffiti carved into the summit rocks, some well over a hundred years old, which often feature in landscape photographs from here and which are also worthy of close up shots. Of less interest is some of the modern graffiti which appears from time to time, usually using spray paint.

If you have time there are pleasant Forestry Commission trails in the woods behind the summit rocks.

How to get here

Black Rocks Country Park is half-a-mile from Cromford. Drive through Cromford up the hill on the B5036 toward Wirksworth, to a left sign posted Black Rocks Country Park and the car park is on your left (pay and display) opposite a cemetery. There are three small car parks in the trees.

Parking Lat/Long: 53.098029,-1.566880
Parking Grid Ref: SK 290 557
Parking Postcode: DE4 4GT (200m)

Accessibility ♿

Paths are level and well-maintained from the car park and along the High Peak Trail in the woodland at the base of the cliffs. There are steep slopes up to the rocks themselves and getting to the top of the rocks can include some walking up easy-angled rocks. There are steep drop-offs at the top of the pinnacles. The country park has a small information centre with public toilets.

Best time of year/day

The summit rocks are north facing so illuminate poorly in winter when the sun is low in the south. In spring and autumn the summit is best in the morning, and in midsummer it illuminates well in the evening. It is well worth a visit on early spring and late autumn mornings when there is a chance of mist in the valley below.

Pine trees at the summit of Black Rocks (VP1). Canon 5D Mk 1, 17-40 at 20mm, ISO 100, 1/40s at f/20. Grad. Oct. © CG

The way up to Black Rocks summit. Sony A6000, 18–200 at 18mm, ISO 100, 1/80s at f/10. Oct. © MR

The pinnacles and cliff faces of Harboro and Rainster Rocks near the village of Brassington are formed of dolomitic limestone, a softer and more eroded rock than the carboniferous limestone to the north.

At Harboro Rocks there is evidence of humans dating back to the last Ice Age and there are scars from mining. It has quite an eery feel to it and although the views from here are tremendous – it is possible to see five counties from the summit – it is somewhat compromised by the adjacent factory and wind farm.

Rainster Rocks has one prominent central tor and is surrounded by a fabulously random collection of hoodoos (pinnacles), ancient hawthorns and tumbledown walls, all full of wonderful detail and offering many photographic possibilities.

The windfarm next to Harboro Rocks won't be to everyone's tastes but makes an interesting background (VP1). Canon 5D, 17-40 at 20mm, ISO 100, 1/80s at f/20. Grad. Mar. © CG

What to shoot and viewpoints

HARBORO ROCKS

Harboro Rocks is somewhat compromised by the immediately adjacent factory and wind farm.
It is is easier to tolerate and compose for the the wind farm than for the factory. The location requires a bit of study but can be very rewarding, with hoodoos and drops offering good subjects that are counterpoint to the ultra-modern wind turbines.

Viewpoint 1 – Harboro Rocks, Wind Farm
The south east corner of the outcrop at Harboro looks toward the wind farm on Carsington Pasture, which has a pleasing symmetry.

Viewpoint 2 – Haraboro Rocks Summit
A pleasing collection of dolomitic pinnacles.

Viewpoint 3 – Harboro Rocks, the cliffs
Some pleasing post-industrial remains merge with natural features to produce some interesting juxtapositions.

Rainster Rocks approach (VP1). Canon 6D, 17-40 at 20mm, ISO 100, 1/20s at f/14. Grad. Jan. © CG

RAINSTER ROCKS

Viewpoint 1 – Rainster Rocks Approach

An excellent composition can be made from the rocky tors immediately adjacent to the approach footpath.

Viewpoint 2 – Rainster Rocks Pinnacles & Walls

The slopes immediately below the summit tor are strewn with pinnacles and broken down walls and reward exploration.

Viewpoint 3 – Rainster Rocks Summit

There are great views out over the Derbyshire countryside over the summit pinnacles

Natural versus human-made counterpoints at Harboro Rocks (VP3). 5D, 17-40 at 20mm, ISO 100, 1/80s at f/20. Grad. Mar. © CG

How to get here

Both locations are close to the village of Brassington 10 miles south west of Matlock.

Harboro Rocks are situated north of Manystones Lane, a mile north east from Brassington. Park on Manystones Lane at a lay-by just the east of the mineral works (Sibelco). Walk back toward the works and follow a footpath by the works that crosses the High Peak Way on to open land and the slope where the rocks are.

Parking Lat/Long: 53.090300, -1.6384113
Parking Grid Ref: SK 242 552
Parking Postcode: DE4 4ES

Rainster Rocks are a mile west of Brassington. From Brassington drive past the church and the Hanging Gate public house. After half-a-mile turn right onto a minor road and park in an obvious lay-by where the road turns a sharp left. An easy walk on public footpaths that leave the road on the corner of the lane brings you to Rainster Rocks, which are immediately in front of you.

Parking Lat/Long: 53.086773, -1.670848
Parking Grid Ref: SK 219 548
Parking Postcode: DE4 4HL

Accessibility

Access for both locations is over public footpaths, which include stiles and gates. Harboro Rocks is more precipitous than Rainster Rocks and care should be taken here.

Best time of year/day

Harboro Rocks is the highest point of ground locally so catches the light at all times of day and throughout the year but it is better suited to a lower sun when the topography is best revealed. They are particularly atmospheric if there in misty conditions.

Rainster Rocks is similarly south facing but set lower in the landscape than Harboro Rocks. Winter is a good time to be here.

Lakes and open water are rare in the Peak District, but in the southern Peak there is Carsington Water, a reservoir that is an important habitat for migrating birds and a great place for bird photography. The visitor centre includes an RSPB information centre and there are bird hides located on its shore. The reservoir is also popular for water sports and fishing. Photographically, this large expanse of water acts like a huge mirror on still days, perfect for reflections, it catches the light well at either end of the day.

Close by is Hopton Hall, dating back to 1414, it is one of the best places to photograph snowdrops in February and roses in the summer.

What to shoot and viewpoints

CARSINGTON WATER

Viewpoint 1 – Visitor Centre Promontory

The visitor centre provides access to a landscaped promontory, the shores of which can be explored. Carsington Water gets very little shelter from the prevailing wind and is rarely calm in its entirety. Pockets of flat calm can be found in and around the visitor centre promontory offering excellent reflections.

Viewpoint – 2 The Water Sports Centre

On a bright, windy day in summer a long lens can be used to photograph sailing boats from the perimeter path.

Viewpoint 3 – The Water Management Tower

At the south end of the reservoir, close to the dam, there is an octagonal water management tower that regulates the water level. On a calm day there is an excellent reflection opportunity here.

HOPTON HALL

Viewpoint 1 – Snowdrops

Hopton is notable for its fabulous display of snowdrops which occur in drifts in the informal gardens in February and for which the gardens are opened specially. Keep an eye on the hall's website for the exact opening dates and times during February.

Viewpoint 2 – The Formal Garden

The beautifully manicured Italianate formal gardens are very accessible. The lower part of the garden has many interesting pathways and statues. In June and July the terraced rose garden is stunning.

The beautiful gardens at Hopton Hall carry interest all year 'round. snowdrops in Feb, flower garden in Jul. © CG

How to get here

Carsington Water is 6 miles from Ashbourne, off the B5035 between Ashbourne and Wirksworth. Park at the visitor centre on the west side of the reservoir a half mile from the B5035.

Parking Lat/Long: 53.061120,-1.642604
Parking Grid Ref: SK 240 516
Parking Postcode: DE6 1ST

Hopton Hall: From Wirksworth take the B5023 toward Middleton-by-Wirksworth before turning left at the Rising Sun public house onto the B5035 toward Ashbourne. After a-mile-and-a-half take a right turn, signposted Hopton. After a further half-a-mile turn left into the hall, which is behind a beautiful, bowed, red brick wall.

Parking Lat/Long: 53.075731,-1.620676
Parking Grid Ref: SK 255 532
Parking Postcode: DE4 2FJ (250m)

Accessibility ♿

The parking at Carsington's main visitor centre is paved and all of the paths around this area of the reservoir are fully accessible.

The footpaths around the gardens at Hopton Hall are loosely surfaced. Most are level although the site is gently sloping. The walled garden has a mixture of sloping paths and steps.

Above: *Carsington has many useful sheltered bays (VP1). Canon 6D, 17-40 at 20mm, ISO 100, 1s at f/14. Grad. Oct. © CG*

Best time of year/day

The perimeter path gives access to all aspects of **Carsington Water,** making it an all year round location, but look for a very calm day if wanting to shoot reflections. Sunrise and sunset can be special here as the water acts as a huge reflector.

Hopton Hall: For snowdrops visit in February, days open are limited. For the summer rose garden the gardens are open Tuesday, Wednesday and Thursday between late June until late August from 10.30am with last admittance at 4.00pm.

Check their website before visiting: **www.hoptonhall.co.uk**

Snowdrops at Hopton Hall. Canon 5D, 400, ISO 200, 1/100s at f/8. Feb. © CG

The high ground between the Derwent Valley and the Ecclesbourne Valley, near the town of Wirksworth, has a lovely, rolling rural feel to it. The highest point is Alport Heights, a popular viewpoint (314m/1030ft) especially looking to the south and west. From its summit you can see the Wrekin (a hill) and the quartzite ridge of the Stiperstones in Shropshire. Further beyond you can see the Berwyn Mountains in Wales and, on really clear days, Snowdonia is visible too. For photography this location is good for long ranging views over rural countryside to distant hills, and is home to a 6m high gritstone tower, the Alport Stone and an old quarry. Radio masts provide unusual studies.

What to shoot and viewpoints

Viewpoint 1 – Radio mast installations
The radio masts will not be to everyone's taste but they are a very unusual feature. They are tricky to photograph and require a wide angle lens.

Viewpoint 2 – The Alport Stone
Slightly to the west below the summit in a small abandoned quarry is the Alport Stone, a 6m high pinnacle of gritstone. This stone has much old graffiti and facing west is illuminated best in afternoon and evenings.

The radio masts (VP1). Canon 6D, 17-40 at 20mm, ISO 100, 1/100s at f/14. Grad. Apr. © CG

The Alport Stone is well positioned for evening shots (VP2). Canon 6D, 17-40 at 20mm, ISO 100, 1/100s at f/14. Grad. Apr. © CG

How to get here
Alport Heights is best approached from Wirksworth. At the Red Lion pub in the town take Caldwell Street and the B5035 to the Malt Shovel pub then a right signposted Alderwasley but then take an immediate right toward Breamfield. Alport Heights is two miles along this road where there are two car parks next to the radio masts and the Alport Stone.

Parking Lat/Long: 53.061109, -1.547258
Parking Grid Ref: SK 304 516
Parking Postcode: DE56 2DQ

Accessibility ♿
The Alport Stone and the radio masts are right next to the car parks. Access to the Alport Stone is down sloping, informal paths which can be tricky when wet.

Best time of year/day
This is a summit site with its best aspect to the west. It is illuminated well all year from late afternoon until sunset.

***Opposite**: The Alport Stone is a brute covered in graffiti but can be dramatic. Canon 6D, 17-40 at 20mm, ISO 100, 1/100s at f/14. Apr. © CG*

An old industrial weaving loom in Strutt's North Mill, Belper.
Canon 6D, 70-300 at 260mm, ISO 1600, 1/6 at f/25. Jul. © CG

If you stand at the top of High Tor above Matlock Bath and look north up the Derwent valley you are looking toward an ancient and wild landscape, home to sheep farmers and once lead miners, where water gathers from the moors and feeds the valleys and dales. Fortunes were made here, especially from lead and copper mining, which funded stately houses and estates such as Haddon Hall and Chatsworth House.

Look south from High Tor down the course of the river Derwent toward Cromford and you are looking at the birthplace of the industrial revolution. Silicon Valley in California changed how we live in the 21st century, comparable technological leaps were made in and around Cromford in the late 18th century.

Here machines were invented that allowed the mass production of manufactured goods, the first factories were built and a sophisticated transport system was developed that allowed global trade and made the UK the richest nation in the world . The area even had its own Steve Jobs, the Lancastrian barber turned entrepreneur Richard Arkwright. Some of the investors that funded these 'start-ups' were the landed gentry who had made their fortunes from mining in the upper Derwent valley.

The area from Cromford following the river Derwent all the way to Derby was judged so culturally important that in 2000 it became a UNESCO World Heritage Site – The Derwent Valley Mills. Some highlights are described below, for more information visit **www.derwentvalleymills.org**.

What to shoot and viewpoints

1. Cromford Mill – 1771 ♿

Along with others Richard Arkwright developed the Water Spinning Frame, a machine using water power and unskilled labour that could produce yarn from raw cotton. Choosing Cromford because of its year-round 'warm'

Cromford Canal. Sony A6000, 18–200 at 41mm, ISO 100, 1/100s at f/8. Oct. © MR

water supply from the lead mines of Cromford Sough, Arkwright and his partners built the five-storey Cromford Mill in 1771. This was the first ever water-powered cotton spinning mill and at its height employed over 500 people working shifts. The mill closed in the 19th century but it was copied all around the world, not just its technology but its working practices, a template for modern factory production known sometimes as the 'Arkwright System'. The mill has been restored and there is a visitor centre. A wander around the complex with a camera finds many features including sluices, leats and the sites of the water wheels, as well as the mill buildings themselves. You can also wander around Cromford, especially around the Greyhound Hotel (built by Arkwright, as was most of the town to house his workers) and the nearby mill pond.

Location: Cromford Mills, Mill Lane, Cromford, Matlock, Derbyshire, DE4 3RQ.   **www.cromfordmills.org.uk**

Cromford mill leat detail in the mill yard. Canon 6D, 70-300mm at 70mm, ISO 1600, 1/1250 at f/5.6. Dec. © CG

Opposite*: The mill yard at Cromford Mill, the mill leat and the bear pit. Canon 5D, 17-40 at 20mm, ISO 100, 1s at f/20. Grad, Dec. © CG*

2. Mason Mill – 1783

Mason Mill was Arkwright's third cotton mill. It was built in 1783 alongside the river Derwent to take advantage of its greater flow of water. The building was constructed from expensive red brick, had more advanced waterwheel technology, and a more efficient internal design to increase production. This was later replicated *'from New Lanark to America, where the central stair tower became the architectural feature of many American mills, albeit often tempered by local style.'* The mill was in operation until 1991 and was a major employer in the area. Today upstairs is a shopping village.

Photographically its strength is the mill's museum basement and its exterior, particularly from the southern side of the river near Willersley Castle. A longer lens can be used to pick a lot of the wonderful details.

The mill's working museum is like walking back in time into an 18th century cotton mill. There are carding and spinning machines, several working looms still producing cloth, and the largest collection of bobbins in the world. Low light dictates a high ISO whilst hand-holding your camera. Also worth a look are the boiler, the steam rooms, and the hydroelectric turbines that supply renewable energy to the entire Masson site, the surplus being fed into the National Grid.

Location: Masson Mills, Derby Rd, Matlock Bath, Matlock, Derbyshire DE4 3PY

www.massonmills.co.uk

3. Cromford Canal – 1794 ♿

Canals then the railways replaced pack horses that were used to transport raw materials and finished goods around the country. The Cromford Canal, completed in 1794, ran for 14 miles from Cromford linking to the Erewash Canal then south to Nottingham. Barges carried coal to Cromford to fuel mills, foundries and for domestic use; then limestone from quarries, copper and lead from mines, and spun cotton thread was carried south. By the late 1800s the canal was in decline as the railways took over freight carriage. The stretch of canal at Cromford is very beautiful, and was restored by the Cromford Canal Society. You will find an abundance of flowers and wildlife here including herons and, if your are lucky, water voles.

Location: Up the road a few hundred metres from Cromford Mill. DE4 3RQ

Shuttles on a loom in the basement of Masson Mill. Sony A6000, 18–200mm at 18mm, ISO 320, 1/60s at f/5.6. Oct. © MR

Masson Mill. Canon 5D Mk 1, 17-40 at 40mm,
ISO 50, 0.4s at f/20. Feb. © CG

4. Leawood Pump House ♿

Two miles south of Cromford there is a grand Grade II listed building with an elegant chimney. It sits adjacent to a Leawood Aquaduct, which carries the canal over the river below. The pump house was used to raise water from the river into the canal above.

5. The Cromford and High Peak Railway, and Middleton Top – 1831 ♿

The Cromford and High Peak Railway, completed in 1831, was built to carry minerals and goods between the Cromford Canal wharf at High Peak Junction and the Peak Forest Canal at Whaley Bridge, then on to Manchester and Liverpool. It was a bold venture as the the steam trains had to climb over a thousand feet out of Cromford up several inclines by the aid of stationary steam engines. Middleton Top is the last surviving winding engine on the line. Positioned high on the hills above the Derwent Valley and with excellent views, the engine house is in excellent repair. **Location:** Rise End, Middleton by Wirksworth DE4 4LS. From Wirksworth drive towards Middleton by Wirksworth. As you arrive at the village, Middleton Top is signposted left, along the road leading to Carsington and Ashbourne.

6. Belper and the Jedediah Strutt – North Mill – 1786/1804 ♿

Jedediah Strutt was another pioneering 18th century entrepreneur and industrialist. Beginning with a farming background, he helped build the foundation of modern manufacturing alongside his sometime business partner Richard Arkwright. Together they abandoned horse power and with Arkwright's water frame set up Cromford Mill. Strutt also developed the Derby Rib machine that increased the production of cotton stockings.

But it was in nearby Belper that Strutt made his biggest impact where he built eight mills. The most impressive being Strutt's North Mill completed in 1786 but burnt down 1803 – mills were prone to fire as cotton dust was highly flammable and fires quickly spread through floor and ceiling timbers. North Mill was rebuilt in 1803 after Jedediah Strutt's death by his son William Strutt to a fireproof design using cast iron beams and Accrington red brick. The mill is one of the first iron framed buildings and precursor of the steel frames used in high rise buildings. A wander around the mills, the river, weirs and North Mill's museum and interior is highly recommended, as is a visit to the imposing East Mill built in 1912. **Location:** Strutt's North Mill Museum, Derwent Valley Visitor Centre, Bridgefoot, Belper, Derbyshire DE56 1YD

7. Heage Windmill

Heage Windmill was completed in 1797 and was in operation until 1919 when it got blown down for the second time in its history. It was restored in the 1970s and again in 2002 after a lightning strike. Now a Grade II listed building, it is the only working six-sailed stone tower windmill in England. It sits in rural countryside next to the village of Heage, and you can photograph it from footpaths that skirt the windmill. The mill opens on weekends and Bank Holidays from April until the end of October if you want closer inspection. You can buy stoneground flour made at the mill from local wheat. For more details visit www.heagewindmill.org.uk **Location:** Heage Windmill, Chesterfield Rd, Belper, DE56 2BH

Belper East Mill. Canon 6D, 70-300 at 170mm, ISO 200 1/200s at f/8. Apr. © CG

Middle top: *Leawood Pump House.* © CG   *Shuttles, bobbins and postcards at Masson Mill.* © CG & MR

Below: *Belper East Mill. Canon 6D, 17-40 at 17mm, ISO 50, 1/30s at f/13. Grad. Apr.* © CG

One man and his dog at the Dovedale Sheepdog Trials. Canon 6D, 70-300 at 250mm, ISO 800, 1/1000s at f/5.6. Jun. © CG

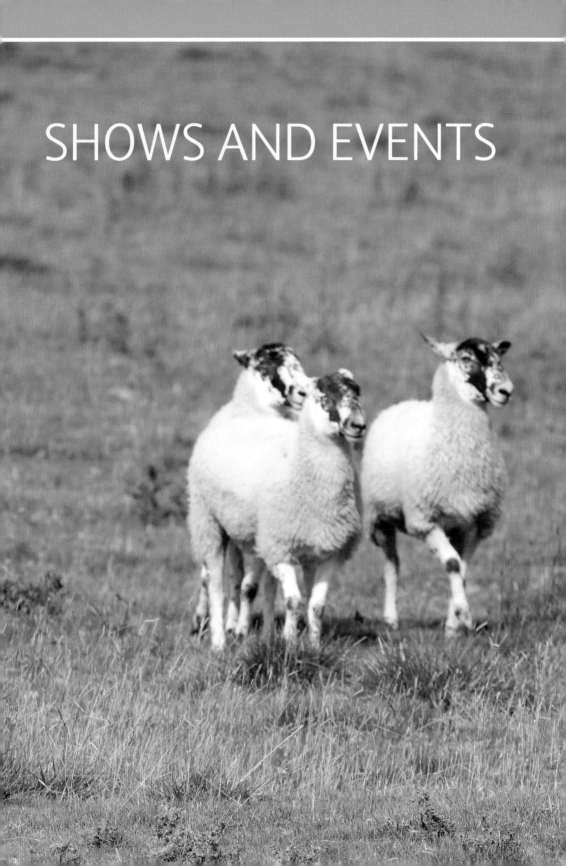

SHOWS AND EVENTS

Well Dressing

Well Dressing is a Peak District custom where village communities create a design made of petals and flowers centred around the village well. The origins are obscure but it predates the arrival of Christianity to Britain and is closely associated with the limestone uplands of the White Peak, where summer water supplies from local springs can be unpredictable. Although now aligned with Christian worship its roots are in pagan thanksgiving and probably made the cross-over when the Romans were here and converted to Christianity.

By the early 19th century well dressing had become quite uncommon but the arrival of the tourist industry revived it and it is now a very important part of the Peak District visitor entertainment schedule.

The designs are created on clay-covered boards into which a design is drawn and then filled-in with petals and flowers. They are impressive and moving, and some of the larger Peak District communities manage to create multiple well dressings. Most well dressing designs are left up for a week to give visitors as much opportunity to see them before the petals fade and their vibrance is lost. Photographically it is best to visit them as close as possible to the blessing date.

The well dressing calendar varies slightly from year to year because they are usually scheduled so that the blessing falls on a weekend. Also, there is no overarching organising committee, with each village being concerned only with its own well dressing and associated celebrations.

WHEN

www.welldressings.com is a useful on-line source of information that lists the annual schedule of well dressings by date.

The complete list of well dressings is substantial and grows every year. We have listed here the most significant Well Dressings within the heart of the Peak District and the approximate order in which they happen.

They're never on the same date but they're always roughly on the same weekend and in the same order.

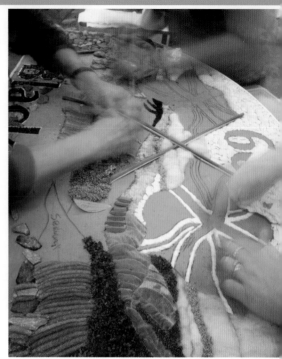

Preparing the Well Dressing at Litton. © CG

May
Tissington, Wirksworth, Middleton-by-Wirksworth, Monyash.

June
Chatsworth, Ashford-in-the-Water, Cressbrook, Flash, Tideswell, Litton, Youlgrave, Rowsley, Bakewell, Hope, Over Haddon.

July
Hathersage, Hayfield, Chapel-en-le-Frith, Buxton, Pilsley (Chatsworth), Little Longstone, Bamford, Great Longstone, Stoney Middleton, Bonsall.

August
Bradwell, Great Hucklow, Taddington and Blackwell, Holymoorside, Eyam, Wormhill.

September
Longnor, Hartington.

Agricultural & Horticultural Shows

The Peak has some of the best agricultural and horticultural shows in the UK with Bakewell, Ashbourne and Chatsworth being very popular. Leek County and Hope Show are smaller but some think are more authentic. All those listed are a treat to go to and you'll get to photograph impressive livestock, local produce, and beautiful flowers and vegetables up close. Plus there will be many country characters in an attendance.

May
Staffordshire County Show
www.staffscountyshowground.co.uk

June
Derbyshire County Show
www.derbyshirecountyshow.org.uk

July
Leek and District County Show
www.leekshow.org.uk

August
Ashover Show   **www.ashovershow.co.uk**
Ashbourne Show   **www.ashbourneshow.co.uk**
Bakewell Show   **www.bakewellshow.org**
Hope Show   **www.hopeshow.co.uk**

September
Chatsworth Country Fair
www.chatsworthcountryfair.co.uk
Hartington Wakes & Country Show
www.hartingtonwakes.co.uk

Hope Sheepdog Trials in Sep. © MR

Sheepdog Trials

Fast moving sheep and dogs. A mid-zoom and a fast shutter speed required.

August
Bamford Sheepdog Trials
www.bamfordvillage.co.uk
Dovedale Sheepdog Trials
www.dovedalesheepdogsociety.org.uk

September
Hope Sheepdog Trials
www.hopeshow.co.uk
Longshaw Sheepdog Trials
www.longshawsheepdog.co.uk
Hayfield Sheepdog Trials and Country Fair
www.hayfieldshow.co.uk

Chatsworth House Events
Chatsworth House had a full itinerary events throughout the year, many of which are great for photography.
For a full listing and dates visit: **www.chatsworth.org**
Here some highlights:
RHS Chatsworth Flower Show
Art Out Loud
Christmas Market
Dodson & Horrell Chatsworth Horse Trials
Chatsworth Country Fair
Bonfire and Fireworks

Haddon Hall Events
Haddon Hall is open from early April through to 30th September plus Autumnal and Christmas opening periods. You can see their event listing at **www.haddonhall.co.uk**

All Events
For a full Peak District event listing visit:
www.visitpeakdistrict.com

Showboy and charolaise, Hartington Show. © CG

There are no motorways and very few major roads in the Peak District and apart from a few hotspots at the weekends the area is a quiet place. Go for a walk on the moors, by rivers, down dales, in woodlands and along the country lanes and you'll find solitude and plenty of wildlife.

With no experience of wildlife photography, most people, with patience and some planning, should come home with photographs and importantly great memories. This brief guide to photographing wildlife in the Peak District covering key species and locations, along with some gear and shooting tips, will give you a head start. For more detailed advice see the books we recommend for further reading at the end of this chapter or book a day with a local wildlife photographer.

Where and What to Photograph

MOORLAND

The Mountain Hare

The mountain hare is found in Scotland with a population south of the border here in the Peak District. You'll find it on the high moorland of Kinder, Bleaklow, the Derwent Edges and Saddleworth moor. In the winter its brown pelage (fur) turns white until the spring and these beautiful animals are easily seen against the moorland – more difficult to spot when it snows. From November onwards if you walk along the Pennine way across Bleaklow starting from the the Snake Pass you will have a high chance of photographing them with a long lens. Once you have spotted one, try approaching from downwind and keeping hidden in the groughs, the eroded peatland ditches.

A mountain hare in winter pelage on Bleaklow. Canon 5D MkIII, 70-300 at 300mm, ISO 1000, 1/400 s at f/5.6. © Stuart Holmes

Opposite: *A young vixen high on the edge of Monsal Dale. Canon 6D, 70-300 at 300mm, ISO 4000, 1/1000s at f/5.6. Jun. © CG*

Red Grouse

The red grouse is a game bird found on moorland. Some moorlands are controversially managed for grouse by heather burning, persecution of wildlife and the placement of feeding stations. Grouse are wary of people and you will often frighten them out of their heather home. They are very common however and if you do see some, find a comfortable spot to crouch in the heather and wait. Some individuals can also be quite bold and you will be able to approach quite close to them. Try any of the accessible Eastern Edges especially Stanage, Win Hill, Kinder and Derwent Edges.

Other Moorland Species

The moors and adjacent farmland are rich with birdlife including golden plover, snipe, meadow pipits, lapwing, skylark and curlew, all of which are best to photograph in the summer – a long lens is mandatory. The rare ring ouzel can be found on Stanage Edge in the summer. On Big Moor look out for the common lizard and adders. If you go on an early morning walk on Kinder at any time of year you may be lucky to spot the silent short-eared owl.

Birds of Prey

Kestrels, buzzards, red kite, sparrow hawks, merlin, peregrine falcon and sometimes hen harriers are all found in the Peak District especially on the moorland areas. To achieve great photographs of these birds in flight you do need a good lens and camera, although you may get lucky if one of these birds is perched on a wall – keep your eyes peeled. Summer mornings are the best times. Try Beeley Moor above Chatsworth which can be especially good for buzzards, the Peak's largest bird of prey, where they are seen soaring above moorland.

Red deer

As described on page 302 in detail, red deer live on Big Moor and at Chatsworth (page 370). At Chatsworth there are also herds of the smaller fallow deer. The prime time to visit both these locations is rutting season in October – the stags will have magnificent antlers then – although they are present and can be photographed year-round. The wilder red deer on Big Moor are harder to approach than the Chatsworth deer. The best time is early morning, especially if there is sun shining through mist.

RIVERS

The Peak District is blessed with crystal clear rivers and streams that are rich in wildlife, especially in the White Peak. Take an early morning walk down the River Wye in Chee Dale or near Rowsley, the lower reaches of the Derwent from Hathersage south and secluded dales such as Lathkill Dale near Youlgrave and Bradford Dale. Many rivers in the Peak are actively managed for wildlife by people like Warren Slaney – head river keeper at Haddon Estates – and local conservation groups; their hard work is paying off. The waters are gin-clear, rich with wild trout and the alkaline waters support plant and insect life that in turn support the fish and other animals.

The flighty heron is common but very alert to any approaching human. Walk slowly and if possible hide behind foliage to camouflage yourself. Weirs are good places to spot herons, especially the Chatsworth weirs. The otter is making a comeback in the Peak and have been spotted at several places on the lower Derwent and the river Wye. You may see one swimming or on a sand bank early in the morning. Similarly stoats can be found along the riverbank. The electric blue kingfisher can be found on the Derwent, Noe, Dove and Erewash sitting quietly on low-hanging branches over the water, suddenly diving in to catch small fish. Dippers are also common flitting from stone to stone foraging for prey along fast-flowing streams and rivers, and also grey wagtails. You will be lucky to see a water vole, their population has declined in the Peak, but they are still there on the Cromford canal, Bar Brook on Big Moor, the river Wye and also you may hear a plop as a water vole drops into a mere on the moors. Salmon are back in the Peak District and if you would like to photograph them they have there own chapter on page 434.

THE WHITE PEAK – FIELDS, HEDGEROWS & COUNTRY LANES

The limestone dales of the Peak have a very old feel to them and many areas are farmed in sympathy with wildlife. High flower meadows are abundant and encouraged. Ash woodlands line deep dales where rare orchids grow and the grasslands of the limestone plateau are dotted by barns and criss-crossed with drystone walls. An early morning or early evening walk are the best times to be out.

A little owl hiding in a wall near Wardlow. Canon 5D, 400, ISO 1000, 1/800s at f/5.6. Mar. © CG

A heron hunts for minnows in the pool at Cressbrook. Canon 450D, 400, ISO 1000, 1/800s at f/5.6. Jun. © CG

Red deer stag on Big Moor in October. Sony A6000, 18-200 at 200m, ISO 400, 1/250s at f/10. Oct. © MR

Brown Hares

Brown Hares can be found everywhere in the White Peak but most commonly on grasslands and they are most active at either end of the day. Often a drive along a secluded road surrounded by fields, in spring when the vegetation is low, will pay dividends. Brown hares can be distinguished from rabbits by their long dark ears, longer hind legs and loping gait. Unlike rabbits they don't have burrows but spend their life above ground. The network of narrow lanes between Bakewell and Chatsworth, and from Hassop to Baslow are both prime brown hare territories. Cars do not seem to faze them and if you stop at a gate you can often see them in the fields. Whilst a long lens is usually essential they do sometimes come close if you are still, especially the young leverets and if you see a prone hare with its ears sticking up above the grass they can be stalked if you stay out of their line of sight, wear dark clothing and stay quiet. If you find a spot with hares, hide down by a hedgerow and you may be lucky and get a shot of one running straight toward you.

Foxes

Whilst urban foxes are bold and quite frequently seen, rural foxes are masters off disguise, incredibly wary of humans and although common, you have to be clever to see one. The best locations are those away from roads where woodland joins open farmland. Look out for areas with paths through grassland. Early morning is best and it is best to stake out a likely spot by hiding in some undergrowth or up a tree. The network of green lanes and footpaths around Priestcliffe (page 352) is good fox territory.

Top: *A red grouse in spring plumage at Stanage Edge. Canon 6D, 70-300 at 300mm, ISO 2000, 1/1000s at f/5.6. Mar. © CG*

Above: *Very colourful in spring and easy to photograph. Chatsworth pheasants. Canon 6D, 70-300 at 250mm, ISO 800, 1/650s at f/5.6. Mar. © CG*

Badgers

Badgers are common in the Peak but are best left to experienced photographers.

Owls

Several species of owl are common in the Peak District. The little owl and the bigger barn owl share similar habitats and are found on farmland, especially in old barns where they nest, they are often seen on drystone walls and fence posts. One of the best methods to spot them is to drive slowly on early mornings where there are old buildings and walls, stopping to use binoculars or good eyesight to spot them in the windows of a barn or sat on a wall, both species are well camouflaged. Evenings whilst the light is still good can also be productive. You will often see the barn owl hovering above meadows hunting for small rodents. Both long-eared owls and tawny owls are common in the Peak but as they are nocturnal it is rare to see them but common to hear their *tu-whit tu-whu* and *ooo…oo..oo.oo-ooo* near mature woodland.

Pheasants

The pheasant is another game bird like the red grouse and were thought to have been introduced to the UK by the Romans. The males are very attractive with their long-tails, rich chestnut, golden-brown and black markings on their body, and dark green head with red face wattling. Females are mottled with paler brown and black. Characteristic of Old England they are attractive birds to photograph especially with an autumnal backdrop or on a misty morning. They add a splash of colour against a drab winter landscape. Pheasants are common across the Peak around the outskirts of many villages and near woodlands, copses and hedgerows. They are easy to photograph if you are quiet and patient but are easily spooked. Chatsworth, especially up behind Edensor village, and around Haddon Hall are a couple of places to be assured of seeing them.

BIRD PHOTOGRAPHY AND WATCHING IN THE PEAK DISTRICT

The Peak District has a rich population of birds and most UK species are represented. Here is a selection of locations and species to get you started.

Carsington Water (page 466) for goldeneyes, tufted ducks, gadwalls, wigeons, teals and coots; Padley Gorge (page 286) for pied flycatcher, wood warbler, common redstart.

The Longshaw Estate (page 286) for pied and spotted flycatchers, wood warblers and green woodpeckers.

Wye Valley (page 344) for redstarts, woodpeckers and ravens.

The Roaches (page 244) for red grouse, curlew and stonechat. Lathkill Dale (page 394) for dippers.

Coombes Valley for redstart, wood warbler, tree pipit and the pied flycatcher.

A seasonal visitor, a fieldfare sporting some frosty plumage. Canon 6D, 70-300 at 300mm, ISO 1000, 1000s at f/5.6. Jan. © CG

Derbyshire gritstone sheep. © MR

Livestock

Sheep are the commonest livestock in the Peak – especially the Derbyshire Gritsone breed with their black and white faces – and there is nothing more cute than photographing lambs frolicking in the spring. It is best to pick an early morning or go for a walk by fields a couple of hours before sunset when the light is at its most golden to photograph them frolicking in groups. Highland cattle can be photographed at the far end of Baslow Edge near Wellington's monument (see page 318) or on Curbar Edge.

FIELDCRAFT

Walking and Stalking

Being quiet and stealth-like and being prepared to dwell in one place is essential to view and photograph wildlife. Go by yourself and without a dog. Wear dark or camouflaged clothing and a hat. Don't wear any perfume or aftershave, and approach from down wind if you can, most wildlife has a keen sense of smell. Walk slowly and silently and be prepared to stop, sit and wait for wildlife to appear – soak in the ambience of being outdoors alone. Be prepared to stalk, it is surprising how close to animals you can get if you crouch and move slowly.

Drive-By

Villager Jim is perhaps the most commercially successful wildlife photographer in the Peak District. Self-taught, his amazing Peak wildlife images result from early morning drives around the Peak – he uses his car as a hide. You can cover a lot of ground in a car, and early in the day traffic is light to non-existent – be aware of other vehicles and don't stop unexpectedly. Stop frequently in lay-bys or in gate entrances to scan the surrounding countryside. Quite often you won't have to leave your car and with an open window you can use your car window sill to steady your camera.

Camera and Lens

The top wildlife photographers spend thousands of pounds on professional camera bodies and lenses. You can however start out with a smartphone camera especially if it has a zoom feature. They are perfectly adequate for taking photos of larger mammals from a distance and close-ups of insects or at a local wildlife park. You will be limited however and next up is a compact camera with a zoom lens which will allow you to photograph wildlife from afar. Compacts such as the Panasonic Lumix, Nikon Coolpix, Sony Cyber-Shot or Canon Powershot which, dependent on the model, have 10x to 30x zoom lenses, can shoot several frames per second and have decent sensors. Above these are the larger bridge cameras, some of which have very long-range telephoto zoom lenses. Second hand DSLRs or Mirrorless cameras can be picked up relatively cheaply and if you combine these with a used zoom lens such as a 70-300mm along with a 1.5 or 2 x converter you would have the perfect starter set-up. Once you get the bug you will soon see the benefit of more expensive equipment.

Settings

Most wildlife photography requires a fast shutter speed, fast autofocus and sensitivity to low light – a high ISO.

If you have compact camera use the sport setting (usually a little running figure) on the scene mode dial that will give you an exposure aimed at capturing action. This setting will give you a high ISO (necessary in low light), a reduced f/stop giving a shallow depth of field (you will

A dozing Cressbrook Tawny Owl sizing me up. Canon 5D, 400, ISO 1000, 1/640s at f/5.6. May. © CG

isolate in focus your subject), auto focus , a fast shutter speed to freeze any action and a high burst rate allowing you to take multiple images and thereby increase your chance of getting a good image.

To get these exposure settings on a manual camera a good general default setting is:

- Shutter Priority
- Partial Metering
- Continuous Autofocus
- Auto ISO
- Centre Focus Point
- Shutter Burst Mode

Select a shutter speed that is at least twice the focal length of the longest focal length of the lens (i.e., if you have a 70-300 lens then select 1/600 sec shutter as a minimum) to avoid camera shake. Auto ISO will preserve the shutter speed for you, but you may prefer to manually choose the ISO to maintain image quality, the lower the ISO the better.

So, once the widest aperture (smallest f/ number) is set and you know what shutter speed you need the only way to achieve the desired shutter speed is to increase the ISO.

Partial metering gives you the best chance of exposing your subject correctly with the minimum number of frames – you may only get one shot. Try a test shot and compensate plus or minus if necessary. Use the centre focal point – it puts the subject in the best part of the lens, giving the autofocus the best chance of working. Shutter burst mode will take lots of shots but relies on accurate autofocus.

Wheatears are common in the White Peak throughout spring and summer. Canon 5D, 400, ISO 1000, 1/640s at f/5.6. Apr. © CG

Shooting and Composition

Once you begin to take wildlife photographs you will just be pleased if you actually get an in-focus shot of an animal. Here are some general guidelines that may help you develop.

- Always be ready to press the shutter. Have your settings dialled in and batteries fully charged.
- Whilst steadying your camera is important it is often better to shoot handheld. Rather than using a tripod steady your camera using something at hand like the top of a wall, a tree stump, a gate, a beanbag or, if you spot something from your car, the top of the window.
- Use your car as a hide: switch off the engine, be quiet and try not to move. Most animals are pretty tolerant of cars – they are used to them.
- Compose your shot so that subject is off-centre and walking/flying into the frame.
- Use walls and any landscape features as leading lines.
- For any close up shots focus on the eyes of your subject.
- Shoot close up tight with a telephoto but also shoot wider to get the animal in context.

WILDLIFE PARKS

The Chestnut Centre

The Chestnut Centre near Chapel-en-le-Frith is a great place to visit and practice taking photographs of wildlife. They have several species of owls and otters, deer, pine martens, wildcats, harvest mice and fox.

www.chestnutcentre.co.uk

The Peak Wildlife Park

The Peak Wildlife Park near Leek has a selection of native wildlife and more exotic species such as meerkats, lemurs, wallabies and the giant sulcata tortoise.

www.peakwildlifepark.co.uk

Further Reading

Photographing Wildlife in the UK – Where and how to take great wildlife photographs by Andrew Marshall (fotoVUE)

Wild Derbyshire by Paul Hobson (self-published)

Wildlife Photography Field Skills and Techniques by Paul Hobson (self-published)

The Wildlife Photography Workshop by Ross Hoddinott & Ben Hall (Ammonite Press)

RSPB Guide to Digital Wildlife Photography by David Tipling (RSPB)

A hummingbird hawk moth feeding on wild garlic in Cressbrook Dale. Canon 6D, 70-300 at 250mm, ISO 4000, 1/1000s at f/5.6. May. © CG

Curlews arrive in the White Peak near Great Hucklow in Mar. Canon 6D, 70-300 at 300mm, ISO 2000, 1/1000s at f/5.6. Apr. © CG

Fallow deer at Chatsworth can be photographed all year round. Sony A6000, 18-200 at 40mm, ISO 400, 1/125s at f/9. Sept. © MR

Above: *A light form of a short-eared owl hunting over Bradwell Moor. Canon 5D, 400. ISO 1000, 1/800s at f/5.6. Feb. © CG*

Below: *The fields around Eyam and Foolow are great places to look for brown hares in spring. Canon 6D, 70-300. ISO 800, 1/1000s at f/5.6. May. © CG*

Biography

Chris Gilbert is a Peak District-based landscape and nature photographer and a photography teacher.

He has always had a keen interest in art, painting and photography and bought his first camera in 1981 from London Camera Exchange in Bishopsgate for £25 with his first paypacket, which also allowed him to afford the film to put in it. Strongly attracted to the paintings of Turner, Heaton-Cooper and Hopper he had always imagined that paint was the medium that landscape was best represented by until he bought Colin Prior's 'Highland Wilderness' in Nevisport in Fort William in 1995, which completely changed his relationship with photography and landscape.

He persisted with both paint and camera until 2002, when the quality of digital photographs began to compete favourably with film, at which point he switched to photography full time, eventually becoming a full-time photographer in 2006. Since then he has been photographing the Peak District and running photography workshops. His work features regularly in the shortlisting stages of national landscape photography competitions. He also works closely with the Peak District National Park Authority Visitor Services through the Peak Photography Gallery at Bakewell Visitor Centre.

Chris lives in Cressbrook, a small mill village perched high above Monsal Dale, right in the middle of the Peak District National Park. He has been running training workshops in the Peak District since 2008.

Ravenseye Gallery
Landscape Photography in the Peak District National Park with Chris Gilbert

Experience and capture the beauty of the Peak District National Park on a day out with Chris either on a Small Group Open Workshop or through a 1:1 coaching experience.

More details at:
www.ravenseyegallery.co.uk
t: 01298 871958
e: chris@ravenseye.plus.com

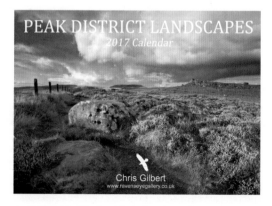

Opposite: *The River Westend winds its way majestically into Derwent Reservoir. Canon 6D, 70-300. ISO 100, 1/15s at f/9. Mar. © CG*

Biography

Mick Ryan is a photographer, writer and publisher based near Hebden Bridge in West Yorkshire.

He began taking photographs at age 18 in 1979 when his parents bought him an Olympus OM-1. With this camera he used to photograph friends climbing in the UK as well as the local landscape in the Ribble Valley in Lancashire.

Later, working as an editor at the climbing magazine OTE and starting the climbing guidebook company Rockfax, he found a commercial outlet for his photography which grew into taking photographs for outdoor companies.

Mick spent most of the 90s in California, USA, writing and publishing climbing guidebooks, returning to the UK in 2006. He worked as the Editor then Advertising Manager at UKClimbing.com until he founded fotoVUE, realising an idea he had in 2000 when living in the Sierra Nevada, inspired by great photographers such as Galen Rowell and Vern Clevenger.

Mick embraced digital photography in 2001, switching from film to memory cards with the Minolta DIMAGE 7i.

He is the author and publisher of several climbing guidebooks including the best selling Bishop Bouldering, is a marketing consultant for several outdoor companies and works with the Adobe suite of graphics programmes.

Mick lived in the Peak District for several years whilst working on this guidebook, and is now busy on a fotoVUE title to the Calder Valley around Hebden Bridge, Haworth and the South Pennines, as well as working with fellow director Stuart Holmes and many great photographers on the growing number of fotoVUE titles.

See more of Mick's work at fotovue.com

On the way up to Kinder by Fair Brook (page 88). Sony A6000, 18-200 at 18mm, ISO 400, 1/125s at f/10. Dec. © MR

If you are a keen photographer or want to take the best photos when out and about or on holiday, **fotoVUE** guidebooks show you where and how to take photographs in the world's most beautiful places.

Website – *www.fotovue.com*

Visit our website for articles on how to improve your photography, view inspirational photographs and learn more about our guidebooks.

- Find out about our books
- Additional viewpoints
- Photography tutorials
- News and special offers
- Inspiration – full of amazing photographs
- Articles and features by leading photographers

Register for the fotoVUE newsletter to get regular updates and offers on our guidebooks.

Exisiting books

fotoVUE photographer-authors use their local knowledge to show you the best locations to photograph and the best times to visit.

- *Photographing The Lake District* – by Stuart Holmes
- *Photographing North Wales* – by Simon Kitchin
- *Photographing Wildlife in the UK* – by Andrew Marshall
- *Photographing Cornwall and Devon* – by Adam Burton
- *Photographing Dorset* – by Mark Bauer

Buy from **fotovue.com**, Amazon, Waterstones, bookshops and direct from the authors.

Forthcoming titles

- *Photographing the Dolomites* – James Rushforth
- *Photographing Scotland* – Dougie Cunningham
- *Photographing South Wales* – Drew Buckley
- *Photographing London* – George Johnson
- *Photographing South West Ireland* – Carsten Krieger
- *Photographing the Snowdonia Mountains* – Nick Livesey
- *Photographing Northumberland* – Anita Nicholson
- *Photographing East Anglia* – Justin Minns
- *Photographing the Cotswolds* – Sarah Howard
- *Photographing the Yorkshire Dales* – Lizzie Shepherd and Oliver Wright
- *Photographing Surrey and Sussex* – Beata Moore
- *Photographing Kent* – Alex Hare
- *Photographing Iceland* – Geraldine Westrupp, Martin Sammtleben and James Rushforth

Check the website for the latest information on release dates.

www.fotovue.com

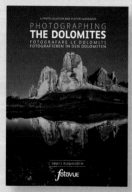
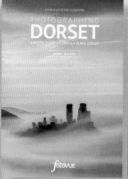

Contact: *mick@fotovue.com* or *stuart@fotovue.com*